The Foundations of Philosophy

The Foundations of Philosophy

Epistemological Self-Consciousness

MICHAEL PÒL MACNEIL

☙PICKWICK *Publications* · Eugene, Oregon

THE FOUNDATIONS OF PHILOSOPHY
Epistemological Self-Consciousness

Copyright © 2025 Michael Pòl Macneil. All rights reserved. Except for brief quotations in critical publications or reviews, no part of this book may be reproduced in any manner without prior written permission from the publisher. Write: Permissions, Wipf and Stock Publishers, 199 W. 8th Ave., Suite 3, Eugene, OR 97401.

Pickwick Publications
An Imprint of Wipf and Stock Publishers
199 W. 8th Ave., Suite 3
Eugene, OR 97401

www.wipfandstock.com

PAPERBACK ISBN: 979-8-3852-2250-6
HARDCOVER ISBN: 979-8-3852-2251-3
EBOOK ISBN: 979-8-3852-2252-0

Cataloguing-in-Publication data:

Names: Macneil, Michael Pòl [author].

Title: The foundations of philosophy : epistemological self-consciousness/ by Michael Pòl Macneil

Description: Eugene, OR: Pickwick Publications, 2025 | Includes bibliographical references and index.

Identifiers: ISBN 979-8-3852-2250-6 (paperback) | ISBN 979-8-3852-2251-3 (hardcover) | ISBN 979-8-3852-2252-0 (ebook)

Subjects: LCSH: Christian philosophy. | Philosophy. | Religion—Philosophy. | Apologetics.

Classification: BR100 M33 2025 (paperback) | BR100 (ebook)

VERSION NUMBER 05/29/25

Scripture quotations marked (AMP) are taken from the Amplified Bible, Copyright © 2015 by The Lockman Foundation. Used by permission.

Scripture quotations marked (AMPCE) are taken from the Amplified Bible (Classic Edition), Copyright © 1954, 1958, 1962, 1964, 1965, 1987 by The Lockman Foundation. Used by permission.

Scripture quotations marked (BYZ) are taken from The New Testament in the Original Greek, Byzantine Text Form, 2005 compiled and arranged by Maurice A. Robinson and William G. Pierpont. This text may be freely distributed.

Scripture quotations marked (BGT): this database is a combination of the BNT and LXT databases. This allows people who want to work with both versions at once to easily do combined searches.

BNT—*Novum Testamentum Graece*, Nestle-Aland 27th Edition. Copyright © 1993 Deutsch Bibelgesellschaft, Stuttgart.

KJV, KJA, KJG Authorized Version (KJV)—1769 Blayney Edition of the 1611 King James Version of the English Bible—with Larry Pierce's Englishman's-Strong's Numbering System, ASCII version. © 1988–1997 by the Online Bible Foundation and Woodside Fellowship of Ontario, Canada. Licensed from the Institute for Creation Research. Used by permission.

LXT—LXX Septuaginta (LXT) (Old Greek Jewish Scriptures) edited by Alfred Rahlfs, Copyright © 1935 by the Württembergische Bibelanstalt / Deutsche Bibelgesellschaft (German Bible Society), Stuttgart. Used by permission. The LXX MRT (machine readable text) was prepared by the TLG (Thesaurus Linguae Graecae) Project directed by Theodore F. Brünner at University of California, Irvine. Further verification and adaptation towards conformity with the individual Goettingen editions that have appeared since 1935 (9th edition reprint in 1971) is in process by the CATSS Project, University of Pennsylvania.

Scripture quotations marked (NASB/NAU) taken from the NEW AMERICAN STANDARD BIBLE, © Copyright The Lockman Foundation 1960, 1962, 1963, 1968, 1971, 1972, 1973, 1975, 1977, 1988, 1995. (NAU) refers to the 1995 edition only.

Scripture quotations marked (NET) are taken from the NET Bible, Version 1.0—Copyright © 2004, 2005 Biblical Studies Foundation.

Scripture quotations marked (NIV) are taken from the Holy Bible, New International Version®, NIV®. Copyright © 1973, 1978, 1984, 2011 by Biblica, Inc.™ Used by permission of Zondervan. All rights reserved worldwide. www.zondervan.com.

Scripture quotations marked (NRSV) are taken from the New Revised Standard Version Bible, copyright © 1989, 1993 National Council of the Churches of Christ in the United States of America. Used by permission. All rights reserved worldwide.

According to the view of Christian philosophy I and others advocate, Christian philosophers should consider the whole range of problems from a Christian or theistic point of view; in trying to give philosophical account of some area or topic—freedom, for example, evil, or the nature of knowledge, or of counterfactuals, or of probability, she may perfectly properly appeal to what she knows or believes as a Christian. She is under no obligation to appeal only to beliefs shared by nearly what common sense and contemporary science dictate, for example. Nor is she obliged first to try to prove to the satisfaction of other philosophers Christianity is true before setting out on this enterprise of Christian philosophy. Instead, she is entirely within her rights in *starting from* her Christian beliefs addressing the philosophical problems in question.

—Alvin Plantinga

. . . the final question is not whether a statement appears to be contradictory. The final question is in which framework or on which view of reality—the Christian or the non-Christian—the law of contradiction can have application to any fact.

—Cornelius Van Til

Having the LORD first in your consciousness is the foundational principle of philosophy.

—Psalm 111:10 (my translation of the LXT)

Contents

Analytical Outline | ix
Preface | xv
Acknowledgments | xvii
Abbreviations | xviii

1 Introduction | 1
2 The Nature, Character, and Purpose of Philosophy | 53
3 A Christian Conception of Philosophy | 119
4 Beyond Anti-Philosophy to Transcendentalism | 195
5 The Christian Presupposition | 217
6 The Transcendental Argument for God (TAG) | 241
7 The Philosophy of Christian Involvement | 268
8 Final Conclusion | 294

Bibliography | 323
Subject Index | 341
Name Index | 349

Analytical Outline

1 Introduction
    1.1 The Foundations of Philosophy—and the Epistemologically Self-Conscious Project
    1.2 The Skeptical Challenge
    1.3 Apologetics
        1.3.1 Apologetics as the Rational Defense of Christianity
        1.3.2 Classical and Evidential Apologetics
        1.3.3 Presuppositional Apologetics
        1.3.4 Subjective Apologetics and Religious Experience
    1.4 The Status and Role of Scripture
    1.5 Epistemological Un-Consciousness and Its Transcendental Critique
    1.6 Transcendentalist but Not Kantian Creative Antirealism
    1.7 Epistemological Self-Consciousness as Augustinian Apologetics
    1.8 Epistemological Self-Consciousness as a Scientific Project
        1.8.1 The Challenge of Perennial Naturalism in the Academy
        1.8.2 The Status of Science—Preliminary Remarks
        1.8.3 The Problem of Induction
        1.8.4 Political Ethics and Science
        1.8.5 Science Is More Than Propositional Statements
        1.8.6 Science as Correlated with Epistemology and Philosophy
        1.8.7 Avoiding the "Tyranny of Science"
    1.9 Philosophy as Transformative
    1.10 Summary and Conclusion
    1.11 Chapter Outlines

2 The Nature, Character, and Purpose of Philosophy
    2.1 Overview

ANALYTICAL OUTLINE

2.2 Origins
2.3 Can We Defend the Tripartite Division of Philosophy?
  2.3.1 The Division of Reason and The Egocentric Predicament
  2.3.2 Epistemic Rights and Epistemic Necessity
  2.3.3 The Struggle for Metaphysics
  2.3.4 The Principle of Verification
2.4 The Nature of Philosophy—Analysis and Synthesis
2.5 The Character—Coherence, Truth, Correspondence, and Objectivity
2.6 The Purpose of Philosophy—Responding to Skepticism
  2.6.1 The Problem
  2.6.2 Descartes, Hume, and Kant
  2.6.3 The Fallibilists
  2.6.4 Realism and the Role of Common Sense
  2.6.5 The Therapeutic Conception of Philosophy
  2.6.6 The Pragmatic Conception of Philosophy
  2.6.7 The Positivist Conception of Philosophy
  2.6.8 The Post-Darwinian Naturalist Conception of Philosophy
2.7 Fallibilism and Modern Science—Universe or Multiverse?
  2.7.1 The Intellectual Challenge of the Concept of Chance
  2.7.2 The New Physics
  2.7.3 Cosmological and Teleological Arguments
  2.7.4 The Fine-Tuning Problem
  2.7.5 Certainty and Reasonable Verisimilitude
  2.7.6 Conclusion
2.8 The Imperative for Epistemological Self-Consciousness
  2.8.1 The Quest for Common Ground
  2.8.2 Beyond Common Ground
  2.8.3 Holism
  2.8.4 The Unity of Apperception
  2.8.5 Epistemological Self-Consciousness and Uncertainty
2.9 Summary and Conclusion

3 A Christian Conception of Philosophy
  3.1 Overview
  3.2 Metaphysics
    3.2.1 Speculative, Descriptive, and Revisionary Metaphysics
    3.2.2 Metaphysics as the Foundation of Science
    3.2.3 Metaphysics as the Organizing Transcendentals

ANALYTICAL OUTLINE

- 3.3 Epistemology
  - 3.3.1 Introduction
  - 3.3.2 A Philosophy of Facts
  - 3.3.3 A Philosophy of Evidences
  - 3.3.4 Overcoming Skepticism
  - 3.3.5 Two Dogmas of Evolutionary Thought
  - 3.3.6 Physicalism
  - 3.3.7 Those That Survive Think Inductively
  - 3.3.8 If All We Have Is Nature . . .
  - 3.3.9 Justified True Belief (JTB), Gettier, and Epistemic Warrant
  - 3.3.10 Plantinga and Warranted Belief
- 3.4 Ethics
  - 3.4.1 Introduction
  - 3.4.2 Ethics, Moral Knowledge, and Worldview
  - 3.4.3 Theonomy and Ethics
  - 3.4.4 Modern Theonomy
- 3.5 Christian "Worldview Philosophy"
  - 3.5.1 Introduction
  - 3.5.2 What Is "Christian Worldview" Philosophy?
  - 3.5.3 The Requirement for a Worldview Transcendental
  - 3.5.4 Evidentialism and Rationalism
  - 3.5.5 The Impossibility of "Right Reason" and "Common Ground"
  - 3.5.6 Plantinga and Van Til on Apologetics—Contrast and Confluence
- 3.6 Summary and Conclusion

4 Beyond Anti-Philosophy to Transcendentalism
- 4.1 Transcendentalism—First Remarks
- 4.2 Transcendentalism and Skepticism
- 4.3 Practical and Theoretical Reason
- 4.4 Worldviews and Ultimate Authority
- 4.5 All Reasoning Is "Circular Reasoning" but Not All Reasoning Is "Viciously Circular"
- 4.6 A Form of Life
- 4.7 The Necessity of a Transcendental Defense
- 4.8 The Transcendental Mode of Criticism
- 4.9 Summary and Conclusion

5 The Christian Presupposition
- 5.1 The Christian Transcendental as the Only True Transcendental

5.2 Contingency and Predestination
5.3 General Revelation and Special Revelation
5.4 Common Grace, Pluralism, and Epistemological Self-Consciousness
5.5 Sovereignty, Indeterminacy, and Natural Law
5.6 Biblical Presuppositionalism
5.7 Summary and Conclusion

6 The Transcendental Argument for God (TAG)
  6.1 Introduction
  6.2 Logical Form and Overview
  6.3 The Distinctiveness of Transcendental Reasoning
    6.3.1 The Conclusion Is a *Transcendental*
    6.3.2 All Reasoning Is Circular Reasoning
    6.3.3 The Scope of the Argument
    6.3.4 The Kant Controversy
    6.3.5 Option "A" and Option "B" Transcendental Arguments
  6.4 Van Til's Transcendentalism
    6.4.1 Presuppositional Apologetics
    6.4.2 From Probability to Certainty
    6.4.3 Indirect Argumentation
  6.5 The Criticisms of TAG
    6.5.1 Global Criticisms of Transcendentalism
    6.5.2 The Nature of TAG
    6.5.3 The Uniqueness Proof
    6.5.4 The Mere Sufficiency of the Christian Worldview
    6.5.5 The "Fristianity" Objection
    6.5.6 From Conceptual Necessity to Ontological Necessity
  6.6 Summary and Conclusion

7 The Philosophy of Christian Involvement
  7.1 Overview and Prerequisites
  7.2 The Imperative for a Political Ethic
    7.2.1 Is Political Involvement Legitimate?
    7.2.2 One Further Possibility—Political Neutrality
    7.2.3 The Lack of a Shared Cultural Reference
    7.2.4 The Importance of Our History
  7.3 The Role of Epistemological Self-Consciousness and Two Basic Principles
    7.3.1 Are We Called to Defend Truth?

- 7.3.2 The Response of Epistemological Self-Consciousness in Brief
- 7.3.3 The Domains of Study
- 7.3.4 Our Civic Responsibility—Recovering It Through Dominion Theology
- 7.3.5 The Theonomic Imperative
- 7.4 Theocracy or Representative Government
- 7.5 Understanding Romans 13
  - 7.5.1 Overview
  - 7.5.2 The Context of Romans 13
  - 7.5.3 Obedience and Submission Are Different Concepts
  - 7.5.4 The Boundaries of Christian Resistance
  - 7.5.5 Christians Can Be Revolutionaries
- 7.6 Final Words

8 Final Conclusion
- 8.1 Summary
- 8.2 Specific Conclusions
  - 8.2.1 Overcoming Skepticism
  - 8.2.2 Philosophy and Science
  - 8.2.3 Christianity, Religious Experience, and Apologetic Philosophy
  - 8.2.4 Transcendentalism and TAG
- 8.3 The Contribution of Our Thesis as Original Research
  - 8.3.1 As Augustinian Apologetics
  - 8.3.2 In Opposition to Scientism
  - 8.3.3 As Synthesis of Van Til and Plantinga
- 8.4 The Wider Relevance of the Research
  - 8.4.1 As Van Tillian Scholarship
  - 8.4.2 For Christian Ethics
  - 8.4.3 As Political Philosophy
- 8.5 Limitations to This Research
- 8.6 Recommendation for Further Research

Preface

THIS WORK IS ABOUT philosophy, and what makes a philosophy distinctively Christian in character, arguing that it is indeed possible for philosophy to conceived of as *first* Christian and not just philosophy done by people that happen to be *Christians*. To that end, we must deconstruct our discipline, understanding how and why it was previously conceived, and then reconstruct it in a Christian fashion consistent with the Christian worldview. Philosophy to be Christian is argued to be *epistemologically self-conscious* philosophy, philosophy that is not just internally coherent but philosophy that reflects the mind of the Christian God as the only true account of reality and *argued in a manner* honoring to the revelation of the Hebrew and Christian scriptures. It argues that a classical division of philosophy into metaphysics, epistemology, and ethics is valid but only when conceived of in a Christian sense and integrated in the Christian worldview. It argues that competing philosophical and scientific accounts are coherent and successful only to the degree that they have imported, consciously or unconsciously, Christian conceptions of the world; thus, rather than refuting the thesis they confirm it. We then apply this insight to what should be the character and practice of a Christian political philosophy.

This book is based on my PhD thesis.[1] While the argument of the book and the thesis is almost unchanged, I do feel the book improved substantially and meaningfully on the PhD version in structure, style, and clarity. Most significantly, it benefitted from an additional, substantial chapter on political involvement detailed in item b. below. Material was reorganized or abridged to meet wordcount limitations, and the requirement to be concise helped rather than hindered the quality of the

1. Macneil, "Epistemological Self Consciousness."

PREFACE

book. For these reasons, I would strongly encourage the interested or stimulated reader to make use of both the full book version and the online PhD version. The PhD version remains useful for scholars interested in the finer details, when needing to copy and paste quotations, or when chasing references, so both versions remain available. Likewise, a section of my blog[2] contains material that never made it into either the final draft of the PhD or this book version but will be of interest to the technical specialist. In more detail, the chief differences are:

a. The footnotes in the PhD version were frequently verbose and added technical cross-references or commentary sometimes tangential to the main argument. For the printed version, footnotes were abridged and focused on supplementing the main argument of the text. Similarly, some of the very lengthy footnotes have now evolved into articles which are found on my blog with the PhD thesis. There was an occasional promotion of a footnote into the main text where on re-reading I thought it particularly helpful to the argument.

b. An entire chapter on political involvement was added back in after being removed from the thesis at the request of the examiners. In my view, this reflected a fundamental difference in philosophical perspective, namely that, for myself, philosophy should be *transformative* rather than just *therapeutic* or elucidatory. From my perspective, the material of this chapter was where we moved from the philosophical coffee shop to the street and so is an *essential* chapter, not only warranted but necessary to complete the philosophical picture I had painted.

It was also an experience to have to rewrite in American spelling, using American punctuation rules and according to the Chicago Manual of Style guidelines—starting life as an engineer, I learned a simple numerical style of the IEEE/IEE; as a trainee teacher I learned the generic humanities style, and then two more proprietary styles internal to my university school! Thus, while I have tried extremely hard to correct the manuscript in line with the CMOS conventions as modified by Wipf & Stock, there might be spelling, grammatical, or typographical errors for which the responsibility will be mine alone.

Michael Macneil, Newcastle Upon Tyne, September 29, 2024

2. Macneil, "PhD Appendices."

Acknowledgments

THERE ARE MANY, MANY individuals to whom I have already given thanks in my PhD thesis upon which this book was based, so I will not repeat that here but will single out Professor Felix Ó Murchadha of Ollscoil na Gaillimhe whose searching criticism of the original draft of made this a far better piece of work. A special thanks also to Dr. David Sullivan (ret.) of Bangor University, North Wales, who was a masterful philosophical mentor during my master's level coursework. Thanks should also go to eminent Van Tillians Prof. Scott Oliphint and Dr. James N. Anderson for their assistance and willingness to help me advance the project; as all of us are interested in authentic Christian philosophy, this input was invaluable. Thanks also to all at Wipf & Stock Publishers for help in bringing this book to life.

Finally, my greatest debt will always be to my Lord and Savior: You have the unique epistemological quality that the more one knows You, the more one realizes that they do not know You as they should; and how much more you need to know that which one does not know: "If anyone supposes that he knows anything, he has not yet known as he ought to know; but if anyone loves God, he is known by Him" (1 Cor 8:2).

Abbreviations

APA	American Philosophical Association
API	American Petroleum Institute
BDAG	(Bauer Debrunner Arndt Gingrich): A Greek–English Lexicon of the New Testament & Other Early Christian Literature
CR	Critical Realism
CVT	Cornelius Van Til
ISO	International Standards Organisation
JTB	Justified True Belief
NGO	Non-Governmental Organization
OPC	Orthodox Presbyterian Church
RC	Roman Catholic
RE	Reformed Epistemology
RV	Reasonable Verisimilitude
TA	Transcendental Argument
TAG	Transcendental Argument for God
UN	United Nations
WHO	World Health Organization
WTS	Westminster Theological Seminary

1

Introduction

1.1 The Foundations of Philosophy— and the Epistemologically Self-Conscious Project

THIS BOOK ARGUES FOR the *necessity* of Christian belief as the presupposition for the *intelligibility* of philosophical and scientific thinking:

a. We give a *description* of reality and its constitution, our *metaphysics*.

b. We give an *account* of reality and the processes of nature, that is our theory of knowledge or our *epistemology*.

c. We then establish what is argued as the only appropriate basis of conduct within our worldview, our Christian *ethics* and how this understanding can then be applied to the political arena.

Agreeing formally with Mahon we assert, "*philosophy [is] properly philosophical only when edifying and* transformative."[1] The transformative process we label *epistemological self-consciousness*. The following are our areas of exploration:

a. Philosophy is conceived of as the *entire* system of human knowledge rather than a specialized addendum to the normal curriculum undertaken only by those with a penchant for abstract intellectual activity.

---

1. Mahon, *Ironist and the Romantic*, 12. Emphasis original.

b. Christian theology is argued to be the *only* system that will lend philosophy so-conceived an intellectual coherence.

c. The parameters for this are both pluralistic in scope and particular in application without contradiction. That is, it corresponds with the world and is internally coherent.

d. The defense of the existence of the Christian God as not only justified or warranted but as *objectively* defensible, rational, *and* true.

e. Competing worldviews or "forms of life" can only be judged as incoherent when subjected to *transcendental analysis*.

f. A worldview is not just a "conceptual scheme" but a much stronger articulation with ontological significance. This helps us overcome some of the traditional problems with transcendental arguments.

In summary, we posit a metaphysic from scripture, we posit a transcendental foundation for knowledge in the transcendent Trinity, and we posit an ethic which we can then apply to the exegetical and practical problems of philosophy. In other words, we then have a philosophical toolbox which will inform our political practice.[2] This work aims to articulate the orthodox, biblical Christian worldview as the only system of thought capable of providing the foundations of intelligibility of reasoning and rationality, in both the private and public spheres of life.

1.2 The Skeptical Challenge

This book stands intelligently but strongly opposed to the skeptical view, except in a strictly qualified sense as an issue of methodological research, and believes that we can live our lives certain of the most important truths regarding the universe. That is, that there are values immanent within all creation that allow us to live in complete harmony within it and with one another. To that end we argue that there are no "brute" uninterpreted facts of the universe (or nature),[3] but all our conceptions and

---

2. John Dewey in 1927 wrote a famous essay called *The Public and Its Problems*. Although he wrote for a decade seeking answers in a Christian context, he was famous for his post-Christian thinking known as *instrumentalism*, a form of pragmatism. He influenced twentieth-century Anglo-American culture to a remarkable degree in education, psychology, politics, and philosophy. He strongly influenced Richard Rorty, who became one of the most influential figures during the last two decades of the twentieth century.

3. I have made a point of juxtapositioning "universe" and "nature" because the

perceptions about the world, how we interpret and evaluate the actions of other external entities alike and unlike ourselves, will be theory-laden and, most importantly, *value* laden. This might seem initially implausible until we consider how naturalism excludes as a matter of theoretical principle that "nature" is the work of a personal God and makes the ethical observations that deny this God *cares* about this "nature" and that the relations of this "nature" reflect God's own character.

In contrast, one of our basic positions is that how we relate to the world around us is at base an *ethical* question, and we are arguing that *only* a Christian ethic ever allows us to properly understand the world around us. We recognize that there is a fundamental difference between employing skepticism as a *methodological* tool of analysis where we systematically evaluate our assumptions with a view to improving our understanding and technological applications of our knowledge, and a skepticism that is a basic *metaphysical* orientation that reality is contingent, disordered, chaotic, and our reasonings are arbitrary, physiologically, or psychologically conditioned responses of our evolutionary history. Indeed, we argue in this work that one of the central purposes of philosophy is really to address this challenge of skepticism in the latter sense, and we devote substantial space to the various responses to this challenge while presenting our own vision.

1.3 Apologetics

1.3.1 Apologetics as the Rational Defense of Christianity

Apologetic philosophy or more simply "Apologetics"[4] is normally conceived of as being concerned with the *rational* defense of the Christian faith against those who oppose it. It was "the defense of the Christian philosophy of life against the various forms of the non-Christian philosophy

---

ordinary language use of the term "nature" refers to the environment of our planet, whereas most philosophers when using the term "naturalism" are talking about the entire physical universe.

4. The classic Greek word from which we get the English term "apologetic" is ἀπολογία (*apologia*). This is not, as in English, a negative after the fact saying sorry for something or some state of affairs. It was rather a reasoned defense of your position before a trial of your peers, a *positive* defense of your position. Thus, Socrates made his *apologia* before the rulers of Athens and the three occurrences in the Christian scriptures (Phil 1:16; 1 Pet 3:15; 2 Cor 7:11), all carry this sense of the word. Further, 1 Pet 3:15 is sometimes considered as the foundational *modus operandi* of the discipline. Thus, "Apologetics" should be understood using this original sense of the word.

of life."[5] The definite article emphasizes the fact that there are non-negotiable foundations to any worldview that claims to be Christian. Part of the argument of this work will be that there may be a great diversity of kind but there remains an *objective* basis for any category claiming to be of that kind. As J. Gresham Machen argued in his *Christianity and Liberalism* (1923), "Liberalism," despite its reuse of the scriptures, was fundamentally a different religion distinct from Christianity because it did not accept biblical doctrines on their own terms but reinterpreted them to fit the post-Darwinian zeitgeist. In that respect, we will explicate and explore the Kuyperian conception of the fundamental antithesis between the Christian and non-Christian worldviews, Van Til's development of it, and our own specific instantiation.

Thus, this work is essentially an apologetic work. It is, depending on your presuppositions regarding the subject, a particular branch of either philosophy, philosophical theology, or theology proper. For example, Richard Rorty, the self-identifying "secular humanist," stated that apologetics "fell off" philosophy in the early years of the twentieth century with "no consequence," i.e., it was *completely irrelevant*,[6] though Rorty was being slightly disingenuous as he elsewhere acknowledged the seminal importance of Christian thought to the West.[7] In contrast, we will be arguing that without apologetics, there can be no possibility of the *intelligibility* of *any* human predication, so it is *completely relevant*; indeed, logically *necessary* and lays the foundation for philosophy.

1.3.2 Classical and Evidential Apologetics

There have been many iterations of apologetics using very different presuppositions. The Old Princeton tradition called for a rational defense of the faith *against* the claims of unbelief. Thus, this was principally a negative or reactive apologetic that wants to duel with the unbeliever using their own terms and presuppositions. The Princeton founders themselves wanted to fit clergymen to meet the cultural crisis, to roll back what they

---

5. Van Til, *Christian Apologetics*, 1.

6. For example, Rorty, *Consequences of Pragmatism*, xlii. Here Rorty considers the "messy dispute" between religion and secularism "settled" (in secularism's favor).

7. Rorty's relationship to religious thought is far from straightforward. I consider it in more detail at Macneil, "Richard Rorty's Iconoclastic Deconstruction of Philosophy."

perceived as tides of irreligion sweeping the country, and to provide a learned defense of Christianity generally and the Bible specifically.[8]

This tradition is also sometimes called "classical apologetics" or "evidential apologetics" though there is an important distinction between these terms. Technically, "classical apologetics" is more correctly thought of as the apologetic tradition originating from the work of St. Thomas Aquinas, specifically his cosmological arguments. "Evidential apologetics" deals with evidential issues such as evidence for the resurrection and the accuracy of the biblical manuscripts. However, the two have become somewhat conflated as they are both variations on the theme that *reasons* are required for the justification of belief and that justification comes from evidence (which is primarily empirical). Thus, some within the Reformed community have grouped them together.[9] Similarly, Warfield in his apologetics asserted that the non-believer must have the scriptures demonstrated and validated as the Word of God by the appeal to *"right reason."* Once this had been demonstrated, then the scriptures themselves could be believed, the autonomous person relinquishes their autonomy, and they accept the absolute authority of scripture and its claim as the authoritative Word of God. The negative nature and defensive posture of this apologetic model should be clear.

1.3.3 Presuppositional Apologetics

The classical and evidential methods have historically been the most influential schools of apologetics until Van Til was credited with a "reformation" of apologetics during his time as professor of apologetics at Westminster Theological Seminary.[10] Van Til's critique argued that the evidential methods have some basic flaws:

---

8. Princeton was founded in 1746 and was one of the nine pre-Revolution colleges. All the "Ivy League" colleges were founded by Protestants. The curriculum, though heavily weighted with theology, was also concerned with educating the whole person and giving people skills for exercising the "dominion mandate" (Gen 1:26; see also Macneil, *Dominion Theology*, 57 ff.) to create a godly culture. Princeton still boasts one of the world's largest philosophy faculties and a functioning seminary (though now very different to the Princeton of the founders). It is of note that Plantinga described it as a "failed [Christian university]" (Plantinga, "On Christian Scholarship" [draft], para. 1) and advocated for a very different model.

9. See, for example, Sproul, Gerstner, and Lindsley, *Classical Apologetics*; Cowan and Gundry, *Five Views on Apologetics*.

10. Bahnsen, "Socrates or Christ," 232–39.

1. It assumes the unbeliever is capable of "right reason," i.e., that the noetic consequences of sin do not substantially interfere with the ability to reason.[11]

2. It assumes there is common, neutral epistemological ground between believer and non-believer upon which each can meet and "follow the argument"[12] where it leads.

3. It makes the Christ of scripture and any of his claims always subject to a standard external to scripture itself. Scripture is no longer the *final* authority but is *subject* to the judgment of human reason. This external substantiation always needs to be satisfied before the claim can be accepted as authoritative and binding on the believer.

We note further:

a. The assumption of (1) cannot be sustained by reference to the text of scripture it is trying to justify. Scripture, particularly the discussion in Rom 8, presents the human person who has not been regenerated by God's grace as *incapable* of right reason.[13]

b. The possibility of (2) is thus negated by the failure of (1)—the believer and non-believer construct antithetical sciences and, as Kuyper explained, "refuse to grant to one another the noble name of 'science.'"[14] Neutrality is a myth as it begs the question by assuming the unaided and an unregenerate human reason is *capable* of judging the claims of scripture.

c. The logical defect of (3) is similarly conspicuous. By implication, *if* what scripture asserts *is* correct, the authority of God is absolute, primary, and self-validating. *If* scripture really *is* God speaking as it claims to be (2 Tim 3:16) then it *must* logically be the absolute and final authority; it is *self-validating* as all ultimate authorities are; there can be no appeal to a higher authority.

---

11. See the discussion of this issue in Plantinga, *Warranted Christian Belief*, 217 ff. This is an important doctrine within Calvinism and the wider Reformed scholarship. Arminian theology is far weaker and unclear on this issue, and thus many Arminian apologists favor a Warfieldian style appeal to a common rationality.

12. This is what might be known as the "Socratic dialogue."

13. In fact, the intense and detailed argument of the first seven chapters of Romans reaches its climax in Rom 8; it is the argument of the need of salvation through grace alone and the futility of human attempts to justify themselves.

14. Kuyper, *Encyclopedia*, 156.

Hence, in contrast to the classical or evidential mode of thought, Van Til from the late 1920s onward argued that Christian philosophy (and thus apologetics) can and should be articulated on a *Christian* basis, intellectually *consistent* with the faith it is defending. He was joined three decades later in this by Alvin Plantinga who was credited as restoring an academic credibility to Christian philosophy that had been lost in the post-Darwinian era of liberal Christianity.[15] Since the late 1950s, Plantinga dealt in a rigorously analytic method and progressively focused from the mid-1960s on the concept of evidence and its relation to belief, arguing that evidentialism rests on a classical foundationalism, which had been categorically demonstrated in the twentieth century, both from within and without the Christian community, as a naïve and an arbitrary position. While historically there have been some attempts to draw from both philosophers, the perceived tensions between their positions and the dismissive attitude of many analytical philosophers, including those identifying as Christian and "Reformed," toward Van Til has meant not enough attention has been given to the important links that can be drawn between them.[16] This work attempts to draw out the complementary nature of their work.

Thus, in lieu of the criticisms of these men, we too must advocate for an alternative model of apologetics, the *presuppositional* model. In other words, this is a *positive* apologetic concerned with presenting Christianity on its own terms, using its native assumptions and presuppositions. However, it immediately needs qualification as to what we mean. Often "presuppositional apologetics" is set against a grouping of all the non-presuppositionalist views,[17] but that is a basic error—"evidentialists" still have presuppositions (often a naïve empiricism) and "presuppositionalists" still use evidence and historical-critical arguments. Van Til was explicit on this last point, recognized also in the philosophy of science, maintaining one must consider the *philosophy* of facts in the apologetic system; facts are "theory laden."[18]

---

15. Sennett, "Analytic Theist," xi–xviii.

16. Anderson, "Cornelius Van Til and Alvin Plantinga," is probably the best example of a working professor actively interested in this linkage. Salazar, *Comparative Analysis of the Philosophical Views of Alvin Plantinga and Cornelius Van Til*, is another example concentrating on the impact of their doctrines of God on their philosophies. I give a biographical summary of the two at Macneil, "Van Til and Plantinga."

17. Sproul, Gerstner, and Lindsley, *Classical Apologetics*.

18. Bahnsen, *Van Til's Apologetic*, 634–62.

It should also be noted that other positions commonly labeled "presuppositionalist" are very different to Van Til's position and sometimes stand in opposition to it or have far more in common with the classical and evidentialist positions than with Van Til.[19] Van Til's presuppositionalism was founded on his philosophical transcendentalism,[20] and thus he was often characterized as offering a *transcendental* apologetic. This transcendental approach makes it possible to argue for an objective proof even when "forms of life" attempt to isolate themselves within an internal language game. We will be arguing in a similar, transcendental fashion which is characterized as analyzing what must be true for there to be knowledge of objects at all, or as arguing indirectly through the impossibility of the contrary, as opposed to direct, discursive arguments.

Thus, this is a strong, positive apologetic approach seeking to argue for Christian philosophy on its own terms, and we will clarify and develop our understanding of presuppositional apologetics as we move through this work. We will seek to demonstrate that it is theologically illegitimate and unfaithful to the testimony of scripture to attempt to use the methodologies, metaphysical and epistemological assumptions of unbelieving humanity to present a rational defense of Christian faith. In summary, the defense must be *presuppositional* and the proof of Christianity *transcendental*.

1.3.4 Subjective Apologetics and Religious Experience

Before we move on to unpacking the concept of epistemological self-consciousness, we should make mention of the importance of the subjective schools of apologetics and the role of religious experience. This is perhaps expedient because of the revival of its influence in the wake of the Pentecostal revival in the first two decades of the twentieth century, the charismatic revivals after WWII, the Christian appropriation of postmodernism in the 1980s, and the "prophetic" mysticism of our

---

19. Bahnsen, *Presuppositional Apologetics*, 137–261. Here Bahnsen provides perhaps the most comprehensive analysis in print of this issue and argues that Van Til is the most consistent of the presuppositionalists.

20. "Transcendentalism" is most immediately associated with the "Critiques" of Immanuel Kant which seek to examine the *preconditions* of the understanding of any predication, or what makes possible any knowledge of the objects of nature. However, Van Til's appropriation of the term was with a strong qualification; see §1.6.

INTRODUCTION

contemporary period.²¹ In some quarters, this irrational or "transrational" mode of apologetics is considered the defense of Christianity which has the greatest claim to authenticity. That is, these "subjective" or "irrational" schools of apologetics defend the idea that "religious experience" rather than reasoned argument *should* be, i.e., to be ethically faithful (or authentic), the basis of the defense of the faith. This is technically known as "fideism"²² (though we do want to qualify that designation somewhat below); fideism generally denies an abstract or common rationality (known to all humanity) can express spiritual truth; we must instead receive it irrationally or intuitively *by faith* or *with a leap of faith*. We find Plantinga and Van Til in broad agreement with each other in asserting that the fideist position has little to commend it apologetically:

> Faith is not blind faith . . . . Christianity can be shown to be, not "just as good" or even "better than" the non-Christian position, but the *only* position that does not make nonsense of human experience.²³

> [The] main competence [of philosophy] . . . is to clear away certain objections, impedances, and obstacles to Christian belief.²⁴

Notwithstanding, fideism has had some highly skilled and passionate defenders throughout Christian history. For example, the ancient apologist Tertullian was famous for this declaration:

> What indeed has Athens to do with Jerusalem? What concord is there between the Academy and the Church? . . . Our instructions come from "the porch of Solomon" . . . Away with all attempts to produce a mottled Christianity of Stoic, Platonic, and dialectic composition! We want no curious disputation after possessing Christ Jesus . . . !²⁵

For Tertullian, the "possessing of Christ Jesus" was not something that could be even a *possibility* that could be reached in the reasonings of the Academy. Similarly, Kierkegaard is the most famous example in

---

21. It might be a surprise to those of us working in a British context that there is a British Council of Prophets: https://www.prophets.org.uk/.

22. Faith is *fide* in Latin; hence *fideism* as "faith-ism," living life by faith. For an academic treatment, see Penelhum, "Fideism." I tried to catch some of the attractiveness of the position in Macneil, "Fideistic Leap."

23. Van Til, *Defense of the Faith*, 66–67.

24. Plantinga, *Warranted Christian Belief*, 499.

25. Tertullian, *Prescription Against Heretics*, VII.

the nineteenth century where the labels "subjective individualism" and "protoexistentialism" have been applied equally to him; central to his thought was the utter inadequacy of "Reason" in dealing with religious experience:

> But what is this unknown something with which the Reason collides when inspired by its paradoxical passion, with the result of unsettling even man's knowledge of himself? It is the Unknown. It is not a human being, in so far as we know what man is; nor is it any other known thing. So let us call this unknown something: the God. It is nothing more than a name we assign to it. The idea of demonstrating that this unknown something (the God) exists, could scarcely suggest itself to the Reason. For if the God does not exist it would of course be impossible to prove it; and if he does exist it would be folly to attempt it.[26]

So, in such cases, it is arguably a legitimate expression of genuine faith, rational within the language game of a community, rather than an irrational intellectual impulse in the face of intellectual challenges.[27] Thus, there is arguably a distinction between fideism and some forms of subjective apologetics. That is, the Christian apologetic system needs to address "the claim Jesus seems to be making is not that he holds a worldview which is true and corresponds to reality, but rather that he himself is the truth."[28] This would seem to make our knowledge of the truth intimately bound up with our knowledge of the Truth himself, and thus, our religious *experience*.

In response, firstly, the question is certainly a pertinent one for the broad Christian tradition where the roles of faith and reason have periodically dominated attempts to articulate a coherent Christian philosophy. For example, Roman Catholicism has remained in some respects more open to the supernatural intrusions as a mode of knowing, and the Catholic tradition has produced some of the most profound mystics.[29] It should also be recognized that primitive Celtic Christianity, with its links to the ancient Nestorian church and thus Eastern Orthodoxy, had a strong mystical heritage. In contrast, the Reformed tradition has

---

26. Kierkegaard, *Kierkegaard Collection*, 131.

27. This was the subject of the debate between Nielsen and Phillips rehearsed in *Wittgensteinian Fideism?*

28. I am indebted to Professor Ó Murchadha for this observation.

29. The works of Madame Guyon and St. Teresa of Avila were particularly impactful on me.

INTRODUCTION

tended to denigrate the miraculous, particularly in the sense of continuing mystical experience in the wake of Calvin's cessationism[30] and the Reformed tradition was frequently excoriated for its inability to celebrate the arts and creativity in contrast to the rich heritage and patronage of the Catholic Church.

However, it should be noted that this is an inaccurate and uninformed generalization,[31] and I would argue it was more a symptom of the degeneration of the Reformed position rather than implicit in it, being corrected to a large degree in the recapitulation of Calvinism in the work of Kuyper during the second half of the nineteenth century up to his death in 1920.[32] Kuyper, in every sense a religious, political, and social reformer,[33] wrote extensively on the arts and sciences as possessing a modality of their own,[34] being a celebration of the character and

---

30. "Those miraculous powers and manifest operations, which were distributed by the laying on of hands, have ceased. They were only for a time. For it was right that the new preaching of the gospel, the new kingdom of Christ, should be signalized and magnified by unwonted and unheard-of miracles. When the Lord ceased from these, he did not forthwith abandon his Church but intimated that the magnificence of his kingdom, and the dignity of his word, had been sufficiently manifested. In what respect then can these stage-players say that they imitate the apostles?" (Calvin, *Institutes* 4.6).

In defense of Calvin, he was reacting against the frequent appeal to "miracles" and "signs" in preference to sound doctrine. He also, correctly, understood the "Apostles of the Lamb," the original Twelve (including Matthias, Acts 1:26), had a unique and special role, never to be repeated. However, he seems not to recognize some offices as continuing, believing they were for the foundation of the Church and the purpose of establishing the Church "everywhere." He believed because the Church was "everywhere," there was no need for, say, the apostolic office (see his *Commentary* on passages such as Eph 4:11; 1 Cor 12:28). Of course, we can formally agree with him that those offices might cease if the Church was indeed *"everywhere,"* but we know now that it is absolutely not the case.

31. For example, see Finney, *Seeing Beyond the Word*, 19–48, for a comprehensive account of the issues surrounding the misrepresentation of Calvinism and the arts.

32. I discuss Kuyper's cultural philosophy in Macneil, "Abraham Kuyper, Culture and Art."

33. Kuyper, one of the most underappreciated intellectual pioneers of the Victorian era, served as the prime minister of the Netherlands from 1901 to 1905, started a political party, founded the Free University of Amsterdam, founded two newspapers, and broke from the state church in founding the Reformed Churches of the Netherlands, while modernizing Calvinism for the modern world. For a representative reader, see Bratt, *Abraham Kuyper*. My book itself might legitimately be considered broadly "Kuyperian" in outlook.

34. He gave a series of lectures in 1898 at Princeton University that outlined his position on how Calvinism related to culture generally. This is perhaps the first definitive statement of neo-Calvinism (systematized later in his *Encyclopedia*) and was highly influential on other Reformed Dutch theologians including Van Til.

nature of God, positioning the person and their relations at the center of philosophical theology to the degree that a recent biographer described his position as anticipating the postmodern a century before Lyotard.[35]

Thus, when during this work I emphasize the "Reformed" interpretation of the Augustinian position, it is not at the expense of these alternative conceptions of Christian thought which have given (and continue to give) us much, though I will argue that I believe the Reformed conception of Augustine, understood best and perhaps, provocatively, distinct from many of those denominations claiming that label, lends itself to the most apologetically satisfying model when developed along the lines we shall be arguing.

Secondly, it is also a pertinent question for me personally as I did not come to faith purely on the basis of being persuaded by rational argument of the legitimacy of the Christian worldview. It was very much an encounter with the "Truth" himself in a mystical vision of the journey to the mount of crucifixion.[36] As a convert to Christianity at twenty-two, I attended a Pentecostal church which was "charismatic" in the literal sense, practicing spiritual gifts such as spiritual deliverance, healing, and prophesy, all of which remain part of my praxis and experience. For over twenty years I attended a fellowship which was predominantly irrational in its approach to the relation of faith and reason, denigrating the latter in deference to the former. Thus, nothing I say in this work should be construed as me being apostate from believing in a living and vibrant faith; it is rather an appeal to an *intelligent*, living, and vibrant faith.

That is, what I came to value and understand was that the minister of the first church, though Pentecostal and charismatic, believed in apologetics proper and dealt seriously with church history, addressing the theory and practice of apologetics; she also suffered the distinction of being labeled a "Pelagian" by critics. Faith needed an intellectual articulation, and it was perhaps inevitable, given my philosophical convictions, that my continued participation in the latter fellowship became impossible regardless of the authentic spiritual experience I enjoyed there and my enormous respect for and appreciation of the leaders. That is, I fully acknowledge the importance of a continuing encounter with the Truth rather than arguing I have perfected my dogma at your expense,

---

35. Bratt, *Abraham Kuyper*, 19.

36. A story I tell with youthful exuberance (this began life in 1990 with lots of potential offense to the critical reader) as an appendix to my (as yet, only self-published) book at Macneil, "Macneil's Guide for the Spiritually Perplexed."

as symptomatic of the most distasteful fragmentation of the Reformed community in 1930 Presbyterian America. Indeed, this work would most certainly be characterized as "post-Reformed" because of the recognition above of spiritual gifts as intended and necessary for the Church today.

Thirdly, it is indeed somewhat paradoxical that objective clarity is mediated through the deepest subjective experience of the Truth himself. However, this paradox I believe can be resolved to a degree by considering that the greatest mystical experience (and indeed the experience of my own conversion) came to me during a contemplation of the scriptures, rather than practicing a set of disciplines *apart* from the scriptures (valuable though such ascetic practices are *with* the scriptures). It should also be remembered that the goal of apologetics is not to bring about a spiritual reformation (which is in the purview of God alone), though it can certainly be a part of that process and Van Til's transcendental terminus might indeed be considered a call to conversion; it is rather to provide a rational defense of our belief.

So, in summary, this work needs a focus, and that focus is on the area of strengthening a rational defense of the faith rather than an exploration of what might be called the phenomenology or spirituality of Christian life, equally important but not the central part of this study. However, in a sense, this categorical division is for analytical purposes only, and we *should never* separate our doctrine from our praxis. This might well provoke many questions as to how our final conclusion is mediated with regard to religious experience, and it will be necessary to reflect on this when we draw the final conclusion of the study and to what degree this weakens our final position. However, we are proceeding on an apologetic basis that assumes a rational defense is warranted and mandated by scripture.

1.4 The Status and Role of Scripture

One of the arguments made in this work will be for the ultimate and self-attesting authority of scripture in the matters of spirituality, doctrine, and ethics. However, it is one thing to *state* this, for such a statement is likely to be considered one of the cornerstones of a generic "evangelical" view of the Bible as succinctly summarized by McGrath.[37] It is quite another to express the *implications* of this in practice for our project here.

---

37. McGrath, *Passion for Truth*, 22–23.

For example, McGrath's analysis focuses precisely on this issue, and he develops a distinctive moderate, evangelical program through that work, critiquing previous systems (particularly the fundamentalist model and the analytic model associated with theologian Carl Henry), but his program is very different to what we develop here.

This is not necessarily a threat to either of us; as scripture itself states, "there are different ministries, but the same Lord,"[38] and people will come to different conclusions as to the meaning of scripture passages, with both claiming the same inspirational authority from "the Spirit." That is, we must recognize that scripture itself did not come to us as systematic theology and it is capable of a diversity of interpretations even among those who have an equal commitment to its truth and authority, whether that commitment is conceived objectively, subjectively, or both. We must recognize that even some cornerstone doctrines such as the Trinity were inferences and emergent theological principles after some centuries of reflection.[39] Thus, whatever system we might derive from scripture has a degree of fallibility even if we believe it is incorrigible to us.

However, I maintain the position that though there might be many possible meanings of scripture, the authors had the intention of communicating *something* specific to us in their narrative (especially when it is written in a pastoral or exegetical genre); even if, with the benefit of hindsight, we might see the Lord communicating something to us quite apart from the intentions of the authors themselves. We see this in the polemical dispute between Paul and James which contrast the very different conceptions of "faith" and "works" with each author using the

---

38. 1 Cor 12:5 (NET).

39. I acknowledge this criticism as Professor Ó Murchadha's here, though in the case of the Trinity I do believe the biblical evidence both linguistically from the Hebrew in Gen 1:1, 26 and in the "Father, Son, Holy Spirit" narrative throughout John's Gospel (e.g., John 14) provide very strong evidence for that conception as a legitimate inference. More technically, in Gen 1:1, "God" (Elohim) is a plural form coupled with the verb *bara* ("create," Strong's #1254) as a singular. While the Hebrew plural was sometimes used to intensify an attribute of the singular substantive, the context offered in v. 26 is emphasizing the plural using a verbal form. To explain the plural otherwise relies on creative imports of a heavenly council who God has invited to create with him (the NET Bible notes for Gen 1:26 are informative at this point). That notion itself is extremely problematic and contested. Rather, philosophically, I believe we at once see the resolution of the "one and the many" problem in the person of God, right at the beginning of scripture as our metaphysical foundation. While this is not conclusive (some have argued it is imposing Trinitarian concepts rather than finding them), I find it philosophically and theologically compelling, in contrast to the weakness of the alternative explanations.

same scriptures but rendering the sense of them in a seemingly antithetical fashion.[40] Our resolution of the dispute with distance will appropriate the insights of both and conceptually distinguish "saving faith" as understood by, say, Luther and faith demonstrating itself in our ethics as articulated by a John Wesley.[41]

So, a polyvalent scripture can still anchor our praxis, and the relevance of scripture is seen concretely later in our work in our section on "Ethics" where the theonomical position seeks to demonstrate how the principles embedded in culturally conditioned narratives remain relevant for us. We can further acknowledge the roles of different genres in communicating not just propositional knowledge but emotive content and poetic allusions; Proverbs is rich with aphoristic couplets and idiomatic constructions which make no sense or are contradictory when considered atomistically.[42] It might have even been the case the author layered the meanings within the text,[43] inviting us to discover those meanings, but that is still distinct from denying the possibility of *any* objective meaning intended by the text. The apostle Paul clearly asserted that language's principal power was the ability to carry meaning:

> There are probably many kinds of languages in the world, and none is without meaning [incapable of carrying meaning]. If then I do not know the meaning [power] of a language, I will be a foreigner to the speaker and the speaker a foreigner to me.[44]

---

40. The book of James seems to follow very closely Paul's argument in Romans on key points, using the same scriptures that formed the key parts of Paul's argument. Paul describes the tension in Gal 2 between himself and James, who had maintained a strict, Jewish form of life post-conversion. Though Paul himself had occasionally accommodated to Jewish scruples (normally with disastrous consequences), by the time Galatians was written, he was clearly unwilling to compromise. If nothing else, this demonstrates the need for a hermeneutic structure when approaching scripture.

41. Wesley expressed this in opposition to some of the strict Calvinism of his time in asserting that there should be some evidence of conversion or of Christian convictions in daily life; it was not sufficient to merely assent to a set of theological propositions or to recite a creed in church. This was also an issue of contention for Jonathan Edwards regarding the immoral behavior of some members of the covenant families of New England. We consider that later in our thesis.

42. For example, "Do not answer a fool according to his folly, lest you yourself also be like him. Answer a fool according to his folly, lest he be wise in his own estimation" (Prov 26:4–5 NET).

43. The Gospel of John is famous for its use of irony and some of its patterns of argumentation were suggestive of Midrashic exposition, with the long, extended discourses.

44. 1 Cor 14:10–11 (NET) with my amplification. The first occurrence of "meaning" translates the word *aphonos* (Strong's #880), which is focusing on the relation of

Thus, taking the Reformers as an example, and the great modern Puritan expositors such as Lloyd-Jones,[45] it is possible to get to a place of strong confidence and certainty over the objective meaning of the narrative while permitting subjective "meanings," senses or interpretations which might valuably be extrapolated from the text. A strong commitment to the propositional mode of knowing provided the strength to the Reformation and the subsequent scientific revolution that dovetailed with it after the stagnation in the physical sciences during the scholastic period.[46] If the Holy Spirit is to "lead us into all truth" and we "[are to] abide in My word . . . then you shall know the truth, and the truth shall make you free"[47] (and the abiding here is in the *logos* rather than the *rhema*), the signification of scripture here would seem to indicate an objective sense and a normative function is implicit *in* the scripture. This would also be supported by the climax of the Sermon on the Mount teaching:

> Therefore everyone who hears these words of Mine, and acts upon them, may be compared to a wise man, who built his house upon the rock. And the rain descended, and the floods came, and the winds blew, and burst against that house; and yet it did not fall, for it had been founded upon the rock. And everyone who hears these words of Mine, and does not act upon them, will be like a foolish man, who built his house upon the sand. And the rain descended, and the floods came, and the winds blew, and burst against that house; and it fell, and great was its fall.[48]

---

speaking the language as a tool of articulation. The second occurrence of "meaning" uses a different word. Here the Greek word is *dunamis* (Strong's #1411), which refers to power as the inner quality of an object. In other words, language has the power of conveying meaning to the speakers; it comes into the English language as the word "dynamite."

45. Though Lloyd-Jones self-identified as an "evangelical," his understanding of the term was far stricter and more in line with the Puritan understanding; see *What Is an Evangelical?* He was an expert on the Puritans (see Lloyd-Jones, *Puritans*) and was considered the foremost example of the expository, exegetical preacher of the twentieth century; an enormous archive of his work is found at https://www.mljtrust.org/.

46. We qualify this statement later as the concept of an independent realm of nature that could be scientifically studied, first articulated with Aquinas, then Scotus, and most radically in Ockham. However, there is a good consensus that the Reformation was a pivotal turning point that made a far friendlier environment for natural science by removing the Aristotelian metaphysics and psychologism that had largely constrained it.

47. John 16:13 (NAS); John 8:31–32 (NAS).

48. Matt 7:24–27 (NAS).

The "words" of Jesus again here are *logos*. What I mean here is that much is made in, say, the Word of Faith movement[49] of the distinction between the *logos* (conceived of as the written Word of God) and the *rhema* (conceived of as the spoken Word of God); with the *rhema* conceived of as the Holy Spirit bringing specific words to the believer or the Church through subjective, religious experience. This is conceived of as the individual or corporate "leading" of the Holy Spirit in the life of the believer or Church. This distinction was employed in this fashion by Jesus in his discussion with Satan: "he answered, 'It is written, Man does not live by bread alone, but by every word that comes from the mouth of God'"[50] where the "word" here *is rhema*. Satan had misquoted and misinterpreted Ps 91 to Jesus, and Jesus corrected the misinterpretation by appealing both to the objective "what is written" and the subjective "what is said."

Thus, by preferring *logos* to *rhema*, I would argue John is talking about something objective here (what I will call "worldview" in this work, originating from the *logos* upon which we are to build our foundation) rather than religious experience.[51] Spiritual experience is not discounted but is tested by scriptural foundations for authenticity; if we accept the biblical narrative, we accept we can be deceived by counterfeit spiritual experience and we need normative criteria to distinguish the two, as well as our inner light. It is on this basis this work proceeds, seeking a solid, objective, scriptural foundation while acknowledging the importance of religious experience in receiving the immediate knowledge of God's will and direction in specific situations where we might have many options or we do not know how to proceed; celebrating the subjectivity and creativity that can flow from scripture that comes to us as narrative while maintaining that same narrative had an objective, intended sense.

1.5 Epistemological *Un*-Consciousness and Its Transcendental Critique

One of the aims of this work is not just to establish the validity of *epistemological self-consciousness* as a concept but also as a methodology to bring others to self-consciousness about their own epistemologies that

---

49. This is not to denigrate that movement; I self-identify denominationally as "Word of Faith."

50. Matt 4:4 (NAS).

51. For the most robust justification for this view, see Bahnsen, *Always Ready*, §§1–26.

they may judge their "worldview" against the standard of rationality and coherence argued herein. As intimated previously, this can only be conducted via a transcendental critique of the opposing worldviews for reasons which we will work out during this work. However, to clarify our aims with a negative example, we should immediately see that one possible logical implication of our posited category is that we are asserting that the opposing worldviews can be (and normally are) epistemologically *un*-conscious.[52] When we state that an individual is epistemologically *un*-conscious, it means philosophically, or at a basic cognitive level, that they are either:

a. *Not aware of the full implications of their theory of knowledge.*

For example, a *consistent* materialist would not be able to persuade us of the legitimacy of their worldview because the laws of logic, a prerequisite of argument, do not fit into the materialist view of the universe. This is because the laws of logic are non-material, universal, and abstract.

b. *Borrowing intellectual capital from those they mean to oppose.*

We do not argue that an unbeliever does not know *how* to count, but rather they can only give a viciously circular *account* of their counting.[53] The fullest sense of knowledge is not just the *how* of an activity but the *why* of the activity. Our claim to "science" fails, I assert, if we cannot justify *why* the process of science is successful.

1.6 Transcendentalist but Not Kantian Creative Antirealism

The astute reader at this point might understand that *transcendental critique* suggests a broad Kantian approach is adopted as the philosophical basis of this work and would thus dismiss it as "unsafe" on that basis, best left in its grave (for we are all analytic philosophers now). However, this is only true in the most abstract sense and should be of no hindrance to the reader who is a realist or finds the Continental schools compelling. With

---

52. It is worth noting here that the term "epistemological unconsciousness" is not being used in the same sense as some Eastern religions might use it, where it refers to mystical modes of knowing. Thanks to Dr. Wali for this comment.

53. Frequently this relies on a tautological appeal to evolutionary theory: *Those that count survive. How do we know that? We survived and we count.*

respect to this important assertion, it is of note that Van Til, to whom this work owes its first intellectual debt, taught that our framework might be broadly considered as "idealist" and our method as "transcendental" but only when those words are understood with their Reformed or Augustinian *Christian* sense.[54]

That is, for Van Til, Kantian thought and idealism in the general sense found their final authority *not* in God's Word but in the *idol* of human autonomy.[55] Van Til agreed with the general transcendental *program* of Kant[56] which was concerned to discover what general conditions must be fulfilled for any particular instance of knowledge to be possible, but the Van Tillian *a priori* finds its ultimate referent in transcendent revelation, not in autonomous deduction of the categories of the understanding. Thus, Van Til considered Kant to have intensified the autonomous attitude of Descartes, who is said to have proceeded from the indubitable of his own existence and proceeded then to God and the world.[57] The

---

54. There is an issue of nomenclature here as to why we want to insist on equating "Reformed Christianity" with Augustinianism; it immediately has the feel of sectarianism and might be argued to be historically problematic. Indeed, we shall shortly argue that Augustine (b. 354) was a member of the church headquartered at Rome; he was a Roman "catholic"; *Saint* Augustine is a "hero" celebrated in the present RC Church.

However, this tension is easily resolved, first on a structural level: the papacy had not developed (though the Roman bishops were attempting to assert their primacy during the time of Augustine, which was the time of terminal decay for the Roman Empire) and there was but one church; but secondly, theologically: it is the theology and philosophy of St. Thomas Aquinas (b. 1225) who, it is argued, stood *directly* against some of Augustine's presuppositions regarding the roles of faith and reason, and it is Aquinas who dominates the basic orientation of RC theology and philosophy today.

Thus, there is no real contradiction; the Reformers in many senses were trying to return to the period before the papacy in which Augustine's work, particularly his mature work, was considered as one of the philosophical high-water marks of the Roman patristic period. Equally significantly for Catholic scholarship, it might also be argued that Henri de Lubac (see the bibliography) as a Catholic reformer of last century was attempting to recover a more orthodox Augustinian view while not defaming Aquinas, instead claiming Aquinas had been misinterpreted in the neo-Thomism of his successors.

55. Francis Bacon (1561–1626), in his rigorous attack on the classical epistemology of his time, also concluded there were "idols" that hindered a true science.

56. Which has intellectual foreshadowing in Aristotle, who argued transcendentally for the law of excluded middle and was revived in the near contemporary arguments against skepticism of P. F. Strawson in the 1960s. Strawson's work, more than any other, was the catalyst for the revival of the interest in the transcendental mode of argumentation and what can be achieved by means of it. We spend extensive time on this in future sections.

57. This is a recurring theme in the work of Van Til as K. Scott Oliphint notes in his editorial notes to Van Til, *Defense of the Faith*, 146n3. For a more charitable and

mind of humanity even became the lawgiver for Kant, not the mind of God, and thus the procedure of Kant stands in direct opposition to that which is presented in this work, which is broadly Van Tillian. Similarly, Plantinga, to whom this work owes its second intellectual debt, also gives us compelling reason to reject any temptation to follow Kant:

> Did we structure or create the heavens and the earth? Some of us think there were animals—dinosaurs, let's say—roaming the earth before human beings had so much as put in an appearance; how could it be that those dinosaurs owed their structure to our noetic activity. . . . And what about all those stars and planets we have never so much as heard of: how have we managed to structure them? When did we do all this?[58]

Indeed, in my basic orientation, I consider myself a realist as Christian philosophy (in which we include theology) is, or at least should be, concerned with the reality which is God's world and in which we live and breathe as concrete persons. Plantinga's epistemology might be considered an elaboration and an expert exegesis of that principle, and I draw heavily from his work in my own position. Fundamental to both our views is that our mind is connected to the world and tells us *real* information about the world because that *is* the way *God created our minds to behave*. This last sentence alone has "nuclear strength" in an apologetic contest: the fundamental philosophical problem of how to connect our concepts with the world is one of the chief problems of philosophy. Nevertheless, we must acknowledge the critiques of Hume and Kant, and one task of this work must be to demonstrate how we unify concept and percept without succumbing to a *naïve* realism or a catastrophic skepticism. For Christians who are not primarily mystics, phenomena and noumena, mind and object, subjective and objective should be categories resolved and unified in God, and we will be demonstrating a reconciliation of these basic philosophical tensions.

---

appreciative reading of Descartes, see Macneil, "Descartes Showed There Was No Need for God."

58. Plantinga, "On Christian Scholarship," 274.

INTRODUCTION

1.7 Epistemological Self-Consciousness as Augustinian Apologetics

By presenting the Christian worldview as the only possible one that maintains theoretical coherence and metaphysical correspondence,[59] this work is essentially an "apologetic" work in the Augustinian tradition where "faith" is considered as the grounding to right reason, rather than reason validating what of faith might be considered "reasonable."[60] Both Van Til and Plantinga self-identified as being within the "broad tradition" of Augustinian philosophy, thus being those who have worked not just *as* Christians who happened to do philosophy but as those who desired to *do* philosophy in an authentically *Christian* way.[61]

While both men have specialized in epistemology, the term "epistemological self-consciousness" is owed most immediately to the work of Cornelius Van Til and to his major interpreter, Dr. Greg Bahnsen (d. 1995).[62] I am employing the term distinct from its strict Van Tillian sense

---

59. We will examine more closely in future sections the "coherence" and "correspondence" theories of truth. The point here is that they need not be considered rival theories at all, as they deal with different aspects of truth, the epistemological and the metaphysical respectively.

60. It is of note that the "early" Augustine, influenced heavily by Greek philosophy as most of the early church fathers were, might be considered to have held the view that faith should be in concord with "right reason." Sixteen centuries later, this was the Warfieldian or the "Old Princeton," view which is a testimony to the longevity and persuasiveness of the position. He steadily moved to the opposite view however, and in his later life he published a series of "retractions" and "corrections" explaining why he had changed his mind. His controversy with Pelagius on the nature of human will and its role in the salvific process was one of the drivers to his change of mind. Similarly, St. Anselm (1033–1109), one of the great intellects of the so-called Middle Ages (who had established a vibrant intellectual center during his tenure at Bec in Normandy), captured this thought in the Latin inscription that prefaced many of his works, "*Fides quaerens intellectum*," translated literally as "faith seeking understanding." This, in a few words, also captures the purpose and the intellectual lineage of my work.

61. For example, Van Til, *Defense of the Faith*, 381; Plantinga, "On Christian Scholarship."

62. While other of Van Til's students such as John Frame (who is still working) have been influential, written on Van Til and developed aspects of his position, only Bahnsen was described by Van Til himself as the "authority on his position." Bahnsen was known as a capable debater engaging in public debates with atheists within the secular academy. A number of Bahnsen's students are still academically, culturally, and theologically active, e.g., Michael R. Butler, Gary DeMar, and Keith Gentry, who might all be credited with developing Van Tillian thought. Following Bosserman (see bibliography), James N. Anderson, K. Scott Oliphint, Vern S. Poythress, Ralph Allan Smith, Lane G. Tipton, and Bosserman himself should all be considered contemporary Van Tillians.

as I also draw on the realism of Plantinga, but it is the position of this work that the solution to the problem of human knowledge and the resulting imperatives are argued to only be provided by the metaphysical foundation of an orthodox, Augustinian[63] Christian understanding and the ethical consequences for a political philosophy are then worked out. It mandates that one fully *understands* their theory of knowledge, its *justification* in metaphysical terms which then *mandates* its ethical consequences.

1.8 Epistemological Self-Consciousness as a Scientific Project

1.8.1 The Challenge of Perennial Naturalism in the Academy

In the interests of due diligence and with proper respect to the merits of the case, it must immediately be admitted that epistemological *un*-consciousness, as seen in the varieties of perennial naturalism, dominates the academy as a normal state of affairs, particularly within the sciences.[64] This immediate challenge requires addressing before we proceed but we can posit that it poses no threat to our thesis. We will demonstrate that its adoption and maintenance within most of the sciences is a result of the post-positivistic naturalism of the academy since the late 1950s which incorporated elements of the otherwise intellectually discredited earlier naturalisms of pragmatism, logical positivism, and logical analysis that dominated Anglo-American philosophy in the second half of the nineteenth and first half of the twentieth centuries. Thus, we will seek to show, that this incorporation, despite the sometimes-fundamental weaknesses

---

63. We could have just as easily used the terms "Calvinistic" or "Reformed" here. As Pawson, "HIS Return," stated, Calvin might be "merely" considered to have put Augustine's theology down in a systematic manner. However, by avoiding naming Calvin, it can avoid the controversy associated with him. In some philosophical circles, the term "Augustinian" is preferred as Augustine was recognized as a philosopher as well as a theologian whereas Calvin is conceived of as an anti-papist theologian first to the eclipsing of all else, no matter how prejudiced and ill-informed such an assessment would be.

64. Often just abbreviated to "naturalism." The term is immediately derivative from the movement that is said to have begun with Thales in ancient Greece (ca. 600 BCE) who attempted to explain the whole of nature (including "the gods") in terms of the natural processes themselves; or, alternatively, that every process of reality (including "the gods") is *necessarily* a natural process, i.e., subject to nature. However it is nuanced, it is at base a form of monism. See Frame, *Apologetics*, 52–54; Plantinga, "On Christian Scholarship," 270–72.

INTRODUCTION

repeatedly exposed in the critical literature (which we examine in detail when we consider the fallibilist perspective on epistemology in §2.6), is an example of prejudice and dogmatism, an attempt to preclude critical examination of the illegitimate philosophical assumptions implicit in the worldview that would otherwise render it obviously incoherent.[65]

Thus, in this work, I contend the exact opposite, that science, to be legitimately categorized as science, must *necessarily* ascend to the level of epistemological self-consciousness built on a robust metaphysics. Whether this should be considered as psychological necessity or logical necessity, with the latter obviously the stronger proposition, is a legitimate matter for debate. That is, we are not arguing that all science must be determined certainly to be considered as science, but I argue in this work that if we *were* to accept the philosophical implications of epistemological unconsciousness where the *possibility* of epistemic certainty is not considered necessary to science, using say the atheist worldview, our attempts at science and philosophy would be, on analysis, rendered incoherent and self-refuting.

1.8.2 The Status of Science—Preliminary Remarks

The discussion above regarding naturalism would immediately suggest that we have a profound definitional and methodological problem regarding what constitutes "science," which is of major importance to our discussion. We can mitigate this though by considering that the linguistic use of "science" was only altered primarily during the post-Darwinian period of the nineteenth century and the opening decades of the twentieth century, when it became intellectually fashionable among the irreligious and anti-religious to cast "science" and "religion" as adversarial and opposing views of reality.

In contrast, when Abraham Kuyper, the great Dutch statesman, educator, cultural critic, reformer, and theologian[66] was writing at the turn of the twentieth century, he employed the term "science" to include

---

65. Both Greg Bahnsen and Michael Butler (who will receive numerous citations in this book) make the point that it is just intellectual prejudice to assert that "unless it is naturalistic, it is not scientific." Plantinga, *Where the Conflict Really Lies*, represents probably the most sophisticated deconstruction and rebuttal of this view to which we will also give attention as necessary.

66. For more about this remarkable and neglected figure, see Macneil, "Abraham Kuyper, Culture and Art."

theology, philosophy, literature, and political economy, in a usage much closer to the modern usage of the term "epistemology."[67] Similarly, he described what we would call "evolutionary theory" (which is generally conceived as "scientific theory") as "the deleterious *philosophy* and consequences of evolutionary naturalism."[68] Likewise, Michael Faraday when he published his revolutionary theories of electricity published them in a journal of *natural philosophy*.[69] The attempt by naturalistic science to define science as that which is naturalistic in its assumptions and methods, demonstrates a principal prejudice.

Thus, I argue that epistemological unconsciousness is to be considered *un*-scientific because it fails as a *rational* explanation of reality which would then imply that naturalism and science are incompatible.[70] However, we have just admitted that the scientific academy views naturalism as normative, and we all still stand in awe of the achievements of modern "science" and furthermore, and rather more subtly, if I have a headache and take an aspirin, who *cares* what the aspirin is doing to my biochemistry if it removes my headache? Or if I merely drive my car, why should I be concerned with *how* the engine works? There seems a *prima facie* justification for epistemological *un*-consciousness both by the weight of the academy and a pragmatic justification by the means of any number of these unsophisticated constructions from everyday life.

We examine that this apparent paradox is resolvable because the naturalist is not, in practice, acting *consistently* with their naturalist principles. They borrow intellectual capital from the Christian worldview and deceive themselves that they need not acknowledge that. The emotive analogies too fare little better, being populist parodies of American pragmatism (see §2.6.6), and are of course unsatisfactory or inadequate simply because:

---

67. Kuyper, "Common Grace in Science." In the early stages of this work in a conversation with Dr. Toby Betenson, I suggested (and he agreed) that the terms "science" and "epistemology" were equivalent; the Latin *scientia*, from where we derive "science," and the Greek *episteme* are both rendered "knowledge." It seems more a matter of the academic discipline, rhetoric, or prejudice to prefer one over the other.

68. Kuyper, "Evolution," 403–40. Emphasis added.

69. Faraday, "Experimental Researches in Electricity."

70. Plantinga, *Where the Conflict Really Lies*, is an extended deconstruction of naturalism and its presentation as unscientific. Some of the most forceful and articulate critiques of naturalism have been made by Plantinga.

a. Medical side effects are sometimes fatal even when the compound offers immediate relief (that is why vaccines historically have needed close to a decade to have been proven safe).[71]

b. Abuse of, say, combustion engines in service beyond their design tolerances can (and do) have catastrophic consequences.

Philosophically, or we might as easily say, "scientifically" (we shall justify further this collapse or merging of categories below), *someone* needs to understand the biochemical effects of drugs to ensure safe use of pharmaceuticals and the mechanical laws applicable under different conditions to design a safe machine.[72] Similarly, we argue that a science which proceeds on a purely pragmatic basis because it just "works" would quickly be unworkable for it begs the question as to *why* it should be useful to us, which must then be decided on a *non*-pragmatic basis. In other words, we most certainly need to be clear of what is meant by our critics when their "science" is showcased as the pinnacle of rationality.

1.8.3 The Problem of Induction

This brings us nicely to the self-contradiction in Hume, one of the fiercest critics. Hume had wanted to apply the empirical methods of Newton beyond physics to provide a basis for *all* of natural science but wrestled with what he saw as an insurmountable obstacle to the justification of inductive thinking, which he rightly saw was providing the basis for a comprehensive natural science in contrast to the metaphysical dogmas that he had counseled, in his most famous passage, "should be cast to

---

71. As the adverse side-effects of the COVID vaccines slowly force themselves into the medical and the public consciousness, this provides a case study as to the perils of pragmatism and political expediency in medical ethics.

72. However, interestingly in engineering there is a distinction between "empirical formulae" and formulae resulting from theoretical (rational) analysis. Empirical formulae result from large scale measurements that are seen to be approximated by a mathematical formula but have no basis in theory; they just "work." In a previous life I worked with modeling fluid flow, which is highly complex and for large scale systems has proven difficult to analyze theoretically with any acceptable degree of predictability and accuracy. However, in the name of safety, ISO and API standards exist that mandate *safe* practice on the basis of the empirical theories. It is perhaps provocative that this "scientific" process is exposed as, at best, semi-rational. However, we should also note that theoretical analysis is preferred wherever possible in virtually every ISO or API standard as a basis for action.

the flames."[73] The force of his criticism was such that it has never been satisfactorily answered by *secular* naturalist thought but Hume also, importantly, realized *he* could not live *consistently* with his own skepticism. In the second of his famous passages, he announces that when the skeptical challenges threatened to overwhelm him, he hit the bar to play backgammon with his friends.[74]

Hume's deconstruction of empiricism was lamented several centuries later by Russell and indeed it was a long, despairing, and sad lament, for Russell could offer no *empirical* argument that would refute Hume. Russell had encapsulated the rationality problem that Hume had identified as the "Christmas Turkey" problem, which I shall give a version of, for I believe it is an excellent illustration of the forcefulness of Hume's criticism of the rationality of induction:

> Imagine you were a turkey in January; every day you hear a bell and you come to realize that is the dinner bell. You hear that bell and, because you have discovered that your universe runs by the law of the bell, you receive food every day at the set time. However, on the first of December, you hear the bell but instead of being greeted with food at the feeding station, the laborers cut your throat with a hatchet.

Your perception of your turkey universe as a uniform spatial-temporal continuum governed by certain scientific regularities came to an abrupt halt. It was merely a *habit of the mind* to see regularity and uniformity based on the empirical evidence of your senses; there was nothing of logical necessity in the experience.

However, the enormous progress of science in the nineteenth and twentieth centuries provides the backdrop as to why Russell temperamentally considered those that took refuge in Hume's skepticism as "dishonest" because they would eat when they got hungry. Russell's point was in essence a pragmatic one rather than a logical or philosophical refutation of Hume—if we took Hume seriously, we would reject that being hungry *necessarily* means that we should eat. That is, unless we are deliberately abstaining from food or have no food, everyone eats when they are hungry. In a similar vein, Ayer, in his seminal work[75] introduc-

---

73. Hume and Steinberg, *Enquiry Concerning Human Understanding*, loc. 2399.

74. In commenting on this passage, Bahnsen asserts that he modeled this approach to life for most of American society (but we could equally add Europe too)—when thinking about life gets you down, hit the bar!

75. Ayer, *Language, Truth, and Logic*. The first edition was published in 1936 in

ing logical positivism to the English-speaking world (see §2.6.7), accused those who used Hume to question the logical status, or more exactly, the *rational respectability* of inductive thinking as guilty of "superstition." Inductive thinking was clearly the basis of science and clearly getting results and that was all there was to it; "nothing else was necessary," i.e., the success of the wider program of "science" was a sufficient justification for Ayer.[76]

This too sounded a lot like the pragmatists with whom the positivists had competed for the heart and soul of twentieth-century philosophy. Dewey had concluded that no answer to Hume was possible, but it was *not important* to find that answer; it was merely a *theoretical* problem, a linguistic or psychological confusion that had no practical significance for our ability to solve our problems of everyday life and so should be ignored. Similarly, when the positivists sidestepped the issue by calling it a "pseudo-problem,"[77] a designation they began to employ for any problem within philosophy or science that seemed insoluble, it was methodologically analogous to the pragmatist dismissal of it as irrelevant. In effect, we will understand that neither could offer anything that would answer Hume. Thus, as we move into the post-positivist period precipitated by Quine's devastating critique[78] of positivism, we will see that Quine himself could offer nothing better than an evolutionary justification of induction, the inadequacy of which we will consider in detail later when we articulate his conception of a naturalized epistemology (see §3.3.5). We will find that there remains no *empirical* or *scientific* justification of induction, but we witness a begging of the question as there was no noncircular explanation as to *why* induction has helped us to survive.

Most notably, we will see that the philosophers of science have remained engaged with the problem of induction; even the briefest introduction to a philosophy of science will describe it as an issue "which keeps us awake at night."[79] Both Schlick and Carnap had extensive treat-

---

lieu of Ayer's involvement with and learning from the Vienna Circle. It was one of the most influential works published in twentieth-century philosophy and set the agenda until Quine's deconstruction of the view in 1953 (though Ayer continued to argue for it through the 1960s). See also chap. 2, n. 44.

76. Ayer, *Language, Truth, and Logic*, 49 ff.

77. Carnap's early principal work the *Aufbau* (1928) has the English title *The Logical Structure of the World and Pseudoproblems in Philosophy*. Similarly, Ayer's discussion of the problem of induction describes it as a pseudo-problem because it is insoluble.

78. Quine, "Two Dogmas of Empiricism," 20–46.

79. Okasha, *Philosophy of Science*, back cover.

ments of it in their original editions of their theories of knowledge; neither of which survived into later editions as a compelling solution. A substantively different approach to the problem was seen in Popper's attempt to interpret science as a discipline of *falsification*, i.e., to recast science in essence as logically deductive. It was an attempt to get around both the positivist problems of verificationism and to "solve" the problem of induction. For Popper, we are to view science as something other than empirical and inductive, reducing the importance of induction, and thus to be more comfortable with the insoluble problem of induction.[80]

However, Popperism had many logical problems of its own, and once this particular genie was let out of the bottle it was a short jump to the position of his one-time student Paul Feyerabend to deny there was *anything* that qualified as a "scientific" method. For Feyerabend, falsification compounded the difficulties for complex webs of propositions[81] and Feyerabend actively endorsed what he called "epistemological anarchy" such that he was designated by some as the "greatest enemy of science."[82] This was not as iconoclastic as it sounds as Feyerabend later clarified to those who thought they saw a rejection of science in his work (and they were many). His appeal was rather to a kind of strengthened pragmatism—let us not be overly concerned with how we arrived at knowledge, just be glad we got there. Thus, the conception of science as somehow implicitly inductive has remained, and this reliance on induction we will see undermines its claims to be the required standard of rationality.

---

80. However, this argument is very weak as the scientist in practice is not really concerned with falsifying the theories of others (though they might do it as a consequence of their work) but is primarily interested in advancing or "proving" the truth of their own theories. Popper's conception of science created quite a stir in the period immediately after publication in English (1959—even though the first edition was published in German in 1935, it lost out to the logical positivism that he was critiquing) but was quickly eclipsed by Kuhn's theories and the naturalism of Quine, both of which were well established by the end of the 1960s.

81. The problem for falsification in these cases is *what precisely* is being falsified? If we have ten propositions but only one is faulty, we cannot say that we have falsified the other nine. See also nn 96, 97.

82. On the face of this remark, you would have expected him to have a kinship with a Rorty or the wider pragmatist movement, but his close associates and friends were philosophers of science (he had a close friendship and professional disputation with one of the most influential philosophers of science, Imre Lakatos, captured in Lakatos and Feyerabend, *For and Against Method*); his dislike for "intellectuals" (including here Rorty, Nagel, and Searle, leaders in the postmodern pragmatist movement) was plain. See Feyerabend, *Killing Time*, 146–47.

1.8.4 Political Ethics and Science

However, and in my view far more importantly, Feyerabend made a supremely important observation about science:

> Science must be protected from ideologies; and societies, especially democratic societies, must be *protected from science* . . . science should be taught as one view among many and not as the one and only road to truth and reality.[83]

Here he is denying any privileged position for science just because it is "science" or to the scientists because they are "scientists," arguing that democracies for their own strength and longevity, should be protected from the excesses of ideologized science. The latter might seem unintuitive until we consider that "scientific materialism" provided the backbone for what became Stalinist tyranny, and the Nazi experimentation in the prison camps was considered by the historic cultural leaders of Europe as genuine science; indeed, it was picked up and given respectability throughout the 1960s within the international eugenics movement.[84] It is also worth remembering that the logical positivist and humanist manifestos of the 1930s had science at the heart of a new paradigm for the progression of human civilization freed from any metaphysical moorings. Similarly, we will see that the behaviorist utopia of Harvard professor B. F. Skinner, which emerged first with his novels in the late 1940s and which he unflinchingly maintained up to his death in 1990, designated concepts such as "freedom," "dignity" and "morality" as relics of a post-Christian era that needed to be purged that a truly scientific "planning" of society might be accomplished.

---

83. Feyerabend, *Against Method*, viii. Emphasis added.

84. The basic principles of eugenics underpinned the "family planning" ideologies and the various frequent excesses of colonial rule around the world. Academic journals that freely used the name persisted through the 1960s, but various scandals such as forced familial separation, *de facto* ethnic cleansing, forced sterilization or abortion of humans judged intellectually "inferior" meant the term lost respectability and is seldom used in a positive sense *openly* today. However, some key components of the philosophy survive in some of the questionable practices of powerful NGOs (particularly billionaire funded foundations) or quasi-UN bodies (bodies that are nominally part of the UN but now function *de facto* independently from it, both financially and governmentally, e.g., the WHO). For example, especially under the guise of "reproductive health" and vaccination protocols, fertility reducing hormones were added for "strategic reasons" to the compounds to deliberately limit population growth in "undesirable" locations. See Macneil, *Great COVID Caper*, §"Ruthless and Immoral NGOs."

Now, it is this ethical dimension to science that makes it necessary for us to reflect on; it will occupy us at various points in this work and plays a significant role for us. Russell wanted to believe that "philosophy could inspire a way of life"[85] but, owing to his engagement with the logical positivism of the Vienna Circle and its project to "clean up" philosophy from its muddled metaphysical speculations, struggled to make up his mind as to what there was left in life to be the targets of our inspirations. Russell's changes in philosophical views were frequent, many, and most basic to the degree he changed his mind frequently as to just what objects constituted reality.[86] Yet he was to be commended in that he was bold enough to argue that there was such a thing as the "real." In a lecture attended by Carnap in which they argued whether the concept of reality was a *pseudo-problem*[87] of philosophy, Russell asked Carnap whether his wife really did exist or whether she was to be considered a pseudo-construction of Carnap's consciousness.[88]

Thus, we argue that we must be prepared to stand on the ground initially carved out by Moore and Russell that we are free to believe in a world in which the grass was *really* there, it was green, and the sky was *really* above us, and it was blue. We are free to escape from the idealist's prison of the real as the perceived, where we are forever separated in the Kantian hinterland from the *Ding an Sich* (the thing in itself), but also from the arbitrariness and skepticism of the positivist and pragmatist alternatives. So, we will see that while the logical positivist and pragmatic

---

85. Russell, *History of Western Philosophy*, 789.

86. Russell, *My Philosophical Development*. This was not a typical autobiography; the introduction by Baldwin contextualizes it well as does Wood's postscript. Russell does not see his frequent changes of mind as problematic but rather as signs of dynamic thinking.

87. As we will study, for Carnap and the other logical positivists who were most sympathetic to him, a *pseudo-problem* of philosophy might be considered a question that could never have a final answer. Any question that could not be disassociated into logical components that would admit of truth claims was to be rejected as *non-sense*. It was because its language was ambiguous that it seemed to be expressing an insoluble proposition; yet, when it is expressed in the ideal language of set theory and logical notation, it is shown to be a linguistic confusion and hence a *pseudo-problem* or no problem at all. Carnap represented the first major push of linguistic philosophy to derive a "perfect" language that would clearly express propositions and thus "solve" the problems of philosophy that had resulted from this obfuscation in normal language. This was his reading of Wittgenstein's *Tractatus* where Wittgenstein asserted that the solution to the problems of philosophy was in their disappearance, when his argument for logical form of reality was properly understood.

88. Carnap, *Philosophy of Science*, loc. 77.

view was to elevate a "scientific view of the world" to ideological status, it was a narrow phenomenological perspective that Quine later exposed as resting on a supremely dogmatic metaphysic. The "scientific view" was indeed a particular view of the world, but it was a barren one, and a tentative and uncertain one at that.

To emphasize this, the logical positivist Neurath had fully appreciated the epistemological frailty of the position, and his famous analogy of rebuilding a ship while at sea reflected the tentativeness and the weak view of certainty at its heart. This analytic turn, though welcome for its rigor, tended to make smaller and smaller units for philosophical reflection and abandoned the traditional synthetic task of philosophy. Similarly, Russell's description of worldview philosophy as "pretentious"[89] accepts this rarefied role for philosophy as the only possible one. However, our argument is that it can hardly be thought impressive that the modern philosopher is seldom interested beyond the narrow circumspection of their specialism, and we proceed to that basis.

1.8.5 Science Is More Than Propositional Statements

Most importantly, by "science" we argue that we are not speaking of just the "natural sciences" such as physics or chemistry where it might be argued that the aggregate of a series of propositions are said to constitute the body of the discipline. In such a view, "scientific" questions could be answered simply using the predicates "true" or "false" with the implication that the wider "truth" (or Truth with the capital T) was the aggregate of all the "true" propositions. This was then said to constitute the "science" of the subject.

This was the influential and novel definition of "science" as offered by Schlick,[90] the putative father of twentieth-century positivism, and is essentially phenomenalistic.[91] This reflected the enormous influence

---

89. Russell, *History of Western Philosophy*, 789.

90. Schlick, *Problems of Ethics*, xiii ff.

91. Though known as the putative father of positivism because of his role in starting the Vienna Circle, Schlick was unusually broad in his perspective, an accomplished physicist and known for contributions to psychology, mathematics, biology, and sociology. His "demolition" of a key component of Kantian thought in his 1922 *General Theory of Knowledge* (with a second edition in 1926) was one of the pivotal events that shaped the "scientific" approach to philosophy that exerted an enormous influence on major figures such as Russell, Popper, and Hempel.

Interestingly, his commitment to realism is often contrasted with other members of

of the "new physics" of Einstein (see §2.6.9) and the working out of its philosophical implications in the Germanophone world, which, with the scattering of its predominantly Jewish intellectuals from Europe during the Nazi era, came to dominate the wider Anglo-American empiricist and analytically oriented philosophies. Schlick himself was one of the first expositors of Einstein's *General Relativity* in 1917 just two years after Einstein published, being commended by Einstein himself for the clarity of his explanation.[92] Schlick was very much the heir of the "philosophical physicists" personified in the work of Helmholtz and Planck, being a PhD student while working with Planck. Consequently, it is perhaps the working definition still assumed, consciously or unconsciously, by most of modern naturalism and hence our need to give it attention here. The philosophical elegance and clarity obtained in his definition of science was his response[93] to the ambiguity, irrationalism and subjectivity of the post-Kantian philosophy that had dominated German philosophy.[94] It was in the service of contrasting "science" with philosophy; he still considered the latter legitimate but *not* scientific by nature because of the questions it asked. The questions of philosophy, which Schlick described as a sequence of physical or psychic "acts," were concerned with

---

the Vienna Circle such as Neurath and Carnap, their later views on language meaning that Schlick's assertions of a "real" world were eventually classified as "philosophical pseudo-statements" by Neurath. Carnap, however, influenced Schlick to soften his commitment to realism, but it was still clear that Carnap paid homage in his work to Schlick; see Carnap, *Philosophy of Science*. Schlick, in short, shows a breadth to his work sometimes not associated with the positivist movement; see Oberdan, "Moritz Schlick."

92. See §§1 and 2 of Oberdan, "Moritz Schlick."

93. For example, see his closing remarks to his introductory preface to his *Problems of Ethics* (xiii). This was written in 1930, almost ten years before an English translation was available. This was the beginning of the period in which logical positivism was to almost dominate analytic philosophy (exerting an enormous influence into a broad spectrum of the humanities) until the mid-1950s with its denial of the meaningfulness of metaphysical statements. We consider this in greater detail later. As I will mention frequently, modern scientific naturalism owes much of its basic hostile orientation to metaphysics from logical positivism. Schlick himself did not see this success of the movement he founded; he was assassinated by a mentally ill former student on June 22, 1936.

94. Indeed, what might be called the wider "Continental" school which it was soon to displace, as the dominant philosophical school in the Anglophone world. Perhaps the most concise and readable account of the difference is found in Glock, *Analytical Philosophy*, 65 ff. A comprehensive assessment of what might be thought of as "Continental" philosophy is found in West, *Continental Philosophy*.

clarifying what was *meant*—they were not knowledge bearing; they were not instruments to recommend one answer over another.[95]

However, such a definition excises huge swathes of the conjectural and imaginative cognitive processes, rarefying what might be considered science, which was precisely what later philosophers of science such as Karl Popper, despite his having attended meetings of the Vienna Circle and possessing a common antipathy with them to metaphysics, would consider fundamental to science.[96] Popper's counterview was substantially obsolescent before it was even published in English by Quine's critique of both the verificationism of positivism and the Popperian alternative *falsification*.[97] For Quine, philosophy was contiguous with science and authentic philosophy was a part of science and what

---

95. A method famously employed by him in his *Problems of Ethics* (1939). Ayer, articulating the same conclusion, concluded "the propositions of philosophy are linguistic in character, not factual ... philosophy is a branch of logic" (*Language, Truth, and Logic*, 57).

96. See the preface to the first English edition of Popper (*Logic of Scientific Discovery*) where Popper (writing in 1959) clearly and explicitly describes his differences with the "language analysts," which is a synonym for the logical positivists. He had initially maintained a degree of affinity with them, having attended meetings of the Circle during the 1930s, and in some respects might be considered as having maintained a similar approach in generality, especially in regarding metaphysical language as "meaningless" while departing in detail. By the time of the publication of the first edition of his *Logik der Forschung* (1935) there were clear differences. Most importantly, Popper believed that philosophical propositions were possible; that is, philosophy was capable of bearing and constituting knowledge. Importantly, by 1969 Popper had admitted metaphysics had a role to play in science specifically and human knowledge generally; see Popper, *Knowledge and the Body-Mind Problem*, 76. In the same work, he also rejected materialism as dogmatic, preferring a view that admitted both mental and physical states.

97. In brief, a scientific statement (or proposition) was one that *in principle* was *falsifiable*. The great advantage over verificationism was that only a single counterexample was sufficient to establish the truth or falsity of a scientific proposition. Popper when formulating this had in mind his experience of working with a psychologist where the same data could be appropriated by rival psychological theories, both claiming to be scientific, as establishing them both. This he felt was too broad and illogical (it denies the law of excluded middle) and was considered by him as characteristic of *pseudo-scientific* theories.

More generally, the problems of delimiting pseudo-science vs. para-science vs. science vs. non-science is admirably attempted in Mahner, "Demarcating Science from Non-Science," but in reading his introduction and then the conclusion, I would argue he struggles to move beyond anything but a very detailed description of the problem and the many different attempted resolutions; rather than quenching the flames of the epistemological "anything goes" bonfire of Feyerabend, he seems to have provided fresh fuel for that fire.

constituted science was itself a "scientific" problem.[98] Quine was relaxed by the implicit circularity that this assumed, which will be important for us when we consider worldview apologetics, where we understand there is a difference between logical circularity and the logical fallacy of vicious circularity. Quine, for very different reasons than the Van Tillians, views circularity in reasoning as inevitable; the issue is rather how tight that circle is before it becomes fallacious.

As radical as Quine was, a more substantive and influential challenge was to come via the work of the philosopher of science, Thomas Kuhn. He challenged fundamentally the view of science as somehow a rational, linear process in perhaps the most influential work on the philosophy of science in the twentieth century, *The Structure of Scientific Revolutions*. Although first published in 1962, it is still a standard work today[99] and has an almost normative status, particularly among those disciplines that are vulnerable to charges of being unscientific and, by association, irrational. Indeed, although not welcomed by Kuhn himself, Kuhn's legacy was to relativize just what might be considered science as a function of historical expediency for a culture and brought the "social" or "soft" sciences such as sociology and psychology much more into the mainstream as legitimate "science."

It also served to demythologize science as *the* rational method of human thought. As noted, for this reason, Kuhn's legacy was maintained much more within the arts generally and their fight with "science" rather than the philosophy of science.[100] Those like Rorty who progressively distanced themselves from professional philosophy and wanted to categorize science in a quasi-Wittgensteinian fashion as akin to poetry strongly endorsed Kuhn.[101] "Science" is simply a manner of speaking about reality with no special privileges accorded to it as specifically or especially rational.

---

98. We shall return to Quine repeatedly. He pushed naturalism as far as it could go which inevitably terminates at a behaviorist view of human nature. Quine himself states he was attracted to a behaviorist explanation of human psychology even in his high school years.

99. The fiftieth anniversary edition was reissued in 2012 with the most recent reprint in 2021.

100. Where though initially significant and influential, he was frequently, and rightly, criticized for a lack of precision and ambiguity in his writing.

101. For example, Kuhn featured prominently in Rorty's *Mirror of Nature* which served to catapult Rorty into fame and infamy in equal measures. He is also heavily featured through Rorty's series *Philosophical Papers*, a four-volume set in which he collated his work into distinctive categories, only completed shortly before his death in 2007. The essay in volume 4 "Philosophy as a Transitional Genre" (89–104) is typical

That said, undoubtedly one of the most important insights emerging from Kuhn and developed in the postmodernism of Rorty was that any description of reality was always made "under a description"; it is always a matter of *interpretation* rather than just the "brute facts." In other words, Schlick's formulation "all synthetic judgments are *a posteriori*,"[102] i.e., judgments are based in and confirmed by a neutral "experience," is seen to be too naïve; we are already begging the question because the "truth" predicate is defined within a system (that defines for us the bounds of "experience") rather than in an abstract and objective fashion.

While we will concur to a degree with this position, we will also qualify it importantly, but we can conclude with many philosophers of science that Schlick's conception *was* too narrow and excludes much of what is now accepted as legitimately scientific. Notwithstanding and of equal importance, the outstanding success of "science" in the last two centuries means we must also be careful before denuding it of too much authority in human discourse as the postmodern critique has encouraged some to do. We will thus proceed to carefully contextualize science for our discussion.

1.8.6 Science as Correlated with Epistemology and Philosophy

Now, regardless of the particulars of this debate over science which we shall revisit as necessary, we will in lieu of our discussion above assert with *prima facie* justification, that "science" in a more inclusive sense is an aggregate term for the theoretical and empirical data of the "hard" (physical) and "soft" (social) sciences. However, we can push further: we might also correlate "science" much more closely with the term "philosophy"; that is, as a synonym for *all* the spheres of human knowledge. This is not just because of the historical equivalence of the usage of "natural philosophy," which was still the common sense of the term even during the early work of Einstein[103] but also because of the philosophical engage-

---

of Rorty's ability to apply his own deconstructive metanarrative to philosophy and philosophers while simultaneously denying there was a metanarrative to be had. The use he makes of Kuhn in that essay is typical of his application.

102. Schlick, *General Theory of Knowledge*, 384.

103. Einstein himself was far more philosophically astute than modern naturalistic science recognizes, recommending a young Moritz Schlick for a professorship but recognizing the difficulty in his appointment as him "not being a member of the established Kantian church." See Oberdan, "Moritz Schlick," who describes the Kantian themes that influenced the physicists and were surprisingly influential on Schlick's

ment of Germanophone physicists Helmholtz, Mach, and Planck, who were all engaged philosophically in a non-trivial manner. It seems little more than prejudice, linguistic convenience, or sociological convention to chop up their work into the "scientific" and the "philosophical."

We can strengthen our assertion by considering that modern compendiums of the philosophy of science demonstrate that science evades a clear definition in terms of either a particular metaphysical approach, a coherent theory of knowledge, even a specific methodology[104] or a rational process. Psillos, after explaining in excess of forty-five thousand words that the scientific concept of explanation is unexplainable, offers us this despairing conclusion:

> In light of the preceding discussion . . . it should be obvious that there is no consensus of what explanation is . . . [a] single and unified account of what explanation is, is futile and ill-conceived.[105]

While this conclusion has a peculiar incongruity in that we are receiving an explanation written by a philosopher of science into why we can never receive a coherent scientific explanation, his subsequent words should provide *us* with hope, even if it failed to do so for Psillos himself:

> Perhaps the only way to understand explanation is to embed it in a framework of kindred concepts and try to unravel their interconnections. Indeed, the concepts of *causation, laws of nature* and *explanation* [emphasis original] form a very tight web . . . hardly any progress can be made in any of those, *without relying on, and offering accounts of, some of the others.*[106]

The implications of what Psillos is stating here as the finishing paragraph to what only can be described as his epic paper in his part of constructing "*the* most definitive . . . ever provided" edifice to (dare I say, "explanation of") "the philosophy of science ever provided"[107] are

---

thinking. It is also of note that Schlick's appointment to the University of Vienna was to the chair of natural philosophy. It might also be noted that Niels Bohr wrote extensively on philosophical implications of his account of quantum theory, known as the "Copenhagen interpretation" (though his work was poorly received in contrast to his physics).

104. A descriptive account of the multiple variations and incommensurate nature of the variations is found in Ladyman, "Ontological, Epistemological and Methodological Positions."

105. Psillos, "Perspectives on Explanation," 170.

106. Psillos, "Perspectives on Explanation," 171. Second emphasis added.

107. Gabbay, Thagard, and Woods, General preface to *General Philosophy of Science*, v–vi.

worthy of another epic paper and certainly reinforce the philosophical presuppositions of this work:

a. We need to understand our beliefs and commitments form an interconnected web.

b. Our explanations will be *circular* in terms of our most basic controlling assumptions.

Taken together, (a) and (b) are the major constituent parts of our *worldview*, though more commonly, the term "conceptual scheme" might be used.[108]

So, we want to assert that science and epistemology, when considered generally, much like theology and philosophy, have the *same* referent (a general account of the universe) as their target material but choose a specific vocabulary and mode of argument when discussing with a particular target audience. Thus, it is sometimes argued that the distinction is, on a technical level, one more of the level of abstraction: when we ask a "philosophical" question we are not looking to the empirical work of a particular science, indeed we cannot, but we are establishing principles applicable to *all* sciences.[109] This is certainly a useful, working definition, but on analysis it begs the question as it already *assumes* a difference; but we have already seen Quine sees no substantive difference between science and philosophy, whereas the positivists denied philosophy any knowledge bearing status (so there would be no metaphysical principles to be had) and yet many physical scientists were historically happy to be known as practicing "natural philosophy."

It is sometimes also said that philosophical knowledge "transitions" to scientific knowledge as the understanding and application of the principles increases within each discipline.[110] This also has a *prima facie* plausibility but lurking behind it is an odor of a pragmatic or an instrumentalist view of knowledge generally. Some "sciences" working through pages of mathematical or statistical analysis will never progress beyond those methods into more "concrete" expressions, but it would

---

108. We will draw a future distinction between these two, with "worldview" being a far stronger term with ontological implications.

109. For example, Bahnsen, *ASC3 Practical Apologetics*, GB1356a–GB1360b. In his magisterial *History of Philosophy* series and his *Introduction to Philosophy* series he employs a similar distinction.

110. Mahner, "Demarcating Science from Non-Science," employs this distinction as one of the lines demarcating science from non-science.

seem sectarian and unreasonable to label them "un-scientific." Thus, in summary, it is perhaps far more convincing that certain groups like to call themselves "scientists" for sociological reasons to distinguish themselves from those they consider "un-scientific."

The designation of being the latter, like that of being a "fundamentalist," is an emotive pejorative with little content because the term is so imprecise. That is, the designation is often merely one of preference or prejudice and is arbitrary in nature. As both Psillos and Mahner discovered, attempting to analyze science in pursuit of clarity in the definition pushes you in a worldview direction. This is precisely the position we will be arguing for: science is defined *only* within the wider context of the entire map of our knowledge, much as Quine described it as a "web" of belief.[111] Some beliefs, near the center of the web are held tenaciously and require overwhelming evidence to be displaced, others at the edge of the web might be lost without affecting those close to the center.

In Wittgensteinian terms, we have several "forms of life," each with their own language games at work here, and we are in danger of being "seduced" by one or the other to the detriment of our cultures. Wittgenstein himself had reflected that in his early years he had attached improper importance to the language game of science but came to understand it was possible to be knowledge bearing in language with no reference to the physical world.[112] As Plantinga too argued, we cannot accuse every community outside of our nineteenth- and twentieth-century Western view of science as being "irrational"; their science is conceived and construed in a different way.[113] Any other conception of science has historically gravitated toward tyranny, both intellectual and political.

1.8.7 Avoiding the "Tyranny of Science"

As we have already noted, one of the modern philosophers of science to deny most forcibly that naturalistic conceptions of "science" should be intellectually privileged before other knowledge gaining activities of humanity was Paul Feyerabend. Indeed, Feyerabend asserted that this

---

111. In Quine and Ullian, *Web of Belief*, we find a view of "science," or more correctly rationality and knowledge, presented in an accessible way as a composite of different activities such as evidence, intuition, and judging.

112. I discuss this in Macneil, "Wittgenstein."

113. Plantinga, *Where the Conflict Really Lies*, preface.

privileging of naturalistic science was "tyrannical,"[114] which was perhaps well illustrated during the COVID-19 pandemic when "following the science" was equated with unjustified lockdowns and the removal of basic freedoms. Dodsworth illustrates this vividly:

> [It's about] how the government weaponised our fear against us—supposedly in our best interests—until we were one of the most frightened countries in the world . . . the behavioural scientists advising the UK government recommended that we needed to be frightened. The Scientific Pandemic Influenza Group on Behaviour (SPI-B) said in their report Options for increasing adherence to social distancing measures,1 dated 22 March 2020, that "a substantial number of people still do not feel sufficiently personally threatened; it could be that they are reassured by the low death rate in their demographic group, although levels of concern may be rising." As a result they recommended that "the perceived level of personal threat needs to be increased among those who are complacent, using hard-hitting emotional messaging." In essence, the government was advised to frighten the British public to encourage adherence to the emergency lockdown regulations.[115]

Feyerabend was likewise concerned with the social boundaries of science and the dangers of the cultural deference to it.[116] This is well reflected in that the head of the pharmaceutical company Pfizer "joked" that "the whole of Israel was a petri-dish"[117] after the Israeli government decided

---

114. Feyerabend's *Against Method* (2010, 1975) is now perceived as on a par with Popper and Kuhn regarding the status and limits of scientific reasoning. His last full book published before his death was titled *The Tyranny of Science*, a transcription of a series of public lectures given in 1992 derived from his lecture course he gave at Berkeley between 1958 and 1990. Though in many senses he was an intellectual chameleon, the justification for his iconoclastic views constantly moving and changing, his constant preoccupation was to demonstrate the myths and misrepresentations surrounding the modern apologies for science. Rushdoony's *The Mythology of Science* is a searching critique in a similar vein dealing specifically with the theory of evolution and the dedication to it by the evolutionists, treating it as on a par with a religious commitment.

115. Dodsworth, *State of Fear*, loc. 107–9.

116. In the follow-up to *Against Method*, *Science in a Free Society* (1978) he broadened his cultural criticism in irreverent fashion and argued that science should be subjected to democratic processes of control rather than science controlling the democratic. It was a challenging argument to make considering the "success" of science, but he attempted it vigorously. It is of note that his widow Paolino stated that he was the most "dissatisfied" with this book at the time of his passing and had wanted to revise it.

117. Sample, "'We Are a Petri Dish.'"

to "vaccinate" its way out of the COVID pandemic; it was a strategy that failed[118] but, remarkably, was unnecessarily repeated in many nations around the world despite of that failure, with similar results of failure. Epidemiologists in nations that argued for a different approach because they believed lockdowns and vaccinations would never deliver what was being promised for them were subject to international vilification with even ceremonial monarchs joining in the criticism and condemnation of any approach that did not endorse the WHO's "official" guidance.[119]

Other dissenting scientists were ostracized, imprisoned, referred to professional bodies, and forced from their employment. Media and social media were mandated to "follow the science" and platforms which marketed themselves as refuges of "free speech" became "scientifically controlled" centers of speech. It was rather like a dystopian, Orwellian novel: "following the science" was clearly subject to a political agenda and it was a tiny subset of science which was followed to the detriment of life and liberty. I explored this abuse of science during the "pandemic" in an extended study,[120] and it certainly seems that Feyerabend's vision that a science out of control would inevitably become tyrannical was almost prophetic, with a privileged subsection of "senior scientists" providing "science" on-demand to allow politicians to pursue immoral actions against their citizens.

This, we argue, reflects the enormous, ongoing cultural confidence in the power of science and the secular State to solve the problems of humanity through this thing called "science" which emerged into the mainstream popular consciousness in the latter half of the nineteenth century[121] and it was a centerpiece of the liberalism of the West in the early twentieth. In early Liberalism, particularly in the British version which was permeated by the messianic pretensions of the Empire before God bringing civilization to the heathen, organized religion provided the moral authority for the State and its justification to the wider polity. However, the heavy reliance of the totalitarian regimes of Nazism and Communism on "science" meant that there grew a reaction to its totalizing naturalism to favor more recognition of the individual and the

---

118. At the time of writing, it was on its eighth wave.
119. Macneil, *Great COVID Caper*, 62.
120. Macneil, *Great COVID Caper*.
121. Though Francis Bacon, as early as 1620, had presented the utopian vision of science as savior in his novel *The New Atlantis*.

subjective, sometimes a violent retreat into subjectivity as in the existentialist movement of Continental philosophy.[122]

This also came into sharp focus during the Vietnam War in the US where the "indiscriminate" use of technology as weapons during the 1960s until the end of the war in 1975 fanned cultural suspicion of science as illegitimate in contrast to recognizing the humanity and dignity of all people. It seemed that cultures were technologically advantaged but no less barbaric. The 1970s were characterized by what seemed like a moral and social decay in the fabric of the West, ethnic conflict within society, and a loss of confidence in "science" and indeed, religion or any other "metanarrative" of an "establishment" to solve these problems of society.

As we also noted previously, it is worth remembering that the ideologies of Marxism and Nazism both privileged naturalistic, value-free "science" in this way as central to their praxis which led to the systematic death of over 120 million in the twentieth century. Having begun his career as part of the Third Reich, Feyerabend can thus be permitted this indulgence for his unique perspective and as one of the most colorful and iconoclastic but original philosophers of science who could simultaneously earn the title the "worst enemy of science." His defense against this accusation is pointed and simple: science must be "subject to public control" (we might say "democratic" control) as it was in previous eras and scientists should not be privileged as a new medieval Catholic clergy, beyond the law and beyond censure.[123] Thus, the importance of the political ethics that emerge from our project, particularly when faced by this type of political challenge.

1.9 Philosophy as Transformative

An interesting contrast can be made between the biblical Hebrew culture and the contemporary Greek culture of the same time with regard to the

---

122. Abraham Kuyper had written repeatedly in opposition to the scientism that was part of the zeitgeist of the latter nineteenth and early twentieth centuries. His epistemology put the person, their relations, and their faith as a central relation. Bratt commented "this sounded postmodern" a century before Lyotard. Existentialism was associated first with Kierkegaard, who emphasized the subjectivity and authenticity of faith rather than objective dogmas; it was then secularized in Sartre as a form of Marxism (treating our very material existence as "absurd") and given a dense and alternative conception by Heidegger (who also exerted some influence on theology).

123. Found in full in his autobiography, completed on his deathbed, Feyerabend, *Killing Time*, 145 ff.

nature of knowledge. As our work is concerning knowledge it is useful to pause and reflect on why we should, or should not, pause and reflect. For the Hebrew, a father was to train his son in a trade and that trade would allow the son to be considered an adult member of society. In that sense, the education of a child was measured by the mastery of a set of skills that allowed the child to be a self-enabling and contributing member of society. Knowledge was expressed in the context of *living* in the world; it was not an abstract or contemplative model of knowledge.

However, a Greek conception might be that a ruler was trained by his "tutor" by exposure to a body of "knowledge" and could learn by rote a set of tenets. On successful recitation they would be considered "educated," but there was no requirement for that knowledge to be grounded or applicable to living in the world. We, to a large degree, have inherited the Greek presumption; we can all remember staying up all night to "revise" for an exam, do the exam, and then forget all what had been "learned" a couple of days later. One argument that we will consider is that it is questionable whether we ever ascended to the status of knowledge, and we shall investigate the requirements for "knowledge" within this work. In a similar manner, in the dying days of the British Empire, it was traditional that British Army officers had no requirement to be trained as regular soldiers with the result that they were spectacularly inept until the radical reforms of Montgomery during WWII that saved the nation from utter humiliation in Africa against Hitler's Rommel. The philosophical contrast was the training of the mind apart from the living of life: some things are only learned through "doing."

This was also the philosophical backdrop to a great dispute in the twentieth century among the educational reformers who argued for comprehensive education against the backdrop of the selective schools; even now, the most radical Left of British politicians will still be seduced into sending their children to "public" schools that are anything but public in the common sense of the word,[124] so that they might receive their training to rule us all as is their birthright. As a child in the 1970s,

---

124. For the non-British reader (and perhaps even for the British reader) the nomenclature is thoroughly confusing. The British "public" school is the equivalent of an Ivy League school in the US: they are independent schools paid for by private fees or endowments, *not* by the government. The US "public" school is the equivalent of the British "comprehensive" school, government funded. Only the highly privileged elite can afford to send their children to the British *public* school, and many of the elites from around the world also send their children to be educated there, particularly diplomats.

INTRODUCTION

this was a live issue for me, and I failed my 11+ for Colchester grammar despite my father's endless drilling me with practice exercises. As Professor Simon put it, I was to be doomed to the "sink comprehensive"[125] only encountering the grammarians as they beat us at rugby as well as any other sport;[126] we knew our place. Such also was the debate between the polytechnics and the universities, with the polytechnics converting themselves to universities during the 1980s for the purpose of instantly gaining kudos in the marketplace even if nothing else but their name had changed. The most supreme irony was that the polytechnics often became "better" universities because of their practical orientation and links with industry. One of my brothers who took the vocational route, picking "vocational" qualifications over the liberal arts degree, is now enjoying the good life down under. Despite many (and probably myself) telling him otherwise, he has not shed any tears missing out on a "broad," liberal arts education. Of course, we might want to defend ourselves that it might just mean he has been desensitized to the important issues of intellectual life as he enjoys the Gold Coast.

Educational theorists often blame Plato at this point—there is gold in some of us, silver in others, the rest are common base metal, and some of us are just plain wood. With the nineteenth-century social-Darwinist twist, each of us *should* know our place; such is the *natural* evolutionary order of things. This is the issue of the mode of philosophizing which has shaped our culture. In testament to our societal failures, my confirmation bias would be to favor the practical over the contemplative conception of philosophy. I *intentionally* chose an old "polytechnic" over the competing university when I trained as a teacher. As a practicing teacher I would often find that the toughest schools in the most "deprived" areas frequently had far better praxis in terms of innovation, curriculum diversity, and care for the individual pupil in contrast to the "posh" schools where the teacher could throw a textbook into the midst of the elite, and everyone would pass with an A while the teacher read their newspaper with merely a "peep hole" that they might maintain order (my mentor during training related such a story to me of his training days). A colleague of mine recounted how her philosophy class spent many hours considering the conundrum "If a tree falls in the forest but no one hears it, does it make a sound?" Now being an engineer and a physicist by training, my instinct

---

125. Simon, *What Future for Education?*

126. Interestingly though, the "Grammar" only played rugby and cricket; "football" (soccer) was too "common"!

was to say, "Be analytical, objective, and clear about your definitions and the problem resolves." I felt the Vienna Circle anointing to clean up philosophy come upon me:

P1: "Sound" is a compression wave itself caused by the disturbance of the uniformity of a medium.

P2: The tree falling disturbs the uniformity of the medium.

Conclusion: a tree falling in a forest makes a sound.

Now please spend all that "saved time" discussing this question to consider rather philosophy that might arrest the catastrophic decline of the West. In similar fashion, when I was training in 1994, I took a psychology of education class where the question, "What is normal?" was posed. I was expecting an intense duel of competing socially defined epithets being offered by us postgraduates militating against the tyranny of the majority, but it was all cut short by the lecturer giving the statistical definition "the highest frequency in a population." This was perhaps in enormous contrast to my psychology of religion teacher many years later who framed "madness" as merely "socially defined," the implication then being we could all be "mad" and not be concerned about it. Perhaps this should be borne in mind with our contemporary discussions of gender and sexuality which increasingly eat up letters of the alphabet.

That is, for myself in my philosophical naivety, such a "ridiculous" contrast regarding the normal would have settled those matters in favor of the practical. With my head still full of formulae from a life as an engineer, there is still something about the clarity and simplicity of a philosophy rooted and grounded in life and living which to me guards against those excesses of academic life.[127] The wider philosophical point then becomes the brutal reductionism of my legacy position: we realize how unfulfilling and perhaps uninspiring such a model of philosophy would be, as Russell mused "in praise of idleness,"[128] reflection has its place for a person to consider the "why" as well as the "how" of existence. Social

---

127. Perhaps demonstrated well by the "Sokal hoaxes" where fake papers advancing bizarre "postmodern" theses were accepted for publication in leading postmodern journals. "Sokal Squared" was a similar recently repeated exercise concentrating on the nascent gender and Critical Race Theory (CRT) disciplines, which I considered more fully in Macneil, "Fake (but Peer-Reviewed) Academic Papers"; despite the ridiculousness and lack of critical peer assessment exposed by the fakery, the academics were unrepentant, labeling it "an attack of the Right."

128. Russell, "In Praise of Idleness."

psychologists too can get far more elaborate than that clean definition of "normalcy" above with bell curves and distributions reducing the "intelligence" of a human population to a single quotient; the "*mis*-measure of man" that rather paradoxically the evolutionist Gould found so objectionable.[129] There is clearly the need for contemplative philosophical reflection here that the philosophy itself might be transformational. Thus, that does not mean I advocate a complete rejection of the contemplative in favor of the pragmatic; as we shall see, pragmatism begs the most important philosophical questions and I reject it as a model of philosophy.

Rather, there is a mediation within the epistemologically self-conscious perspective of what is asserted in the name of philosophy as to its relevance for solving the problems of society and culture more generally. In this sense, we would be wise to argue for a transformative model of philosophy, both as a matter of education of the mind and how to live in the world. By turning our pure mathematics into applied mathematics, we appreciate the beauty and value of the pure, so also with philosophy. Blackburn makes this critical judgment that expresses a similar imperative:

> We are not going to agree with the great postmodernist slogan made famous by Jacques Derrida: *"Il n'y a pas de hors-texte"* ("There is nothing outside the text"). [It appeals only to those] sufficiently divorced from the activities of life (at least at the times when they are writing about life) to really begin to imagine themselves in a virtual reality, the sealed world of their own beliefs and sayings.... The cure, as Wittgenstein saw very clearly, is to remember, and perhaps to practise, the practical techniques and skills of doing things in the real world.[130]

However, what we are considering so far above is philosophically agnostic. From a Christian perspective, Christian philosophy is transformative not just in a definitional fashion but in a phenomenological one also. If, as Descartes also wrote in his notebook, "the fear of the LORD is the beginning of knowledge"[131] this refers not just to intellectual or cognitive knowledge but the practical skills of life. The Hebrew language has a set of words which reflect these different senses of knowledge:

---

129. Gould, *Mismeasure of Man*.
130. Blackburn, *Truth*, 169–70.
131. Prov 1:7 (NAS).

> The noun . . . (*da'at*, "knowledge") refers to experiential knowledge, not just cognitive knowledge, including the intellectual assimilation and practical application. . . . It is used in parallelism to . . . (*musar*, "instruction, discipline") and . . . (*khokhmah*, "wisdom, moral skill").[132]

In his rationalism, it might be questionable that Descartes took these different senses of knowledge to heart, but he certainly argued that the atheist was unable to argue for a systematic theory of knowledge,[133] though equally others felt able to invert Descartes arguments and present an atheistic version. The most profound claim of biblical knowledge is the knowledge of salvation, the spiritual and intellectual response to the simple argument of Paul:

> But what does it say? "The word is near you, in your mouth and in your heart" (that is, the word of faith that we preach), because if you confess with your mouth that Jesus is Lord and believe in your heart that God raised him from the dead, you will be saved.[134]

Here the Greek verb σῴζω (*sōzō*) translated "saved" has wide philosophical application with a field of meanings such as rescue, liberate, keep from harm, heal, and preserve. In this conceptual sense, it is almost an exact equivalent to the Hebrew word *shalom* (בְּשָׁלוֹם) emphasizing the phenomenology of the concept for the believer. The regeneration and the renewal of the individual is then the transformative force within a culture, the restoration of the dominion mandate given to humanity in the Genesis narrative.[135]

However, even with the regeneration of the individual that remains outside of a political organization, you will never transform or even reform a society, a far broader theonomical understanding is needed and we will examine this in more detail in later sections. As Cope argues, political naivety is endemic in the wider evangelical consciousness.[136] Societal "transformation" has a magical ring about it: all the problems of culture and society will be solved with everyone getting "saved." In contrast, the Reformers, in opposition to modern revivalism, had a multigenerational

---

132. NET Bible translators' note for Prov 1:7.
133. Descartes, *Meditations and Other Metaphysical Writings*, 99–104.
134. Rom 10:8–9 (NET).
135. This was the subject of my master's dissertation: Macneil, *Dominion Theology*.
136. Cope, *God and Political Justice*.

perspective. It is of note that most twentieth-century revivals throughout the world, especially in the West, impacted wider culture very little in marked contrast to previous centuries. Indeed, within a few years of the "revival" there was virtually no trace of its impact to be found in metrics even as basic as church attendance.[137] So our designation of philosophy as "transformative" is not at the expense of contemplation or rational reflection, but rather the litmus test of what our philosophy brings to living in the world. We prefer something that is at least relevant to the solving of human problems.

1.10 Summary and Conclusion

In this chapter we have introduced some of the definitions, themes, and the methodological assumptions we are going to be following in this book. First, we indicated our rejection of metaphysical skepticism: we take the position that the world as God's world is knowable to us, God provides us with senses that allow us to live in the world by coming to a knowledge of the world. We also introduced the important concept that all our reasonings about the world are "theory laden" and that those theories will be derivative from the values; those values in turn are implicitly assuming a particular metaphysic. For our work, this assumption is of a personal God that cares about the universe, our world, and each individual person.

We then offered this work as an apologetic work and examined the definition of apologetics and considered that apologetics can be conceived of as consisting of both objective and subjective aspects. We asserted our position as arguing for what has become known as the "presuppositional" apologetic method, which has the central methodological principle that the faith must be defended in a positive manner consistent with the faith, rather than relying on a negative, defensive method dependent on a foreign epistemology drawn from evidentialism or classical apologetics. We

---

137. For all its fame, the "last" Welsh revival of 1904–5 which has an enormous apocryphal status as the catalyst for other revivals around the world, such as the LA Azusa Street revival (1906–8), had little long-term effect on Welsh culture. Similarly, Azusa Street gave birth to Pentecostal denominations, but American society as a whole continued its degeneration. The Great Tent evangelists after WWII and the Toronto Blessing of 1994, for all their fame and notoriety in Christian circles, all failed to impact wider society as vehicles of reformation. Indeed, Canada, apparently a continuing center of the "blessing," is transforming itself into a totalitarian "liberal" state and is criminalizing Christian orthodoxy, prohibiting the preaching of certain passages.

then examined the role of scripture and religious experience within the apologetic framework and argued that an apologetic model consistent with scripture should assume scripture as the foundation for all reasoning. We concluded that a post-Reformational model was necessary to properly incorporate the role of religious experience, particularly with regard to spiritual gifts, but argued that scripture mandated an apologetic that rationally defended the faith. We distinguished between the biblical usage of *logos* and *rhema*, concluding that although there was implicit plasticity in a narrative, the biblical narrative clearly intended itself to be understood in an objective sense as well as us responding subjectively to it and for us to build our foundations upon what we understand. Thus, our basic orientation within this work was to argue that the Christian worldview was objectively defensible, while also noting that the aim of an apologetic discourse was not necessarily the conversion of the opponents, but that the account offered was intellectually sufficient to refute the charge of irrationality.

In order to posit how we might seek to offer an objective proof of the Christian worldview as the only coherent worldview, we introduced Kant and the transcendental mode of reasoning. We immediately asserted that while agreeing with the basic program of Kant to discover what general conditions must be fulfilled for any particular instance of knowledge to be possible, we do not agree that he was successful. We examined how Kant and Hume are asymptotic for the limitations of understanding in modern philosophy and particularly the significance of the problem of induction. We argued that induction was the foundation of natural science but would only be justified by a Christian metaphysic. We then examined in detail the paradigm of naturalistic science, the dominant paradigm of our time asserting that its naturalism offered no basis for a true science which has historically encompassed all the domains of human knowledge. This again we connected with the necessity for a worldview founded on a Christian metaphysic because there are implicit ethical assumptions within our science that cannot be avoided. Naturalistic science was exposed as tyrannical both in its excesses of the totalitarianisms of the twentieth century and our contemporary context of the recent pandemic.

We thus assert that one of the principal benefits of epistemological self-consciousness is that it recognizes the autonomy of every sphere of human knowledge but does not permit the autonomy of any sphere to operate in a moral vacuum. We understand this as one of the seminal insights of Kuyper and in lieu of our collapsing of the rigid boundaries between science, epistemology, theology, and philosophy, we can justifiably concur with him that the designation "science" must be taken to include the hard and soft-sciences, theology, "philosophy," literature, and political economy in order that we do justice to *what* we know as well as *how* we know—in other words, a holistic and a non-naturalistic account of science.[138] Hao Wang, most definitely a philosopher who remained within the wider analytic tradition but viewed the analytic school as inadequate to the task of philosophy in his later period,[139] expressed the imperative for this distinction and the correlative need for a wide cognitive field for our scientific vision concisely:

> Quine's emphasis on empirical psychology is related to his idea of a "liberated epistemology," which proposes to make the study of language learning a successor subject to epistemology. But I take his proposal to be in the tradition of asking *"how I know,"* rather than *"what we know."*[140]

We noted that if there is admitted a functional difference in preference to a theoretical one for these categories, then it would seem to be that many philosophers believe that the level of abstraction in which they operate is a higher than that of the scientist who is dealing with *phenomena*. However, we understood that this immediately begged the question as to why dealing with "phenomena" might be considered a definitive attribute of the scientist; there are many "theoretical" scientists who seldom deal with phenomena. Thus, on the basis of a similar assessment, we concur with Quine, who considered the distinction between philosophy and science much as he considered the distinction between the analytic and the synthetic, merely one of convenience. Thus, we assert that the dispute of a difference between science, the humanities, and philosophy is in the final

---

138. Kuyper, "Common Grace in Science," 441–60.

139. This was self-identification on the part of Wang, e.g., Wang, *Beyond Analytic Philosophy*. He was a confidant of and expert on Kurt Gödel (1906–78) whose "incompleteness theorems" were perhaps the most important pieces of mathematical philosophy of the twentieth century, and perhaps of all time, in which he demonstrated that classical mathematics lacked a rational basis, i.e., certain statements accepted as true could not be *proved* as true. It also demonstrated that mathematics could not be derived from logic, refuting the logicism of Frege and Russell. Gödel felt he had disproved nominalism in mathematics (favored by many positivists and post-positivist naturalists such as Quine) which considered mathematics to consist "solely in syntactical conventions and their consequences." That is, he had a conception that mathematics was *objective* (a descriptive science) and about the real world. See Kennedy, "Kurt Gödel."

140. Wang, *Beyond Analytic Philosophy*, 208. Emphasis added.

analysis a linguistic one, not a theoretical one; we can take "science" in its broadest sense as encompassing human knowledge in its entirety.

This is not to deny the legitimacy or value of the individual subjects or their autonomy as spheres of knowledge over which they are sovereign but recognizes that there is a unifying ethical principle that coheres the spheres and provides an interpretative framework of reality.[141] "Science" is thus a close synonym of "philosophy" which we now take to define and articulate more closely that we can see what to demand from epistemological self-consciousness. We can freely claim to be advocating a scientific thesis and a thesis concerned with the concrete, real world of experience, as well as with the world of ideas and concepts. We can thus express formal agreement with Kant in his conclusion regarding practical[142] reason:

> In a word, science (critically sought and methodically directed) is the narrow gate that leads to the doctrine of wisdom, if by this is understood not merely what one ought to do but what ought to serve teachers as a guide to prepare well and clearly the path to wisdom which everyone should travel, and to secure others against taking the wrong way; philosophy must always remain the guardian of this science, and though the public need take no interest in its subtle investigations it has to take an interest in the doctrines which, after being worked up in this way, can first be quite clear to it.[143]

In summary, and of great methodological importance for us, we see that Kant attempted to tie his metaphysics, epistemology, and ethics together. While we noted that both Van Til and Plantinga defer to agree that he achieved this coherently, consistently, or convincingly, we can certainly agree with Van Til that Kant's transcendental program seeking the preconditions of understanding on this tripartite basis should remain appealing to us, even if we disagree with his autonomous method[144] and

---

141. This was considered one of the most significant aspects of Kuyper's thought to guard against the ecclesiastical hegemony of either the Catholic or Protestant churches while maintaining the central importance of a biblical worldview throughout culture. See Kuyper, "Sphere Sovereignty," 461–90.

142. "Practical reason" is reason applied to (or the reason of) how we should act, i.e., a synonym of ethics; "theoretical" reason is reason applied to (or the reason of) how we should think, i.e., our ideas and concepts.

143. Kant, *Critique of Practical Reason*, 130.

144. It is somewhat of a dogma in Van Tillian circles to describe Kant's method as "autonomous" (neatly explained in Theodore M. Greene's introductory essay to Kant's

INTRODUCTION

final conclusions. We can also discern from this passage that Kant believed there was a moral responsibility of philosophers to have worked through the problematics that confront humanity and to have offered ethical solutions. For this reason, also, we undertook a consideration of the transformative role of philosophy and its contemplative role, emphasizing the importance of keeping the practical dimension in mind. It is the challenge of working through this process that will be undertaken in this work.

1.11 Chapter Outlines

- In chapter 2 we examine some of the historical issues within philosophy and identify some important features of reason and rationality.

- In chapter 3 we begin working out the taxonomy of a Christian philosophy within the tripartite framework. We consider in detail the work of Plantinga in providing a framework for warranted Christian belief, its limitations, and why it is necessary to supplement his work with the positive apologetic of Van Til.

- In chapter 4 we examine transcendental reasoning in general and the significance of worldview for the reasoning pattern. Particular attention is paid to the circularity problem and the role of ultimate authorities in our noetic structure.

- In chapter 5 we deal with the more theological variables of our philosophic equation and how these inform our transcendental approach. These are the "big issues" of post-Reformational Christianity and our philosophy should be compatible with them.

- In chapter 6 we deal specifically with the Transcendental Argument for God (TAG) as Van Til's form of transcendentalism and consider the varieties of objections to it. The TAG aims to demonstrate the necessity rather than just the sufficiency of the Christian worldview as the prerequisite for intelligibility.

Religion (1960/1793)), meaning without reference to God, or in a more nuanced sense, "not finding its final reference point in God but the mind of autonomous man" (Bahnsen, *Practical Apologetics*, audio recording).

- In chapter 7 we consider the political implications of our philosophical perspective in a critique of traditional evangelical thinking for the Christian philosopher.
- Chapter 8 summarizes what we have learned and identifies an outstanding research question emerging from our study.

2

The Nature, Character, and Purpose of Philosophy

2.1 Overview

IN OUR INTRODUCTORY DISCUSSION we minimized the distance between science and philosophy and inferred that science is inherently philosophical and vice-versa. We concluded it is more a question of language and audience than a fundamental difference in the subject matter. We also concluded that philosophy and science are both knowledge bearing and have a referent of the entirety of human disciplines, not just the empirical sciences. However, as confidence in the power of science was challenged by a decay in culture and world conflicts which were increasingly technologically sophisticated but no less barbaric, we recognized that the postmodern malaise had entered philosophy and science, arguing that rationality was largely arbitrary. In response, we recognize that this makes it imperative that Christian apologetics is able to offer a coherent answer to this skepticism, cynicism, nihilism and irrationality but, and this is of critical importance in our approach, in a manner *consistent* with the faith it is defending, which our work will argue can only be presuppositional.

Thus, we now need to explore how philosophy *has* been conceived and then decide how it *should* be conceived in that presuppositional, robust fashion that our worldview is both warranted scientifically *and* philosophically. In this chapter we deal with the former "has"; the next chapter deals with the latter "should." We will undertake here an historical and thematic analysis of philosophy, focusing particularly on the analytic turns of the twentieth century. This is not because "Continental" philosophical perspectives such as phenomenology, existentialism, or postmodernism have nothing to teach us or were not of equal importance, but simply because it would not be possible to give an account with sufficient depth of deep and complex thinkers such as Heidegger, Sartre, or Lyotard.[1] Our final conclusions are also not weakened by our failure to consider these; we could have based our analysis on the Continental schools and come to very similar conclusions as to their failures to be coherent or adequate in the demands we want to make of philosophy in our work.

2.2 Origins

Philosophy is *commonly* conceived of in the "Western tradition" as starting with Thales of Miletus circa 626 BC, the first of the pre-Socratic sages of ancient Greece. However, it is more accurate to state that he was the first of the proto-*naturalist* philosophers that attempted to explain phenomena with a reference only to what was found in nature with no recourse to supernature. Unsurprisingly, for Thales, on an island surrounded by water, everything was posited, *naturally* enough, to be constituted of water. However, among his philosophical peers in his direct succession, it was not long before the implicit monism of this position fractured to give rise to a more *elemental* view drawn from nature, where the basic elements became air, fire, and water. As strange and bizarre as the formulations of these philosophers were, these thinkers are almost universally revered with unadulterated awe as captured here by an enlightened contemporary one-time physicist:

> The roots of all physics, as of all Western science, are to be found in the first period of Greek philosophy in the sixth century B.C., in a culture where science, philosophy and religion were not separated. The sages of the Milesian school in Ionia were not concerned with such distinctions. Their aim was to discover the essential nature, or real constitution, of things which they

---

1. I acknowledge the critique of Professor Ó Murchadha of an earlier draft at this point, and the suggestion that my purpose could be served by considering only the analytic tradition.

called "physis." The term "physics" . . . meant . . . originally, the endeavour of seeing the essential nature of all things.²

Effusive as this is, it might seem implausible to assert that *all* of Western science (which we should also note included philosophy and religion) owes so much, but Professor Jonathan Barnes, once eminent professor of ancient philosophy at Geneva, in a standard text on early Greek philosophy offers a scholarly corrective to such critical reticence:

> The importance of the Presocratic thinkers [lies] in their astonishing ambition and imaginative reach. Zeno's dizzying "proofs" that motion is impossible; the extraordinary atomic theories of Democritus; the haunting and enigmatic epigrams of Heraclitus; and the maxims of Alcmaeon . . . the thoughts of these philosophers seem strikingly modern in their concern to forge a *truly scientific vocabulary* and a *way of reasoning*.³

Now, leaving aside that Zeno made an elementary error in not distinguishing infinite time slices and finite distance; or that Democritus's atomic theories bear only a pauce linguistic similarity to chemical theories⁴ or that the "perpetual flux as taught by Heraclitus is [intellectually] painful, and science . . . can do nothing to refute it";⁵ or that the extant maxims of Alcmaeon are very few indeed; we seem to be ignoring the great philosophers of other ancient civilizations such as the Indo-Chinese empires (the advanced epistemologists Dharmottara and Gaṅgeśa spring to mind)⁶ and the Babylonian Empire (known for their astronomical measurements, not just their astrology) and the broader traditions of the Eastern "wise men" and sages (the "wise men of the East"),⁷ fragments of whose literature still survive;⁸ we must ask ourselves, "Why the Greeks?" The answer is in that other element of ancient Greek philosophy that

2. Capra, *Tao of Physics*, 22.

3. Barnes, *Early Greek Philosophy*, back cover. Emphasis added.

4. Democritus actually has a completely different sense to his terms and, in my view, should not be considered a precursor to modern atomic theory.

5. Russell, *History of Western Philosophy*, 65.

6. As Nagel, *Knowledge*, 58, notes, Dharmottara anticipated the Gettier problem with *specific* examples of his own; Gaṅgeśa gave a detailed causal theory of knowledge.

7. Cf. Job 1:3; Matt 2:1 (NAS). The NAS note on this verse is illuminating: "Pronounced may-ji, a caste of wise men specializing in astrology, medicine and natural science."

8. The book of Job is recognized as the most ancient biblical composition and may have a relationship with the "Babylonian Job," an earlier composition meditating on the righteous and suffering.

made it so paradigmatical for all that followed in its wake, its "discovery" of "humanism." The autonomous spirit which distinguishes it is seen in the famous maxim of Protagoras (485–415 BC) who famously asserted, "Man as the measure of all things." This was in direct contrast to the behest of the gods, or some other supernatural composite, and it is this combination which inspires such worshipful adoration from all those who crave autonomy and freedom from divine discipline or sanction.

Now, the objection might be made that the designation "proto-naturalism" for these opening eras of Greek philosophy was anachronistic. It is certainly true that I am not implying by using this designation that is does *not* mean that "God" or the "gods" disappeared from the vocabulary of these thinkers though it seems clear that by the time of the post-Socratic Epicurus it had matured into a strong materialism, an important characteristic of modern naturalism. It is correct that the pre-Socratics Thales, Heraclitus, and Democritus all employed the "gods" as an explanatory principle, but it was to give a nominal metaphysical justification for something they were positing. Democritus, for example, wanted to explain the "swerve" in the fire atoms in terms of the activity of the gods; Thales and Heraclitus equated motion and change with divine activity evident of the immanent, animating presence of something "god" or "divine" in the matter itself. Kenny notes that Heraclitus was famous for his *Logos* principle but, unlike the apostle John, his *logos* was not personal but "divine" in some abstract fashion, categorically distinct from Zeus.[9] That is, the "God" principle was not conceived of on the basis of a person with whom one communed or had any kind of moral obligation to, even when in the case of Heraclitus there were hints of a "divine law" that should inform *political* practice, the first hint of a law within nature itself. This is certainly of interest to us within this work and it is to Heraclitus's credit that he shares that ethical concern for *some* kind of firm foundation for reasoning, but his *Logos*, his divine principle, was a *logical* necessity to complete the system or to provide a fix where all rational attempts had failed, or where the light of reason had not yet been able to penetrate the metaphysical or epistemological darkness.

Thus, it was only in desperation that Plato resorted to the myth of the demiurge to backfill his system of which he had been the most effective critic to prevent a total collapse and a re-surrender to the relativism and moral cynicism of the Sophists. His project, on this level endorsed by

---

9. Kenny, *New History*, 18.

Aristotle, was the attempt to offer a systematic and coherent philosophy of reality to arrest what they saw as the terminal decay of Greek culture in light of the disaster of the Peloponnesian war. Yet he maintained a contempt for the mythology of Greece which he saw with ample justification merely as an amplification of human traits[10] and not as a model of ethical purity; his famous Euthyphro dilemma was a polemic directed to address the moral scandal of the behavior of the gods. Certainty regarding the objects of knowledge and the nature of reality was a prerequisite to their program of reviving Greek culture and to counter the relativism and moral cynicism of the Sophists, but God was an addendum *after* the fact; an account was sought in nature and by human reason alone wherever possible.[11] Many centuries later, Pascal was to criticize Descartes in a similar manner in the period conceived of as being reanimated with the glory of Greek philosophy:

> I cannot forgive to Descartes that in all his philosophy he would have liked to dispense with God, but he did not accomplish to contrive to forbear God's hand in giving ever so slight a push to set the world in motion. After that, Descartes had no use for God.[12]

So, in summary, we are using the term "proto naturalist" to characterize the mood and general drift of Greek philosophy rather than as a precise analytic term; naturalism is unequivocally a notoriously elastic term. Even when qualified as one of many, mutually exclusive naturalisms, it evades coherence. Thus, the noted philosopher of science Bas van Fraassen,[13] who I would argue distilled down naturalism into a single phrase like "there is no such being as God" and writing later in a Christian context, it was a *specific* conception of God which would consequently classify as "naturalisms" many forms of thought that would claim to have a theistic basis or would use the word "God."[14] That is, "God" much like Feuerbach was to assert, was a projection or an abstraction

---

10. Bahnsen, in *Practical Apologetics*, notes with some humor that the problems of the gods were human problems, Zeus's nagging wife but one.

11. Frame, *History of Western Philosophy and Theology*, 177, 179–80.

12. Sainte-Beuvre, *Port Royal*, 1052.

13. Van Fraassen is credited with "restoring respectability to anti-realism in science." His influential theory of constructive empiricism presented in his 1980 book *The Scientific Image*.

14. Van Fraassen, "Haldane on the Past and Future of Philosophy," 177–81. This is a particularly cogent and interesting response article.

from the natural world; theology was "merely" anthropology, though for Feuerbach "Humanity" *was* a legitimate object of worship.[15] So, religion was not supernatural, but natural. Thus, it is not a straightforward term, even for empiricists who believed they were assuming a "naturalist" context. Our main point in using this designation is that there seems an unreasonable adoration of Greece on the part of its modern apologists who have forcefully but, arguably unsafely, equated science with naturalism and consider the classical Greek philosophy as their inspiration.[16] We will see that Van Fraassen is joined by Van Til and Plantinga in rejecting forcefully that equation, and I believe that rejection is persuasive, legitimate, and sound.

However, let us end on a more positive and appreciative note for Greece. We must value that both Plato and Aristotle understood the need for a coherent system of philosophy that correlated metaphysics, epistemology, and a theory of values. Plato was seeking to avoid the ethical and political scandals of the Peloponnesian era by providing a sure foundation for knowledge. This he rightly saw would arrest the cultural and moral decay by providing an objective metaphysical and epistemological account, which in turn provides the basis for a normative ethic. Our work will basically concur with these categories and his cultural aims but by demonstrating that the Christian theistic basis will allow us to succeed where he failed. Thus, the point remains that these broad streams of humanism came to form what we think of as "classical" Western philosophy and the spirit of modern secular science.[17] We will now proceed to examine in detail this conception of reason with a view to demonstrating its inadequacy and incoherence, to clear the way for our positive presentation of epistemological self-consciousness.

---

15. So, Feuerbach was perfectly willing to agree with his contemporary Schleiermacher that the experience of "total dependence" on an object outside of yourself *was* the essence of religion, but the object of that dependence and worshipful adoration for Feuerbach was the natural potentiality of humanity itself, not a supernatural God. Marx and Engels were greatly influenced by Feuerbach in their naturalization of religious experience.

16. Van Fraassen, "Naturalism in Epistemology," 63–96.

17. Again, eulogized in Barnes, *Early Greek Philosophy*, xviii.

2.3 Can We Defend the Tripartite Division of Philosophy?

2.3.1 The Division of Reason and The Egocentric Predicament

This post-classical conception of rationality asserted the requirement for a coherent theory of knowledge (epistemology) with a basis in an established theory of what is real (metaphysics); one can then decide how one should relate to and behave in the world (ethics). Philosophers have tended to label themselves as "ethicists," "metaphysicians" or as "epistemologists," but in contrast we are arguing that this is a basic error; these categories should not be thought of as hermetically sealed off from one another but are interdependent.

For example, it is straightforward to express the *prima facie* interrelatedness and interdependence of the three components by considering that we cannot possibly have a theory about *how* we know until we can fix *what* we know. Succinctly, *meta*-physics seems necessarily to precede the objects of *physics*, the raw component targets of epistemological theories. Yet, in the reciprocal fashion, until we can understand *how* objects are to be constituted (a *theory* of objects), we will struggle to describe reality at all. Here, epistemology seems necessarily to precede metaphysics. Similarly, an *ethical* action implies that we are relating to entities outside of ourselves and so we are assuming an ontological posture that accepts the existence of an external world and an epistemological position that assumes we can possess moral knowledge.

We should not skip over the enormous philosophical import of the last paragraph—we have here captured some of the most fiercely contested ground in the history of philosophy. There are still those who argue we can never move beyond the egocentric predicament and establish with certainty any other existence but that of our own mind. This is known as *solipsism* and is not as disreputable in philosophy as one might instinctively think,[18] with Thornton arguing that solipsism is not commonly argued only because "philosophers failed to accept the

---

18. Bertrand Russell relates some personal correspondence where the person he was writing to wrote back with surprise that there were not more solipsists like herself; empiricists have commonly had problems with justifying the external world and other minds, needing to rely on explanations from analogy—*"I have a mind, you seem to be behaving like me, so you must have a mind"*; they are hardly convincing and are certainly vulnerable to criticism. Some also consider Berkeley to be arguing for a form of solipsism and Descartes's starting point to be solipsistic.

logical consequences of their own most fundamental commitments and preconceptions" which he takes as "abstraction from 'inner experience.'"[19] If inner experience is conceived of as subjective, then moving outward to a real, *objective* world presents a major problem, perhaps *the* problem of philosophy.[20]

2.3.2 Epistemic Rights and Epistemic Necessity

In this respect, and of particular interest to the Christian philosopher, is that Plantinga took the unusual strategy in one of his earliest full-length books[21] to argue that belief in God was on the same level of rationality (or certainty) as belief in other minds. We do not believe it is irrational to believe in other minds though we cannot *prove* it in a non-circular fashion; hence, it *is* rational to believe in God. This was proved not to be a transitionary doctrine on Plantinga's part; in writing the new preface to the 1990 edition he maintained, with some qualification,[22] his conclusion was "quite correct."

Just how distinctively "Christian" such a strategy is, is most certainly an interesting debate with some within the Reformed community such as Butler[23] criticizing him of falling short of the requirement to demonstrate the *necessity* of Christian belief as the presupposition for the intelligibility of philosophical and scientific thinking.[24] This criticism is pertinent and we examine the detail of it, but I do believe Plantinga's work should be viewed as a whole to mitigate the force of it somewhat; that is, he pushed the boundaries of Reformed thought[25] but started and finished in

---

19. Thornton, "Solipsism and the Problem of Other Minds."
20. Kenny, *New History*, 616–19.
21. Plantinga, *God and Other Minds*, xii.
22. Nevertheless, it was quite a major qualification concerning his later distinction between *justification* and *warrant*. We consider this conception in some detail in a future section.
23. Butler, *On Plantinga*, MB200–MB210.
24. We will develop this line of criticism as well as Plantinga's positive apologetics in future sections.
25. His formulation of a "Free Will" defense regarding the problem of evil (1974) was considered objectionable in conservative Reformed circles. However, Plantinga was arguing as a logician and was contesting the claims of leading atheologians that the presence of evil disproved the existence of a good, omnipotent, and omniscient God. He dismissed the argument on its own terms; he was judged to have succeeded in this regard, even among the serious atheists.

THE NATURE, CHARACTER, AND PURPOSE OF PHILOSOPHY

Calvin College which he described as his "spiritual home."[26] In his early period, he was known for his analytic rigor in meeting the unbeliever on their own ground and demonstrating that more was being claimed than is logically possible from their arguments.

His strategy in that early period was fundamentally that the believer was within their "epistemic rights" even on the unbelievers' terms, i.e., *rational* to continue to believe as they did. This, quite correctly, can be perceived of as a negative apologetic and is vulnerable to the charge of being a sophisticated skepticism.[27] However, in his middle period during the early 1980s, he strengthened this position as part of the Reformed Epistemology movement and closed out that period in the next decade with a three-volume opus, the final volume of which can be viewed as the most mature and positive presentation of a sophisticated apologetic for the rationality of Christian belief.[28] Though his account relied on a naturalistic epistemology[29] it was backed by a supernaturalistic metaphysic; thus, Plantinga certainly viewed his own work as within the Reformed Augustinian school of philosophy despite freely admitting he did not believe it was possible to demonstrate *philosophically* that Christian belief was *necessarily* true.[30]

Thus, Plantinga self-consciously limits his apologetic (and it seems the scope of *any* apologetic philosophy) as to demonstrating the *reasonableness* of Christian belief rather than its necessity. As one of the key tasks of this work, we will be demonstrating how it is possible to move beyond this terminus using a specific version of transcendental reasoning associated with the apologetic system of Cornelius Van Til.

---

26. He spent the years 1963–82 there and from 2010 as emeritus professor. Interestingly, he spent 1982–2010 at Notre Dame which, though a Catholic university, he defended as having some of the finest Protestant thinkers.

27. As a reviewer printed on the cover of the 1990 edition of *God and Other Minds* noted.

28. At this point (2000) he preferred to describe it not as "Reformed Epistemology" (perhaps because of its sectarian ramifications as he had moved from Calvin to Notre Dame) but as the "Extended Aquinas/Calvin (A/C)" model. In fairness, it owes far more to Calvin than to Aquinas but is uniquely his as it drew criticism as to just how "Reformed" it was, e.g., Jeffreys, "How Reformed Is Reformed Epistemology?" Others like Butler argued he had departed fundamentally from Calvin and Reformed thought.

29. It was naturalistic in the sense he argued for it as a faculty of perception, i.e., as a part of the human person apart from any supernatural regeneration of the person. The presence of sin affected its operation but did not prevent it. However, the faculty was considered *God-given*, which is a rather different context for naturalism to operate in.

30. Plantinga, "Augustinian Christian Philosophy," 291–320.

2.3.3 The Struggle for Metaphysics

To consider carefully the legitimacy of the classical categories of metaphysics, epistemology, and ethics, especially in the light of the seemingly insoluble problems of circularity and interdependence we have noted above, is an obvious prerequisite of any argument we might seek to build on them. Some philosophers have advocated abandoning these categories in favor of alternative conceptions. Still others have abandoned reason altogether and looked to emotion, intuition, or some other variation of subjectivity, fideism, or relativism. Similarly, others have considered reason irrevocably chastened and assigned it a subsidiary role. We will encounter some of those philosophers and their positions in later sections to analyze and evaluate their positions, but it is the working hypothesis of this work that we can immediately admit the legitimacy of ethics and epistemology without too much hesitancy; there is a *prima facie* case that we require a theory of knowledge and a theory of how to behave toward others, even if we considered it purely a pragmatic or conventional matter, or part of our psychology.

However, of the three areas, metaphysics has had the most sustained attack on it as a legitimate branch of philosophy. Metaphysics is concerned with the most important questions of existence and reality. For this reason, it has often been characterized by speculative, mystical, religious, and irrational thought, with the early British empiricist David Hume[31] characterizing the metaphysical tradition thus:

> If we take in our hand any volume; of divinity or school metaphysics, for instance; let us ask, Does it contain any abstract reasoning concerning quantity or number? No. Does it contain any experimental reasoning concerning matter of fact and existence? No. Commit it then to the flames: For it can contain nothing but sophistry and illusion.[32]

---

31. We must immediately qualify our designation of Hume as an empiricist. Hume was accused by Russell of a "destruction of empiricism" (Russell, *History of Western Philosophy*, 646) in the sense that Hume's desire to be a pure empiricist drove him to a radical skepticism and a rejection of the *principle of induction* upon which empiricism and much that counts as scientific reasoning rests upon. However, as Russell rightly notes, Hume *in practice* wanted to maintain a *reasonable* approach to understanding the world rather than provide a justification for the irrationality and subjectivity of those like Rousseau, Schopenhauer, and Nietzsche.

32. Hume and Steinberg, *Enquiry Concerning Human Understanding*, loc. 2399.

It is often argued that Hume was the father of such disdain for metaphysics in the eighteenth century and that the subsequent "suspicion" among natural scientists regarding any philosophical position that invoked metaphysical authority originated with him. However, this seems to be overplaying Hume's influence, particularly during his lifetime.[33] In essence, a desire to be free of metaphysical dogmas, particularly the religious kind, was distinctive of the period beginning with the Renaissance, through the Reformation and into the early modern period; generally accepted as constituting what is called the Enlightenment,[34] with each subsequent iteration of the Enlightenment project modifying metaphysics to a more palatable form for its own purposes. Rather, it was only with the paleopositivism of Comte, and the Darwinism that had been influenced by it, which then found mature expression in the logical positivism and the "new physics" of the early twentieth century (which explicitly rejected Kantian and Hegelian metaphysical idealism), that metaphysics faced its largest challenge. The metaphysical religious narratives were being fundamentally challenged and accused of being false under the weight of common-sense, empirical "science." It was only *then* that Hume became a late-canonized saint for all the positivist and postpositivist movements, with his insights providing a limiting, psychological threshold of understanding beyond which the "new" science and a "cleaned-up" philosophy could not legitimately progress.

In essence, during the early part of the twentieth century after the massive expansion of natural, *empirical* science following its successes during the nineteenth, there was a concerted attempted by the logical

---

33. Hume, *Dialogues Concerning Natural Religion*. Interestingly, this was published posthumously by his nephew in 1779 despite being completed by Hume as his last piece of work in 1761. Hume had declined to publish, wishing to "live quietly and keep remote from all clamour" for the closing years of his life after frequent confrontations in his career. The contents were considered incendiary by all who knew of the work; see Aiken's introduction to Hume's *Dialogues*.

34. For example, Francis Bacon, a century and a half before Hume, had elegantly identified many of the metaphysical "idols" of the human tribe and originated a worldview in which "science" (meaning empirical science) was idealized. Inductive, empirical science was seen as salvation from prejudice and tyranny, as he wrote both in his philosophical treatise of 1620, the *Novum Organon*, and in his utopian novel, *The New Atlantis*. Bacon, in many ways, was far more influential than Hume, second only to Newton in developing a distinct conception of the practice and application of a "scientific" philosophy, that is, a *scientific worldview*. Yet, in principle, they did not find the concept of God objectionable, even the Christian God, though both were arguably theologically heterodox and had little tolerance for clericalism or dogmatism, as was the case with most early moderns.

positivists and their fellow-travelers in the new analytic philosophy[35] to finally dispense with "metaphysics" on the basis that it was misunderstanding the structure and the function of language and was thereby logically *non*-sense. Ayer, the first to popularize the position in the English language, stated this position thus:

> Our object is merely to show that philosophy, as a genuine branch of knowledge, must be distinguished from metaphysics. . . . We . . . define a metaphysical sentence as a sentence which purports to express a genuine proposition, but does, in fact, express neither a tautology nor an empirical hypothesis. And as tautologies and empirical hypotheses form the entire class of significant propositions, we are justified in concluding that all metaphysical assertions are nonsensical.[36]

2.3.4 The Principle of Verification

However, this basis of the logical positivist conception of meaning, the *principle of verification*, that held a proposition was only meaningful *if and only if* it was, in principle,[37] empirically verifiable, was fundamentally untenable as it excluded all types of propositions which clearly had meaning but had no direct connection with the natural world or did not *rely* on the natural world for verification or falsification.[38] As we noted above, it also had the radical consequence of dispensing with much of ethical theorizing as "*non*-sense," a position which even Bertrand Russell, perhaps the most well-known member of the positivist movement[39] and

---

35. Analytic philosophy is often conceived of emerging as a distinctive school with Moore and Russell at the turn of the century; with Frege and his revolutionary work on the logic and language as the historical precursor. See Glock, *Analytical Philosophy*, ch. 1.

36. Ayer, *Language, Truth, and Logic*, 41.

37. This concession was made by the "softer" logical positivists to permit scientific theories where the verification was logically possible but practically improbable or very difficult to accomplish in practice.

38. This was the essence of Wittgenstein's criticism of it, which should carry particular weight as the verification principle itself was initially known as *Wittgenstein's* verification principle (Monk, *Ludwig Wittgenstein*, 286–87). Wittgenstein had radically changed his conception of how language worked, remarking that in his early work he had over-emphasized the "language game of science." That is, there are *other, meaningful* ways of talking about the world which would not be considered "scientific" but *would* still be considered rational.

39. Some care does need to be exercised with too readily appropriating Russell into

the figure who dominated philosophy in the first half of the twentieth century, was careful to qualify:

> There remains ... a vast field, traditionally included in philosophy, where scientific methods are inadequate. This field includes ultimate questions of value; science alone, for example, cannot prove it is bad to enjoy the infliction of cruelty.[40]

However, the most devastating critique of the verification principle was that the principle itself was not based on any process of empirical verification. In other words, it *exempted* itself from its *own* criteria and was thus shown to be nothing more than a *dogma*, and, paradoxically, a *metaphysical* one at that. So, in Neurath, metaphysics could indeed "disappear without a trace"[41] but he failed to perceive that the denial of metaphysics was paradoxically a metaphysical plank which he would also allow *a priori* as a building block for his famous raft of human knowledge.[42] It suffices us to say at this point that when adjustments were attempted to the principle, including by Ayer himself then ten years later after his initial statement of it in response to the criticism of it, he had to concede that metaphysics could not so simply be deleted from philosophy as "nonsense":

> Although I should still defend the use of the criterion of verifiability as a methodological principle, I realize that for the effective elimination of metaphysics it needs to be supported by *detailed* analyses of *particular* metaphysical arguments.[43]

---

the movement. It is undeniable he was a foundational member of the Vienna Circle, but his later conception of philosophy as needing more than *just* logical analysis sets him apart in my view. The affinities and differences are evident in the essay "Logical Positivism" (1950), which in its closing pages also describe its own inconsistency and inability to justify its own presuppositions.

40. Russell, *History of Western Philosophy*, 788.

41. Neurath, "Protocol Statements," 92.

42. Logical positivists were universally robust in dismissing even the *possibility* of "synthetic *a priori*" knowledge; see Schlick, *General Theory of Knowledge*, 384. All knowledge was knowledge of particulars gained through experience or analytic propositions. That said, there were significant differences—Neurath, Carnap, and Schlick were sometimes considered as rival factions within the positivist movement because of Schlick's commitment to realism, which certainly suggests *a priori* commitments. Neurath and Carnap both considered the realism-antirealism debate a "pseudo-problem," i.e., a problem caused by linguistic confusion or convention, and thus without content. The untimely death of Schlick curtailed the influence of those that favored his approach.

43. Ayer, *Language, Truth, and Logic*, 16. Emphasis added.

That is, Ayer is here conceding that there is nothing *fundamentally* irrational or "non-sensical" with metaphysically based arguments but rather, as we should all reasonably accept, it is the actual *quality* of the metaphysical argument made that needs to be evaluated with whatever rational criteria is required for that domain. In effect, Ayer was attempting to respond to the fault-lines that were beginning to appear in the positivist edifice that had near dominated post-war scholarship across a variety of disciplines.[44] However, within seven years of this revision of 1946, it was to suffer the devastating critique of Quine which demonstrated emphatically that logical positivism rested paradoxically on metaphysical dogma.[45] Thus, despite this totalizing faith of the logical positivists, who had considered themselves the most rigorous and consistent of the empiricists, their presuppositions came to be seen as crudely inadequate philosophical views, being established on a principle that is asserted *independently* of experience and is thus self-refuting in the most basic, logical sense.[46]

As a result, metaphysics was slowly rehabilitated into philosophical discourse, with the positivist school fragmented by the end of the 1950s.[47] However, positivism passed on much of its basic methodology onto the naturalism that was its direct successor, and the metaphysical approach of scientifically minded philosophers is significantly different than the speculative metaphysics which was so loathed by the empiricists such as Hume and rejected by the positivists. Thus, introductory texts on metaphysics such as Mumford earnestly seek a kind of methodological respectability

---

44. In the second edition of *Language, Truth, and Logic*, he acknowledged in the introduction (p. 5) the youthful excesses of the first edition. While in the second edition he maintained that the viewpoint was "still substantially correct," he was to reflect in later work that it was "predominantly incorrect" but had served a "valuable cathartic purpose."

45. Quine, "Two Dogmas of Empiricism," 20–46.

46. It should be noted that its successor, methodological naturalism (MN), suffers from precisely the same problem—if *all* there is, is nature, why do we believe what nature tells us? This is sometimes called "Darwin's doubt." We will examine this problem in more detail.

47. Ayer (1959) wrote his introduction to *Logical Positivism* as editor with the view that the post-positivist philosophy of Quine and Goodman, and the continuing work of members of the logical positivist school such as himself, Carnap, Neurath, and Hempel, were a development of the position. However, logical positivism is generally considered to have been devastatingly critiqued by Quine in his "Two Dogmas" (1953) and should be taken as marking the end of the movement.

which owes most of its inspiration to a respect for the scientific method, even when they assert it goes beyond the capability of science.[48]

Henceforth, in conclusion, for the purposes of our study we can conclude that metaphysics is defensible as a legitimate discipline of philosophy and so we have preserved philosophy in its tripartite understanding. This is not to deny there seems to be some circularity in our definitions and there will be some problematics to work through. However, it is our position that the Christian scriptures provide a unique resolution of this circularity in the biblical narrative and so we will build our worldview with this understanding.

2.4 The Nature of Philosophy—Analysis and Synthesis

After the fall of logical positivism, a mature and reflective Ayer, freed from the passionate zeal of his youth some thirty years earlier that had concluded that logical positivism was the *only* true way of philosophizing, noted insightfully:

> It is especially characteristic of philosophers that they tend to disagree not merely about the solution of certain problems but *about the very nature* of their subject and *the methods* by which it is to be pursued.[49]

Nevertheless, despite this new-found charity to his fellow-philosophers, Ayer remained *committed* to the same fundamental mode of philosophizing of his youth and should be credited as to never have become completely apostate from his totalizing faith in empiricism.[50] As we have seen, empiricism holds that all knowledge derives from our senses and so is a comfortable bedfellow to naturalism which deals with nature as the measure of all things. Ayer was adamant that philosophers should not consider themselves as doing any kind of "research" but were merely "to clarify the propositions of science by exhibiting their logical relations"[51] and, as we saw in the previous section, that the only *meaningful*

---

48. Mumford, *Metaphysics*, 98–108.

49. Ayer, *Logical Positivism*, 9. Emphasis added.

50. Ayer edited a second edition of a compendium of logical positivist thought in 1966 (despite Quine's dismantling of it in 1953) and clearly continued to regard that the naturalism of his contemporary philosophers had in a large measure been shaped by the logical positivist program. Plantinga, *Where the Conflict Really Lies*, in discussing the tenor of naturalism in the early chapters of his book, concurs with this. See n. 47.

51. Ayer, *Language, Truth, and Logic*, 32, 33.

propositions were ones which could be *verified* by reference to the physical universe.

The effect of this tendency was to radically rarefy philosophy (and science) to replace it with *scientism*, the belief that the only *genuine* questions (as opposed to linguistic confusions) were questions that *science* could answer or alternatively, the only questions *worth* asking were the questions that science *could* answer. This is thus revealed as a normative *ethical* position and really approximates a religious commitment on behalf of its advocates. Thus, as Ayer believed in nailing his colors somewhere and should be commended for doing so, I, with similar brotherly zeal in direct opposition to his rarefied view of twentieth-century empiricism, believe the process of critical interpretation, evaluation, alongside the solving of human dilemmas and the presentation of solutions, *is* a critically important part of the business of philosophy and the philosopher.

Yet, it must be immediately admitted, perhaps because of the enormous influence of this empiricism of the positivists in the disciplines of science and with the post-Kantian and post-Kuhnian skepticism of the humanities in twentieth-century philosophical thought, it is a model of philosophy that has had few supporters in the contemporary or popular conception of philosophy. That is, it has few supporters in either the analytic or the Continental perspective after the revolutionary changes in philosophy and culture generally at the start of the century. In the words of the most influential Anglo-American of the first half of the twentieth century, Bertrand Russell, such a vision of the task and practice of philosophy is a "pretentious" and "dogmatic" conception.[52]

However, we can disarm Russell's criticism by considering what has become of the modern analytic tradition of which Russell was a founding member. That tradition has virtually abandoned the synthetic function for mere "clarification" of the issues we might discuss, or "therapy" rather than a "solving" of the problems we clarify. To refute this and to defend the synthetic task as essential to the philosophic task, we need look no further than to the eminent G. E. Moore, Russell's fellow insurrectionist in the fight against idealism and one whose rigorous analytic method provided the inspiration for a generation of philosophers.[53] Moore rec-

---

52. Russell, *History of Western Philosophy*, 789.

53. The *Journal of Philosophy* 57.26 (Dec. 22, 1960). It contains contributions from several significant philosophers of the twentieth century who are not so much expressing agreement with Moore's positions but championing his rigorous method and the quest for clarity in philosophical discourse.

ognized that synthesis was a basic, necessary function of philosophy: "[one of the tasks of philosophy is to present] a general description of the Universe."[54] Here we understand "description" was not mere enumeration of phenomena but also the wider interrelations and a reasoned account of reality. Moore was a committed realist, and that realism was for working with the world, not to suffer in subjection to it in ignorance. Thus, we must proceed on Moore's basis and accept the challenge of giving a rational account of our world and our place in it.[55]

In summary, mere analytic "clarification" is most unsatisfactory for the conception of the work of a philosopher unless we can progress to offering salvation from those problems. We can also with inquisitorial curiosity wonder how philosophy once stripped of "dogmatic pretensions" might possibly for Russell be able to "suggest and inspire a way of life."[56] It seems incoherent because elsewhere Russell had:

a. Insisted philosophical problems *had* been solved[57] and that he had further solutions (though few in the philosophical world seemed to agree with him leading to his gradual eclipse in post-War philosophy).[58]

b. That the major problem of philosophic and cultural discourse was with the timidity of the clear-minded in being confident enough to argue with the absolutist bigot or obscurantist religious fundamentalist.

c. He complained mid-century that logical positivists were too *"narrow"* in their outlook and that they had a *"technique which conceals problems instead of helping to solve them."*[59]

---

54. Moore, *Some Main Problems of Philosophy*, 1.

55. Much more could (and should) be written to justify this conception of philosophy, and subsequent sections will offer some justification for it, but not the space it would warrant in a dissertation focusing on metaphilosophy. Wang in *Beyond Analytic Philosophy* offered an insightful critique and an appeal for the broad philosophical project from within the analytic tradition while urging a position beyond it, perhaps captured in his words "From how I know to what we know" (§19). He considered modern naturalism to be answering the former question and neglecting the latter, which he viewed as the most important and the truly philosophical one. He believed Gödel (a close friend) to have made progress with the latter.

56. Russell, *History of Western Philosophy*, 789.

57. Russell, *History of Western Philosophy*, 752.

58. Russell, *My Philosophical Development*, 9–11.

59. Russell, "Logical Positivism," 380–81. Emphasis added.

All this shows that Russell *himself* believed that a *worldview* springing from one's philosophy was one of the purposes and goals of philosophy; in his pre-positivist apologetic for philosophy, he explicitly said so.[60] To believe that he lived his life apart from his philosophical beliefs is implausible at best; we might also observe that in his post-positivist work, which was from the 1950s onward, he was much more a political and cultural intellectual activist than an academic philosopher. Further, the sheer volume and breadth of what he called his "philosophical work" was captured in an authoritative anthology,[61] which would suggest the business of the philosopher is *indeed* a broad wrestling with the problems of culture, an analysis and a synthesis that moves us in the direction of solutions.

2.5 The Character—Coherence, Truth, Correspondence, and Objectivity

We are arguing that any philosophical system or account should have the following set properties to be considered comprehensive:

a. *Coherence*: in a philosophical system, this is the property that it is internally consistent, that the different parts are logically compatible with one another.

 For example, if it is asserted that there is no resident meaning in a text, but a text is used to communicate the content of your philosophy with a view to converting the readers to your way of thinking, you are being incoherent. Blackburn made that very clear in his critical discussion of postmodernism:

> There are amusing episodes of radical postmodernists who suddenly forgot all about the death of the author and the indefinite plasticity of meaning when it came to fighting about copyright and the accuracy of translations of their own works.[62]

b. *Truthfulness*: as I wrote elsewhere, "There is not a subject in philosophy that has such a noble and contentious history than that of

---

60. Russell, *Problems of Philosophy*, 111 ff.
61. Russell, *Basic Writings of Bertrand Russell*.
62. Blackburn, *Truth*, 170.

THE NATURE, CHARACTER, AND PURPOSE OF PHILOSOPHY

the subject of truth and how to reconcile reality (or nature) and our perception of it."[63]

Just what "truth" is and its relationship to reality is a function of the philosophical system itself but the challenge to be "truthful" is never far from the attention of a philosophical school, even for the philosophical iconoclasts like Rorty that would like to bury it without trace.[64] In contrast, I take a very strong view of the possibility and the reality of truth in this work, following Plantinga in this:

> We all really know (unless thoroughly corrupted) that there really is such a thing as truth ("objective" truth, that being the only kind there is) and that it is of fundamental importance to us and foundational to our noetic structures.[65]

c. *Correspondence*: the property of describing the world in some way, a discernible set of states in the world or having an analogue in the world.

This is not to deny that correspondence is a difficult concept and how problematic it might be when we admit degrees of correspondence; but there is a strong intuitive sense that there is such a concept that does useful work for us.

d. *Objectivity*: The idea of objectivity, that there is a subject-independent world about which things can be said and to which our philosophy represents in some concrete sense, is essential to our view.

However, objectivity can also be more abstract dealing with *concepts* that are subject-independent. "Objectivity," as noted in the quote from Plantinga above, is strongly associated with conceptions of truth; what is true independent of the subject or "true" for all of us, *that* is the objective.

It is important each of these properties is present. For example, both Leibniz and Spinoza had coherence in their systems but are considered "dream philosophies" in the sense they fail the objectivity or truth test,

---

63. Macneil, "Feeling Good About Truth," 2.

64. As captured in the title *Take Care of Freedom and Truth Will Take Care of Itself: Interviews with Richard Rorty*, a collection of interviews with Rorty spanning over two decades. For Rorty truth was "merely a property of individual sentences" and there was "nothing of philosophical interest that could be written about it."

65. Plantinga, Afterword to *Analytic Theist*, 357.

which might be conceived of as the twin test of correspondence and coherence. Unlike the conventional pitting of these theories as oppositional to one another,[66] we recognize with Bahnsen that the former deals with the *metaphysics* of truth, i.e., what truth *is*, how it is constituted; and the latter deals with how we *know* something is true, that it fits into a wider theoretical framework, i.e., the *epistemology* of truth. Similarly, Blackburn is again helpful here, capturing both elements of the truth test:

> It is the things that explain my words that are their reference, and give them their truth. [Donald] Davidson went wrong by wondering what justifies a belief, in the abstract . . . John's explorations and investigations, his situation, his observations, experiences, what he has seen and heard, smelled, touched and felt, are all potentially part of the answer. . . . The cure . . . is to remember, and perhaps to practise, the practical techniques and skills of doing things in the real world.[67]

However, what is being argued here is not pragmatism in disguise but rather an appeal to what might be called a "critical realism"[68] that ties what we believe to the world we live in. Whatever our philosophy claims to be, it should be grounded, even mediated, in both our mental and physical experience of and existence in the world. In contrast, pragmatism (see §2.6.6) formally emphasizes the usefulness of any philosophy by its instrumental or practical utility but prejudges, like the positivist, questions relating to the real/unreal/ideal and the good/bad/moral/immoral, as *irrelevant* "pseudo-problems."[69] That is, they are problems *too difficult* to solve and therefore *cannot* be *genuine* problems, for all *genuine* problems *admit* of a solution. They have camped by the skeptical gorge and consider it uncrossable. Yet to consider the challenges of skepticism

---

66. For example, idealists who held that the "real" was the "mental" or the "rational" had historically favored a coherence theory of truth—all the elements needed to cohere as an account of reality. Similarly, realists who emphasized a physical world apart from our mental life that is mediated to us through our senses (though some naïve realists deny that experience is "mediated" through our senses as that implies a rational process) had favored a correspondence theory of truth, each propositional claim is tested against the world.

67. Blackburn, *Truth*, 169–70.

68. "Critical realism" is a philosophical school and a moderate response to skepticism. We examine critical realism more closely in a future section.

69. Carnap introduced the concept of the *pseudo-problem* as a sub-essay in his *Aufbau* (1928). Dewey wrestled with many of the same problems and came to similar conclusions: who *cares* about Hume's skepticism as a *theoretical* problem; what matters is that we can solve the *practical* problems of humanity.

as simply irrelevant is to *disengage* from the process of philosophy. Addressing the skeptical challenge is one, if not the key, challenge of philosophy for in answering skepticism we give reasons for *what* we believe, *why* we believe it, and what we *should* believe. It is to a more in-depth consideration of skepticism that we now turn.

2.6 The Purpose of Philosophy— Responding to Skepticism

2.6.1 The Problem

Modern Western philosophy might be said to have begun with Descartes, who positioned epistemology, in the sense of the basic possibility of self-consciousness or self-*knowledge* and the relation of the self to the rest of reality (i.e., a *metaphysic*), at the center of the philosophical process. Descartes was famous in his method for proposing *the* way of philosophizing was the method of doubt: by considering what could be doubted one would *intuit* what is certain.[70] Since then, skepticism has been reproduced repeatedly in all manner of senses such that we might conceive of philosophy as an attempt to answer the problem of skepticism or to collapse into it. Thus, for Descartes raising the problem, we can be thankful.

However, collapsing into a general skepticism hardly commends itself to a healthy intellectual life or even a practical honesty, but skepticism has proven notoriously difficult to vanquish. For example, Russell writing his last major philosophical work was disturbed by the metaphysical skepticism of the early twentieth century and argued for a tempering of the Cartesian method of doubt rather than its implications being pushed to their logical limits:

70. Descartes published the method informally to the general populace (in French) in his *Discourse on the Method* (1637) and more formally in Latin for the academy and for his ecclesiastical critics in his *Meditations on First Philosophy* (1642). In contrast to many of his critics, contemporary and modern, he did not in his *cogito* consider himself to be merely presenting a syllogistic proof; in that understanding he is plainly guilty of the logical fallacy of circular reasoning. Rather, for Descartes himself, "[one] does not deduce existence from thought by means of a syllogism but recognizes it as something self-evident by a simple intuition of the mind ... if he were deducing existence by means of a syllogism, he would have to have had previous knowledge of the major premise," AT 7.140. In agreement with Butler, *Transcendental Arguments*, I believe it could be argued that his *cogito* was a conceptual transcendental argument rather than a syllogism.

The fact that I cannot believe something does not prove that it is false, but it does prove that I am insincere and frivolous if I *pretend* to believe it. Cartesian doubt has a value as a means of articulating our knowledge and showing what depends on what, but *if carried too far it becomes a mere technical game in which philosophy loses seriousness.*[71]

However attractive Russell's intent and temper is to us, as a logician he could not have possibly justified this statement as settling the issue. His logician opponents certainly did not, pointedly ignoring him after the 1950s, and he eventually admits elsewhere he can give no *logical* refutation of such skepticism, "against the thorough going sceptic I can advance no argument except that I do not believe him to be sincere."[72] Thus, if we are searching for strong, logical certainties we remain extremely dissatisfied with the weakness of his final position.

Additionally and most seriously, a special kind of metaphysical skepticism, particularly associated with the post-Darwinian world and the nihilism of Nietzsche, objects to any possibility of there being objective *moral* knowledge; that our attempts at defining normative behaviors are arbitrary social constructs and moral knowledge is an impossibility.[73] This had devastating socio-political consequences: in the words of Abraham Kuyper, lamenting the descent of Europe into chaos and then war, "all eyes in Germany had turned to Nietzsche." The philosophies of Nazism and Communism that he and Hegel had inspired left an ethical void that American pragmatism and relativism needed to fill with at least some conventional or situational conception of socially constructed wisdom for the new democratic family, if all hope was not to be lost of reclaiming the Liberal consensus in the nations threatening to succumb to the rise of this totalitarianism.[74]

71. Russell, *Human Knowledge*, 161. Emphasis added.

72. Russell, "Logical Positivism," 382.

73. Willard, *Disappearance of Moral Knowledge*, offered perhaps the most detailed analysis of how this view became normative in twentieth-century philosophy, then provided a substantive rebuttal of it.

74. Nietzschean scholars, such as Diethe and Holub, are at great pains to distance his thought from that of the Nazis, blaming his sister Elisabeth Förster-Nietzsche for being centrally responsible for Nietzsche's reputation as a belligerent and proto-fascist thinker. One of the apocryphal stories is that Hitler gave Mussolini copies of Nietzsche's works to him as a present on his sixtieth birthday in 1943. Whatever the truth of that, it is clear Hitler thought well of Nietzsche's work and mourned his sister at the shrine she built to her brother, though we should equally recognize this is an *ad hominem* argument that does not logically connect Nietzsche with Nazism.

Similarly, Plantinga demonstrated to us the problems with the grounding of rationality on this basis means that there are those who argue that human knowledge is *always* tentative and truth, or a true and complete science, remains forever beyond our reach. It should be obvious such a position is antithetical to a Christian ethic that maintains the present authority of a normative scripture. Consequently, it is of upmost philosophical and cultural importance to us that skepticism, if not completely refuted, is reduced to an indefensible scandal:

> And this leads to the scandal of skepticism: if I argue to skepticism, then of course I am relying on the very cognitive faculties whose unreliability is the conclusion of my skeptical argument.[75]

Thus, as an epistemological position or a metaphysical stance, we will argue vigorously against it throughout this work. Hence, let us consider the three figures that really set the contours of the debate over skepticism and the track of Western philosophy ever since.

2.6.2 Descartes, Hume, and Kant

Descartes's exercise of *skepticism* was suitably moderated by the conviction of his *cogito*, in which he had believed he had reestablished the firm foundation for knowledge after dismissing Aristotelian metaphysics. However, Descartes's difficulties were many, even among those not immediately hostile to his program for ecclesiastical reasons (both Catholics and Protestants), and the Cartesian program, despite the efforts of his disciples and successors, was considered terminally devastated by the later Kantian critique of it.[76] Kant's "critical philosophy"[77] is considered as

---

Professor Ó Murchadha indicated to me that Nietzsche had spoken against German nationalism, and it is a tendentious argument to make to link Nietzsche with Nazism. I accept the substantial force of this but would still argue that however the relationship is conceived, Nietzsche provided a rich *source* for the "philosophers" of National Socialism, as Holub himself acknowledges. Similarly, Marx had appropriated Hegel's basic metaphysical position of history as moving toward a great consummation. There were also "right wing" Hegelians who emphasized the role of the State as the salvation of men; Hegel had asserted the State was *God walking on earth*. They secularized the concept and devolved the salvation of men to the State.

75. Plantinga, *Warranted Christian Belief*, 219n29.

76. The dismissal of the *cogito* is seen first at A348/B406 of Kant's *Critique of Pure Reason*: "[the *cogito*] with respect to its achievements we cannot entertain any favourable anticipations."

77. Kant's later philosophy was called "critical" philosophy because his most famous

the "central text of Western philosophy"[78] and Russell grudgingly wrote that even in the late 1940s Kant was "generally considered the greatest of modern philosophers."[79] Interestingly, Kant in critiquing the Cartesian program was doing so as part of the process of *answering* the radical skepticism of his contemporary Hume who we noted was the first to formulate a program that desired to excise metaphysics from philosophy and to turn epistemology into mere psychological habit.[80] We saw he had a particularly dim view of the Rationalist project, considering their work only fit for the flames.[81] In contrast, he wanted to apply the empiricism found in Locke (1632–1704) and Berkeley (1685–1753) to the problem of knowledge. Empiricism held that all knowledge is *perceptual* (that is, grounded in empirical experience) and he advocated for what he called the "[Newtonian] Experimental Method of Reasoning"[82] to the problem of human psychology and the processes of reason.

However, in his rigorous analytical consistency, he was driven to a catastrophic skepticism for he concluded that *causal* reasoning, the basis for inductive science, was merely a "habit of the mind." Hume had thus concluded that there was no reasonable (rational) grounding of reason; it was a tight circle of logical fallaciousness. We really could know *nothing* in the sense there was no *rational* basis to rationality, "reason when considered an abstract view, furnishes invincible arguments against

---

work was a trilogy of "Critiques": *Critique of Pure Reason* (1781/1787), *Critique of Practical Reason* (1788), and *Critique of the Power of Judgment* (1790). Further, much of his work post the publication of the first critique was clarifications and reworkings. Of note here is the *Opus postumum* which Kant considered his most important work, but which remained unstudied, only reaching publication in a critical edition by the University of Cambridge in 1993. The editorial introduction is itself an exemplary exercise in Kantian scholarship and the context of the work.

78. Kant, *Critique of Pure Reason*, back cover.

79. Russell, *History of Western Philosophy*, 677. My own undergraduate philosophy lecturer told our class that he had an entire examination paper just on Kant.

80. It is of note that Quine some three hundred years later also took refuge in psychology, but this time the behaviorist version, to try to deal with the knowledge and science problem. We will consider the details of Quine's naturalization of epistemology and ontology later.

81. After Descartes, modern Western philosophy divided at two major views—Continental Rationalism and British Empiricism. Rationalists reasoned from self-evident premises to the non-self-evident; empiricists held knowledge was perceptual. Kant was motivated to mitigate the skeptical conclusions of Hume with regard to empiricism and the credibility problem of the Rationalists; see Macneil, "Kant, Rationalism, Empiricism."

82. This was the original subtitle to Hume's *Treatise of Human Nature* (1739).

itself."[83] Philosophy and science were to be dispatched to the Humean Crematorium for disposal; his skepticism threatened to unravel even the *possibility* of knowledge which Kant appreciated would be devastating to science and he was determined to avoid. Thus, Kant was awoken from his "dogmatic slumbers"[84] while acknowledging the force of Hume against both the empiricist and rationalist conceptions of reason; he wanted to mitigate against Hume's conclusions:

> It remains a scandal to philosophy, and to human reason in general, that we should have to accept the existence of things outside us (from which after all we derive the whole material for our knowledge, even for that of our inner sense) merely on *trust*, and have no satisfactory proof with which to counter any opponent who chooses to doubt it.[85]

The central feature of the Kantian "answer" to Hume was his division of reality into a noumenal realm beyond the human mind and a phenomenal realm of experience upon which the mind *imposed* its understanding.[86] Science was strictly phenomenal, but at least it was salvaged as a possibility. However, this had the consequence of forever putting the knowledge of reality as it was in itself (*Ding an Sich*) as beyond the reach of the human mind and Kant's science was not *discovery* of natural laws but *imposition* by the psychological processes where the mind was the "lawgiver of nature." Kant's solution to the predicament might also be conceived of as a strengthening of the egocentric one as he internalized still further Descartes's starting point of an awareness of his own existence.

This conception, Kant's "Copernican revolution,"[87] evoked a long sequence of nineteenth-century philosophers who responded to Kant's critique either negatively, preferring in a Schopenhauer or a Kierkegaard

---

83. Hume, *Dialogues . . . Of Miracles*, 7. Hume had this sentence in the mouth of Philo who is not generally assumed to be representative of his views, but the consensus among Humean scholars was that this was the inevitable terminus of the skeptical view that Hume followed to where it led.

84. Kant's *Critique of Pure Reason* was intended to be his answer to Hume as noted in his *Prolegomena*, loc. 813.

85. Kant, *Critique of Pure Reason*, Bxln. Emphasis original.

86. Scruton, *Kant*, 57–59.

87. Kant used this allusion in the preface to the second edition of the *Critique of Pure Reason*, Bxvi, by which he indicated his radical reversal of the priority of the object and the understanding. The object conformed to the understanding, rather than the understanding conforming to the object.

mysticism to rationality,[88] or positively by "rescuing" and "improving" rationality as in Hegel.[89] Later, the analytic schools that came to dominate twentieth-century philosophy rejected Kant's conception of a noumena and asserted phenomena was all we have. We will now examine these distinctive streams that flowed from the various responses to Kant, giving specific attention to that analytic tradition.

2.6.3 The Fallibilists

The central issue when dealing with the skeptic is that they can argue that the attempts to defeat skepticism always assume what they, the skeptic, is not prepared to grant and thus are deemed to be "circular" in some way. As Russell freely admitted, he could see no way of escape from Hume's skepticism, and the naturalist too will always have that predicament.[90] Thus, one "solution" to skepticism is to accept its presence but to mitigate its force in some way. This has been the favored approach of contemporary scientifically oriented epistemology and is known as *fallibilism*, which can be conceived of in a number of different ways, but which we might usefully outline it in this way:

1. The principle that knowledge is not certain but is always open to revision in the light of new arguments.

   This is attractive as it recasts philosophy as contiguous with science in the sense of methodological equivalence.

---

88. The existentialism of Kierkegaard is sometimes considered a conscious capitulation to the subjectivism in Kant but owes more to his reaction against Hegel. Kierkegaard was especially disgusted by Hegel, considering his work idolatrous, arrogant, and conceited. Schopenhauer too reacted strongly to Hegel, even attempting to hold lectures at the same time in direct competition to him, but is noted for failing miserably in the attempt.

89. Hegelian philosophy is sometimes characterized as the "last word in idealism," a new dialectical form of reason.

90. Both Schlick and Carnap considered Hume as somehow asymptotic to a theory of knowledge. Schlick removed most of his defense of induction from the second edition of his *General Theory*, viewing it as inadequate in his preface to the second edition. Carnap in his *Aufbau* also admitted the logical weakness of induction ($105) and considered Hume as correct in denying causality as anything but a functional description of the perceptual world. It is of note that Russell did not find the account of Carnap persuasive, despite Carnap having referenced Russell's account of Cause.

2. We can have knowledge on the basis of defeasible justification, justification that does not *guarantee* that our beliefs are correct.[91]

This is attractive because it wants to preserve a claim to knowledge rather than cede to skepticism.

However, there is a catastrophic weakness admitted by the school itself:

> It is unclear how to formulate fallibilism precisely . . . it is surprisingly difficult to describe the level of fallible justification required for knowledge *in a clear and non-arbitrary way* . . . fallibilism does not necessarily escape skepticism. A theory might be fallibilist while still espousing standards too demanding to be regularly met.[92]

This clearly pinpoints incoherence at the heart of the concept, and it is of not much use to us to dwell specifically on the specific technical debates within the various inflections of fallibilism. It is enough for us that to a greater or lesser degree, fallibilism is assumed in most philosophical schools (which is one major factor in why we judge them inadequate) and we will often identify fallibilism implicit to a greater or less degree in the sections below.

2.6.4 Realism and the Role of Common Sense

With the retreat of idealism at the beginning of the twentieth century there was the emergence of the analytical schools and confidence initially grew in the realistic view; that is, the world is both describable and directly knowable. For the realist, to argue otherwise was non-sensical, as Moore famously posited as he lifted up his hands and declared the external world to exist on the basis of common sense.[93] This was to be

---

91. See, for example, Hannon, "Skepticism, Fallibilism, and Rational Evaluation," 172–94.

92. Hannon, "Skepticism, Fallibilism, and Rational Evaluation," 173. Emphasis added.

93. Moore's famous proof of the external world is worth repeating: *MP1 If hands exist, then there is an external world. MP2 Here are two hands.* Conclusion: *There is an external world.* Of course, this is a summary of a much fuller argument presented in Moore, *Selected Writings*, ch. 9. He was most famous for his rejection of idealism and his defense of common-sense realism. The argument was defended as recently as Otero, "Purposes of Reasoning." Moore was also highly influential in bringing Wittgenstein in from the philosophical cold in 1929; Wittgenstein repeatedly indicated he

repeated with great sophistication by Moritz Schlick, who dismissed the entire Kantian thesis at the end of a gloriously constructed critical argument in one sentence:

> Thinking does not create the relations of reality; it has no form that it might imprint upon reality. And reality permits no forms to be imprinted upon itself, because it already possesses form.[94]

However, all was not well in this newly rediscovered "real" world and Schlick conceded seconds after its triumph that realism is found in philosophy by *degree* only:

> We are bereft of any hope of arriving at absolute certainty in the knowledge of reality. Apodictic truths about reality go beyond the power of the human faculty of cognition and are not accessible to it. There are no synthetic judgments *a priori*.[95]

This last proposition was to prove particularly problematic and unraveled under the weight of criticism within a few decades of its positing, being defended only by the logical positivists in their most vociferous period. As Kenny noted, the possibility of and the "nature of synthetic judgements *a priori*" was a, if not *the*, principal problem of philosophy and is implicitly assumed by most hypothesizing and patterns of reasoning.[96]

Consequently, there was something also profoundly unsatisfactory for realism to be so easily confounded by the skeptical challenge in Schlick's formulation after he conducted such a painstakingly careful argument.[97] Likewise, many found Moore's defense of common sense compelling. However, a naïve or "common sense" realism is easily shown to be untenable, particularly for the believer despite its popularity among evangelical Christians.[98] We can understand this better by considering

---

valued Moore for his conversational power and his interrogative style. Moore is one of the few men to have had an entire issue of the *Journal of Philosophy* (57.26, Dec. 22, 1960) dedicated to him at his passing.

94. Schlick, *General Theory of Knowledge*, 384.
95. Schlick, *General Theory of Knowledge*, 384.
96. Kenny, *New History*, 618.
97. Blackburn, *Truth*, contains an excellent and accessible account of the various forms of realism as responses to skeptical criticisms.
98. Bahnsen, *History of Philosophy*, rather pointedly makes the point that nobody defends naïve realism today except the evangelical church and all the naïve realists are in the evangelical church. Though overstated, the popularity of the "classical" proofs, despite their serious philosophical shortcomings, demonstrates well the problems of a naïve realism.

that one reaction to Hume was in his contemporary Reid's "common-sense" realism that posited that our senses and perceptions were God-given and thus basically reliable. For that reason, it is also known as *reliabilism* and led to the view that "common sense" could be a guide for science and rationality. The early American colleges were heavily influenced by this view and there is a direct lineage to the evidential apologetic school.[99] The main problem with it arose when "common sense" was given expression by Darwin's hypothesis which he had allegedly formed based on his voyages and empirical studies. The force of common sense *seemed* to undermine the claims of scripture with the result of a rapid secularization or liberalization of many of the protestant colleges.[100] This was not just an American problem but was repeated in many Christian centers in Europe and missionary centers further afield.

2.6.5 The Therapeutic Conception of Philosophy

The therapeutic conception responded to the fallibilist turn of analytic philosophy during the twentieth century by redefining philosophy as simply *a* way of thinking about matters, rather than as a substantive research project that *establishes* the limits and content of human knowledge. Schlick reading and collaborating with Wittgenstein during the period 1927–33 had progressively developed an understanding that the purpose of philosophy was not knowledge *about* the world in the sense of metaphysical theories but knowledge *of* the world through empirical methods.

Wittgenstein's *Tractatus* had famously instructed one to only speak on what could be spoken about[101] which was taken by Schlick to dismiss metaphysics or otherwise speculative thought from philosophy in favor of the "new philosophy" of clarification.[102] Ayer labeled Wittgenstein's middle period as "therapeutic positivism" and other scholars

---

99. Yale, Princeton, Harvard, and most of the "Ivy League" colleges (analogous to the UK "Oxbridge" status) were all founded by Protestants. The great Princeton theologians Charles Hodge and B. B. Warfield were heavily dependent on the Reidian "common sense" view. Hodge explicitly asserted that "Providence" (or a Christian context) was not necessary to underpin a belief in common sense; it really was "common" to all humanity.

100. Some moved first to Unitarian positions or to liberal theology, while others fully secularized. Kuyper's Free University of Amsterdam had secularized by the 1930s, barely fifty years after its founding as a Christian university.

101. Wittgenstein, *Tractatus Logico-Philosophicus*, §7.

102. Oberdan, "Moritz Schlick," §7.

also interpreted Wittgenstein in this way during the 1940s.[103] However, Wittgenstein had written to Ayer protesting this interpretation and in his later period distanced himself publicly from positivism and this early understanding of his work. Monk makes the case that this was a secular appropriation of Wittgenstein who was far more mystical in intended sense, if not in the grammar, of the conclusion of his *Tractatus*.[104] That said, it was also clear he had been attracted to Schlick's Circle and its positivism as a way of *doing* philosophy during his early phase, despite expressing dissatisfaction with their interpretation of the *Tractatus*.[105]

Whatever its origin in Wittgenstein and its relationship to the logical positivists, the therapeutic conception has had an enormous and long-lasting influence on the analytic philosophical movement. However, in its contemporary, somewhat diluted form, it is sometimes caricatured, accurately in my view, as a "flight from certainty" or "an escape from [the necessity of] reason[ing]."[106] It merely diagnoses and does not treat the terminal patient, considering it improper a treatment should be prescribed but holding we might learn something from observing their death. It is considered so inappropriate within academic philosophy to suggest that philosophy and philosophers, firstly *could* and secondly *should* generate solutions to the problems they seek to clarify. Thus, it is perfectly *acceptable* to discuss the philosophy of religion in some abstract sense, but it is totally *inappropriate* to assert that one conception deserves the attribution of truth and thus our intellectual submission to it, whereas the others do not.

---

103. It was certainly fashionable for a time to consider Wittgenstein's "method" in this way; see Farrell, "Appraisal of Therapeutic Positivism (I)" and "Appraisal of Therapeutic Positivism (II)." However, Wittgenstein himself had replied strongly to Ayer in a personal letter unfavorably regarding this assessment (Monk, *Ludwig Wittgenstein*, 356–57) although Ayer does not mention it, even in his own intellectual biography of Wittgenstein (Ayer, *Wittgenstein*).

104. Monk, *Ludwig Wittgenstein*, 255–98.

105. See Macneil, "Wittgenstein," for more consideration of his relationship to the positivist movement.

106. These were the themes explored in an accessible manner in a series of essays by Schaeffer, compiled in *He Is There*. Schaeffer was sometimes eschewed by the secular academy as a pseudo-intellectual because he refused to write for the academy, preferring a direct and popular apologetic style. However, his insights were recognized by important figures such as Van Til, Bahnsen, and Packer within the Christian academy even if they disagreed with him or criticized his lack of accuracy and rigor in places. Bahnsen devotes substantial space (Bahnsen, *Presuppositional Apologetics*, 272 ff.) to critiquing Schaeffer's version of presuppositionalism as wanting, while recognizing Schaeffer's immense insight into the general drift of intellectual history.

While this would immediately be of concern to most Christian philosophers who above all else *should* be seeking to establish the legitimacy of a Christian ethic based upon Christian knowledge founded on a Christian metaphysic, it is by no means a concern unrecognized outside of the Christian community. Philosopher and educator Paul Arthur Schilpp[107] addressing the American Philosophical Society in a presidential address of 1959 had his speech reported thus:

> Schilpp's address accused philosophy in the analytic tradition, which then (as now) dominated the philosophical profession, of a *"contemptuous dismissal of ethics and of social and political philosophy,"* which he saw in turn as a manifestation of a broader *"reluctance . . . to make any contribution to man's existing dilemmas."* Philosophers, Schilpp argued, have a duty to help guide society by offering it the best available ethical and political wisdom. *"Most of the great thinkers of mankind,"* he said, *"seem to have believed wisdom was a good thing not merely for living the good life, but necessary for the development and running of society and of the state. This being the case, ethics and social and political philosophy occupied a considerable portion of their interest and work."*[108]

Thus, for Schilpp, the philosophical task *should* be conceived as of giving a general account of the interrelationship between the three traditional categories; what, in the language of this work, we have already designated as a "worldview"—a coherent account of our place in the universe and our relationship to it.

So, in summary, we can see that the therapeutic conception of philosophy does not, after all, offer us any mitigation of skepticism but seems rather to have surrendered to it. There is a tacit if not explicit assumption that we cannot be certain but maybe we can be clear on what we can perhaps we cannot be certain about. Stated this way, we can see there is an incoherence running through this conception for we can never truly be *clear* in our understanding unless we can give an *account* of the objects of our perception.

---

107. It may be unfair to judge Schilpp as outside of the Christian community. He remained a Methodist minister until the end of his life but was also known for his radical internationalism, governing role in the ACLU (of whom John Dewey was the first patron), and his championing of world government. As I have argued in "Politics, Church and State in the Post-Trump Era," such a conception of government should surely be considered antithetical to a biblical view of government.

108. Willard, *Disappearance of Moral Knowledge*, xii–xiii.

2.6.6 The Pragmatic Conception of Philosophy

It is with William James and John Dewey that the pragmatic movement is most strongly associated though the pragmatic maxim had initially been posited by Pierce, a logician and an experimental scientist by training and practice.[109] James was an accomplished anatomist who proceeded to become a professor of psychology and then progressed to a professorship in philosophy. He was thus a formidable intellect who made major contributions to both psychology and philosophy. However, his focus remained psychological in orientation, in the explication of belief formation which clearly intersected all kinds of philosophical issues regarding warrant and truth. He also had a motivation to defend a certain view of moral and religious thought where he posited that we often believe and are compelled to act with insufficient theoretical grounds but that alone did not delegitimize our actions. Central to his conception was the *evaluating* of the *practical effects* of a course of action.[110]

Thus, the fallibilism and sophistication of James is very clear, and he influenced Dewey significantly. However, his ongoing influence was muted by Dewey's innovations regarding the pragmatic maxims and the fact that he was also defending a Victorian pietism which was intellectually falling out of fashion. In contrast, Dewey grew up in an evangelical environment but was apostate by the turn of the twentieth century from his early attempts at developing a Christian philosophy.[111] That said, some view him as secularizing aspects of Christian ethics, replacing divine prerogatives and

---

109. Pierce believed the pragmatic maxim best explicated scientific theories to the degree Pierce preferred the term "pragmaticism" to distinguish himself from James. However, James and Pierce were good friends and Dewey had been taught by Pierce. This was thus an amicable family squabble; all three made central to their thinking the same pragmatic maxim that it is the practical effects of an object or action that need to be considered in understanding it and evaluating it.

110. This was seen vividly in his response (1896) to Clifford's *Ethics of Belief* and applied generally to religious belief.

111. For the decade 1884–94 John Dewey worked with the church in Ann Arbor and the Christian Student Association at the University of Michigan. Rockefeller, *John Dewey*, is considered one of the best accounts of Dewey's complex relationship to religion. The review by Shea, *On John Dewey*, a Deweyan scholar, of Rockefeller is also an excellent source of information on Dewey's basic orientation with regard to religion. Shea makes the important point that Dewey never had much enthusiasm for orthodox Christian doctrine despite his evangelical upbringing, being a "perfect case ... for [J. Gresham Machen's] thesis that theological liberalism is not Christianity but ... the religion of secular uplift" (*On John Dewey*, 75).

duties with human ones, and he believed passionately, and some would say religiously, in the connection between philosophy and life.[112]

Building on the pragmatic maxim, he asserted that the traditional epistemological "problems" of philosophy aiming to supply a coherent account of knowledge were *irrelevant*.[113] Dewey and the pragmatists who followed him considered words like "true," "false," "good," and "bad" not to be objective in reference but subjective and relativized by considering their effects and the fallibilism present is implicit in the renunciation of the traditional categories. Dewey, indeed, went further judging the utility of philosophy as to how it enables us to reach "our goals." What mattered was whether we had a set of intellectual tools with which we could control our environment and solve our socio-political problems.[114] Dewey's "version" of pragmatism he preferred to call *instrumentalism*; his view was a broad application of the pragmatic maxim to all the problems of society providing us with "instruments" to control and shape our environment. Dewey's emphasis could thus be perceived as sociological, and some refer to him as a sociologist though his work was of far wider scope and depth; his influence on American and Western democratic culture generally was substantial, some would say the dominant undercurrent of modern statism.[115]

The logical problem, though, as with all American pragmatism, which is also another critical weakness for *all* non-Christian philosophy, was the philosophical problem of defining what *should* be "our goals."[116] This necessarily needs to be done outside of the pragmatic maxim as it deals with conceptions of necessity and *value*. It is an *ethical* question. Similarly, it is paradoxical that Dewey himself argued for a *particular* view of education, i.e., an educational *theory* and asserted that the *proper*

---

112. Shea, *On John Dewey*, describes Dewey's religion as replacing God with the problems of the Public and the clergy or fellow believers with the naturalists and the humanists.

113. Dewey was probably the major influence on American culture generally, particularly in political philosophy. Logical positivism was far more influential in the philosophy of science though there was substantial common ground between them. Pragmatism had a revival of sorts beginning in the 1970s and still has supporters among the top tier of American philosophers such as Putnam and Nagel. It is very much an American movement.

114. Dewey, *Public and Its Problems*.

115. Rushdoony, *Christianity and the State*, loc. 466 ff.

116. Russell makes a very similar point in discussing Dewey in *History of Western Philosophy*, 778.

conception of education (what *should* be the end) was in accordance with that theory.[117] In arguing for a *particular* conception, he was asserting it in a theoretical fashion and thus outside the pragmatic maxim that judges on results.

It is on this point that pragmatism fails the coherency test for it can never on a *pragmatic* basis have a self-evident conception of "ends"; it is *always* begging the question. Rather like Russell expressing a view that by admitting a *single* principle outside of empiricism we can establish empiricism (whereas we would effectively deny the -ism of empiricism), Dewey and the pragmatists want to predefine "our goals" and then proceed but effectively bankrupt their position in doing so.

2.6.7 The Positivist Conception of Philosophy

Kant's account of science as "imposition" rather than "discovery" was becoming progressively implausible as natural science emerged strongly and grew in confidence in the period following his death. By the middle of the nineteenth century, the influence of Comte's paleopositivism[118] and the phenomenalistic emphasis of the early twentieth century saw Schlick's emphatic rebuttal of Kant in asserting reality imposed its form on our mind, rather the Kantian mind imposing its categories on the world.[119] This Kantian posit was viewed as most unsatisfactory because it separated humanity from the possibility of objective knowledge and rested on the doctrines of transcendental psychology. This reliance on transcendental psychology was judged as particularly problematic in Kant's thinking which even modern neo-Kantians such as Strawson now

---

117. Dewey, *Democracy and Education*.

118. "Paleopositivism" is used to distinguish it from the "logical positivism" of the twentieth century. Logical positivism had little in common in detail with paleopositivism other than its elevation of science into scientism with their respective manifestos. Positivism rejected any conception of the *noumenal* (which was Kant's way to leave the door open to a moralistic religious faith), thus privileging phenomena and dismissing theocentric religion. Comte was unapologetic in advocating for a new religion of humanism (acknowledging the failure of the French revolution because he viewed its brutality as inadequate in its view of the sensitivities of the human subject). There still exist positivist "churches" in some countries committed to a moral reformation. In his naturalism, he exerted substantial influence on Darwin and many proto naturalists.

119. It is clear at this early point in his career Schlick was a realist. In later years his realism weakened owing to the influence of Carnap, who considered the realist/anti-realist problem a "pseudo-problem" caused by the obfuscation implicit in an imperfect language.

deem as unsafe, his derivation of the categories and his choice of formal categories as open to debate. There was also an awareness that there is something fundamentally unintuitive in Kant's conception of science as the *imposition* of modes of understanding on the world. That is, "science," if it is anything, is generally accepted to be a *process*; it was considered by its practitioners as a process of *discovery* rather than imposition.

Thus, it was difficult to describe the work of Faraday regarding electricity, which was to revolutionize the world, or the mathematical equations of Maxwell modelling the propagation of electromagnetic waves that provided the basis for modern communication technology, as somehow not "discoveries" about nature but rather the "imposition" of the mind of humanity on them. Thus, as natural science developed and technology was produced by the application of such science in second order disciplines such as engineering, it became increasingly apparent that to view science as the mind *imposing* order on the world seemed more dogmatic than an authentic philosophical account.

Yet Schlick, even in his triumphant refutation of Kant, in a very important manner strengthened Kant's metaphysical agnosticism to outright atheism, jettisoning apodictic truths as "beyond the power of human cognition." In rejecting metaphysics, he argued that the knowledge of particulars was all we had.[120] Subsequently, the logical positivist movement (of which Schlick was the major founder) rarefied philosophy as they sought empirical purity and threatened to cull even ethics as a philosophical category, reducing it to mere emotion without literal meaning.[121] "Positivism" seeks to bypass the need for a metaphysical basis for philosophy (in that sense they might be considered extreme global skeptics regarding metaphysics) by simply positing that the methodology of philosophy (modeled after science) seeks merely to *organize* the phenomena of nature on the basis of the objective evidence of the senses, and not to "explain" it in any fashion.[122] Thus, Sir Isaac Newton, who revolutionized the scientific world of his day, is sometimes considered as the protopositivist on the basis of his remark that he would not "dare to feign a hypothesis."[123]

120. Schlick, *General Theory of Knowledge*, 384.
121. Ayer, *Language, Truth, and Logic*, 102 ff.
122. Russell, *History of Western Philosophy*, 783, 789.

123. The interpretation and ambiguity surrounding this remark and the doubt that can be cast on it as a manifesto for strict positivism is discussed accessibly in Carey, "Hypotheses Non Fingo." It must be pointed out that Newton's legacy was not

The idealized version of his method was allegedly to provide just a sufficient model to explain a particular "fact" of nature from the empirical evidence and to postulate no further. The scientist merely "organizes" phenomena gathered on the basis of observation or experimentation rather than attempting to explain it beyond what the evidence permits. Thus, an implicit assumption of this school is the supremacy of empirical methods; they are considered more reliable and safer than the deductions of the rationalists. Positivism thus attempted to mitigate skepticism by describing the traditional "big," conceptual problems of philosophy as *pseudo-problems* that disappear once we tidy up our language.[124] However, as we found in §2.3.4, the glaring anomaly of this metaphysical position that rejected all other metaphysical positions was that the postulate of verifiability was not a criterion that was itself *empirically* verifiable. They had rarefied philosophy of its most important content, eventually replacing all speculative metaphysical dogma with a single metaphysical dogma of there being no metaphysics.

Additionally, the logical positivists had a similar *ethical* problem to Dewey and his instrumentalism. Though they wanted logical rigor and the application of the *scientific* method to the problems of society, positivism could not *justify* as to why the scientific method applied to our social problems *should* be desirable. This was even more so the case after the bloodthirstiness of the "scientific" regimes of Communism[125] and Nazism[126] which, ironically, also led to the effective disbanding of the school as many members of the school became Jewish exiles to the

---

in experimental science but for his grand mathematical theories and his "hypotheses" regarding light and gravity. Even if his intention was to be experimental and positivistic, his practice stood in stark contrast to that intention, something that is frequently missed when people talk about "Newtonian science" as a model of experimental science.

124. This is in large part inspired by Wittgenstein's *Tractatus*, see 6.5ff; especially note 6.521, "the solution of the problem of life is seen in the vanishing of the problem." It was developed and expressed much more forcefully in *Aufbau* by Carnap, who had been "excited" after a conversation with Wittgenstein.

125. A first order primary source for Communism and its relation to Nazism is found at the Weisbord Archive, https://www.marxists.org/archive/weisbord/index.htm. Albert and Vera Weisbord were American Communist revolutionaries, noted for their education and activism. The archive section on philosophy explicitly exegetes the "scientific" vision and advocates positivism. Albert's discussion of the origins of National Socialism are elucidating as he was writing while it happened and in retrospect.

126. Stein, "Biological Science," explicates in great detail how biological science was *foundational* to the Nazi view of humanity and their political program.

US.[127] Yet, the positivists believed their manifesto, alongside the humanist manifestos of the same period, were "better" than what went before but on their own criteria, there seems no possible justification for *why* we should think it so. Their ethical position is thus arbitrary and question-begging. However, we have already indicated that the catastrophic deconstruction of logical positivism was to come from within their own ranks. In 1953 Quine[128] (an intimate collaborator in his early period with Carnap) published an epoch-making paper in which he demonstrated that logical positivism was founded on two dogmas, *analyticity* and *reductionism*.[129] This was to prove terminal for the movement though it heavily influenced the methodological naturalism that emerged from the philosophical naturalism of Darwinism that we will examine next.

2.6.8 The Post-Darwinian Naturalist Conception of Philosophy

For the major schools of philosophy in the first part of the twentieth century, the bottoms fall out of what we might call an *ethical* theory of what and why we should value as a culture or how and why we should behave in a particular way. This is primarily because any conception of ethics seems to require a non-natural, metaphysical assumption about the character of reality, the relations within it and the flow, even the meaning or purpose of it, which had traditionally been provided by some non-scientific

---

127. Carnap, like many members of the Vienna Circle, took refuge outside of Europe in the US as Nazism took hold in Europe. He made a point of working on a Sunday *because* it was a religious day; the Nazis had at times appealed to the Christian scriptures (especially the book of John, which could be easily misinterpreted with its extended polemical tone against "the Jews"), and the Nazis used theologians such as Luther, whose polemics had been used as justifying their actions against the Jews. Additionally, some Nazis had deep connections with sections of the Catholic hierarchy, who later helped senior figures escape to South America. It was thus not surprising that many of the Jewish members of the Vienna Circle rejected religious metaphysics and Christianity in particular, forcefully.

128. Quine generated a large corpus over nearly fifty years and was arguably one of the most influential of the post-positivist "scientific" philosophers of the second part of the twentieth century known for his behaviorism, his rigorous logicism, and his naturalism. *From Stimulus to Science* was a concise distillation of his views, published just five years before his death; he continued being philosophically active shortly before he died.

129. Quine, "Two Dogmas of Empiricism." "Analyticity" was defined in this paper by Quine as "truths ... grounded in meanings independently of matters of fact." "Reductionism" was defined in this paper by Quine as "each meaningful statement is equivalent to some logical construct upon terms which refer to immediate experience."

meta-theory, i.e., a philosophical theory of "nature" or a religious view of "creation." However, Darwin postulated that *natural selection* was the mechanism of a *natural process* of evolution,[130] providing *prima facie* a *scientific* and a naturalistic meta-narrative. With an evolutionary view of humanity, Darwin made it possible to be "an intellectually fulfilled atheist" (as reported in Professor Dawkins's words to A. J. Ayer over a candlelight dinner at an ancient Oxford college founded to train preachers).[131] As positivism and pragmatism waned, naturalism turned more explicitly to the Book of Darwin to be the missing intellectual piece that allowed the atheist to have a "coherent" worldview and for eminent philosophers such as Quine to "find hope in Darwin" that blind chance is hurtling us toward an inevitably better world.

Ethics is explained in terms of "evolutionary advantage" for those who are moral. However, there lies the problem. As G. E. Moore demonstrated, it is a logical fallacy in naturalism to believe we can move from what *is* to what *ought* to be the case. The self-vitiating nature of naturalism was also demonstrated forcefully by Lewis[132] and Plantinga concurred—if *all* we have is naturalism, there is no *reason* or necessity for us to believe that what nature tells us is neither good nor bad;[133] it becomes at best an arbitrary choice or preference. Plantinga captures the problem of naturalism and the possibility of knowledge perfectly:

> Despite the superficial concord between naturalism and science—despite all the claims to the effect that science implies, or requires, or supports, or confirms, or comports well with naturalism—the fact is that science and naturalism don't fit together well... there is *deep unease, deep discord, deep conflict.*[134]

The basic problem with any naturalistic argument is that it is self-vitiating with regard to rationality; reason gets subsumed into behavioral or cognitive science or evolutionary necessity. There is absolutely no reason to believe in the *authority* of the pronouncements of reason

---

130. This is an important point regarding the questionable status of evolutionary theory as a *scientific* theory. Evolution has a prehistory almost as ancient as philosophy itself.

131. Dawkins, *Blind Watchmaker*, 6. The primary purpose of most academies at the ancient universities was initially to educate preachers for the ministry; see Rivers and Wykes, "Dissenting Academies."

132. Lewis, *Miracles*, ch. 3.

133. Lewis, *Miracles*, 17–36; Plantinga, *Where the Conflict Really Lies*, 309 ff.

134. Plantinga, *Where the Conflict Really Lies*, 309. Emphasis added.

when we drill down into its foundations and find they are naturalistic any more than we would trust the "reasoning" of a monkey. Thus, it should be evident that the conception of truth in naturalism is problematic and for those philosophers who seriously considered it, such as Quine, a rarefied disquotational view of truth is all that remains. As Quine puts it, "'snow is white' is true, if and only if, snow is white"—unquoting *p* is true gives us *p*. Further, as he was apt to do, Quine felt this foreclosed the matter for further philosophical discussion:

> There is surely no impugning the disquotation account. . . . Moreover, it is a full account: it explicates clearly the truth or falsity of every sentence.[135]

In fairness to Quine, he then proceeds to distinguish between truth and warranted belief,[136] where the latter might be seen to impugn on the traditional content of philosophical debates about truth, allowing Quine to assert that truth is simply a matter of two valued logic.[137]

As with much of Quine's method of philosophizing, we gain clarity at the cost of rarefying the content but cannot help to feel we have just deferred the discussion to a later section or my next book on that subject. However, Quine is refreshingly candid in places regarding the rather knotty problems of philosophy: "I have no definition of empirical content to offer for such theories, but it *seems* to make *reasonable intuitive* sense."[138] The remarkable lack of precision and commitment to subjective idealism implicit in these remarks should be of comfort to those so burned by Quine's projects to naturalize both epistemology and ontology.

2.7 Fallibilism and Modern Science— Universe or Multiverse?

2.7.1 The Intellectual Challenge of the Concept of Chance

We began by noting that fallibilism is an attempt to deal with skepticism by admitting that our knowledge will be incomplete or partial but still has sufficient warrant. However, we have found that fallibilism in

---

135. Quine, *Pursuit of Truth*, 93.

136. We consider Plantinga's conception of "warrant" when we consider epistemology proper; see §4.3.7.

137. Quine, *Pursuit of Truth*, 93–94.

138. Quine, *Pursuit of Truth*, 95. Emphasis added.

practice under pressure from the uncompromising skeptic capitulates to and in effect, compounds the deadly, general skepticism of the twentieth century, forming what North described as the "epistemological crisis" of the "new" university. In its practice of denying certainty, a unity of human knowledge, a devaluing of "knowledge for knowledge's sake" and most recently in the twenty-first century, profitability over academic expertise; we find fallibilism a grossly inadequate underpinning for either science generally or epistemology specifically. On this basis, the modern university has been described as an *anti*-university, actively promoting chaos, contingency, and chance as the only "sure" principles of reality.[139] We need to consider why such an unintuitive and seemingly anti-intellectual position has maintained the ideological credibility it has. This we shall explore by considering and evaluating its most exotic form, the *multiverse* postulate.

2.7.2 The New Physics

Most remarkably, this disunified and unordered conception of reality was given its initial intellectual plausibility by the "new physics" of the early twentieth century which seemed to show stochastic processes,[140] indeterminacy, and subjectivity at the sub-atomic level. This was found attractive by those who, for various ideological reasons, wanted to generalize and characterize *all* of reality as contingent and subjective. Quantum processes also seemed to be affected by the process of observing, i.e., they were asserted as lacking objectivity in an absolute sense; they were by nature subjective. In quantum speak, the act of observation seemed to "collapse the wave function" to "actualize" a "particle" in a particular location. Famous experiments such as the double slit experiment seemed to show the presence of a particle in two different places at the *same* time and demonstrating a wave-particle duality,[141] i.e., it had a "fuzzy" onto-

---

139. North, "Epistemological Crisis," 3–4. North's essay is an exposition of this viewpoint, opening with quoting Snow's blind faith in chance.

140. A "stochastic" process is a seemingly random one but is capable of characterization. There are also detailed mathematical description possible for such processes; see Rodrigues and O'Reilly, "Statistical Characterization," the latter being the lecturer for my own undergraduate course on stochastic processes.

141. See Polkinghorne, *Reason and Reality*, 85–98; and Polkinghorne, *Quantum World*, for accessible accounts of these issues from a theological perspective. His views are particularly interesting as he spent most of his life as an elementary particle physicist but resigned his chair at Cambridge to train as a priest. *The Quantum World* was

THE NATURE, CHARACTER, AND PURPOSE OF PHILOSOPHY

logical status. One interpretation of this physics asserted that it denied the law of excluded middle, one of the tenets of classical logic.[142] With logic consequently viewed as purely conventional and faulty, reality was apparently elusive, fluid, and un-fixed. This also flowed well with the postmodern zeitgeist of the age in which the dogmatic religious meta-narratives were collapsing under the weight of various pluralist and liberal responses to Darwinism. That is, some of the postmodern narrative tended to cast existence as "ironic"—meaning that all our conceptions of ourselves (and reality generally) are tentative, we should not take life that seriously, and we should abandon the foolish project that seeks a comprehensive understanding.[143]

However, the "extended meaning" (we might say philosophical implications) of such physical theories cannot reasonably be appropriated to the deconstructionist cause in defense of chance, contingency, and chaos. It is certainly correct that there are two basic positions regarding the ontological status of the proposed quantum states, i.e., are they *actualized* or just a convenient *model*? Penrose firmly asserts the "objectivity" of the quantum state vector[144] as telling us something about the real world whereas Hawking denied quantum physics offers us anything other than convenient models.[145] However, *both* Penrose and Hawking feel able to write popular accounts of the history of the universe; that is, Hawking clearly believed there is a *meaningful* story to tell about the universe.

In contrast, for the thorough going deconstructionist, it is a staple that there can be *no* history for it is not possible to understand the world from the outside, there is no objective position from which to view the world. However, the logical fallacy is plain: just because we cannot be close enough to every historical account to give a fully objective account

---

described by Penrose, arguably considered with Hawking as the most influential of the mathematical physicists, as "a delightful book written at a popular level without any misleading over-simplifications" (book endorsement). Part of Polkinghorne's motivation in his early accounts was to counter the appropriation by Capra, *Tao of Physics*, and Zukav, *Dancing Wu Li Masters*, of quantum physics as evidence for a view of the universe more aligned with Eastern religious thought. See also Macneil, *Are Science and Theology*, esp. ch. 4, for a discussion of this issue.

142. Associated most directly with Niels Bohr, the Danish physicist, and also known as the "Copenhagen Interpretation" of quantum theory. Bohr was especially interested in the philosophical implications of quantum theory though his philosophy is considered of a far poorer quality than his physics.

143. Rorty, *Contingency, Irony, and Solidarity*, 73–74. See also §3.3.2.

144. Penrose, *Emperor's New Mind*, 268.

145. Hawking and Penrose, *Nature of Space and Time*, 1.

does not mean we cannot be close enough to understand the various dynamics at play and to assert a reasonable account with the expectation of a good degree of objectivity.[146] Historical analysis and synthesis remain a worthwhile endeavor that are ignored at the price of the future; even our folk wisdom teaches us that if we ignore the mistakes of the past, we will repeat them.

However, there is a far more substantive and robust refutation of the deconstructionist position that can be made. Theories of the "very large," that is the cosmological or relativistic theories, were showing a remarkable amount of "tuning" of the universe which was taken as strengthening the case for determinism in natural law, for it appeared the universe was *necessarily* as it was. For example, Wilkinson describes how Martin Rees's *Just Six Numbers* had indicated a *remarkable* tuning in the basic physical constants of the universe and that *all* these constants not only needed to be the values they were but *needed* to be that as a group.[147] Anyone with an understanding of probability appreciates the near impossibility of such an event as the individual probabilities, themselves considered infinitesimally small, are multiplied together for the overall probability.[148]

2.7.3 Cosmological and Teleological Arguments

As Polkinghorne also noted, this was *prima facie* attractive to those seeking evidence for divine design and still features predominantly in evidential style apologetics.[149] I do not intend to consider these "classical" proofs in any detail for I believe they all share a fundamental *logical* weakness, and this can be explicated quickly here. Any "design" arguments (also known as cosmological or teleological arguments) are logically very weak

---

146. See Blackburn, *Truth*, ch. 8.

147. Wilkinson, "Multiverse Conundrum."

148. That is, if there were six events with an individual probability of occurrence of 1 in 6 (1/6), e.g., rolling a die and it turning up a 1; the probability of rolling six dice and *all* of them turning up 1 at the *same* time is 1/6 x 1/6 x 1/6 x 1/6 x 1/6 x 1/6 = 1/46,656. One of the major problems with conventional evolutionary theory is that the probability of a functioning cell emerging by "chance" was estimated by mathematicians as $10e^{-300}$, i.e., 0 followed by 300 decimal zeroes. For all intents and purposes, this is an impossible event, even allowing for the geological timescales commonly employed in evolutionary theory.

149. As found in "Old Princeton" apologetics associated with names such as B. B. Warfield and E. J. Young. However, they are also associated with St. Thomas Aquinas and form the default mode of Romanist apologetics.

as they do not *necessarily* point to a *single* designer and even if they did, it would not necessarily be to the specific "God" the monotheist would require. Design arguments also suffer from the problem that they are attempting to postulate something about the supernatural world from the natural world, which, as Kant put it, is also logically fallacious—we could only move to a designer that is part of the natural world or there would be more in our premises than in our conclusion.

That said, design arguments *do* work for the *believer* in a devotional sense,[150] serving as evidence from natural revelation because we *already* have the correct presuppositions and can give glory to God for his creation. That is, in my view, they work as exegesis for believers but are weak as logical proofs for unbelievers, i.e., they are not a medium for natural theology. This is not to say that they are still very popular in apologetic settings and are capable of a sophisticated defense,[151] but I do believe they have insoluble logical problems.

2.7.4 The Fine-Tuning Problem

However, the undeniable fine-tuning of the universe did (and does) present an enormous *logical* challenge to the physicalist, the evolutionist, and the general naturalist. As the case for fine-tuning got louder, the need for a response got stronger. It came in a particular interpretation of quantum theory which posited that any *possible* state *does* exist, and each combination would be a "universe" dimensionally isolated from the other, each with their own laws of physics.

That is, the intoxicating feature of the multiverse concept for the physicalist is the proposition that all *possible* worlds (each resulting from

---

150. It has been argued that Aquinas's use of these arguments should be understood in his theological context. That is, he was not arguing, as it is often understood, that by considering his arguments as an *un*-believer you could be converted to a believer by the force of reason alone (St. Anselm in the 1100s believed he had come up with arguments of that kind, but these did not withstand critical examination, commendable and impressive though they were). Rather it is a rational argument for a believer who already has the correct presuppositions. For this reason, Plantinga, *Knowledge and Christian Belief*, considers that Aquinas and Calvin had much more in common epistemologically than is normally permitted in either Protestant or Roman dogmatics, such that Plantinga changed the designation for his theory from "Reformed Epistemology" to "Christian knowledge on the A/C model." See chap. 2 n. 28.

151. For example, in Swinburne, *Existence of God*. Plantinga notes he has progressed the case for natural theology beyond its classical boundaries, but it remains a staple of Reformed thought that a natural theology is not possible.

a particular combination of quantum states) *do* exist but in a disconnected fashion. "Reality" was conceived of as a collection of universes, i.e., a *multiverse* and because there was considered an infinite plurality of quantum combinations, one combination would generate a universe like our own with the conditions for life. If "nothing" can split into "matter" and "antimatter"[152] we have an entire materialist conception of the universe that has no requirement for "God" to even "light the touchpaper of the universe."[153] Thus, the fine-tuning problem is "solved": *our* universe, despite its remarkable fine "tuning" *must* exist if *anything* exists at all, even if classical probability theory had suggested the near impossibility of that state. This is obviously supremely attractive for the atheist materialist, but Wilkinson cites the problem with it well:

> The exceedingly indirect nature of the evidence probably means the multiverse will remain at the furthest border of *speculative science* for some time to come. As for the fine-tuning problem, the Lewis/Tegmark infinite multiverse idea seems to solve it, but anything more specific such as string theory[154] just deflects the problems up to the next level of speculation.[155]

This is a loaded criticism, as "speculative" science is hardly the rigorous, "hard science" the physicalists want to pretend physics is. It hardly demands epistemic submission because of its compelling evidence. It is arguable, as Penrose asserted, that there is *no* evidence, just pre-theoretical "toy theory"[156] conjecture, and it is difficult to imagine any path that

152. The point being that the combination of matter and antimatter results in annihilation and a null energy state.

153. This was a phrase used by Stephen Hawking in an interview I watched which follows the contours of *The Illustrated A Brief History of Time*, ch. 8. Hawking renounced any belief in an inflationary-deflationary model of the universe that he had first developed with Penrose, favoring a "steady state" model of the universe that was consistent with the non-theistic and naturalist conceptions. It is of note few of his peers followed him in this, despite its atheological attractiveness.

154. It should also be noted that Stephen Hawking was less than enthusiastic about string theory at the time of his debate with Penrose, claiming it lacked predictive power. It may well have disappeared into obscurity if it had not been for the "graviton" equation, established independently, emerging from string theory during its application to another problem. Consequently, we might still hear of "string theory," or perhaps more correctly a *particular* version of string theory (M-theory) in the philosophy of physics today.

155. Wilkinson, "Multiverse Conundrum." Emphasis added.

156. "Toy theory" might seem to make it trivial but technically refers to a radically simplified cosmological model dealing with only the details the researcher is trying to explicate and ignoring all else. Such radical simplification, even if backed by impressive

would turn that conjecture into a theory that would even be granted the status of reasonable verisimilitude.[157]

We should also note that there are deep philosophy of physics issues skipped over with barely a nod here in these exotic accounts. It sidesteps the definition of "matter" and "antimatter" which are extremely problematic with antimatter possibly better described as a "virtual" mathematical construct with no physical analogue.[158] It is also worthy of note here that the matter/anti-matter/dark-matter problems were motivators that prompted Hawkins to propose a "steady state" model of the universe[159] rather than an inflationary-deflationary one that he had famously formulated with Penrose in 1970. On the inflationary universe hypothesis, 98 percent of the required mass of the universe demanded by the theory appears to be "missing." "Dark matter" was added as a concept to provide a cosmic fix for the model—matter that has not been detected but must be there for the theory to be tenable; black holes were once thought of as favorite candidates as reservoirs. However, as more was learned about black holes, this has not been maintained.

The dark matter problem was a driver for new cosmological theories that dispense with it. Hawking was not able to de-convert many of his peers to the non-inflationary view, after the forceful elegance of his work with Penrose (most still hold an inflationary model), though he asserted that early quantum effects removed the need for the "singularity" at the start of the inflation and the end of the expansion, a phase which was still necessary to generate the multiverse with suitable characteristics for life. Further to this case in point, we find that Hawking advertised himself in the more serious literature as a "positivist" because he did not view his work as describing reality in any sense but merely as a model and it was *irrelevant* as to whether there was a corresponding physical

---

mathematics, hardly seems compelling as a comprehensive account.

157. "Reasonable verisimilitude" (or RV) is a designation favored by "critical realists" such as Polkinghorne to any theory that cannot be proved apodictically but is nevertheless considered as approximating the truth. In *Are Science and Theology*, §2.3.4, I offer a brief but salient account of critical realism. Although my thought has clearly moved on, there are still plenty of similarities between the arguments made here and there.

158. Penrose, *Road to Reality*, 67. His popular account of his revised view is given in Hawking, *Illustrated Theory of Everything*.

159. Paradoxically, "steady state" models were common in medieval religious models that viewed the universe as created. As I understand it, Hawking's later model is a steady-state view but with a beginning quantum era as he describes in the revised version of his *Brief History of Time*.

object,[160] i.e., the universe *as it is in itself* might be completely different from that predicted by his theories.

This is illustrated with brutal clarity by the philosophical weakness of the "infinite universes" position admitted in Hawking's final paper before his death, in which Hawking described his revised multiverse theory as still a "toy model." His motivation for offering a revised version was to limit the required number of universes so that the theoretical problems of the "infinite" universe requirement could be mitigated.[161] However, by weakening the *possible* universes, he aided the plausibility of those who favored some kind of design hypothesis which the infinite model had initially served to counter after Rees's probability analysis. So, despite Hawking being famous for and advertising a "theory of everything,"[162] it seems there is actually very little but speculative conjecture of a vastly simplified model of the universe which is expressed in complex mathematics that did not convince his most able peers.

Thus, Penrose after a full decade of debate with Hawking describes the ultimate paradox of modern physics: "it is a common view among many of today's physicists that quantum mechanics provides us with *no* picture of reality at all,"[163] an opinion remaining confirmed thirteen years later from within quantum physics in a most emphatic manner by Glattfelder.[164] We might thus feel distinctly unimpressed and unthreatened if this is the worldview of the most creative minds in the philosophy of physics, particularly if the best explanation of "what there is" has but the status of a "toy theory." We must assert it is a metaphysical presupposition that motivates such a position, not a discursive scientific process. Goff admits this bluntly:

> If, in the earliest period of our universe, our laws were shaped by the right kind of probabilistic process, the many worlds theory could furnish us with enough variety of laws across the many worlds so as to make it likely that one would be fine-tuned. *We don't yet have evidence that our laws were shaped by such a process.* But *if the alternative is the postulation of a supernatural creator, then this seems like the more plausible proposal.*[165]

160. Hawking and Penrose, *Nature of Space and Time*, 1.
161. Hawking and Hertog, "Smooth Exit from Eternal Inflation?," 147.
162. Hawking, *Illustrated Theory of Everything*.
163. Penrose, *Road to Reality*, 782. Emphasis original.
164. Glattfelder, "Ontological Enigmas," 345–94.
165. Goff, "Did the Dying Stephen Hawking?" Emphasis added.

Goff here is appealing to nothing other than naturalistic *prejudice* as the basis for his "plausibility," which mirrors the evidentialist believer's preference for a supernatural creator hypothesis. Neither possesses superior logical force.

2.7.5 Certainty and Reasonable Verisimilitude

In our brief account above, it is evident that we have ample *prima facie* warrant to reject both skepticism and fallibilism as a normative basis for our epistemology, surprising ourselves that the latter offers an unworkable alternative to skepticism, either suffering from arbitrariness of criteria when defining its position or being vulnerable to skepticism when it makes strong knowledge claims. This is not to deny that it might indeed be true that secular and non-presuppositional epistemologies, including those claiming to be theistic, are forced to conclude "we are all fallibilists now,"[166] as any attempt to ground epistemology on infallible criteria seems impossible on a non-circular basis and sometimes viciously so.[167] We will seek to substantiate this *prima facie* warrant into the philosophical necessity for epistemological self-consciousness as we progress through this work, but our point here is that to fully grasp the significance of Schilpp's criticism of analytic philosophy noted above is the challenge to not be philosophically timid and for us to reengage with the big problems of philosophy once again. Concisely, it is to understand the possibility of *certain* knowledge and the ability to apply it.

That said, there might indeed be, and I would say there definitely are, domains of knowledge where our knowledge is always perceived of as developing or limited and might, in a sense, be argued as "uncertain." Yet, that admission is not an imperative for skepticism; rather our basic philosophical and psychological orientation remains epistemologically self-conscious and scientific in the sense we believe our knowledge is always progressing *toward the truth*; truth remains a *legitimate goal* of our inquiry.[168] The important philosophical distinction here is that we can

---

166. Hannon, "Skepticism, Fallibilism, and Rational Evaluation," 174n3.

167. Quine when discussing the problem of induction in the *Web of Belief* openly admits that "science" justifies induction but that "the sciences" themselves are founded inductively. Many attempts to reimagine science are, in fact, motivated by the inability to justify the notion of induction.

168. Polkinghorne, *Quantum Physics and Theology*, 1 ff. This was also the title of a famous paper by Donald Davidson, contra Rorty's attempted reading of him as

claim *certain* foundations for our claims to the possibility of knowledge, while recognizing we do indeed *learn* through analysis and experience such that our knowledge *grows*.

Thus, critical realists (CR) like to call this basic orientation *reasonable verisimilitude* (RV), and Polkinghorne makes this the centerpiece of his approach.[169] Polkinghorne's work demands serious engagement for, as a senior scientist who then trained as a priest but who also remained scientifically and theologically engaged, he brings a refreshing perspective, and he provides a persuasive case, contra Hawking, that the "true Theory of Everything... is trinitarian theology."[170] He is also a committed realist in that he believes the experimentally driven physical research does indeed "discover" something that is *really* there. This presents quantum physics with a far more objective sense and helps us escape from the meandering conjectures and exotic fantasies surrounding quantum physics that seem to gain intellectual respectability because the speaker once did something for science.[171]

Yet, he does believe his approach is *mediating between postmodernism and modernism* so his knowledge claims, though he considers them as having strong ontological significance and truth value, are unlikely to refute the self-conscious skeptic. Where to draw this line between modernism and postmodernism, if it is accepted as a legitimate possibility, cannot be seen as an objective process. Polkinghorne leaves himself open to critique on this basis and vulnerable to claims of subjectivity. It would appear the CR/RV position gets pulled into the black hole of fallibilism if the skeptic pushes hard enough.

2.7.6 Conclusion

In our analysis above of the various recapitulations of the fallibilist positions, we find that when they are driven to epistemological

---

sympathetic to postmodernism. Of course, as a disciple of Quine, Davidson's conception of truth needs careful explication.

169. Polkinghorne, *Quantum Physics and Theology*, 6.

170. Polkinghorne, *Quantum Physics and Theology*, 110.

171. For example, see Goswami, *Visionary Window*. There is a significant movement that endeavors to "combine Western science with Eastern mysticism [to create] a new scientific paradigm" (back cover). Lewis in his science fiction fantasy *That Hideous Strength* had the sub-text that it is only a short step from a strong commitment to "science" to a mystical view of the universe as somehow possessing a soul or to "science" taking on a God-like character.

self-consciousness, these "scientific" formulations are seen to be woefully inadequate and unsatisfactory as to the nature of reality and a theory of knowledge. Their associated ethical implications, which became plain in the generalization of a "chance" principle and the denial that any certain moral knowledge is possible, are thus also brought into question. Thus, our intermediate conclusion must be that the messianic promises made of empirical "science" in all these philosophical forms are ill-equipped to deal with skepticism and cannot form a firm foundation on which to build a society. The clarity we have obtained at this juncture also demonstrates the effectiveness of our methodology of moving them to epistemological self-consciousness. Thus, we will now consider some of the more rationalistic concepts that emerged in post-Reformational and Enlightenment modes of thought, that is, both secular and Christian innovations, and apply the same critique to them with a view to providing a bridge into our wider program of epistemological self-consciousness.

2.8 The Imperative for Epistemological Self-Consciousness

2.8.1 The Quest for Common Ground

The Renaissance and Enlightenment mindsets drew heavily on the Greek mindset, literature, and philosophy with which we began our discussion. The era is often popularly conceived of and taught as a "rediscovery" of this classical or "golden age" of Greek culture with its emphasis on humanism and autonomy in contrast to the Catholic hegemony. However, it should be noted that the relationship with the Catholic Church during the period was not always adversarial; there was a large patronage of universities by the Church and some of what was considered the Christian Renaissance was acclaimed as some of the best work of the period, but it *was* true that the lack of progress in science was the exception to the general advancement in other parts of culture.[172] Rather paradoxically, this was not so much to do with the Catholic hegemony but rather with the dominance of Aristotelianism and its teleological accounts of science within the academy.

---

172. Some commentators have suggested "medical" science was the exception to this rule, with substantive progress being made during this period.

Yet it certainly remains defensible that it was with the work of Plato[173] (429–347 BC) and his pupil Aristotle (384–322 BC) that the Western early modern tradition owes so much. It was also true of later thinkers such as Epicurus (ca. 300 BC), in whom we see the first strong articulations of naturalism and atheological skepticism which were to feature in some Enlightenment thinkers such as Hume. Hume found Epicurus's atheological argument from evil compelling: "Epicurus' old questions are yet unanswered. Is he willing to prevent evil, but not able? then is he impotent. Is he able, but not willing? then is he malevolent. Is he both able and willing? whence then is evil?"[174] Pelagius believed he was following Augustine when he answered that question with the concept of human freedom[175] and it has had some forceful defenders in our contemporary generation of philosophers.[176]

It should be of no surprise then that we see a series of Catholic philosophers who, like some of the early church fathers, were heavily influenced by Greek thought and imported that conception of reason. Leaving out the long historical sequence before him, this "scholastic" tradition was seen to have its most articulate and rigorous working out in St. Thomas Aquinas (1225–74). In apologetics it is asserted that it was Aquinas's appropriation of Aristotle that sets the basic orientation of Catholic thought that continues to the present with, it is said, its general principle of a *common* reason providing the grounding for apologetic argument; the outreach and appeal to the unbeliever is on the basis of discursive argument; the claims of Christianity will be demonstrated to them through direct arguments with premises that can be accepted by both sides.[177]

---

173. A. N. Whitehead, one of the most eminent philosophers of the first half of the twentieth century, wrote thus: "The safest general characterization of the European philosophical tradition is that it consists of a series of footnotes to Plato. I do not mean the systematic scheme of thought which scholars have doubtfully extracted from his writings. I allude to the wealth of general ideas scattered through them" (*Process and Reality*, 39).

174. Hume, *Dialogues Concerning Natural Religion*, 63.

175. Ó Murchadha, *Formation of the Modern Self*, 30.

176. Plantinga, *God, Freedom and Evil*, was considered a milestone in a modern defense of the argument in mitigating the criticisms of Mackie and Flew which had dominated the non-positivistic atheism-theism debate in the first two decades after WWII. Flew caused a scandal in the atheist community when, in 2004, after fifty years of atheological scholarship, he announced he had changed his mind. I distinctly remember my first philosophy lecturer commenting that "it demonstrates that he is still thinking." The story is told in Flew, *There Is a God*.

177. For example, Leo XIII in 1879 made it mandatory for Catholic institutions

THE NATURE, CHARACTER, AND PURPOSE OF PHILOSOPHY

Thus, Aquinas's "Five Ways" from his *Summa*[178] is the archetypal examples of the method, all being variations on the cosmological principle, providing the foundation to what came to be called natural theology—a proof for God's existence derived from nature alone. In this respect, Aquinas, in this rational innovation, precipitated a radical departure from his own position by those less cautious in their theological commitments. For this reason, we need some important clarification and qualification to correctly understand the track from Aquinas into what might be called "natural theology" and the evidential method of apologetics if we are not to misrepresent Aquinas; there is some question regarding whether natural theology is an innovation from his work rather than an expression of it.

Prima facie it is not difficult to recruit a traditional understanding of Aquinas to the evidentialist cause. For example, in his *Summa contra Gentiles* he argues he "must have recourse to natural reason, since the gentiles do not accept the authority of scripture."[179] The first four books of the *Summa* make no appeal to "revelation" other than to confirm the conclusions reached by *reason*. We might be tempted to argue that we had already seen a similar pattern in Anselm (1033–1109), who argued impressively on the basis of "reason alone" for "faith seeking understanding" but in an important sense, for Anselm as most certainly with Augustine, faith was seen to *precede* reason. The traditional interpretation of Aquinas in many Reformed accounts of Thomism (and indeed many conservative Thomist thinkers for the best part of five centuries) was that he reversed this priority, i.e., that reason provides the grounding for faith.[180]

---

that taught philosophy that Aquinas was "to be taught as the only right one," and Russell had offended many Catholics by a BBC broadcast in the 1930s when he criticized Aquinas. Some reforms and councils since have softened the dogmatism somewhat, especially since the 1960s Second Vatican Council. However, Pope Benedict as a philosophy professor (though he was perhaps better known as a theologian) maintained a strict division at the "modern" philosophy, which he said began with Descartes. He was also noted for rolling back some of the reforms of the 1960s that had muddled some of the Catholic dogma.

178. *Summa theologiae*, his most important and well-known work, composed 1267–73. An authoritative, online English translation is found at https://www3.nd.edu/~afreddos/summa-translation/TOC.htm. His second most important work was the earlier *Summa Contra Gentiles* (1259–65); a parallel Latin-English version is found at https://isidore.co/aquinas/ContraGentiles.htm.

179. Aquinas, *Summa Contra Gentiles* 1.2.

180. De Lubac, *Augustinianism and Modern Theology*, 113–14.

This traditional account of Aquinas asserts that we know by revelation through grace or by reason and that God can be known in both ways, but with God in his essence considered as incorporeal, proof of God through reason will always be indirect. Aquinas was empirical in orientation and had no desire to appeal to intuition to substantiate the rational knowledge of God; it is through the senses that reason mediates the world. From these principles, God consequently cannot be directly known by reason but must be known by analogy and remotion.[181] Thus, the famous arguments early in his *Summa* proceed backward through the chain of causality to God.[182] His core argument was that if all objects were contingent, by definition there must have been a time where they did not exist; but because they do exist there must be some necessary object (which we will assign to be God) that *caused* them to come into existence. These contingent objects were the objects of nature which Aquinas enveloped such that they had a functional separateness and independence from the divine nature, i.e., suggestive of a theory of natural law. It is this conception of a realm of *pura naturalis* ("pure nature") which was to precipitate what became both a theological and a scientific revolution.

Dupré describes his innovation as developing in subsequent thinkers in terms of a theory of secondary causes, "a conception of nature as fully equipped to act without divine assistance."[183] However, this must be considered an innovation rather than an exegesis of his account as Aquinas was always careful to avoid the separation into two independent or parallel accounts; the two constituted a single reality directed toward a supernatural end. This elucidates the alleged tension in Aquinas that had so disturbed Russell.[184] For Russell, Aquinas's appeal to reason was "insincere" because the conclusion was "fixed in advance," i.e., *from revelation*. Aquinas seems to be being accused by Russell of being Augustinian. However, equally, Aquinas in his dependence on Aristotle was vulnerable to the criticisms of Aristotle's conception of the "universal" as embedded in the "particular," where the active intellect extracts the universal from the particular and that "form" was held, instantiated, within the intellect.

This was philosophically problematic; it was at best paradoxical to assert the presence of a universal in a particular by definition and there

---

181. This is sometimes known as the *Via negativa* ("the negative way"), proceeding to the knowledge of God by what he is not.

182. Butler, *On Plantinga*, pt. 3.

183. Dupré, Introduction to *Augustinianism and Modern Theology*, xii.

184. Russell, *History of Western Philosophy*, 452–54.

was a search for how such a position could not just be mitigated but avoided altogether. To deal more effectively with the problem of universals and particulars, there was a movement toward *nominalism* where the universal is merely considered a convenient linguistic label. When combined with a voluntaristic account, first articulated by Scotus but radically in Ockham, a division between nature and grace was making a naturalistic account not just possible but the foundation upon which, according to Dupré, Catholic, Lutheran, and Calvinistic thought were to unconsciously proceed.[185] Thus, it was in the work of Aquinas's interpreters Cajetan and de Suarez in the sixteenth century that formalized this division between nature and grace, with a priority given to naturalism, to the near exclusion of the spiritual. It is this naturalistic form of Thomism that characterizes evidential apologetics within a Catholic, a Reformed, or an evangelical context. This Lubac wishes to expose as a faulty exegesis of the thoughts of Aquinas while simultaneously acknowledging that it was a dominant conception within Thomist theologians only facing a concerted reappraisal in the first half of the twentieth century.[186] Lubac's thesis was that a return to an Augustinian foundation would be compatible with a correct reading of Aquinas,[187] thus it is this "aberrant" version of Thomism that lends itself to evidentialism. Rather provocatively then we might consider the implicit reformation of Lubac as compatible with our own aim of restoring the properly Christian foundations of rationality, though this would be something that would need to be examined further in a separate work.

Thus, it becomes more interesting for us that Plantinga identifies the "germ" of what Calvin labeled the *sensus divinitatis* in Aquinas, and he described his own epistemological model[188] as the Extended Aquinas/Calvin (A/C) model, in preference to the earlier "Reformed Epistemology" moniker. It must be noted that though he spent a considerable period at Catholic Notre Dame after Calvin,[189] it is still implausible this change

---

185. Dupré, Introduction to *Augustinianism and Modern Theology*, xi.

186. De Lubac, *Augustinianism and Modern Theology*, 112–15.

187. De Lubac, *Augustinianism and Modern Theology*, 275–78.

188. Plantinga, *Warranted Christian Belief*; Plantinga, *Knowledge and Christian Belief*.

189. He returned to Calvin, "his intellectual and spiritual home," in 2010 after spending 1982–2010 at Catholic Notre Dame. He was still teaching part-time in 2012 and was awarded the Templeton Prize in 2017.

of nomenclature may have been merely a concessive political gesture.[190] It is certainly contrary to Plantinga's personal testimony in response to anticipated criticism when joining Notre Dame in which he endorsed Notre Dame as being home to some of the finest Protestant thinkers also. That is, the traditional demarcation between Catholic and Reformed thought is not as clear-cut as many accounts suggest. It should also be noted that the pre-eminence of reason is not peculiar to the neo-Thomist apologetics challenged as heterodox by Lubac, and it is readily found in Reformed thought. They become issues of emphasis rather than substantive difference and this is one of the reasons that Van Til was so forceful in his rejection of it, or at least in the priority given to "evidences." "Evidences" are not *self*-evidential, facts are not "brute" facts, so evidences are founded on a philosophy of evidences. These important issues we consider later in this work.

So, in summary, despite the complexity of the theological landscape we have sketched above which denies the simple separation of Catholic and Reformed thought, history still teaches us that it is on the naturalistic assumption which theologians and philosophers have proceeded and which we will demonstrate is unsupportable. Implicit in this position is that the "principle of reason" was considered general and universal; there was a "common intellectual ground" on which an argument could be undertaken and worked through on the basis of reason alone. However, with Lubac we can concur, "the dualism engendered by an obsessive notion of 'pure nature' was not without its uses"[191] if for no other reason than to confute artificial teleological accounts which had hampered the progress of natural science. It was thus in the wake of the Reformation proceeding as Dupré hinted in a mode friendly to *pura naturalis* assumptions, that there was a major expansion of science as Aristotelianism lost its grip, even among the Catholic scientists.

It was rather the *papal* reaction to Galileo that caused serious complications for the Catholic scientists; the censuring of Copernicus was actually *after* his work had been assimilated to a large degree by the lower levels of the Church.[192] Similarly, Lubac was first censured by Pope Pius XII in 1950 seeking to articulate what was already a nascent repositioning

---

190. Plantinga, "On Christian Scholarship," does, however, demonstrate an acute sensitivity to his Catholic context.

191. De Lubac, *Augustinianism and Modern Theology*, 275.

192. I discussed this more fully in "Descartes Showed There Was No Need for God."

in Catholic thought,[193] a decision effectively reversed when Pope John Paul II appointed him a cardinal in 1983.[194] So, much as secularists like to set in opposition science and religion, or the sectarian Reformed want to castigate the Catholic hegemony for their stifling of science, the situation was and is far more complex and nuanced. The battle is rather at the worldview level independent of sectarian allegiance, and it is that which we are seeking to articulate ultimately in our work.

2.8.2 Beyond Common Ground

Thus, it should be apparent to us that a more sophisticated rationality was required to support orthodox Christian premises while maintaining the important contact with the real world. This was not to be found in the Fundamentalist movement that emerged as a reaction to the Liberalism of the academy, who chose instead to withdraw from mainstream academic life for close to half a century until the early 1970s. Similarly, the American Reformed Christian world splintered into various denominations after the reorganization of Princeton by a denomination seeking to liberalize their theology, and it was to be from Calvin College, a locus of the Dutch-Reformed tradition, that something of a renaissance in Christian scholarship emerged out of the philosophy department, particularly in the figures of Alvin Plantinga and Cornelius Van Til, who both studied under Harry Jellema, recognized by both as a highly influential teacher of Christian philosophy.

Plantinga's work can be seen as analytic philosophical theology developing a far more robust reliabilism with a careful and sophisticated development of Reid. In Plantinga we see that alongside a metaphysical commitment to realism, there is not a denial of the interrelatedness of the

---

193. De Lubac, *Augustinianism and Modern Theology*, ch. 9, is an historical justification of his position as a position more correctly orthodox than the accusation by the traditionalists of his heterodoxy.

194. Though Lubac himself asserts there was never any formal papal sanction and goes as far to quote it positively, though rather cryptically, in *Augustinianism and Modern Theology*, 274. However, his Order most certainly viewed the cyclical as a censure, and he was forbidden from publishing or teaching as a Catholic. See Hulse Kirby, "7 Persistent Myths," for a modern perspective on the specifically contentious issues in Lubac's theology. As noted, Lubac was rehabilitated by Pope John Paul—a Catholic theologian noted the Church never rescinds its previous papal bulls (executive decisions by the pope) because the pope is considered "inspired by God" and thus "cannot err"; they simply issue new ones which override them.

subject, their world, and the world around us. There is the ethical presupposition of standing in God's world and being accountable. This avoids the lapse, like the positivists and the naturalists, into skepticism, scientism, or both. In contrast, Van Til was in the broad Dutch neo-Calvinist tradition, and his philosophical theology can be seen as seeking to build upon the seminal work of the great Christian theologian and statesperson of the late nineteenth and early twentieth centuries, Abraham Kuyper. Kuyper had recapitulated a Calvinist philosophy of life fitted for modernity while vigorously rejecting the various faces of modernism. He argued with great force against the Darwinist, Liberal, and the emerging socialist metanarratives that had come to dominate the philosophical zeitgeist and the wider cultural milieu which we have considered earlier when discussing the influences of Darwinism and modern naturalism. However, with the backwash of Arminian revivalism, the obscurantism and cultural ghettoism of the dispensationalist premillennialism of the emerging Fundamentalist movement, it made his profound and intellectually rigorous message anachronistic and unappealing to the wider anti-intellectual Christian consciousness, even at the time he was expounding it.

In contrast to this emergent New Evangelicalism, Van Til offered an orthodox, Reformed but sophisticated development of Kuyper while simultaneously arguing for the objectivity of Christianity, the latter a distinctive of the "rival" Reformed Princetonian Warfieldian view, developing his position from the mid-1930s onward.[195] He was to lay the ground for a dramatic reentry of conservative Christianity into the public square without ever being directly involved in the Reconstructionist movement he spawned.[196] He had helped develop the epistemological basis for the program to counter the inadequacy of the Christian consciousness, which had been ill-equipped to counter the flow into either mysticism or liberalism, and the subsequent loss of political influence to the pragmatism of John Dewey in the US and to far worse in Europe. As we have already seen, the old Liberalism of the European empires disintegrated as the rational nihilism of Nietzsche was given teeth in the Nazi movement.

---

195. Kuyper and Warfield were contemporaries and had met when Kuyper lectured when visiting Princeton; they were good friends. However, Warfield had written a preface to a colleague's introduction to apologetics in which he criticized Kuyper's presuppositionalism. Kuyper and Warfield were the opposite poles of the Reformed community with respect to apologetics, but both were enormous intellectual figures in neo-Calvinism. We will repeatedly examine the differences between the two and Van Til's novel synthesis; see also §3.5.5 for the detailed analysis.

196. This was the subject of my MA dissertation, *Dominion Theology*.

Thus, with Plantinga and Van Til there was to be an intellectual turning point in the early 1950s. Plantinga was just beginning his career, Van Til was maturing into popularizing his position. Their influences were felt in very different spheres but both were Reformed thinkers arguing for Christian philosophy from Christian premises. We will examine in detail in future sections what they brought to the table, but we have already intimated in our preliminary discussion that we will need to follow first Plantinga and then Van Til to salvage any hope for a *rational*, Christian philosophy.

2.8.3 Holism

In our survey above, we have found that the basic problems with fallibilism are that of *incoherence* and *arbitrariness*, displayed both in philosophy and so-called scientific conjecture. If you cannot mitigate skepticism at a basic logical level, the skeptic will always defeat you as the lines you need to draw for your theorizing they can legitimately reject. Thus, it is no wonder that Schilpp, addressing the APA at the intersection of the pragmatic, positivist, and naturalist philosophies, was so scathing in his criticism of modern analytic philosophy and why this work will continue to argue antithetically to tolerating the scandal of skepticism.

Even the finest naturalist philosophers such as Quine retreat into fallibilist language at points of difficulty but then proceed past the difficulty on the basis that the difficulty is solved by "reasonable intuitions."[197] If the intuition really *is* reasonable, it might reasonably not qualify as an intuition but as a judgment; just as Quine's use of the term "intuition" elsewhere has a qualified, technical meaning distinct from the somewhat irrational implication of the term.[198] However, he does seem arbitrary in sometimes using it in the sense of something beyond our conscious reasoning process as more of an "informed guess," *so much for rigor*! We are not being rude to Quine here but merely imitating the master who famously dismissed modal logic and various other important problems of philosophy with the phrase "so much for X."[199] Yet, conversely, there is something very profound and important to be found in Quine.

197. Quine, *Pursuit of Truth*, 95.
198. Quine and Ullian, *Web of Belief*, 92.
199. Not everyone agreed with him on those "so much for" points, especially when they had just written a whole book on modal logic. See specifically Plantinga, *Nature of Necessity*, appendix 1.

In his emphatic repudiation of logical positivism, Quine reopened the door to metaphysical questions as *legitimate* questions and brought into sharp focus the richness of our cognitive picture and the elaborate taxonomy of our rationality. One of Quine's arguments in two dogmas that was so revolutionary was his "holism." It was the *whole* of our statements about the external world that should be confirmed or infirmed and not the individual statement "taken in isolation from its fellows."[200] This was a radical break with the logical atomism that had been characteristic of the empiricist movement in the twentieth century.

He proceeded to describe his philosophy concisely in a textbook for young students and it serves as a concise primer on modern rationality conceived of in terms of a scientific holism.[201] He uses the "web" as a metaphor and it is a particularly well-chosen metaphor: the web is multifaceted but has a center that is the most important section, giving it its coherence and strength, with every part of the web linked to it. It provides the lens through which all else is interpreted and evaluated.[202] The web can suffer substantial damage to the periphery but retains strength and offers coherence provided its core remains undamaged. Thus, although a naturalist and an atheist, Quine is of great interest to us because he talks in his work about a "view of nature" which, in the semantics of our thesis, we will call a "worldview."[203] Thus, taken with the work of Kuhn in the following decade and perhaps foreshadowed in the work of Popper a decade before, we consolidate our conclusion reached in our discussion of fallibilism that modern "science" struggles not just to define itself, but

---

200. Quine, "Two Dogmas of Empiricism," 43.

201. Quine and Ullian, *Web of Belief*. This was originally written as an English course but proved so popular with philosophy courses that the authors rewrote it to align more closely with the audience. Quine believed that philosophy and science were coterminous. Thus any "non-scientific" philosophy was not really philosophy at all as it could add nothing to human knowledge, which Quine had equated with the "whole of *science*." It is of immediate note that Quine recognized the *circularity* of this position but considered such circularity *inevitable*: all *genuine* problems are construed in *scientific* terms and are soluble by *scientific* methods. "Circularity" likewise plays a significant role in our future discussion.

202. We will later refer to this as an interpretative principle or a "presupposition."

203. Invaluable reading in this respect is his "Autobiography," a highly compressed account written for a composite work. The full autobiography, *The Time of My Life* (published by MIT Press), grew to over five hundred pages. As Quine explains in a postscript to the shorter version, it took around twelve years for the Festschrift in which it was included to come to press, by which time the full autobiography was about to be published, so he did not update it.

THE NATURE, CHARACTER, AND PURPOSE OF PHILOSOPHY

also its fundamental arbitrary nature and its weak claims to objectivity.[204] We confirm that an idol has been made of "modern science" as the oracle of truth when its inner circle knows its own reality is very different.

2.8.4 The Unity of Apperception

The challenge we are repeatedly seeing in our discussion above is the problem of the construction and the unity of knowledge which Kant was unable to reconcile. When Kant's famous aphorism "Two things fill the mind with ever new and increasing admiration and reverence, the more often and more steadily one reflects on them: the starry heavens above me and the moral law within me"[205] gets quoted, it is often with a sense that it is a profound mystical or religious insight. Perhaps there is an element of Kant's own religiosity there, but it is more readily understood as an admission of the total failure to reconcile the principles of the natural world with the principles of the inner, perceptual world. This is owing in part to the equally as significant insight that percept and concept were in a circular relationship to one another. He recognized that the unity of apperception, that process of explaining how knowledge gets structured in the mind, had been dealt with poorly by philosophers.

Nevertheless, his solution to Hume's skepticism by simply reflecting Hume's despairing conclusion as the answer to Hume turned out to be no solution at all; he pours concrete around his feet and forever separates the noumenal, phenomenal, and noetic realms with the implausible thesis that all minds conform to the transcendental categories. Even for the contemporary neo-Kantians such as Strawson, this thesis was too psychological and problematic.

Thus, for the Van Tillian, Kant's motivation of attempting to establish the transcendentals of human understanding was the correct project but ultimately succumbed to and formalized the skepticism that had awoken him from his dogmatic slumbers only to sleep twice as soundly. In contrast, Van Tillians agree with him that the stakes are high for the possibility of knowledge; for Hume's deconstruction of reason, captured in his conclusion "when considered as an abstract view it furnishes invincible arguments against itself,"[206] destroyed the possibility of knowledge.

---

204. Mahner, "Demarcating Science from Non-Science," 515–75.
205. Kant, *Critique of Practical Reason*, 129.
206. Hume, *Dialogues . . . Of Miracles*, 7. His conclusion has since been a thorn in

There seemed to be no rational basis for rationality, and we *can* formally agree with Hume that considering reason as the abstract, *autonomous* human reason, will *indeed* destroy the possibility of a coherent theory of knowledge. Thus, we will work through the argument that Van Tillian transcendentalism using the transcendental of the ontological Trinity as a transcendent transcendental seeks to provide the solution to this problem of knowledge where Kant's transcendental failed.

That is, what we seek to work through is that the imperative for epistemological self-consciousness is that we can be certain that our metaphysical claims about the nature of reality, those claims being guaranteed by the inscripturated Word and the character of God. We are not direct foundationalists in the autonomous sense of scientism but are foundationalist in the indirect, transcendental sense when "transcendental" is interpreted in a specific Christian context with a specific referent. Only then can the problem of knowledge be solved.

2.8.5 Epistemological Self-Consciousness and Uncertainty

For the Christian philosopher, and we have endeavored to show for *any* philosopher wishing to be critical and aware of their own presuppositions, the main divisions of philosophical inquiry are not hermetically sealed off from one another and that intellectual coherence is only obtained when one understands this interrelatedness and can articulate it. That is, they have come to a place of *epistemological self-consciousness*. This does not minimize the role or necessity of analysis as articulated so strongly by Russell, but rather presses it into the service of the synthetic function as articulated by Moore.

That is, without synthesis, analysis is rarefied and bare, the philosophy it produces is sterile or at best, shallow, reducing in Rorty's words to "poetry" or "cultural politics" rather than a body of knowledge and understanding.[207] By "shallow" we do not mean it is without merit or significance, but for Rorty as the "post-analytic" philosophical standard bearer of the "postmodern pragmatist" movement, philosophy is simply a matter of "speaking about" the target subject matter in a particular way;

---

the side of all empiricists and rationalists alike; his challenges cannot be met without the transcendental of God's existence making sense of reason, the logical imperative for this book.

207. Rorty, *Philosophy as Cultural Politics*, ix–x.

the "solution" lies elsewhere.[208] Here we find the antithetical position to that argued in this work—much of modern philosophy seems to consider it as a "given" or of a matter of disciplinary orthodoxy that *we can be certain of nothing*, except of course that we *can* be *certain* that *we can be certain of nothing*.

Now, for the purposes of clarity we have stripped down the sometimes exotic and complex formulations of the fallibilism at the center of the perspectives above to get at the logical core and expose its logical frailty, while hopefully avoiding the construction of straw men. Sometimes we *are* constrained to deal with *probabilities* and *reasonable verisimilitude* (as maintained by some critical realists), as well as the empirical methods of the Bayesian schools for interpreting new evidence. We can still acknowledge the value and worth of this work when working in the different spheres of life.

That is, accepting Kuyper's principle, we understand that each sphere or modality of life has a degree of autonomy and its principles; the religious does not dictate to them, but it is legitimate to stand as the ethical guardian and to robustly engage in critical challenge when necessary.[209] In contrast, it is the univocal *naturalism* of these schools that we challenge that never permits them to move beyond discussions of probabilities rather than *certainties* and we end up in that philosophical cul-de-sac of Neurath's sailors. Such methods are plainly ill-equipped to deal with ethical questions such as value and moral knowledge.

While we might not be able to ascertain complete confidence in our various sciences, that then does *not* mean that our foundations, metaphysical, epistemological, and ethical, completely collapse. As Plantinga noted, just because classical epistemological foundationalism was found wanting that does not imply, as Rorty asserted, that *all* foundationalism is refuted. In the same manner for ethics, Blackburn concurs where he argues very strongly for the moral imperative based on a robust commitment to ethical knowledge on the basis of a convictions regarding right and wrong both historically and in our shared world.[210]

---

208. The way Rorty saw himself as the postmodern, pragmatist, post-philosophical, bourgeois liberal is captured well in the interviews with him in *Take Care of Freedom*. Rorty was described by Blackburn (a peer and one of his severest critics) as "unusually well informed." See Macneil, "Richard Rorty's Iconoclastic Deconstruction," for a comment on his iconoclastic philosophical project which began after the publication of his *Mirror* (1979).

209. Kuyper, "Sphere Sovereignty," 461–90.

210. A concise summary is found in Blackburn, *Ruling Passions*, 279 ff. The

2.9 Summary and Conclusion

In this chapter, we began where it all began for philosophy (in the Western tradition at least) with Greece. We asked the simple question "Why the Greeks?" We argued that the humanism, proto-naturalism, and autonomous or self-sufficient mindset of the Greeks was what made them the progenitors of the dominant stream of what reemerged in the Enlightenment rebellion against religious authority and has become the dominant intellectual temper of our time. We argued that naturalism needs to be understood as an imprecise category and as an elastic term. We stressed that a culture could still speak with language that sounded theistic but, in that context, God was a projection of human traits and could be considered naturalistic. We argued that naturalism is best taken as describing the drift of Greek culture into what we now call scientific naturalism with its empirical assumptions; we noted Epicurus was one of the first philosophers to articulate that view. We indicated that a strong critique has been made of this equation of naturalism with the scientific and it was our intention to explicate this. However, we did want to acknowledge the importance of the Greek taxonomy of rationality for us and we concurred with the tripartite view of philosophy as metaphysics, epistemology, and a theory of value (that is, ethics *and* aesthetics).

We then considered the most serious "problem" with this conception, that there was an interdependence between the terms and that this circularity had led to an intense hostility to metaphysics and its attempted eviction from philosophy first by Hume and most recently by the logical positivists; we examined in some detail the presumptions of the positivists and the eventual reason for the failure of their project, being that its central principle, the verification principle, exempted itself from its own criteria. We could thus assert the legitimacy of metaphysics as a branch of knowledge. We also saw that the "problem of other minds" was one of the fundamental challenges for philosophy and this introduced us to how the issues of epistemology were central to Western thought. We saw how Plantinga exploited the tension to argue that a Christian could not be considered "irrational" because a belief in God was on the same level as the belief in other minds. We saw how this provided the backdrop to his overall Reformed Epistemology—Extended Aquinas/Calvin project which terminated in a

---

position is applied to the problem of truth more generally in Blackburn, *Truth*, and he specifically singles out Rorty's position as ethically bankrupt. Rorty acknowledged Blackburn's critique in a footnote in later compilations of his papers.

THE NATURE, CHARACTER, AND PURPOSE OF PHILOSOPHY

sophisticated argument for the rational acceptability of Christian belief but with no necessity. This was also the first mention of Van Til's project to argue for the *necessity* of Christian belief for rationality.

We considered how logical positivism after its fall gave way to scientism, the view that the only legitimate questions were questions that science could answer, or alternatively what we asserted was the *ethical* view that the only questions *worth asking* were the questions science could answer. This we noted was devastating for philosophy in that it reified it of content, converted ethics into a descriptive process, and denied synthesis as a legitimate function of philosophy in favor of analysis or a mere description of relations. This helped us assert the need for a synthetic function of philosophy and our belief that one of the chief tasks of philosophy was to frame a worldview, a comprehensive account of reality and its relations. We also equated this with our stated aim at the start of this work that philosophy should be *transformative*; we do not merely want to analyze and clarify problems but also to assist in solving those problems.

We then proceeded to map out what we should expect from a philosophical theory; we demonstrated a commitment to realism and an objective reality. We considered correspondence, coherence, and truth as necessarily objective, rejecting any subjective conceptions of truth as confusing warranted belief with truth. We understood how a commitment to realism helps distinguish philosophies between internally coherent "dream philosophies" and philosophies, using Wittgenstein's dictum, "rooted in the practice of living in the real world." Again, we are noting here the need for philosophy to be transformative and relevant to living in the world but not merely pragmatic; noting the fundamental weakness of pragmatism was a dogmatic commitment to a preconception of what was "useful" or "beneficial." Recognizing there were various problems with realism, we then took a deep dive into skepticism and argued that philosophy historically could be considered a series of responses to skepticism.

We considered that modern philosophy was founded on the methodological skepticism of Descartes but recognized that his skepticism was qualitatively different than the metaphysical skepticism that Hume was driven to in his desire to be rigorously empirical. We considered how Kant wanted to mitigate that skepticism and how the consensus among Kant scholars was that he did so by separating reality into the noumenal and phenomenal. Science was concerned with the phenomenal, the way things *appear* to us and that was the limit of our knowledge. We might have useful posits such as God which belonged to the noumenal realm, but they were beyond proof or knowledge. We considered how Kant was the turning point of the subsequent philosophy; some argued for mysticism as the route to the knowledge of the noumenal in preference to his chastening of rationality, others rejected the noumenal realm and asserted phenomena was all that we had.

We considered the preference of twentieth-century philosophy for fallibilism, the view that skepticism can be accepted but mitigated in some way. However, we noted the varieties of fallibilism, even in the sophisticated theories of modern physics that seemed to demonstrate indeterminacy and chance at a microscopic level, were not categorical or convincing arguments with the two giants of modern physics, Hawking and Penrose, having mutually exclusive metaphysical conclusions. There was no "scientific" answer, but our very conceptions of reality are theory laden and have a fundamental metaphysical commitment that is pretheoretical. We saw that the most exotic naturalism of the multiverse postulate was exposed as a metaphysical prejudice.

We then examined how we might structure our own Christian metaphysical commitment, and whether there was a possibility of a "common ground" with the unbeliever where we can meet and resolve our differences. We found the traditional arguments of natural theology were logically fallacious. We saw that the principal issue was one of the relative roles of reason and faith, particularly which one was to be considered primary. We considered the Augustinian view that faith would provide the grounding for reason and the alleged reversal within the neo-Thomist position that faith should be first demonstrated to be reasonable. The latter was shown to be the catalyst for a view of nature as in a distinct realm subject to its own laws, which in turn would lead to the dominance of a non-spiritual view of reality and the retreat of Augustinian apologetics. This became cemented as a "commonsense" rationality and was the context for the emergence and domination of evidentialist and classical apologetics which were empirical and naturalistic in their approach. However, the same epistemological commitment became catastrophic to Christian philosophy when Darwin published his findings which seemed to indicate that on the same commonsense basis, the metaphysical accounts of Christian scripture were at best mythical. This led to a rapid liberalization and secularization of previously conservative colleges, unable to refute Darwinism and the consequent withdrawal of conservative and orthodox Christian influence from the public square.

We noted that both within the Catholic communion in the work of Lubac and from within the Reformed communion in Van Til and Plantinga, there was a renewal of the Augustinian view which precipitated a movement toward epistemological self-consciousness. Lubac challenged the concept of a pure nature that could be understood independent of God's revelation and providence. Plantinga demonstrated the weakness of the Darwinian position, in that its naturalism was self-vitiating; where is the rationale for believing what nature tells us? We noted that within philosophy generally there was a rejection of positivist dogma and the acceptance of the theory-laden principle; a gradual rehabilitation of metaphysics, with philosophers like Quine arguing for a holism and an interconnected web of beliefs. We understood that with Van Til this holism is given a scriptural and a Christian context and that he asserts that only transcendental reasoning is able to mediate the truthfulness of rival worldviews and deal with the unity of apperception problem that Kant had been unable to resolve. In contrast, Plantinga argues that the way forward is with a radically overhauled Reidian foundationalism; a commitment that the world really is as it appears to us and that our faculties will give us knowledge of the world. While this does not provide an objective philosophical proof, it is internally coherent and rational. Thus, we begin to see a Christian philosophy is possible and indeed desirable, the consensus among the fallibilist was that our rationality needs a rationale, but none could be found for it—thus, the imperative, *we* must offer one.

Thus, the next tasks of our work must be to demonstrate how Christian "worldview" philosophy, which is necessarily apologetic, provides that rationale. Yet, it is important to assert immediately that we are not arguing for a static view of knowledge, to replace pragmatism with dogma or requiring that one is forced to accept from a range of competing *a priori* views of the world. Rather, we shall be arguing for the *objective* reasonableness of the Augustinian (or Reformed) understanding of Christianity and seek to establish the view that it is the *only* fully coherent and, thus, truly *rational* view to hold. We will be arguing *transcendentally* that it provides the basis of *all* rational thought and is *implicit* in *all* rational thought whether or not the subject recognizes it. We will be arguing that *all* human beings are creatures of God, made in his image and *to the degree* that they behave and think rationally in conformance to that image, they are able to construct a scientific view of the world reflecting the revelation of the order in the mind of the Creator. This is the heart of an apologetic philosophy.

So, as we brought the philosophical positions considered above to a place of epistemological self-consciousness, it became evident that:

1. They are inadequate as theories of reality.

2. Any attempt to dispense with metaphysics asserts a particular metaphysical dogma and is thus incoherent.

3. We must argue that *only* a *specialized conception* of the model reflected by the classical tripartite conception of philosophy, the Christian theistic worldview (and that further refined to the *Augustinian* tradition), is the *only* position that is not rendered incoherent and has a legitimate claim to rationality.

Regarding 1 and 2 we might find a broad, if grudging and an often hidden, implicit, acknowledgment within reflective philosophy, because we have indeed managed to generate such a diverse and wide range of philosophical perspectives to address this inadequacy and the incoherence. That it might be solved by 3 is what we must now turn to address for many would consider any reference to theistic solutions to the problems of knowledge as either a return to the past or "theology not philosophy." However, it is only by establishing the theological foundation that we can rescue any conception of philosophy and save it from the abyss of postmodern deconstructionism and paralogism.

3

A Christian Conception of Philosophy

3.1 Overview

WHAT WE WILL ENDEAVOR to accomplish in this chapter is to build on the understanding of philosophy in the previous chapter and to work our way toward what a distinctively Christian conception of philosophy requires. From the assessment of the previous chapter, we can safely assume a "traditional" division of philosophy as offering the most holistic account but here we want to precise it with the concepts that will help to make it a robust philosophical account.

First, we clearly distill the categories we have been assuming in our previous critical discussion, modifying and clarifying where necessary. Such is the importance of our refutation of the skepticism regarding metaphysics, which suffered repeated philosophical assaults during the twentieth century, that we must put a spotlight on the relation between the wider fields of human knowledge, science, and metaphysics. It is a principal and important relation if for no other reason that the language game of science, and particularly *naturalistic* science, is the dominant paradigm of our time.[1] If we cannot show that what we believe is *scientifically* respectable or at least defensible, or if we are unable to persuasively deconstruct or recontextualize the credibility of a naturalized metaphysics

---

1. As Bahnsen notes, some atheological apologists believe that a statement is not to be considered scientific *unless* it assumes naturalism.

or a naturalized epistemology, we will struggle in the philosophical and wider cultural marketplace.

Our ultimate strategy will be to establish the necessity of a transcendental criteria for rationality *generally*; we can then demonstrate that the confidence in a "scientific worldview," whatever that *might* mean in its details, is only defensible as a generality with a Christian metaphysic as its foundation. We then firmly place the epistemological self-consciousness project in the appropriate context, that of worldview philosophy.

3.2 Metaphysics

3.2.1 Speculative, Descriptive, and Revisionary Metaphysics

Ladyman, in a contribution to what was conceived of as the "most comprehensive attempt to provide a philosophy of science,"[2] offers a definition of metaphysics as "the theory of what exists [ontology] . . . the most fundamental questions about being and the nature of reality . . . whether there are objective natural kinds [categories] . . . [or whether] there are laws of nature."[3] Thus, temporarily leaving Ladyman's own exposition aside of a scientifically oriented metaphysics, it is easy to see why "metaphysics" can easily become a speculative, amorphous, imprecise, and loaded term easily associated with mystical or occult accounts of the universe and the supra-rational interrelation of its objects, sometimes being pushed to posit an irrational denial of all distinction, a monism posited against the direct evidence of our perceptions.[4]

That is, metaphysics and science often end up being contrasted, even by the more moderate and informed practitioners. Consider this account of Mumford, who, as a metaphysician, wants to define metaphysics for us:

> Science is based on observation, which is often its starting point and the ultimate arbiter of the truth of a theory. Metaphysics, while it's concerned with the world, is not so much concerned with that part of it that can be observed. *What we can see with our eyes is of little help in metaphysics, or philosophy in general. The evidence of the senses is not what decides whether a*

---

2. Kuipers, *General Philosophy of Science*, back cover.
3. Ladyman, "Ontological, Epistemological and Methodological Positions," 303.
4. As, for example, in many forms of Hinduism and Buddhism where the aim is to *intuit* the oneness of all being.

A CHRISTIAN CONCEPTION OF PHILOSOPHY

philosophical theory is to be accepted or rejected. We considered, for example, whether a table was just a bundle of properties or was a substance underlying and holding together all those properties. We should note that we cannot decide between these two theories on the basis of observation.

It is not as if we could actually remove the properties of a real object and find a propertyless substratum. What would one look like, given that it was propertyless? *Our questions are not, therefore, scientific ones . . . what we do in metaphysics is indeed above and beyond physics.* It is above in its level of generality; and it is beyond the observational investigation of the world, thinking about the features that rationally the world should or could have.[5]

Thus, Mumford wants to drive a thick wedge between science and metaphysics, or more specifically, between physics (broadly conceived as the theory of the physical) and metaphysics. However, he also wants to distinguish between philosophy and science on the basis that science is an *empirical* process, which we have already demonstrated in our discussion is a highly contentious position. The sociological dimension of his self-identification as a "metaphysician" might be the best explanation for such a naïve view. It seems scientists are not the only ones that want to demarcate their subject from its competitors.[6] We can rightly be critical of him here:

a. It would be a particular type of arcane philosopher or religious mystic who would not be concerned with what their eyes do see, or to deny that what they see with their eyes has no bearing on philosophy.

b. For a realist, one of the principal tests of a philosophical theory is its relation to reality and, excepting the absolute idealists, most idealists would also be concerned with how their concepts are tied to the intersubjective world, however conceived.

c. As we demonstrated previously, to separate philosophy from science is not an objective procedure, it is a matter of arbitrary criteria, prejudice, or linguistic convenience (and probably a combination of all three). That is, it is logically impossible to distinguish between whether or when a physical law which has an organizing feature should be considered "metaphysical" or "scientific" without begging the question.

5. Mumford, *Metaphysics*, 100.
6. Mahner, "Demarcating Science from Non-Science," 515–75.

In summary, Mumford in his account of metaphysics is demonstrating for us what should be properly called "speculative" metaphysics, the rather more secularized and respectable form of "religious" metaphysics. When reading Mumford, one senses his desire for the procedure which he wants to defend to be considered "scientifically respectable," but one is then easily frustrated by the passages above where he seems to be suggesting no such reconciliation is possible. This makes it easier to understand why metaphysics was the target of extreme dismissal by Hume in the eighteenth century and by the logical positivists in the twentieth century.

However, as we also noted, that dismissal was later demonstrated by the devastating critique of Quine as nothing but itself a *metaphysical* position which *dogmatically* asserted the single principle that denied all metaphysics. In response, Quine himself proposed a revolutionary[7] "naturalized," descriptive metaphysics (quickly followed by a "naturalized epistemology"[8]) which had a degree of scientific and logical respectability and was established by himself and others of similar naturalist convictions. This was to provide a functional ontological foundation[9] for science, informing the practice of it by what is most properly called *methodological naturalism*.[10] Quine's metaphysics were austere and limited in scope indeed, but for that reason were eminently respectable and acceptable to the naturalist project. Ladyman's account with which we began this section belongs broadly to this naturalistic tradition, but he also clearly demonstrates in his discussion the multitude of sometimes contradictory assumptions and mutually exclusive perspectives possible beneath that umbrella of naturalism. Exactly what entities were admitted and how they exist or relate to one another, if indeed at all, makes it somewhat fluid, arbitrary, and subject to change with the paradigm shifts of science.[11]

---

7. There is some question as to how "revolutionary" we should consider Quine's approach. For all the disdain that was heaped on Aristotle, Quine's *behaviorist* theory of knowledge was, like Aristotle's, a *psychological* solution to the problem of knowledge construction.

8. Quine, "Epistemology Naturalized," 69–90. Although this never appeared until 1969, Quine in the introduction makes it clear that he had already formulated and presented this view by 1965.

9. Quine, "On What There Is," 1–19.

10. Plantinga, *Where the Conflict Really Lies*, 168ff.

11. The informed reader might smell a Kuhnian emanation at this point: his concept of a "paradigm" as a hermeneutic tool to interpret science and especially the progress of science. Kuhn will play a significant role in our future discussion.

Thus, the Quinean model seemed overly austere in contrast to the ambitious metaphysics of those who were seeking some kind of a recovery of the generality of description[12] and even explanation or "revisionary" improvement of the understanding of the world[13] in the post-positivist period. There was, and always will be, a deep dissatisfaction for the worldview philosopher with the incongruity of lodging at the Humean philosophical dead-end of there being no reasonable basis for reason, enduring the Kantian psychologization of reason, which then degenerates further into a Quinean, behaviorist account encompassing the whole of nature and learning. Unable to solve the intransigent problems of knowledge, they are dissolved by subsuming them under another science.

That is, Quine liberated the world from the dogmatism of logical positivism, only to return to their altar of the *pseudo-problem* for worship as he paid homage with behavioral psychology as the successor subject to epistemology. His naturalist followers appealed to evolutionary science as their hope, but Plantinga then proceeded to strongly argue that naturalism and evolutionary theory were *incommensurable* at the logical level that should have been of fundamental importance to Quine.[14] There was a scholarly (and sometimes unscholarly) argument with Plantinga over the details,[15] but that led to his refinement of the argument over the best part of two decades. There is now a substantive agreement about the force of these anti-naturalistic arguments when conceived in the detailed Bayesian fashion[16] or as a broader conceptual argument, as found for example also in Lewis[17] and as revised in his interpreter Reppert.[18] It would appear to be a metaphysical prejudice, a religious commitment to an atheistic scientism, that keeps us in the Humean cul-de-sac.

---

12. Taylor, *Metaphysics*, xv ff. Like P. F. Strawson, Taylor asserted he was being descriptive rather than attempting a *theory* of metaphysics. However, both men undoubtedly advanced metaphysics as a theoretical discipline, Taylor in his arguments regarding fatalism (52–62), and Strawson's use of transcendental arguments in *Individuals* set off the debate about the merits of transcendental arguments which is an argument form leveraged later in this book.

13. Lawson-Tancred, Introduction to *Metaphysics*, loc. 158.

14. Plantinga, *Where the Conflict Really Lies*, 307 ff.

15. Fitelson and Sober, "Plantinga's Probability Arguments," 115–29.

16. Plantinga, *Warrant and Proper Function*, ch. 12.

17. Lewis, *Miracles*.

18. Reppert, *C. S. Lewis's Dangerous Idea*. Reppert clarifies and refines Lewis's argument.

THE FOUNDATIONS OF PHILOSOPHY

Further, the austere answers of Hume and the naturalism he influenced are far more inadequate in other ways important to us as philosophers who do not merely think of philosophy as the handmaiden of science[19] but, to borrow Russell's phrase, as an *inspiration to a better way of life*.[20] We find unlikely support for our contention in ironically one of the most visionary and prophetic of the twentieth-century public intellectuals, Aldous Huxley, who in his philosophical writings had once argued for a complete negation of metaphysics in a negative, atheistic existentialism. In sympathy with Russell, he advocated for an "erotic revolt" that the moral restrictions "imposed by Moses" might be undone as mere conventions. In rejecting such a "Christian" view of the social and economic order, society could be liberated and more just when reconstituted on a socialist basis. However, later in his life, Huxley in an unusually cogent piece of writing argued as early as 1937 that Hume's view decimated vast swathes of human experience as "meaningless" when these experiences were what brings *meaning* when faced with the "angst" of meaninglessness. "Meaninglessness" was no longer the pathway to emancipation but a negation of being and becoming, the social emancipation an illusion as "The Party" was elevated as an infallible organ of tyranny.[21] In doing so, he paralleled Wittgenstein's latter rebuttal of the positivist interpretation of his view of language in the *Tractatus*[22] and their political application of it in their manifesto.[23]

So, in summary, it behooves us to refuse to surrender to an intellectual powerlessness and skepticism about the world; we are seeking to understand nature, master and reshape it. That is why this work has no reticence in arguing for a strong metaphysics and we now proceed as to

---

19. In medieval conceptions of philosophy, it was orthodox to consider philosophy as the "handmaiden of theology." The only legitimate practice of philosophy was to support Church dogma. Similarly, for the post-positivists and many who favor an empiricist flavor to their metaphysics and especially for their epistemology, they see no purpose for philosophy other than in the explication of science. We might call this part of the *worldview of scientism*, and we can see some characteristics of a religious commitment on the part of the believers.

20. Russell, *History of Western Philosophy*, 789. Russell's exact words were "philosophy does not cease to suggest and inspire a way of life."

21. Huxley, *Ends and Means*, 267, 273 ff.

22. See Macneil, "Wittgenstein and Religious Language."

23. *Wissenschaftliche Weltauffassung*—"the scientific view of the world." This was title of the 1929 manifesto of the Vienna Circle which also fed into the first Humanist Manifesto (1933).

how metaphysics can legitimately provide a foundation for science and our epistemology.

3.2.2 Metaphysics as the Foundation of Science

In the previous section, we rejected substantially Mumford's definition of metaphysics, but we can affirm with him that metaphysics will supply interpretative tools, ordering functions and concepts. This process is inevitable, and most philosophers of science after Quine would accept that we always *interpret* the data that might come to us from the phenomenal experience through a conceptual scheme or what we will eventually label a "worldview." We will see why equating a "worldview" with a "conceptual scheme" alone is not wholly adequate, but our point here is that metaphysics aims to help rescue our conceptions of a *meaningful* universe, an understandable cosmos and thus informs how we *should* behave in it.

We have already seen how Huxley as representative of a caste of young intellectuals desired to cast the universe as "meaningless" so that we can swap places with God as the locus around which reality revolves. However attractive that this atheistic moral nihilism of Nietzsche and the scientific socialism of the Marxists was to both the young Huxley and the young Orwell, as it was to generations of Romantics, radicals, and libertines on different Continents, it was replaced with the dark pessimism of his *Brave New World* and of Orwell's *1984*, both of which saw no limit on the moral self-justification and appropriation of executive power by the State empowered by the inevitable flow of history toward its utopian consummation; this was all too easy to be co-opted by those otherwise with the more classical Liberal view, for the State, is, after all, "a minister of God to you for good."[24] To avoid this tyranny and the merging of Church, here broadly conceived as even the secular "civic religion," and State,[25] is the political challenge that is before us, a metaphysic must provide a context for action and a guide to our morals.[26]

To this end, Viktor Frankl, a survivor of Auschwitz and other concentration camps, vividly reminded the post-Holocaust world of the

---

24. Rom 13:4 (NAS).

25. See Sookhdeo, *New Civic Religion*.

26. Explored in a distinctive fashion in Murdoch, *Metaphysics*. Although Blackburn describes her "religious" thesis as "implausible," this reflects Blackburn's anti-religious prejudice; Murdoch's work *was* serious and provocative on this subject.

immanent freedom and dignity of the human person which would only come from a metaphysical awareness of one's value and place in the universe.[27] Rather than choosing the absurdism of Sartre or the moral nihilism in the embracing of sexual licentiousness of a Huxley or a Russell[28] in response to their existential condition, the existentialism of Frankl, which grew into an entire school of psychology and psychiatric practice, focused on the individual discovering, encountering, and embracing the *meaning* of their existence. This was found and expressed most of all in maintaining the dignity and nobility of their humanity in the face of the greatest and gravest of indignity, evil, and ignobility that confronts one.[29] He asserted that the concentration camp had merely one aim and that was to dehumanize, such that a person seeks merely to survive at the cost of all moral sense which would then justify their treatment as subhuman animals by their captors,[30] rather than answer the questions that their very existence asks of them.[31] Both the Nazis and the Communists believed their programs to be "scientific," with religious moral sentimentality washed away by Nietzsche and the salvific manifestos of the logical positivists deified science.[32] It was not just legitimate, but *incumbent* in

---

27. Frankl, *Man's Search for Meaning*.

28. Russell in his youth described his sexuality as "un-Victorian," rejecting Christian ethics of virtue with many like-minded young intellectuals of the period such as Huxley. They embraced sexual "freedom," which translated for Russell as many affairs and four marriages. This was a significant factor in his immediate dismissal from City College in New York in 1940, where after protests he was judicially judged "morally unfit" and was unable to take up his appointment. However, he (like Huxley) markedly tempered the excesses of his lifestyle in later life. As Irvine, "Bertrand Russell," noted, he believed sex, though a basic need (and thus not confined to the boundaries of monogamy), should not be removed from "serious emotion and from feelings of affection." In a particularly moving piece of writing at the end of his life, he described his life as one of seeking for love (and eventually finding it) with one of his daughters also noting that most basic need in her father.

29. Frankl, "Logotherapy in a Nutshell," 101–36.

30. The Nazis would make documentary style films within the ghettoes demonstrating the inhumanity of Jew to Jew. This was especially so in the activity of Jewish collaborators. This helped provide the 'logic' for their later extermination in the camps.

31. This question of moral sense is explored deeply by Iris Murdoch in *Metaphysics*. She was known for her literary accomplishments, her keen sense of aesthetics, and her moral philosophy. She wrote much about metaphysics and demonstrated how metaphysics enriched the philosophical landscape. She interacted with existentialism and wrote various critiques eventually seeking a firmer foundation for moral philosophy; see Murdoch and George, *Existentialists and Mystics*, a collection of those essays and shorter articles.

32. It was somewhat ironic that the *Wissenschaftliche Weltauffassung* of the Vienna

this new era to make the *scientifically* informed judgments regarding the inferior races, particularly when it is for the noble aim of regenerating humanity.[33]

Similarly, philosophically and theologically, naturalistic science struggles to arrest such an internally coherent *account* of brutality if it is limited to the methods of empirical science. The empiricist model of science posits itself as descriptive rather than analytical, but if we have no analysis there can be no synthesis, no organizing of our observations into a framework where it can be understood and interpreted; we then have no moral conscience in that thing we call *science*. This is what Plantinga and Lewis more generally call naturalism refuting itself by its own presuppositions.[34] So, in what sense does it make sense to refer to metaphysics as the foundation for science? We can discern this indirectly by returning to Mumford and correcting what he describes as the organizing "worldview" feature of metaphysics:

> We have been trying to understand the fundamental nature of reality . . . Science also seeks to understand the nature of reality, but it does so in a different way. Science looks for some general truths, but they are also concrete, whereas the truths of metaphysics are very general and abstract . . . the philosopher's answer will be at the highest levels of generality. They may say there are particulars that fall into natural kinds, there are properties, changes, causes, laws of nature, and so on. The job of science, however, is to say what specific things exist under each of those categories. Metaphysics seeks to organize and systematize all these specific truths that science discovers and to describe their general features.[35]

While we have already taken issue with Mumford's strict dichotomy between science and philosophy viewing it as untenable, we can permit

---

Circle had such an effect on Nazi ideology as most of the members of the Circle were Jewish and left for the US during the 1930s.

33. Heidegger was to write (1935) that his initial involvement with the Nazis was because he saw in the "inner greatness of the movement" a chance for the "regeneration of the people." This was not just for the German *Volk* but a technological overhaul of Being of all humanity. This was properly *religious* in intent (Heidegger went onto to influence theology). He was not alone; many Germanophone intellectuals, including Jung, were fellow travelers for a time before admitting they "goofed." Wheeler, "Martin Heidegger," provides an excellent summary of the complexities of this argument.

34. Plantinga makes this argument in *Where the Conflict Really Lies*, Lewis in *Miracles*.

35. Mumford, *Metaphysics*, 99.

the methodological variation and the functional differences between the two without incoherence. We would also want to challenge this naturalistic notion of "abstract"; like Murdoch argued[36] our values are never distinct from, but rather spring from, our metaphysical assumptions. We would also want to challenge that it would be possible to come up with "specific truths that science discovers" without first having the organizing metaphysic in place to help us *interpret* those facts; we never encounter "naked facts,"[37] we always view reality through whatever metaphysical lens we assume. However, Mumford is correct to identify metaphysics as providing an organizing function. Most importantly, that metaphysical lens will also organize our conceptions of value.

3.2.3 Metaphysics as the Organizing Transcendentals

So, in summary and to this end, metaphysical concepts such as causality, probability and possibility, time, personality, identity through time, eventuation, mind, and matter legitimately provide organizing *transcendentals* of experience—that is, they make **all** experience coherent and understandable because they are *presupposed* for the purposes of intelligibility. The organizing principles of metaphysics attempt to unify the human field of knowledge by systematizing the human sciences but also attempting to explain *why* science itself is successful as a methodology or, being rather more Wittgensteinian and critical, seek to identify what are the "family resemblances" between the many different sciences which might explain their success. They must also provide a justification for the values with which science is conducted. Thus, we will understand as we develop our understanding of our Christian version of transcendentalism, that it is only with the addition of the ontological Trinity that there is a transcendental justification for these transcendentals and a value base for our actions, if we are to rescue ourselves from the skeptical challenge of arbitrariness, moral nihilism, ethical relativism, and dogmatism.

---

36. Murdoch, *Metaphysics*.

37. Historically, "naked facts" as a concept was associated with the empiricism of Locke. The mind is viewed as the *tabula rasa* upon which experience creates simple ideas, grouping into complex ones, eventually coalescing into the understanding. This is now generally described as "naïve" empiricism and has few contemporary defenders.

3.3 Epistemology

3.3.1 Introduction

Epistemology for our purposes is conceived of as the theory of knowledge, "concerned with . . . the analysis of knowledge and its relationship to belief and truth, the theory of justification, and how to respond to the challenge of . . . skepticism"[38] but also, and importantly for the development of this work, *warrant*. This term is particularly important for us as a study in Christian philosophy as the definition and exposition of the term by Plantinga was considered "one of the major accomplishments of twentieth century epistemology."[39] Our aim in this section is to distill these highly complex issues in a non-trivial way and with enough detail that we can provide a robust grounding for our theory of knowledge and thus provide the underpinning for epistemological self-consciousness.

3.3.2 A Philosophy of Facts

"Belief," "fact," and "truth" are complex concepts in need of analysis and clarification. There are elaborate extended theories of belief which we shall not examine as they are not relevant for us here, for we can immediately recognize with Bahnsen that "knowledge is a subcategory of belief: to know something is, *at least*, to believe it."[40] It is the subcategory we are concerned with, not the padding. Most generally, a belief might be characterized as:

> A *positive* cognitive attitude toward a proposition, an action-guiding mental state on which a person relies (whether intermittently or continuously) in his theoretical or practical actions and plans.[41]

In our emphasis, we are noting that *volition* is involved in belief. That is, we view belief such that a person *will* act upon their beliefs but that does not mean they are necessarily conscious of those beliefs; they

---

38. Ladyman, "Ontological, Epistemological and Methodological Positions," 303.

39. Plantinga, *Warrant and Proper Function*, book endorsement.

40. Bahnsen, *Van Til's Apologetic*, 159. Emphasis added. Bahnsen notes that Wittgenstein rejected this view, asserting that knowledge and belief were distinct categories. Few have followed Wittgenstein in this view; it is difficult to dismiss that connection between belief and knowledge established by Plato, problematic as it has been.

41. Bahnsen, *Van Til's Apologetic*, 160.

might have subconscious beliefs or beliefs which are too difficult to verbalize or are sublimated beneath layers of pain. A person might insist they "believe" X, Y, or Z but then their actions demonstrate otherwise. Somewhat paradoxically, someone may hold what they consider to be a belief in their *conscious* mind, but their actions show a different and stronger (or more *positive*) commitment to another set of *subconscious* beliefs. We should also recognize that some beliefs are held based on deduction or inference from other beliefs, while some beliefs are considered incorrigible or infallible to us; that is, they are not held on the basis of substantiating evidence or they are considered to be self-evidencing; they are *basic* beliefs. For example, Calvin held that belief in God was properly basic, and to avoid impiousness, the *only* appropriate way to believe in God.[42]

Now let us consider factuality. Most importantly, we need to recognize immediately that what constitutes a particular "fact" about the world *will be a function* of our epistemological position (thus, our beliefs) *and* our metaphysical commitments. That is, our *philosophy* of facts governs our treatment of evidence and whatever basicity, deduction, induction, or inference we might defensibly make from those facts. This also has the implication that *what* is even accepted as deductive or inductive is also governed by our presuppositions.

This was established beyond reasonable doubt by the work of Quine and most notably Thomas Kuhn in the post-positivist period; he argued that there are no such things as "brute facts" as had previously been argued by many of the logical positivists and to some extent, empiricism generally, but that our very observations of the world were "theory laden" or "worldview dependent."[43] Kuhn argued convincingly that contrary to a naïve empiricism, a "fact" is not an abstract, objective entity that is independent of our perception and conceptualization of it or even its cultural context. In the contemporary language of the philosophy of science

---

42. Calvin, *Institutes* 1.4.1. Here Calvin uses the term "manifest" in the terms of the natural revelation in creation rather than implying a natural *theology* which posits positive evidential inference from nature to God.

43. Kuhn, *Structure of Scientific Revolutions*, 111–34. This became known as simply *Structure* in conversation. It is difficult to underestimate Kuhn's influence and impact at the time of publication. Though a philosopher of science, his legacy was primarily in other disciples (especially non-scientific ones) who felt his work de-privileged science as a unique, objective enterprise. That is, Kuhn struggled to escape the relativist implications of his work and ran into problems with his more general thesis of the incommensurability of scientific paradigms. Thus, although an extremely important milestone in the philosophy of science, he was by no means the last word.

we explicate this when we assert that "facts" are never naked sensory data (for we can just as well argue philosophically just what the term "data" might mean);[44] they are interpreted within a conceptual framework (or, in Kuhn's terms, a normative *paradigm*)[45] that renders them meaningful. This might be better explained as the basic distinction between "seeing" and "seeing *as*": an aborigine in a first-contact encounter will have the same phenomenological experience as us if we were to show them a television but would not have the same perceptual process and might have a very different idea of our television. It might *reasonably* be rendered a portal to the spirit world.

Thus, "theory laden" or "worldview dependent" are givens in our discussion, and the latter phrase will become increasingly important for us as we focus the discussion; there is no other way by which we can conceive of the problem in a rigorous, transparent, and coherent manner. There is also an indissoluble relationship between truth and factuality. Nagel puts the intimate and important connection this way:

> Some philosophical claims about knowledge have turned out to be confused or self-undermining, but other findings about knowledge, like its *special connection with truth*, have stood the test of time.[46]

It would seem reasonable to assert that all facts should be truths about the world and some theories of truth would indeed declare we have merely expressed a tautology in that assertion. However, all truths are not necessarily (logically) facts, unless we permit abstract truths with no material analogue into our theory of truth. That is, "facts" are perceived as having, if not a necessary, a special or strong connection with reality;

---

44. For example, it is common in Information Theory to distinguish between "information" and "data." "Information" is conceived of as "data" that has been organized in some way. If sensory data or "stimulus" is where we start (as in Quine, *From Stimulus to Science*), we have already imposed a preunderstanding on our "facts."

45. "Paradigm" first appears in Kuhn's *Structure* on 11 and is what he called "normal science," a stable iteration of a particular science. Kuhn was originally a physicist, and paradigms were easy to discern in physics—Baconian, Newtonian, Einsteinian quantum physics and the Quantum Field Theory (QFT) of Hawking/Penrose. Ian Hacking in his introductory essay to the fiftieth anniversary edition thus questions how applicable his model is generally to the other sciences but does not question the basic concept of a governing paradigm which became influential far beyond the sciences.

46. Nagel, *Knowledge*, 116. Emphasis added.

"truth" can be conceived broadly (in terms of theoretical coherence) or narrowly (in terms of correspondence or disquotation).[47]

We should remind ourselves from a previous discussion that these are then not two oppositional theories of truth as frequently conceived but are addressing different questions, one dealing with the *metaphysics* of truth (what *is* truth?), the other with how we *know* something is true (within the context of a theory), the *epistemology* of truth. It is our theory of the world, or *worldview* that gives us both a test *for* and the conditions *of* truth; it is not merely a "conceptual scheme" but makes ontological commitments. Thus, Quine would speak of our "theory of nature" as giving meaning to any proposition or factuality about the world.[48]

The question then before us becomes *how* we test worldviews for coherence and truthfulness if all are epistemologically self-contained and we are not to surrender to relativism and arbitrariness. For example, Rorty would appropriate Kuhn to attempt to deconstruct any normative conception of reality and ethics on the basis *everything is under a description* and concluded the only position we should hold is a certain tentative, ironic view of our predicament in the world (we think in lieu of Sartre's starting point that our existence is just "absurd"); we should not take life, and certainly not philosophy, too seriously.[49] However, in Blackburn's critique[50] of Rorty, he asserts this is just moral cowardice and Rorty himself spilled much ink in later years arguing the importance of "ethics" and for a particular political vision[51] with the utmost sobriety and through both academic and popular media.[52]

---

47. See Macneil, "Feeling Good About Truth," for an in-depth examination of truth, particularly its ethical dimension. See Audi, *Epistemology*, 245 ff. for an account of the coherence and correspondence theories of truth.

48. Quine, *Theories and Things*, 22–23. For Quine a "fact" was not even an epistemological issue; it was an issue of fundamental ontology, i.e., you do not argue over the definition of a fact, the collection of facts is just what constitutes science.

49. This was the background Rorty sketches in introducing his second major book, *Contingency, Irony, and Solidarity*.

50. Found in an extended fashion in Blackburn, *Truth*. Rorty acknowledged the force of his criticism (at one point) in a footnote.

51. Rorty, *Philosophy and Social Hope*. This was a collection of essays during the 1990s during a period just after the zenith of his success. He could never live consistently with the almost nihilistic implications of his views (*Contingency, Irony, and Solidarity*, xv) and in the decade after spent a lot of time arguing about "ethics" in attempting to tame the postmodern monster he had unleashed.

52. Jeffries, "Richard Rorty: The Man Who Killed Truth" was broadcast on BBC4 on Nov. 7, 2003.

Hence, we should be able to immediately appreciate the importance of factuality. Some consider "God" to be the most substantive and important "fact" of the universe upon which all others "facts" depend and have their origin:

> We may say, then, that we seek to defend the fact of miracle, the fact of providence, the fact of creation, and therefore, the fact of God, in relation to modern non-Christian science . . . that *we are seeking to defend Christian theism as a fact*. And this is really the same thing as to say that *we believe the facts of the universe are unaccounted for except on a Christian-theistic basis*.[53]

This will be the view that we will be defending and advancing. However, others forcefully reject God is *any* kind of "fact" other than that of a delusion or shared mistake:

> The difficulty for the religious community is to show that its agreement is not simply agreement about a *shared mistake* . . . it is clear that particular religious beliefs are mistaken, since religious groups do not . . . agree and they cannot all be right.[54]

We will consider the resolution of the dispute as we progress, but the principle of "worldview dependent" perception and conception is biblical, Christian, and sound; Calvin had grasped this many centuries earlier when he spoke of the "spectacles of Scripture" enabling us to "[gather] up the otherwise confused knowledge of God in our minds, having dispersed our dullness, clearly shows us the true God."[55] In this case our description is scripture, and "everything" is the created realm.

3.3.3 A Philosophy of Evidences

Our previous discussion concluded that worldview considerations govern the very perception of our experience and govern our interpretation of data. A traditional naïve view of evidence as being weighed in the balances of a neutral scientific practitioner engaged in disinterested research and marching us ever onward toward truth and objectivity is most certainly found wanting. This was the basis of the concern that this confidence in empirical methods remained so strong in Christian apologetics that

---

53. Bahnsen, *Van Til's Apologetic*, 37–38. Emphasis added.
54. Martin, *Atheism*, 345. Emphasis added.
55. Calvin, *Institutes* 1.6.

it reduced any apologetic claims to discussions of probabilities of truth rather than certainty. Thus, let us consider the reformational move that Van Til made to reshape the landscape of Christian apologetics.

Van Til emphasized that he was not rejecting traditional *evidential* arguments such as the cosmological or ontological proofs and historical arguments for the resurrection, but that he was not going to use them in a linear, sequential manner to demonstrate the proof or truth of God's existence. This is because as we noted previously, as standalone, *apologetic* arguments they are logically very weak and limited in what they can establish. To illustrate further, there is nothing *necessary* derived from the *fact* of Christ's resurrection other than a man who was dead had come back to life for reason or reasons unknown *unless* we have *already* believed the scriptural narrative that interprets it for us.[56]

Indeed, the proof or truth of God's existence had rather to be assumed for those arguments to have logical force and so, consequently, will have very little apologetic value for the conscious skeptic. Thus, for Van Til, the appropriate apologetic method is to seek to uncover the presuppositions that make experience itself possible and to discover the only worldview that supports those presuppositions.[57] That is, as we had previously posited, he concurred with Kant about the transcendental question but proceeded to answer the question with a transcendent transcendental framework rather than using the tools of transcendental psychology.

This becomes an epistemological principle of principal importance that allows us to escape from the circularity problem caused by the interdependence of metaphysics and epistemology. There was the constant challenge in the history of philosophy of whether metaphysics must proceed epistemology or vice versa. How can we *know* objects unless we have a theory of objects? Yet how can we define a theory of objects unless we *know* what an object i*s*? This circular argument "tormented and obsessed" epistemologists such as Chisholm.[58] Only in the conception of a God who is Trinitarian, both immanent and transcendent, can this problem of being above and within creation, as both a unity and a

---

56. For example, Barbara Thiering (*Jesus and the Riddle*) in an academically "respectable" higher-critical thesis, asserted that Jesus did not actually die, but was buried in a cave, revived by the magician Simon Magus, married, had three children with Mary Magdalene, divorced, and finally died in Rome. Plantinga, *Knowledge and Christian Belief*, 102–3, gives us some other choice examples.

57. We examine this "worldview" thinking more closely in §3.5.

58. A classic statement of this problem is found in Chisholm, *Problem of the Criterion*, 3.

diversity, be solved. He is both the one and the many, the whole and the particular; or to use the Van Tillian term, the "concrete universal."

This is a term which Van Til derived from idealism. Van Til had claims to be an expert on Bernard Bosanquet (1848–1923) whom Van Til "deemed the most advanced and sophisticated idealist of his generation"[59] and interacted with F. H. Bradley, one of the last and most influential of the British idealists. Thus, it was a controversial term for him to use but it was only the willful refusal of critics to engage with the additional (or completed) sense he was giving the term that made it so. Van Til directly responded to the contradiction implicit in this term by agreeing that idealism could never resolve this contradiction if it proceeded on naturalistic or atheistic assumptions. This is because it worked from the assumption that "Man and the Absolute" were correlative, whereas for Van Til, Christian theism considers it necessary that God is self-contained, requiring only himself.[60] This was Van Til's nuancing of his understanding and his solution to the "one and the many" problem which had been one of the most intractable problems of unbelieving philosophy, e.g., are universals merely linguistic conveniences or have they metaphysical status (do natural kinds exist?) and if only particulars exist, how are we able to communicate in a contingent universe governed by chance?

For Van Til "kind" was what it was because God *thinking* of an object makes it what it is; his thinking is then constitutive of the particular objects of reality. This would be in contrast to human thought which was always derivative in its concepts from God's conceptualization and subsequent actualization of the world. There is thus a tight correlation and interdependence between his metaphysics and epistemology in which both spring from his Christian theism: "... God, who gives life to the dead *and calls into being that which does not exist.*"[61]

So, in summary, despite epistemology often being taught as if it was a self-contained discipline, we can conclude even at this stage that this is misguided and incorrect. It would be inconceivable for a materialist to

---

59. Quoted in Bahnsen, *Van Til's Apologetic*, 9n15.

60. Van Til, *Defense of the Faith*, 1–24.

61. Rom 4:17 (NAS), emphasis added. There are interesting exegetical issues with this verse as discussed in the NET notes for it, though they are slightly unclear as to the difference in the renderings. The literal Greek is καλοῦντος τά μή ὄντα ὡς ὄντα ("calling the things not existing [or not being] as existing [being]"), which has the interesting philosophical issue regarding the ontological status of non-existing objects, i.e., what is implied in using the sign "thing," something which was discussed much in linguistic philosophy by Russell, Quine, and the positivists and was revisited by Plantinga also.

maintain a supernaturalistic metaphysics; they would intuitively opt for an empirical hypothesis. Thus, we have established that metaphysics and epistemology are linked, and further that this circularity is *only* resolved by the mind of God as the origin of both correspondence and coherence. Our presuppositions govern how we handle the evidence of our senses and push us in the direction of transcendental philosophy.

3.3.4 Overcoming Skepticism

When we considered skepticism previously it was within the context of how the response to skepticism had generated several different philosophical schools, each of which with their particular approaches to reality were attempting to mitigate it in some way; we might say we examined the epistemology of the various skepticisms. Yet we did not consider skepticism *itself* (we might say the metaphysics of skepticism) or its ethical dimensions. It is by adding these dimensions that we shall demonstrate how that makes it possible to answer far more comprehensively the skeptical challenge.

Here we examine in detail the two main forms of skepticism, and in the process of navigating through the turbulent waters we encounter the Christian philosophy of Gordon Clark who used a skeptical premise to build his theory of knowledge and his apologetic approach. However, we find his positions untenable and a dangerous, immoral application of a skeptical premise. We then proceed to examine how considering the psychology of skepticism proves an effective tool to dismantle most of its force. We then arrive at a terminus that suggests a transcendental critique is the only route forward to dismiss any residual logical force of the skeptical argument.

Recollect that Ladyman, writing as a philosopher of science, helpfully focuses the epistemological project as directly concerned with, as one of its primary goals, the task of countering skepticism: "Epistemology is the theory of knowledge and as such is concerned with . . . how [we] respond to the challenge of local . . . or global skepticism."[62] Implicit in Ladyman's account is the assumption that unless the skeptical challenge can be mitigated, there can be *no* robust science and in lieu of our previous conclusions from §2, we can forcefully concur with that judgment; though unfortunately, there is little to find in his account other

---

62. Ladyman, "Ontological, Epistemological and Methodological Positions," 303.

A CHRISTIAN CONCEPTION OF PHILOSOPHY

than a repetition of the various attempts we have already seen to mitigate it. However, we can still usefully apply his definition as a starting point for our own discussion.

Primarily, his definition tells us that skepticism comes in two specific forms: *local* and *global*. That is, it is conceivable someone has difficulties in accepting the absolute certainty of individual "facts" but *claims* to be non-skeptical and instrumentalist in their general approach to reality. This we would call *local* skepticism that is mitigated in some way in practice. In direct contrast to this, we *can* all imagine a stubborn or lazy apologist for idleness who wants to camp out at the Humean caravan park, claiming we have no reasonable basis for reason; that is, there is no purpose or meaning to life other than what we give it, so let us eat, drink, and join Hume himself in playing backgammon until we die![63] This would be a global claim.

Whether this global claim of epistemological impotence can be maintained without collapsing into incoherence we will probe shortly for it would seem *prima facie* to be an abandonment of our epistemic *duties* and, as a Sartre or a Camus would put it, make the starting point for our existence in the world an absurd one.[64] Such a position is one we cannot afford to entertain; we already have the records of the dissipation and destruction suffered by such Romantic thinkers as Rousseau, Shelley, and Byron who downgraded reason in favor of feeling.[65] Even if we cannot precisely formulate just what is *wrong* with global skepticism of that sort, it is the moral disappropriation that follows in its wake that should immediately make us incredulous and become our strongest lever against skepticism.

So, in lieu of our introductory remarks above, there is arguably a difference between a local skepticism as a *method* (as say employed by

---

63. The biblical reasoning of Paul is identical in 1 Cor 15:32, "If the dead are not raised, let us eat and drink, for tomorrow we die." Paul on many occasions expresses a similar thought, "If we have hoped in Christ in this life only, we are of all men most to be pitied." Paul was certain of his metaphysics and his claims to knowledge, "For this reason I also suffer these things, but I am not ashamed; for I know whom I have believed, and I am convinced that He is able to guard what I have entrusted to Him until that day" (2 Tim 1:12). The perfect tense of "believe" in the Greek emphasizes this was a life-changing decision and encounter for Paul.

64. Both Sartre and Camus subscribed to what might be called versions of *absurdism*; see Aronson, "Albert Camus."

65. A profound, controversial, and provocative account is provided by historian Paul Johnson in *Intellectuals*, which is a salient, rabid deconstruction of the intellectual caste.

Descartes) and by someone considering skepticism as a *metaphysical feature* telling us something about the way reality is constituted or of our conceptual relations to reality (as in Hume). Thus Strawson, who spent large sections of his career challenging the legitimacy of skepticism in the latter sense, nevertheless accepted the legitimacy of the former:

> The sceptic is, strictly, not one who denies the validity of certain types of belief, but one who questions, if only initially and for methodological reasons, the adequacy of our grounds for holding them. He puts forward his doubts by way of a challenge—sometimes a challenge to himself—to show that the doubts are unjustified, that the beliefs put in question are justified. He may conclude, like Descartes, that the challenge can successfully be met; or, like Hume, that it cannot. . . . Traditional targets of philosophic doubt include the existence of the external world, i.e., of physical objects or bodies; our knowledge of other minds; the justification of induction; the reality of the past.[66]

That is, by a *local* skepticism we are challenging, perhaps by some kind of hypothesis, counterfactual or thought experiment, to what degree (if any) a particular "fact" of the world, recollection or memory can be held to be "true," incorrigible, or infallible. In contrast, the global skeptic, because he tolerates no metaphysic has no *logical* boundaries to his skepticism, will live his life in an intellectually schizophrenic manner; because he nevertheless must act as if there were certain elements and laws of nature that constrain him.[67]

So, whereas local skepticism can be a practical gateway into knowledge, *global* skepticism, the metaphysical form of skepticism, is the assertion that claims to knowledge are beyond the reach of the human mind. All that remains are contingent features of the world and the coherence of the world as a whole is beyond the powers of human cognition. However, there are also variations of severity and tenor of the global skeptics. With Hume's criticism as asymptotic to their theories of knowledge, such a claim was normative for the logical positivist movement of the twentieth century we met earlier in this work, with both Schlick and Neurath offering versions of it. However, Schlick and Neurath had no motivation

---

66. Strawson, *Scepticism*, 2–3.

67. Plantinga does note that there is a minority view of Hume that he was not a skeptic at all and that his conclusion was best described as a pragmatic one—we *must* live ignoring our skepticism. However, there is little doubt that he was (and is) the putative progenitor of the skeptical clan.

A CHRISTIAN CONCEPTION OF PHILOSOPHY

to be morally cynical or intellectually lazy, there's was a mitigated global skepticism with Ayer labeling it a "thoroughgoing phenomenalism";[68] the positivist movement was wanting to be the *scientific* view of the world. This was a long way from the deliberate nihilism of a Huxley or a Sartre. Their unmitigated global skepticism was a much stronger claim; it would suggest an undermining of the entire scientific and philosophical project.

How can such a claim even be formulated in an intellectually respectable manner? Well, some have argued based on the unreliability of our senses in *particular* instances that we can thus *never* trust our senses. However, this seems to be committing the basic logical fallacy of hasty generalization, so it is of some interest that Christian *logician* Gordon H. Clark argued precisely this[69] when presenting a major revision of his neo-Platonist epistemology for which he had gained a considerable reputation.[70] Clark's revised theory asserted that man's only knowledge was knowledge contained in the Bible or knowledge deduced from what is contained in the Bible, arguing in the final major works of his career for fideism as the only option for the Christian philosopher. Fideism,[71] or "dogmatism"[72] as he preferred to label it, was where we accept that the central or basic claims we make as part of our epistemology are unprovable and accepted as axioms, *unprovable* presuppositions:

> The only personal solution to this logical impasse is a change of heart on the part of one of the contestants. Agreement can be obtained only by one party's repudiating his premises and accepting the other's presuppositions . . . the change is something logic [argumentation] cannot do. God alone is able.[73]

His reasoning was that secular philosophy could not give an account or justify any single item of human knowledge; therefore there was

---

68. Ayer, *Language, Truth, and Logic*, 31.
69. Clark, "Wheaton Lectures," in *Philosophy of Gordon H. Clark*, 25–124.
70. Nash, "Gordon Clark's Theory of Knowledge," 125–75.
71. A general account is provided in Penelhum, "Fideism."
72. Clark and his followers had argued to distinguish "dogmatism" from fideism, but Clark, in his final book, *Three Types*, 104, *did* finally describe his position as fideist, accepting dogmatism *was* a form of fideism. Clark was a competent logician and held to a neo-platonic view in the early part of his career. His confidence in logic was absolute, "In the beginning was the Logic, and the Logic was with God and the Logic was God" (his translation of John 1:1 in his *Logic*). He commits the etymological fallacy here; *Logos* was not used in the sense which "Logic" was used until a number of centuries after John wrote those words.
73. Clark, *Historiography*, 337.

no knowledge available to man via his senses or deduction except what is revealed in the Bible or deduced from what is in the Bible:

> The term dogmatism therefore designates that method of procedure which tries to systematize beliefs concerning God, science, immorality, etc. on the basis of information divinely revealed in the sacred writings. . . . If now one appreciates the present status of the argument, the dogmatic answer to the question can easily be given. The present status of the argument is the choice between dogmatism and nihilism.[74]

As just noted, Clark had adopted this position from his previous logicism which had gained a substantial following among a distinct group of conservative presbyterian apologists[75] after he became grounded as a neo-Platonist would with some of the imponderables and paradoxes that Plato was all too aware of. Nash's essay included in the 1968 Festschrift for Clark was primarily concerned with Clark's original epistemology which had gained him so much scholarly respect and in explicating Clark's difficulties in wrestling with these Platonic conundrums, but he added an appendix dealing with Clark's revised view, declaring it in short shrift incoherent.[76]

This response was echoed in an identical manner by Bahnsen[77] because it assumes empirical methods offered no possibility of knowledge and yet we would need to read the Bible (an empirical process) to obtain the biblical knowledge. Although Clark did not deal with this objection immediately, deflecting his opponents with a challenge to contradict his deconstruction of empiricism (which was forceful), his later attempts appealed to forms of intuitionism and to the immanent presence of the knowledge contained in the scriptures in the human heart. However, as Butler then noted, it "then makes the scriptures themselves redundant"[78] for their revelation is prescient in the human subject.

More seriously, from the point of view of Christian worldview philosophy, the most dangerous consequence of this position was that there are no normative ethical boundaries for our conduct. Whereas Clark

---

74. Clark, *Three Types*, 8, 139.

75. These were centered around Trinity Divinity School, which is still the main source of Clark's material under the auspices of the Trinity Foundation.

76. Nash, "Gordon Clark's Theory of Knowledge."

77. Bahnsen, *CVT and Gordon Clark*.

78. Butler, *On Plantinga*.

or his followers[79] would never countenance such a move as Reformed Christians, they could not offer an argument against it because his final move was undeniably a fideist one. Specifically, all proof is conceived of as being within a system of proof and it is the sovereignty of God, not an apologetic argument, that Clark offers as his ultimate rationale. As Bahnsen noted, apologetics as a philosophical defense is destroyed by this expression of global skepticism.[80]

It is not difficult to see the perversity of such a view and the nefarious applications for the unbeliever that is available through such a view. The desire for the facsimile of justification for irrationality in our worldview has been a recurring feature in Romantic and post-Kantian philosophy. Huxley expressed this vividly and simply in his retrospect and frames it specifically as originating from the desire to reject a Christian view of the world:

> For myself, as, no doubt, for most of my contemporaries, the philosophy of meaningless was essentially an instrument of liberation.... We objected to morality because it interfered with our sexual freedom; we objected to the political and economic system because it was unjust. The supporters of these systems claimed in some way they embodied the meaning (a Christian meaning they insisted) of the world. There was one admirably simple method of confuting these people and at the same time justifying ourselves in our political and erotic revolt: *we could deny that the world had any meaning whatsoever.*[81]

However, rather paradoxically for Huxley, he found the rejection of the Judeo-Christian principles was catastrophic. He found that one of the

---

79. Clark taught at Trinity Divinity School for many years, and it became the focus for opposition to Van Til's apologetic when Van Til criticized Clark for failing to recognize the Creator-creature distinction, which led to a bad-tempered argument during the 1940s that culminated in Clark leaving the OPC. Trinity Divinity School still has zealous Clarkians to this day who still take exception to Van Til's criticism of Clark's position and evidence that Van Til was "neo-Orthodox." As Bahnsen, *CVT and Gordon Clark*, indicates in clarifying the political, theological, and philosophical issues around that controversy, it would have been most peculiar for Van Til to be caricatured as neo-Orthodox by the Clarkians when he was the most forceful exposer of that movement as heterodox and no friend of evangelical Christianity, even being complemented on that fact by some of his most forceful apologetic opponents.

80. Bahnsen, *CVT and Gordon Clark*. The final ten minutes of this presentation are a forceful rebuff of what Bahnsen see as the ultimate problem with Clark's position. This audio presentation follows the contours of Bahnsen, *Van Til's Apologetic*, 669–72.

81. Huxley, *Ends and Means*, 273. Emphasis added.

strongest *practical* objections to his global skepticism was that it opened the door to the very political tyranny which he had wanted to avoid:

> By the end of the twenties a reaction had begun to set in—away from the easy-going philosophy of general meaninglessness towards the hard, ferocious theologies of nationalistic and revolutionary idolatry. . . . The universe as a whole remained still meaningless, but certain of its parts, such as the nation, the state, the class, the party, were endowed with significance and the highest value . . . [and] . . . can have *only* evil and disastrous results.[82]

The political dimension we will begin to consider in more detail in the subsequent section when we deal directly with ethics, but we should at least get a sense of the interconnectedness of one's ethical theory with one's metaphysic and theory of knowledge.

We can also make a further observation that narrows the legitimacy of skepticism still further. A skepticism regarding our senses is incoherent for another basic, *methodological* reason. It is in the *additional* observations of our senses, perhaps informed by additional understanding from theoretical analysis, that often corrects our *previous* observations or leads us to additional theoretical reflections. That is, a radically new theory formulated through "edge-case" analysis previously dismissed as "experimental error" is not at all uncommon in the history of science, physics especially.[83]

Further and perhaps conclusively, if we assume the global skeptic wants to *convince* us all to become global skeptics, they will need to believe they "know" global skepticism to be the case. In other words, they are requiring that they can be *certain* that there is *no certainty*. No matter how this is presented in the philosophical or scientific literature,

---

82. Huxley, *Ends and Means*, 274. Emphasis added.

83. Einstein's early quantum theory predicted that the photons of light which he said made up a light *wave* (it was normative in the contemporary physics of his time to consider an entity to be either a wave *or* a particle; it would be a logical contradiction to be both), having a nominal mass, would be bent by a gravitational field. He predicted a detectable delay in comparison to the Newtonian equation in viewing an eclipse of Jupiter because of the slight bend of the light that would become significant because of the vast distances involved between the Earth and Jupiter. It was confirmed with a remarkable degree of accuracy to ten decimal places. Previous microscopic "quantum" effects such as this, which were so small they had been dismissed when measuring on the macro-scale, were found to be present when researchers revisited previous datasets where they had dismissed the aberrations as limitations of the measuring apparatus.

A CHRISTIAN CONCEPTION OF PHILOSOPHY

"sometimes under the guise of newly introduced technical vocabulary,"[84] there is a basic incongruity in this position that is at its most obvious with primitive skepticism, and furthermore, if we push it harder to demand an *account* of the skepticism, we should now see is implicit in *any* form of skepticism. Too often the skeptic is assuming directly or indirectly, consciously, or subconsciously, *that which they are seeking to refute.* Plantinga attacks Hume on that basis:

> And this leads to the scandal of skepticism: if I *argue* to skepticism, then of course I rely on the very cognitive faculties whose unreliability is the conclusion of my skeptical argument.[85]

Looking forward to our future discussion, we will see that in Van Tillian terms, this is recognized as a failure of skepticism under *transcendental* critique. Transcendentalism is important to argument in a much more basic sense of making argumentation *itself* possible and coherent, so a transcendental argument is categorically different to a deductive or an inductive style argument. Thus, we will need to consider transcendentalism in much greater detail but for our purposes now, the transcendental is that part of our knowledge structure that makes rationality reasonable and completely disarms the skeptical challenge.[86]

So, in summary, we should, on an ethical basis, immediately label the primitive global skeptical view as both incoherent and destructive. We can also note at this point a very important feature of the skeptical challenge, that as soon as we talk methodology, and try to apply the global skeptical premise, we find we cannot without instantiating specific cases and we find that we are now talking about "local" skepticism. In Wittgensteinian terms, the solution to the problem is the disappearing of the problem once we have clarified exactly what we mean. That is, as soon as we attempt to state a more moderate form of global skepticism that asserts that there is no *certainty* available to us, or that all our scientific conclusions are subject to "revision," we have moved to a consideration of local skepticism. Global skepticism then appears as a principle with absurd consequences and thoroughly impractical because

---

84. Nagel, *Knowledge*, 55.
85. Plantinga, *Warranted Christian Belief*, 219n29.
86. In fairness, it should be noted that not all philosophers will accept the legitimacy of the transcendental mode of argument, which is why we will consider it in a chapter on its own.

we can never articulate any of its consequences or implications without self-contradiction.

We can reinforce this conclusion reminding ourselves of our previous section dealing with skepticism, where we can now recognize local skepticism as characteristic of the genus *fallibilist*. In that section we have already seen that the various fallibilist schools failed to be internally coherent when they were looking for a plausible *account* of the possibility, or an account of, the knowledge that we are aware or *know* we possess regarding the world. Thus, even a local skepticism on anything but a methodological level as a hypothetical tool cannot be acceptable to us. That is, local skepticism is not warranted in a *moral* sense as a gateway into a general skepticism even if in some abstract, absolute logical sense its referent cannot be refuted because of the possibility of error. In a reciprocal fashion, we may not be able to claim absolute certainty for certain kinds of measurements, inductions, or observations regarding the physical world but that does not morally warrant us to give up experimentation and having a psychological confidence and an ethical commitment to improvement.

So, our knowledge, even if it is changed, adapted, or replaced with new formulations, is still *certainly* available to us through a combination of a transcendental principle, empirical and deductive processes. They are sometimes supplemented by abductive or probabilistic analyses, and we do not have to choose between them. They often answer different questions, are often complementary, and are parts of our epistemic toolbox. Thus, we should have seen in our analyses here and in our previous section regarding the various secular responses to the challenge of skepticism, that epistemological error results when one principle is chosen to the exclusion of all others.

To reiterate, we find that global skepticism seems to be a concept that lacks content and application; it is an abstraction masquerading as a category. As soon as we try to apply it, it concretizes into local skeptical arguments which if conceived in anything but as a hypothetical tool (rather than as a statement for which there is no way the question could be answered), it would render the achievements and procedures of human science and research illegitimate. In contrast, for us, the pursuit of truth and warranted verisimilitude remain legitimate goals of research. Thus, as a further step in our argument, this is surely a discussion of what is *valuable* to us and not just a matter for logic.

That is, we can see that a rebuff of skepticism is pushing us in the direction of ethical considerations and in the direction of a coherent, integrated, worldview philosophy. If we attempt to deal with skepticism in a naturalistic or purely propositional fashion, we arrive at a philosophical impasse unable to dislodge the skeptic. Yet the moral imperative is to dislodge the skeptic just as it is the moral imperative to have the courage to condemn the prison camp guard at Auschwitz.[87] That is, if we remain personally and collectively committed to progress, that is we believe it is something we *should* do, our incomplete or tentative moves toward "absolute" certainty do not prevent us from acting as if we were "certain" at important milestones along the way and acting in a way that demonstrates our moral commitments.[88] It only warrants a skeptical despair and an amoral impasse to the morally cowardly or the apathetic in the face of the great potential of our progress as a race. We can at once be confident of the truth we know now while we understand that we might know the same truth in a more complete or robust fashion in the future, but we can remain confident that we have still encountered and know the truth at the present time. Blackburn expresses this thought well:

> Perhaps we never found logos or a "first philosophy," an underlying foundational story telling us, from somewhere outside our own world view, just why that world view is the right one. But perhaps we have learned to do without that, just as we learn to retain our hard-won confidences, without closing our minds to any further illuminations that the future may bring. Above all, I hope we have become confident in using our well-tried and tested vocabulary of explanation and assessment. We can take the postmodernist inverted commas off things that ought to matter to us: truth, reason, objectivity and confidence. They are

---

87. This is the argument James Conant makes against Rorty in "Freedom, Cruelty, and Truth," 268–342.

88. This argument is elegantly made by Blackburn in his critique of Rorty and postmodernism at numerous places in Blackburn, *Truth*, e.g., §§ 6.8, 8.6. In criticizing Rorty's position he pushed very hard on this point, recalling Aristotle's maxim that if "our ethics permit murder, there is something wrong with our ethics"; an observation Wittgenstein had also reflected on when he asserted that philosophy must be lived and thus judged through the processes of life itself; it is our "form of life." Blackburn took very seriously Rorty's quip "truth is what your contemporaries let you get away with," and as he noted, "it is shocking enough to be something Rorty's contemporaries wouldn't let him get away with" (*Truth*, 31). Blackburn's critique of Rorty and postmodernism in general was perhaps the most sustained and thorough one in the literature; see also Macneil, "Richard Rorty's Iconoclastic Deconstruction."

no less, if no more, than the *virtues* that we should all cherish as we try to understand the bewildering world about us.[89]

Notice how Blackburn uses metaphysical and epistemological terminology and correlates that with ethics. This is a good example of "worldview" thinking. For Blackburn, his assertions are ethical and fall within that worldview to justify them, even in the face of epistemological skepticism. Skepticism becomes far more of a *psychological* choice and an example of epistemic irresponsibility than it is a philosophical necessity. For example, Hume, on his own admission, answered his own thoroughgoing skepticism by playing backgammon with his friends and living day to day *ignoring* his skepticism. Hume's failure in the final analysis was an ethical one, not a logical one, and was caused by his metaphysical prejudice. We do not permit ourselves that indulgence within epistemological self-consciousness.

Yet we *do* acknowledge there is a further step in discrediting skepticism on a logical level. This we defer to when we discuss the transcendental mode of argumentation for answering the skeptical challenge, for this enables us to establish the rational basis for reason and then to argue that we are able to have *objective* certainty about the existence of the Christian God and that it is *provable*, rather than merely an evidential or probabilistic claim about the existence of "a God" (though we might now understand we would be within our epistemic rights to claim we are not irrational in believing in God). For the time being, we can now assert that psychologically, skepticism holds no compelling appeal for us to be epistemologically cautious. However, skepticism has historically been born out of naturalism pushed to its logical limits, so we now move to consider why naturalism is more generally incoherent to further invalidate the skepticism built on it.

3.3.5 Two Dogmas of Evolutionary Thought

In titling this section as I have, I am playing on the title of Quine's famous refutation of logical positivism, *Two Dogmas of Empiricism*. Quine, as we have already noted, was one of the most innovative and influential postpositivist philosophers of the second half of the twentieth century, famous for both his radical behaviorism and proposing a naturalized metaphysics and a naturalized epistemology as a replacement and mitigation of

---

89. Blackburn, *Truth*, 220. Emphasis added.

the dogmatic criticisms he had leveled in that famous paper. Thus, let us examine the reasons why we should also immediately reject any form of his *naturalized epistemology* even when first argued by such eminent naturalists as himself.

Firstly, it must be said that the naturalist model uses evolutionism (and particularly *natural selection*) as a quasi-religious device, rather like an atheological hermeneutic that allows the flow of science through time to be given structure and reasonable *meaning*—no statement regarding counterintuitive complexity or conceptual confusion is not capable of clarification by appealing to natural selection. Further, I would argue that historically, evolutionary thought was and remains today primarily a metaphysical dogma in its *entirety*. Most significantly, it predates Darwin, even in its modern scientific incarnation, with Darwin himself in extant correspondence admitting he was riding a wave of popular sentiment regarding the inevitability of human progress and improvement which had become a strong theme in the paleopositivist philosophy of Comte, and similar socialist and humanistic thinkers inspired by the French Revolution.[90]

Conceptually, it has roots in the very origins of the pre-Socratic tradition (though it must be recognized to what degree is a disputed claim[91]) but both evolutionists and creationists have agreed on that assertion for very different reasons. What changed with Darwin was that it got a scientific makeover and a proposed *mechanism* ("natural selection") was offered; but, on detailed inspection of Darwin's text, on the most tentative basis and with minimal evidential support.[92] Even during Darwin's lifetime, it was considered *scientifically* implausible and with the work of his contemporary Mendel on genetics undermining a central claim of his theory,[93] it was only with the deliberate scholarly suppression of Men-

---

90. There is a major Darwin correspondence project due to complete collation of his correspondence (numbering in excess of 8,500 letters); see University of Cambridge, "Darwin Correspondence Project." Darwin had been impressed by the work of Comte as his naturalism strengthened later in his life.

91. Zuiddam, "Was Evolution Invented by Greek Philosophers?," 68–75. I feel Zuiddam never quite expunges the thesis of the origins of naturalism (and hence evolutionism) with the pre-Socratics, which was blatant by the time of the post-Socratic Epicurus. His "retrospect" at the end of the paper and its footnotes perhaps admit as much, but the paper is a provocative and cautionary read.

92. Bahnsen, *Evolution (Scientific and Theistic)*. In this recording, Bahnsen gives a rigorous and thorough critique referring to the paucity of the empirical evidence. Darwin only offered two instances in his *Origins*.

93. It was only with Huxley, *Evolution: The Modern Synthesis*, that an attempt was

del's work and the aggressive scientific zeal of Thomas Henry Huxley,[94] "Darwin's bulldog," that Darwinism was maintained as a credible thesis.

The scientific plausibility problem did not go away. Historically, as paleontological evidence mounted during the twentieth century and the embarrassment of the major gaps in the fossil record became the major issue for the most serious evolutionists, there was an urgent internal search (though not a trace of it was or seen in mainstream school textbooks and graduate introductions) for an alternative model of evolutionary thought. Following almost seventy years of theory and counter theory, it arrived in 1972 with Stephen J. Gould proposing a major revision known as *punctuated* evolution. The sophistication of presentation and subtle sophistry of the revised theory was quite magnificent, Gould himself describing it as the paradox of the "insulation from disproof" without realizing that was because he was still reasoning in a tautological manner on a key philosophical and explanatory point, explaining the gaps in the fossil record as a result of periods of rapid change followed by "quiet" periods in evolutionary history, that *therefore* we would expect to see no evidence of intermediate forms.[95]

However, there is *no* "therefore" in this account; he is simply affirming the consequent. Clearly, this was not a hypothesis which was then tested against the evidence confirming the predictions of a theory but rather a pseudo-hypothesis that was fit to the evidence to give the desired end-result. However, it *was* a major repudiation of Darwinism based on the lack of paleontological evidence, and this *was* a direct contradiction of gradualism and the mechanism of natural selection *as well as* a deconstruction of many of the competitor views to his own. Philosophically, it was in essence a more sophisticated borrowing of the concept of rapid revolutionary change from Marxism[96] by a scientifically capable and credible researcher[97] (it had previously been attempted dogmatically

---

made to reconcile Mendel with *neo*-Darwinism. By this point "classical" Darwinism had been quietly shelved.

94. Aldous Huxley was his grandson, as was famous biologist and synthetic evolutionist Sir Julian Huxley.

95. Gould, *Evolutionary Theory*, 755–64.

96. Gould discusses this very interpretation in *Evolutionary Theory*, appendix A.

97. Gould wrote one of the best critiques of socio-biology in his *Mismeasure of Man*, which was a direct assault on a genetic basis for reducing intelligence and the potential for human improvement to a single measure (the IQ). The later edition contained a critical response to Murray and Herrnstein's *The Bell Curve*, which equated social inequality with intelligence measured using similar assumptions. He also

A CHRISTIAN CONCEPTION OF PHILOSOPHY

by Marxists aware of the evidence problem), but it utterly cemented the tautological structure of evolutionary thought. Even more astonishingly, we would not know of the scientific poverty of the theory[98] reading our standard textbooks, but as Gould openly states, "it is a metaphysical commitment on our part."[99] Thus, tellingly, when Neo-Darwinists speak of "natural selection" today they mean something *very* different from natural selection as the principal mechanism of evolution. Apparently, we have a choice of two dogmas, gradualist evolution or punctuated evolution, both claiming to be Darwinian but mutually exclusive.[100] Similarly, Plantinga demonstrates this dogmatism in his critique of Dawkins's arguments:

> For the nontheist, undirected evolution is the only game in town, and natural selection seems to be the most plausible mechanism to drive the process. Here is this stunningly intricate world with its enormous diversity and apparent design; from the perspective of naturalism or non-theism, the only way it could have happened is by way of unguided Darwinian evolution; hence, it *must*

---

intersected with religious themes in a serious, non-trivial way. Gould's thinking was far more nuanced and capable than his theory of punctuated equilibrium would suggest with his work describing extremely thoroughly the inadequacies of Darwinism and the imperative for its revision; it was just his own theory was equally as inadequate and philosophically bankrupt. He, like Dawkins, had a level of commitment to evolution as fact, in his own words "a metaphysical assumption," which could only be described as *religious*, defining "religious" as the dominant presupposition in one's life.

98. Such is the religious and dogmatic zeal of the evolutionists that the mere *attempt* of a major exhibition at a National History Museum in 2019 to highlight some problems with the theory caused a national level debate, accusations of religious fundamentalism, and right-wing conspiracy theories undermining serious science.

99. Gould, *Evolutionary Theory*, attempts a metaphysical analysis at various points during his explication of his revised theory. His tome runs to almost fifteen hundred pages, and it is to his credit that he recognizes the underpinnings of evolutionism in its major forms are always metaphysical and pretheoretically so. What is so vivid in his exposition of his revised theory is how thoroughly he discards competing theories of evolution such as Dawkins's *Selfish Gene* thesis (calling it a "fallacy"), Lamarckian "myths," and a detailed refutation of individual innovations through the twentieth century by just about every significant evolutionist up to the late 1960s. He first proposed his theory in 1972 and was totally committed to its inevitability and correctness as a matter of historical determinism.

100. The exchange between Dawkins and his allies with Gould and his allies was (and remains, even after Gould's death) particularly caustic. The important substance of the debate, however, is found accessibly in Sterelny, *Dawkins vs. Gould*. Gould was "happy" to return in kind Dennett's ill-tempered rubbishing of his work. It is of note that Sterelny is a philosopher, and in the final summary at the end of the book we sense that clearly; this debate is about the presuppositions of a *worldview*, not about the "evidence."

have happened that way; hence there *must* be a Darwinian series for each current life form.[101]

That is, Plantinga argues here that the presuppositions of naturalism simply provide a dogma with which to deal the question of origins and the diversity of nature and concludes it will not allow us to "follow the argument where it leads."[102] In contrast, the theist *might* want to countenance some form of guided evolution as the means to creating a Darwinian series which is then interpreted as a creative act of God; for other reasons they might be unwise to do so (it would require a creative hermeneutic to reconstruct historical biblical claims, which have all proved philosophically embarrassing[103]), but they *could*.

Secondly, the unnerving fallacy that Plantinga exposes in naturalist thinking is that even *if* we grant the naturalist that natural selection was somehow epistemically justifiable and biologically possible in some non-astronomical scale,[104] that does not mean it was *necessarily* the case as argued in, for example, New Atheism. It just does not follow that we can argue as Dawkins did in the *Delusion* that because God as a supremely complex being is thought of being "improbable" that evolution by natural selection is *more* probable (presumably because it demands less complication) and thus *must* be the case.[105] Rather, a metaphysical presupposition will be implicit in answering that question; as Dawkins indicated himself, he was inverting the probability argument frequently made by believers for his own purposes, but we can observe that neither inflection of the argument has superior logical force, and the logical force of the argument in either form is particularly poor on critical examination. On a trivial level, Dawkins's conundrum is rather like having eight options before us, all with a low probability, but being required to choose one. At the very least, our epistemic rights permit us to withhold commitment until we are convinced by substantiating evidence or a compelling logical argument.

That is, there is a basic problem, even if we accept that there are Darwinian sequences or even if we admit natural selection, that in itself does not establish a design-free universe and require us to accept the

---

101. Plantinga, *Where the Conflict Really Lies*, 24. Emphasis original.

102. Plantinga, *Where the Conflict Really Lies*, 24.

103. Rabbi Jonathan Sacks attempted this strategy with Professor Dawkins at the BBC RE:Think festival on Sept. 12, 2012 (see Sacks, "Jonathan Sacks and Richard Dawkins"). Sacks has to concede the historicity of Genesis as do liberal Christians.

104. This is questionable. See Macneil, "Evolutionary Theory."

105. Quoted in Plantinga, *Where the Conflict Really Lies*, 28 ff.

naturalist presupposition. However, the most glaring philosophical fallacy is to treat the hypothesis of God as if it was the *same* as any other *scientific* hypothesis. Dawkins explicitly stated this fallacy as his opening assumption and has oft repeated it.[106] Yet, in discussing ultimate authorities, there is no way we can stand outside of that authority otherwise we would be asserting that the human mind has the superior authority, and it would be the ultimate authority, usurping God. Dawkins has fundamentally begged the question in even framing the argument as he does, and it is an error oft repeated in unbelieving polemics across the arts and the sciences. The fundamental assumption of unbelieving thought is the ancient Greek prejudice we began our study with, *the unaided intellect can judge the ultimate issues of reality*; as Lewis stated, it is "God [that] is in the dock . . . God may be acquitted but the important principle is that [men are doing the judging]."[107]

So, in summary, a sneering Dawkins or a mocking Dennett claims much more for the evolutionary argument than it can deliver, even if we grant them a hearing for the sake of the wider case being argued, for as Plantinga rightly states, "*Argumentum ad Derisionem* is hardly an approved argument form."[108] What we are beginning to suspect is that naturalism is taking on the characteristics of a dogma, or as we noted previously, Gould's "metaphysical commitment" that is pre-theoretical. I believe in the following three subsections we can establish that beyond reasonable doubt.

3.3.6 Physicalism

The most extreme form of naturalistic epistemology is known as physicalism. *Physicalism* is the position that all processes, even mental ones, *eventually* reduce to physical processes—that is, all is physics! Though popular with a particular clique of physicists (implausible though that might seem!) and a sect of naturalist philosophers, it understandably draws substantial criticism from non-physicists unhappy that their branch of science is viewed as a downgraded science, and the more holistic philosophers unhappy at the rarefaction of the human experience.[109]

---

106. For example, Dawkins, *God Delusion*, ch. 2.
107. Lewis, *God in the Dock*, 244.
108. Plantinga, *Where the Conflict Really Lies*, 38.
109. Rarefaction was considered a merit by the logical positivists and in its putative

Similarly, epistemologically, it then follows that all knowledge forming processes can be reduced to neuroscience or evolutionary psychology and problems of epistemology become problems for another branch of science; this was the strategy of the "naturalization" project of Quine. However, when the neuroscientist or the psychologist is asked to give an *account* of the knowledge forming process, all that can be offered is "evolutionary advantage" which, as we noted above, is a "miserable tautology."[110]

3.3.7 Those That Survive Think Inductively

The more respectable and sophisticated naturalism found in a Quine or in a Goodman suffers from a similar weakness to the crude form found in Dawkins. Quine especially, for all his exposure of the dogmatism of positivism, seems to be arguing for a softer but equally pervasive set of naturalist presuppositions justified or explained by some tautological recourse to evolutionary theory. Quine's conception of induction is a perfect example; let us paraphrase: *we think inductively, and we have survived; thus, those that have survived, have survived because evolutionary advantage resulted when they thought inductively.* This is a repeatable formula for any natural characteristic or phenomenological event—it persisted or was beneficial because it offered evolutionary advantage and evolutionary advantage resulted from its presence, so what is present is present, a miserable tautology indeed. Quine readily admitted such reasoning was begging the question:

> The answer [to the riddle of induction] is best sought in terms of natural selection. An innate sensitivity to certain traits, and insensitivity to others, will have survival value insofar as the traits [of prediction that the future will be like the past] that are favored are favorable to prediction [but] [n]either the projectible traits nor the traits favored by natural selection are easily characterized, and the relationship between them is more tenuous still. *Further, when we appeal to biology and theories of*

---

successor, the naturalist program. Indeed, rarefaction *meant* making it congenial to a naturalist, scientific account. Interestingly, Huxley in *Ends and Means*, esp. chs. 14 and 15, writing at the zenith of logical positivism, completely rejected this rarefaction though he had once been enamored by the scientific and humanistic worldview. Huxley never signed the first Humanist Manifesto that was published just as he released his *Brave New World* in 1932.

110. A phrase for which we thank Kant, who used it when discussing the traditional arguments for God's existence.

neural organization we appeal to science that is itself grounded, in large measure, inductively.[111]

Thus, there is surely nothing subtle about the circularity; it *viciously* begs the question in the most tautological fashion. That is, if we can never explain *why* or *what* the specific evolutionary advantage was, such reasoning is always viciously circular. It was simply a presupposition or limiting notion necessary to support the naturalist program.

3.3.8 If All We Have Is Nature . . .

Interestingly, one of the most searching critiques of naturalism was provided by C. S. Lewis in his *Miracles*, the second edition of which benefitted from the robust critique of Elizabeth Anscombe of the first. Lewis has not received the recognition he deserves for his philosophical thought with a major factor being the mistruths spread because of the debate with Anscombe.[112] In brief, he asserted that if nature is all we have, there is absolutely *no reason* to accept what nature says on an epistemological level unless we have a supernaturalistic metaphysics. This position was defended in the most robust manner by Plantinga in which he acknowledges the debt to Lewis's formulation of the argument against naturalism.[113]

In making his case, Plantinga notes Darwin himself was uneasy about the emerging naturalism of his viewpoint and the consequences it held for the status of reason, asking: *if all was nature, why would we trust the reason that arises from that same nature?* That is, just how far do we need to be up the evolutionary tree for our reason to be reliable? On this basis, Plantinga noted that Quine, Ayer, and Dawkins all "found hope" in Darwin as providing a hermeneutic in evolutionary thought

---

111. Quine and Ullian, *Web of Belief*, 88–89. Emphasis added. Quine in this passage is referring explicitly to the influential work by Nelson Goodman, *Fact*, where he challenged an evolutionary explanation of why certain inductions would have survival value. Quine is honest enough to admit there is no satisfactory solution to what Goodman has argued that is not begging the question. As Gould spoke of his own pretheoretical commitment, Quine demonstrates the same metaphysical commitment to *some* version of evolutionary theory.

112. Lewis helped found the Socratic Society at Oxford, which hosted some of the liveliest debates of the era. The Anscombe-Lewis debate is the subject of much misrepresentation; see Macneil, "Lewis and Anscombe Debate." Anscombe complimented Lewis on his revised argument.

113. Plantinga, *Warrant and Proper Function*, 237n28.

but notes the hope is far less robust than they want to admit for the very reason that Darwin and Lewis perceived—there can be no *natural* justification of nature because justification is always conceptual in character and thus beyond nature *by definition*. It *reflects* on nature; it is apart from nature, and it is an abstraction of thought.[114] So, in this short but I hope fair and salient account of, as Lewis would say, "the cardinal problems of naturalism,"[115] we find naturalism as self-vitiating and evolutionary thought as a dogma. We can now proceed to seek firmer epistemological foundations elsewhere.

3.3.9 Justified True Belief (JTB), Gettier, and Epistemic Warrant

Robert Audi in his authoritative introduction to epistemology offered us this definition of epistemology which will help us frame one of the most influential and persistent working definitions of knowledge, the JTB thesis:

> Epistemology, or the theory of knowledge, is concerned with how we know what we do, what *justifies* us in believing what we do, and what *standards of evidence* we should use in seeking truths about the world and human experience.[116]

This connection of truth, evidence, and justification can be traced all the way back to Plato and is thus known as the "classical" definition of knowledge. Despite not being without serious problematics or controversy, some of which were articulated by Plato himself and the most important of which we will consider immediately below, it has, nevertheless, for many philosophers remained a substantive basis on which to found much epistemological discussion.[117]

For example, in Descartes and then Locke, this definition was associated with a reliance on some form of justification through *evidentialism*, where for a belief to be responsibly held, i.e., to fulfill one's epistemic obligations or duty, you should have *good reasons* for the beliefs you hold. Likewise, this was the view forcefully argued by nineteenth-century

---

114. Plantinga, *Warrant and Proper Function*, 216–38.
115. Lewis, *Miracles*, ch. 2.
116. Audi, *Epistemology*, i. Emphasis added.
117. See for example Chisholm (*Problem of the Criterion, Theory of Knowledge*) who spent most of his career trying to resolve the problematics surrounding it. In his own words, he was "obsessed with the problem."

polymath William Kingdon Clifford,[118] who asserted it was a moral duty incumbent upon all to have good reasons for what is believed. It is of note that he then dismissed "faith" on the grounds it lacked such justification which chimed well with the Darwinist thesis that had been advanced a few years before he wrote.

However, the most significant challenge to the JTB thesis (though it had its historical precursors) were the "Gettier problems." Gettier's tiny three-page article[119] spawned an encyclopedic response which remains a live issue for epistemologists who in one way or another still consider epistemology as a legitimate category.[120] He had demonstrated in an elegant fashion using some simple parables that belief, truth, and "simple" or first-person evidential justification ("I saw that, heard this," etc.), otherwise known as "internalist accounts" which emphasize the first-person involvement in the "knowing" process, were not sufficient (and, on the contra-externalist accounts, not even *necessary*) grounds for knowledge.[121] For example, someone may have personal *justification* for a belief that was *contingently* correct, e.g., they observed a stopped clock (formed a justified belief regarding the time) that just happened to be correct at the instant of observation (i.e., true). Yet with our God's eye view and the additional information available to us, the fulfillment of JTB conditions would not mean that they had come to knowledge of the time.[122] Those elements of belief, justification, and truth were *necessary*, but not *sufficient*, and two thousand years of Western thought regarding knowledge crashes unceremoniously to the ground. As Plantinga noted, "the havoc he ... wrought in contemporary epistemology has been entirely salutary."[123]

There was clearly a need for a "fourth element" and many accounts have attempted to append an additional criterion. For our purposes, we need but note that even in the face of a "blizzard of rival theories" that emerged to try and improve on its shortcomings, those theories proved too complex or problematic to replace what they were trying to improve

---

118. Clifford and James, *Ethics of Belief and Will to Believe*.

119. Gettier, "Is Justified True Belief Knowledge?," 121–23.

120. A significant epoch in this literature was its documentation by Shope, *Analysis of Knowing*.

121. Nagel, *Knowledge*, 61.

122. This was a famous example by Bertrand Russell in 1948. Other examples are provided by Nagel, *Knowledge*, 46–49, 58.

123. Plantinga, *Warrant and Proper Function*, 32.

upon.[124] Yet, Plantinga has probably, more than any other epistemologist, given as full an analysis as possible as to the problem of knowledge and an "answer," or more accurately, an alternative conception of knowing as an answer to the Gettier problems, and it is to this we now turn as an important building block toward epistemological self-consciousness.[125]

3.3.10 Plantinga and Warranted Belief

Plantinga develops a broadly Reidian[126] framework in his own theory. Plantinga considered Reid "substantially correct" in his account and his basic approach to reality, which was a commitment to *realism* and *reliabilism*. The former refers to the belief in an objective external world and the latter to the belief that properly functioning cognitive faculties give you access to that world. However, Reid's philosophy used a particular conception of "commonsense realism," and we should all realize that "common sense" is a problematic concept, as it is usually indexed to a form of life within a culture, or even a subculture.[127] Thus, Plantinga strengthened the account of Reid in two volumes[128] before developing his account of warranted *Christian* belief in a third.[129]

Plantinga's arguments reject internalist accounts of knowledge as inadequate, but it is important to understand that he substantively modified and enhanced the rival externalist school such that belief in God

---

124. Nagel, *Knowledge*, 55 ff., 114–16, ch. 4.

125. It should also be noted that Plantinga showed that others had already posited specific scenarios which would be recognized as examples of "Gettier" problems long before Gettier was even born, e.g., Russell's clock (1912) and Meinong's (d. 1920) conditioned auditory hallucinations (*Gesamtausgabe*, 398–99). There were also examples in ancient Indian and Chinese philosophy. However, Gettier managed to summarize concisely the problem.

126. After Thomas Reid, who in Plantinga's view, was a "much neglected" contemporary of Hume. In his preface to *Warrant and Proper Function*, Plantinga acknowledges his debt to Reid. Nichols and Yaffe, "Thomas Reid," provide an excellent overview of Reid's work and influence. There is substantial extant communication between Reid and Hume, who were Scots contemporaries.

127. For example, in modern "pluralistic" or "multicultural" societies, each ethnic community will probably have its own conception of "common sense" or what is normative and acceptable behavior.

128. Plantinga, *Warrant: The Current Debate*; and *Warrant and Proper Function*.

129. In *Warranted Christian Belief*, 218–27. Plantinga effectively exegetes Reid's critique of Hume and exposes what Plantinga calls the "scandal of skepticism": we rely, assuming the reliability of the faculty of reason, to reach our skeptical conclusion *about* reason.

A CHRISTIAN CONCEPTION OF PHILOSOPHY

could be considered both basic and epistemically responsible. Externalism holds that knowledge is essentially a "relationship between a person and a fact,"[130] noting that a person can be quite unaware of the origin of their knowledge (thus failing the primary internalist criteria), e.g., they know that Everest is the highest mountain but have no recollection of *why* they know that. That is, they *may* have had evidence at some point to come to that belief or they *may* have accepted it based on testimony or some other authority. Despite their failure to meet internalist criteria, most of us would be happy to concede that they really *did* know something about Everest.

However, externalism suffers from what is known as "the Generality Problem." The externalist must grant that there is some discriminating faculty within the individual that makes it possible to establish that relationship and to discriminate between the true and just what appears to be true because of contingency. The theory is only robust if there is a specific faculty that can assess the reliability of the mechanism in those cases, but most assessments will be made on the criteria of vision, hearing, or some other relatively *general* faculty. Thus, as Nagel notes, because first party justification is deemed to play no role:

> If we carve up belief-forming processes so narrowly, then any true belief will count as knowledge. How do we hit the target of describing the mechanism and its context at just the right level of detail?[131]

Hence, a pure externalist account will be problematic and so Plantinga does not deny that internalist conceptions such as justification will play no role, but he strengthens, or better subsumes, the internalist conception of justification to *warrant* (which has additional externalist and reliabilist underpinnings). "Warrant" becomes what must be added to truth and belief to ascend to a claim of knowledge. He conducts the details of this argument at great length in his *Warrant* trilogy[132] and presented a helpful, abbreviated form in a simplified, retrospective summary volume.[133] We will trace the salient features of this model below.

---

130. Nagel, *Knowledge*, 61.
131. Nagel, *Knowledge*, 66.
132. Plantinga, *Warrant: The Current Debate*; *Warrant and Proper Function*; and *Warranted Christian Belief*.
133. Plantinga, *Knowledge and Christian Belief*.

Firstly, Plantinga makes the important distinction between *warrant* and *justification*, with warrant being the stronger term. Justification, for Plantinga, is the locus for what Gettier problems revolve around and concretely for Plantinga, someone is *justified* when they have "not flouted one's epistemic duties" by properly considering the available evidence in the formation of their beliefs and the subsequent progress of their "downstream experience" which permits them continued justification.[134] However, as the Gettier scenarios demonstrate, the possibility remains of a dissonant component that misdirects commitment to a generally false but contingently true, justified belief. Warrant for Plantinga is the defeating of this dissonant component from the cognitive environment with a stronger definition:

> The claim is that such belief . . . originate[s] in cognitive faculties that are functioning properly in a suitable environment according to a design plan successfully aimed at producing true beliefs.[135]

This, as we have noted, owes much to Reidian reliabilism, but Plantinga strengthens Reid by reducing the reliance on the fluid concept of common sense and adding the concepts of a design plan ideally suited for the epistemic environment successfully aimed at truth. What he means by this is that correctly functioning cognitive faculties could be following a design plan, but that design plan could be aimed at say, survival, rather than the truth. In this case, the claim to knowledge would fail, which would seem to be intuitively reasonable—we know that when survival becomes a priority, an organism might quickly behave instinctively or selfishly rather than in a dispassionately rational manner.

Plantinga also overhauled the "proper function" requirement, expounding the "proper" to assert that a naturalist account of warrant can only be supported by a supernaturalistic metaphysics, thus importing a theistic premise as functionally necessary for a rational system:

> The fundamental idea is that God provides us human beings with faculties or belief producing processes that yield these beliefs and are successfully aimed at the truth; when they work the way they were designed to in the sort of environment for which they were designed, the result is knowledge or warranted belief.[136]

---

134. Plantinga, *Warrant: The Current Debate*, 10 ff.
135. Plantinga, *Knowledge and Christian Belief*, 30.
136. Plantinga, *Knowledge and Christian Belief*, 89.

Thus, turning specifically to Christian beliefs, he asserts that as a form of theism, we can be warranted, that is, *rational* in our faith. That was a substantial achievement and was enough for his work to be noted as "one of the major accomplishments of twentieth century epistemology" by one of his epistemological peers.

Now some such as Butler have critiqued Plantinga that his initial account of warrant[137] was "naturalistic";[138] this is accurate in the sense Plantinga conceived of warrant in term of cognitive functions (part of our *natural* makeup), common to all of us and readily admitted he was offering a *naturalistic* epistemology *but* cojoined with a supernaturalistic metaphysics.[139] I would assert that his emphasis here though was in the conjoining, the epistemology does not stand alone but should be considered with the metaphysics, which is precisely the direction we want to travel in epistemological self-consciousness. Additionally, God is conceived of as providing us with these faculties and central to Plantinga's argument is Calvin's *sensus divinitatis*, conceived of as a cognitive function that works to present a belief in God that is properly *basic*, i.e., not arrived at via inference from evidence; much like perception, memory, and *a priori* knowledge.[140] Plantinga then relies heavily on Calvin's theological account of it, as seen from the exegesis of the key biblical passages.[141] More generally, he describes one of the focuses of his project as developing "Calvinist Epistemology,"[142] and I believe we can see in his most mature work Plantinga is offering an apologetic that is not neutral and not wholly negative. It is also not clear that Butler's criticism would be sustained if we import Bas van Fraassen's critical definition of naturalism,[143] which reduces to "there is no such person as God"[144]

---

137. Plantinga, *Warrant and Proper Function* and *Warrant: The Current Debate*.

138. Butler, *On Plantinga*.

139. Plantinga, *Warrant and Proper Function*, 237.

140. Plantinga, *Knowledge and Christian Belief*, 35; the full account is found in Plantinga, *Warrant and Proper Function*, chs. 3–7.

141. Plantinga, *Knowledge and Christian Belief*, 30–35. This is the highly abridged version of the full argument found in Plantinga, *Warranted Christian Belief*, 167–356.

142. Plantinga, "Self-Profile," 55–64.

143. Van Fraassen, known primarily as a philosopher of science, is very provocative on this point, asserting that a robust definition of naturalism is extremely problematic to formulate.

144. Quoted by Plantinga, *Warranted Christian Belief*, 227. Bas van Fraassen is known for his seminal work in the philosophy of science and his theory of *constructive empiricism*, which was an anti-realist conception of science, positing that a scientific

which would appear a long way from Plantinga. Strawson is also careful to indicate the "elastic" usage of the term and its interpretation.[145] So, the accusation of being a "naturalistic" account is not on its own conclusive with regard to the claim that Plantinga was offering an insufficiently Reformed epistemology.

Butler's further and stronger claim is that this is not a "biblical" epistemology, or more specifically, an epistemology drawn from scripture. He wants to contrast Plantinga with the apologetic method of Bahnsen. Bahnsen explicates and exegetes at great length the scriptural basis for his method[146] with his distinctive analytic style. However, rather paradoxically, Butler's criticism of Plantinga on a Van Tillian basis might have been leveled at Van Til. Bahnsen had wanted to correct the "deficiency" admitted by Van Til that he regretted never demonstrating in detail the scriptural basis for his apologetic.[147] I would argue something similar is going on with Plantinga; Plantinga *is* assuming a Christian basis (and I would say "strongly assuming" if we believe his own intellectual and personal autobiography[148]) but we do not find a Bahnsenite threading of scriptures together in his work. We rather, like Van Til, find profound works of philosophical theology. There are papers where he pulls in quotes from Paul, the exegesis of Calvin or something from Anselm, Aquinas, or Augustine, or makes the case against a natural theology from Rom 1:18. So, it seems Plantinga can claim rather better theological credentials than those that Butler is willing to grant him at this point.

However, Butler makes another, and I believe the strongest, most serious criticism of Plantinga. It is that his apologetic is merely *theistic* rather than Christian, strong in its negative function but weak in putting forward a positive apologetic. That is, we might view his project as merely establishing the *rationality* of Christianity as a basic belief but conceding that the non-believer *could* be just as rational.[149] We should be happy to

---

theory aims to be empirically adequate only. Van Fraassen is also of note for being an advocate of transcendental arguments, which will be considered later in this book.

145. Strawson, *Scepticism and Naturalism*, 1.

146. Bahnsen, *Presuppositional Apologetics* and *Always Ready*. The former is the more academic development of the latter, which was only rediscovered posthumously by Bahnsen's family clearing out his office after his premature departure from heart failure.

147. Berkhower had criticized him on this basis and CVT responded directly acknowledging the fault in his Festschrift; see Geehan, *Jerusalem and Athens*, 203–4.

148. Plantinga, "Self-Profile," 33 ff.

149. Butler, *On Plantinga*.

concede that this seems to be the position that Plantinga would be seen as arguing for through his early work into the middle period of the RE movement.[150] The reason we would want to challenge this as his final position is because Plantinga himself seems to have had recognized this criticism and moves in his *Warrant* trilogy from establishing some general notion of warrant to its application for theistic belief and then specifically for its application to *Christian* belief. Most significantly, he also deals directly with the challenge of religious pluralism with the clear presupposition that Christianity *should* be considered true and warranted:

> From a Christian perspective, this situation of religious pluralism is itself a manifestation of our miserable human condition . . . . A fresh or heightened awareness of the facts of religious pluralism . . . could serve as an occasion for a renewed and more powerful working of the belief-producing processes by which we come to apprehend [the truth of Christianity and our obligation to God]. In this way knowledge of the facts of pluralism could initially serve as a defeater; in the long run, however, it can have precisely the opposite effect.[151]

Thus, he explicitly deals with what he calls "defeaters" to Christian belief, conceived of as an argument that undermines the *basicity* of a belief by demonstrating its falsity:

> If the believer concedes that she *doesn't* have any special source of knowledge or true belief with respect to Christian belief—no *sensus divinitatis*, no internal instigation of the Holy Spirit, no teaching by a church inspired and protected from error by the Holy Spirit, nothing not available to those who disagree with her—*then*, perhaps . . . she will have a defeater for her Christian belief. But why would she concede these things? She . . . *should* ordinarily think . . . that there are indeed sources of warranted belief that issue in these beliefs. . . . She believes, for example, that in Christ, God was reconciling the world to himself; she may believe this on the basis of what the Bible or the church teaches . . . it is the work of the Holy Spirit to convince our hearts that what our ears receive has come from him.[152]

---

150. A further discussion of the development of Plantinga's "middle period" is found in Plantinga, "Reformed Epistemology." As noted already, our discussion here moves past this period, to his most mature work which bears the slightly awkward Extended A/C (Aquinas/Calvin) designation.

151. Plantinga, *Knowledge and Christian Belief*, 113–14.

152. Plantinga, *Knowledge and Christian Belief*, 113–14. Emphasis original.

So, it seems problematic to characterize Plantinga's theological terminus as purely theistic; he certainly has Christian theism in mind. Notwithstanding, Butler makes the further criticism that Plantinga's conception of warrant moves from the general to the specific with the final move for Plantinga *to* Christian belief. That is, it is a naturalistic account from the bottom up. Plantinga can certainly be interpreted that way and concedes as much with an important qualification; he always requires a metaphysical foundation of theism but finishes with a clear explication of Christian belief:

> When I speak here of Christian belief, I mean what is common to the great creeds of the main branches of the Christian church . . . the *theistic* component of Christian belief [but] also the uniquely Christian component.[153]

Butler asserts that a Van Tillian or truly Reformed apologetic would go to the scriptures, establish warrant from the scriptures, and then build their epistemology from the top down in a presuppositional manner. Butler explicates this in his presentation immediately after discussing Plantinga, noting his approach as a "truly Reformed epistemology . . . we derive our epistemology from the Bible for it to be a biblical epistemology."[154] Butler also makes the important point, examined and argued at length in Jeffreys,[155] that Plantinga has modified and extended Calvin's conception of the *sensus divinitatis* and allows it to play a far larger role in his thought than Calvin permitted in his. The implication is thus that Plantinga cannot be considered sufficiently "Reformed" in this regard. Yet, even if we grant this contention, this does not in itself delegitimize Plantinga's extension of the concept any more than it does Van Til's extension and refinement of Calvin's thought.[156] Where Butler is more difficult to answer is in arguing that Plantinga is using a different concept of the *sensus divinitatis* altogether, suggesting it is knowledge *gaining*, in opposition to Calvin asserting all men *already* have knowledge of God. I believe the answer at this point is that both Butler and Plantinga have defensible positions—we have an issue with begging the

---

153. Plantinga, *Warranted Christian Belief*, vii.

154. Butler, *On Plantinga*, MB208–MB210.

155. Jeffreys, "How Reformed Is Reformed Epistemology?," 419–31.

156. The "theological" question is much more whether Plantinga has a *biblical* defense of his position. As Bahnsen provided the detailed exegesis for Van Til, it may be required that Plantinga's thought would need the attention of a theologian to defend it (if possible).

A CHRISTIAN CONCEPTION OF PHILOSOPHY

question as to what precisely Calvin meant by *knowledge*. His discussion seems to involve both an *a priori* and an *a posteriori* conception of knowledge, combined also with "instinct" and conscience:

> That there exists in the human minds and indeed by natural instinct, some sense of Deity, we hold to be beyond dispute, since God himself, to prevent any man from pretending ignorance, has endued all men with some idea of his Godhead, the *memory* of which *he constantly renews and occasionally enlarges*, that all to a man being aware that there is a God, and that he is their Maker, may be condemned by their own conscience when they neither worship him nor consecrate their lives to his service.[157]

Calvin proceeds to expound this *sensus divinitatis* in a polyvalent fashion. Plantinga freely admits he is *extending* this conception and precising it within a specific framework of modern epistemology. He, I would argue, is emphasizing the knowledge *gaining* noetic process, which is rather different than Butler's Van Tillian metaphysical criticism, though Butler is a fine analyst also. Calvin is certainly proceeding in his argument in a systematic fashion, but his categories are not those of modern analysis. We thus must caution that Butler's criticism is not proved as a defeater for Plantinga.

In summary, I would argue that largely what we see here is a linguistic distinction between the analytic philosophical method of Plantinga and the presuppositional apologetic of a Van Tillian more aligned with the *methods* and *vocabulary* of Idealism.[158] Anderson concurs broadly with me there[159] and has probably made use of both positions sympathetically though well known as a Van Tillian. Plantinga's controlling methodology is to "answer the fool according to his folly that he not be wise in his own estimation" whereas the Van Tillian method is "Do not answer a fool according to his folly, lest you yourself also be like him."[160] Just as these two scriptures are not contradictory but occur as a couplet for our benefit, we should see the legitimacy of both approaches, just as we appreciate

---

157. Calvin, *Institutes* 1.1. Emphasis added.

158. Van Til was characterized (accurately, I believe) by Bahnsen as "using the vocabulary [and] logic of idealism but in a way that the idealist logicians could not because of their own non-theistic presuppositions" (*Van Til's Apologetic*, 45–46, 167–69). Van Til expounds this in *Systematic Theology*, ch. 2.

159. Anderson, "Cornelius Van Til and Alvin Plantinga," and "If Knowledge Then God."

160. Prov 26:4–5 (NET); cf. Plantinga, "Self-Profile," 33.

the polyvalency of Calvin's account. The Van Tillian defends the faith in a manner consistent with the presuppositions of scripture; Plantinga deconstructs and exposes the presuppositions and the consequences of the arguments of the unbelieving opponent, frequently demonstrating their limitations and the faults of their arguments.

It seems we are in danger of making a philosophical mistake by the forced juxtaposition of the two apologetic approaches as if they were mutually exclusive options; their motivations and goals are different but largely complimentary (as Butler also indicates in recommending aspects of Plantinga's work)—Plantinga provides the detailed analysis, Van Til provides the high-level transcendental proof. It is one of the weaknesses of the Van Tillians, as noted by Bahnsen himself, that there can be a laziness when it comes to the detailed argumentation in refuting an informed (even if very wrongly informed but nevertheless articulate) opponent. It is not sufficient to jump directly to the final transcendental refutation missing out serious evidential or scientific objections that have been answered by equally serious research.[161] We might not need evidence on our own terms within our own community, but we must certainly argue the point with our opponents rather than just accuse them of incorrect presuppositions and autonomous reasoning, no matter how perfectly correct that assessment would prove (as we will demonstrate in future chapters). It is just not a *complete* account or rigorous intellectual refutation of their culpability.

Notwithstanding, there remains an important substantive difference between Plantinga and Van Til as captured in Butler's final criticism of Plantinga as an epistemology that does not prove the *necessity* of Christianity, merely its sufficiency. This is salient and pertinent as we note that Plantinga considers it "beyond the competency of philosophy" to demonstrate the truth of Christianity despite his own strong, personal conviction of its truth.[162] Plantinga mitigates what he believes rational argument can establish; he believes that Christian belief is in the final analysis formed in a way that supersedes what rational argument can

---

161. Van Til said as much in response to a question as to why he did not apply detailed historical criticism of his opponents: he answered it was because his colleagues in other departments had the expertise to do it much better on an historical basis than himself. His skill and gift were in philosophy, and he would proceed on that basis.

162. Plantinga, *Warranted Christian Belief*, 499; *Knowledge and Christian Belief*, 126.

accomplish; he does not believe he establishes the *truth* of that belief though he believes it *is* true:

> I won't argue that [Christian] belief *is* true, although of course I believe that it is. The fact is that there are some very good arguments for [Christian] belief, arguments about as good as philosophical arguments get; nevertheless, these arguments are not strong enough to support the conviction with which serious believers in God do in fact accept [Christian] belief . . . these arguments are not strong enough to confer knowledge on someone who accepts them.[163]

Now, I do believe that Plantinga is being particularly nuanced here and I still believe his position remains a Calvinist one.[164] The Calvinist will always maintain that it is the sovereignty of God and the grace of God that brings one to salvation and not a rational argument, it seems Plantinga has drawn the line between the philosophical and the theological here—thus, the limiting of the competence of philosophy:

> But *is* it true? This is the really important question. And here we pass beyond the competence of philosophy. In my opinion, no argument with premises accepted by everyone or nearly everyone is strong enough to support full blown Christian belief.[165]

There is also the equivalent coda in the full statement of his arguments:

> Here we pass beyond the competence of philosophy, whose main competence . . . is to clear away certain objections, impedances, and obstacles to Christian belief. Speaking for myself and of course not in the name of philosophy . . . it does, indeed, seem to me to be true, and to be the maximally important truth.[166]

So, in summary, we can acknowledge Butler has the formal right to criticize Plantinga as wanting in the final analysis for proving the objective truth of Christian belief, but he equally should (and I would say further that he *does*) acknowledge the strength and force of what

---

163. Plantinga, *Knowledge and Christian Belief*, x.

164. I detect a hint of Kierkegaardian existentialism in Plantinga here; a "leap of faith" seems to be required. Both of his 1958 published papers (his first) dealt with existentialist themes, though he was always a rigorous analytical philosopher in method. See Macneil, "Fideistic Leap," for a broader discussion of Kierkegaard.

165. Plantinga, *Knowledge and Christian Belief*, 126.

166. Plantinga, *Warranted Christian Belief*, 499.

Plantinga has given us in defending the faith.[167] However, in agreement with Butler, it necessitates we must follow Van Til if we wish to proceed to an objective proof of the existence of and the necessity of the Christian God as the guarantor of knowledge, as required by epistemological self-consciousness.

We will examine the transcendentalist approach of Van Til in subsequent chapters, which allows Van Til to assert that the only possibility for coherence in human predication is the necessary existence of the Christian conception of God.[168] However, we need another thread to our philosophical garment if it is to serve us in the most demanding winters and it is the ethical or our theory of values. Ethics, or our theory of values and of what is valuable,[169] grounds our philosophy by testing it against the world we dwell in, so it is to that we now turn.

3.4 Ethics

3.4.1 Introduction

Ethics is almost always prefixed with a qualifier: *classical, situational, secular*, and *rule-egoism* being four examples reflecting distinct conceptions of ethics that have at one time exercised an influence over Christian ethicists.[170] All these schools still fall within the remit of ethical discussions, for sometimes ethics is treated more as a descriptive science than a prescriptive process. We should also note that these terms are already something of an aggregation; there are distinct schools within Christian ethics and secular ethics which have reflected on one another, cross-pollinated one another, and importantly, aggressively rejected one another.

---

167. Butler acknowledges in early assessments (1997) the substantial contribution of Plantinga and his criticisms of unbelieving philosophy. In later work, he seems far more ambivalent toward Plantinga though still acknowledging his status, accomplishment, and contribution; see Butler, *Biblical Presuppositional Apologetics*. In his latter presentations he was frustrated that Plantinga had not progressed in his understanding of Van Til over a period of twenty years.

168. Bahnsen, *Van Til's Apologetic*, 715.

169. Butler prefers to consider ethics as a subheading of a wider theory of values, with aesthetics as a sister category. As Wittgenstein noted, "Ethics and aesthetics are one" (*Tractatus* 6.421) and I will mean both.

170. Ramsey, *Christian Ethics*. This is an older but an excellent quality primer by some of the most influential ethicists of the early post-positivist period where philosophical thought regarding ethics was again expanding beyond the confines of verificationism and psychologized ethical discourse.

Thus, there is no way we can do justice to the *detail* of the variation of ethical perspectives and why they diverge as they do, but rather we will do justice to the guiding ethical principles of *our* thesis and why it is authoritative for us, and why such a detailed enumeration of rival ethical theories is then rendered superfluous.

Ethics is most basically "the surrounding climate of ideas about how to live. It determines what we find acceptable or unacceptable, admirable, or contemptible ... what is due to us, and what is due from us, as we relate to others."[171] That is, it is the constitutive material of our *moral knowledge*. Whereas a "moral" act is considered the "right way" to act, an *ethical theory* is the theory that defines *why* it should be the right way to act. Thus, Van Til spoke of "the Christian view of human action or behavior."[172] This will include our *Christian* conceptions of "good" and "bad" actions, virtue and vice, justice and injustice, and the *Christian* criteria which are proposed to judge such actions. Ethics is also inherently *political*, how we organize and govern ourselves or permit ourselves to be governed flow inexorably from our ethical conclusions.

Of course, any comprehensive treatment of ethics would demand far more space than is permitted here but we can give just enough of an argument to demonstrate that we can reject the positivistic and naturalistic psychologizing of ethics. Like Willard, we refute the abolition of moral knowledge and boldly assert its reality; we thus do not merely describe what ethics might be, but we reason and argue to the point that we might prescribe what our ethics *should* be.[173] Our ethics are not just a manner of behavioral conditioning, exotic socio-biological psychology[174] or

---

171. Blackburn, *Being Good*, 1.
172. Van Til, *Defense of the Faith*, 74.
173. Willard, *Disappearance of Moral Knowledge*, viii.

174. Zak advances the thesis that the hormone "oxytocin" explains our moral behavior, "Am I actually saying that a single molecule ... accounts for why some people give freely of themselves and others are cold-hearted bastards ...? In a word, 'yes.'" (Zak, *Moral Molecule*, 11). He remains an entrepreneur and a professor in good standing, still pioneering this new "science" (neuroeconomics, immersion neuroscience); see https://pauljzak.com/. He claims the full authority of twenty years of "peer reviewed" research. As a philosophical exercise, this field provides great examples to test against Mahner's "Demarcating Science from Non-Science" criteria for distinguishing science from pseudo or non-science.

In view of the "peer reviewed" status of this research, I would be amiss to omit the general point that "peer review" is not always an objective process but reflective of far wider interests, sometimes informal censorship of dissident scholarship, sometimes reflective of the kudos gained by publishing your "revolutionary" paper, sometimes purely of your corporate buying-power, sometimes as a means of political control.

relativized to our cultural situation or personal feelings (though all are factors to consider) but an outer expression of our inner convictions regarding our place in the universe and our relation to the God of scripture and one another. For the epistemological self-conscious, our objective referent must be the revelation through the narrative of scripture. Yet, this is not merely memorizing the Ten Commandments but appreciating the elaborate and detailed exposition of those principles in the Law and the narratives of scripture. The ethical life for the Christian is the life lived in harmony with the mind of God, but let us first walk the path to this as the only logical terminus for the ethical life. That is the aim of this section.

3.4.2 Ethics, Moral Knowledge, and Worldview

Perhaps more than any other area of study in philosophy, ethics is the interface between philosophical belief and action. A basis for and a theory of ethics is required for us to live in the world and with one another. The challenge is presented to us is that which Aristotle clearly lays before us:

> But not every action nor every passion admits of a mean; for some have names that already imply badness, e.g. spite, shamelessness, envy, and in the case of actions adultery (*moicheia*), theft (*klopê*), murder (*androphonia*).... It is not possible, then, ever to be right with regard to them; one must always be wrong.[175]

This we might interpret as *if our ethics end up condoning adultery/theft/murder there is something wrong with our ethics*. However, in our modern context, the debate surrounding birth and death,[176] particularly regarding abortion and euthanasia, witness to the fact that not everyone agrees with everyone else where ethics is concerned. In Aristotle there is something *a priori* in his conception of ethics *and* something of an active, psychological commitment demanded of the actor, known as *hexis* in his writing, a term found also in Plato reportedly from Socrates's conception of knowledge.[177] It refers to a personal ownership of and responsibility

---

175. Aristotle, *Complete Works*, EN II.6 1107a8–15. Here the references are to Aristotle's division in the *Complete Works*; Aristotle's principal ethical writings are also found in *The Nicomachean Ethics* which has a helpful contextualizing introduction.

176. Blackburn, *Being Good*, §§8–9.

177. Sachs, "Aristotle: Ethics."

for your conduct, a resonance rather than a dissonance between your theory of your world and your practice of life.

Ethics is, in any *reputable* conception, about the *how* we live *and* the *why* we live the way we do. Now "reputable" is a loaded term but, like Willard argued with a high degree of plausibility, much of twentieth century ethics *was* in disrepute. Beginning with the analytic method of Moore and the positivistic conceptions of Schlick, ethics was reduced to a descriptive science, i.e., a set of propositions considered "true."[178] These were the psychologized conceptions of ethics that pursued knowledge only (i.e., description) that had a putative debt to Watson's behaviorist accounts of psychology,[179] which were then pushed to greatest extreme in the psychological theories of Skinner who believed we could engineer a perfect society, because human behavior was, after all, *entirely* a matter of *conditioned response*. The disrepute results because in such an understanding there is *no* moral culpability because one's behavior was an *inevitable* consequence of one's environment. Thus, if there is a "fault" it is that of "society"; more specifically, the fault is that social engineers and cultural visionaries who have been *too timid* and have allowed concepts such as freedom, dignity, and democracy to obstruct the scientific path to an ordered and peaceful world.

Now, this immediately begs the question as to *why* such a world as envisaged by Skinner and his fellow travelers *would* be desirable. *Why* would we consider an "ordered and peaceful" world preferable to a "free, dignified, and democratic" one—this is an ethical question, and we should demand the answer rather than accept these as poles of a dilemma. Why choose between these two? In my view, this is a *false* dilemma; a "free, dignified, and democratic" society in no way implies a disordered and a non-peaceful society, unless the order and peace we seek is that modeled by North Korea.[180]

---

178. Schlick, *Problems of Ethics*, 1.

179. Watson first presented his theory in 1913 in an article in *Psychological Review* and established a distinct school of psychology that viewed human behavior as governed by scientific laws and thus being entirely deterministic. Quine was to recount how impressed he was in reading Watson, and his influence on Quine's rejection of mentalistic accounts of language and his general psychologized perspective on naturalizing epistemology and ontology cannot be underestimated.

180. Skinner presented his utopian vision in his novel *Walden Two* (1948) and the philosophical statement (or "post-scientific" justification) of his program in *Beyond Freedom and Dignity* (1971). See Macneil, "Skinner's Utopia."

Particularly for Christian worldview philosophy, these views should not escape the need for ethical evaluation and rebuke, and for the epistemologically self-conscious, their coercive and autonomous character stands utterly opposed to the freedom and liberty within the scriptures that form our foundation.[181] Thus, to fully grasp the nettle of the real nature and purpose of ethical reflection, we should understand the inseparable nature of our metaphysics (being *of* the world), our epistemology (our *theory* and thoughts *in* the world), and our ethics (what we *decide* to do being *of* and *in* the world). All these are presuppositions that control our thinking about and action in the world. The aggregate of these we might also call our *worldview* which will increasingly feature in our discussion as epistemological self-consciousness develops.

3.4.3 Theonomy and Ethics

In the view of this work, the core of Reformed normative ethics can but be "theonomical." It *integrates* our ethics with our epistemology and with our metaphysics; they become a coherent package rather than viewed as disparate categories. Bahnsen helps us understand why this is a preferable approach:

> If the law of God is the moral ideal to be followed . . . and if the practice . . . is contrary to it, what measures [will correct] the situation? This question, as every other question, must be addressed by the law of God itself. The moral code not only sets forth standards to be followed . . . it lays down principles of conduct to be followed by those who wish to *bring about* [reformation].[182]

The *theonomical* ethical position asserts the primacy of the scripture in ethical matters rather than the primacy of the autonomous human intellect. The intellect is not to be ignored as if this was merely a dogmatic commitment, the intellect is rather to be used as a *tool* and applied with the *presupposition* of working through the material provided in the scriptures and systematizing it while properly regarding the Creator-creature distinction. It is this conception of *theonomy* and the role it plays in

---

181. Much more could and should be said on the imperative for freedom and liberty as central to the Hebrew and Christian scriptures; see Macneil, "Politics."

182. Bahnsen, "Theonomic Position," 52.

A CHRISTIAN CONCEPTION OF PHILOSOPHY

defining our ethical theory and informing our practice that diffuses what Van Til called "the labyrinth of ethical literature."[183]

Theonomy in the most general sense is associated with Reformational confessions, especially those of the Puritans and more specifically the Westminster Standards of 1647. Theonomy is formed from *theos* and *nomos*, classical Greek words for "God" and "law"; so theonomy is simply a preference for "God's law" in contrast to *autonomy*, formed from *autos* and *nomos*, meaning "self" and "law." God's Law in this sense[184] is conceived of as being scripture alone and all of scripture:

> It is necessary for the Christian to maintain without any apology and without any concession that *it is Scripture, and Scripture alone*, in the light of which all moral questions must be answered. Scripture as an external revelation became necessary because of the sin of man. No man living can even put the moral question as he ought to put it, or ask the moral questions as he ought to ask them, unless he does so in the light of Scripture.... There is no alternative but that of theonomy and autonomy.[185]

Now, we do need to qualify the sense of "autonomy" that Van Til uses here and that we are employing. Most vividly, "autonomy" became well known as Kant asserted it as the basic intellectual attitude of the Renaissance with Kant arguing that a condition of moral culpability must be the autonomy of the human subject. We should feel comfortable agreeing with Kant, for as Paul also acknowledges, there is a conscience in a person that at once accuses them or declares them innocent. Every person has a personal responsibility before God and is judged on the basis of *their* decisions. There are indeed further serious and complex theological issues of the noetic effects of sin and the necessity of grace to draw the fallen subject to receive salvation and yet the maintaining of their moral culpability. We examine those issues more closely in §5, yet the principle is sound.

Autonomy can also be taken in a more positive sense as shown in the Amplified Version rendering of 2 Cor 9:8:

---

183. Van Til, *Defense of the Faith*, 74.

184. Sometimes in biblical studies "the Law" is taken to just refer to the Pentateuch (the five books of Moses); similarly, "the Law and the Prophets" describes just the collection of the Pentateuch and the prophetic books. However, in the theonomical sense, "the Law" is just a shorthand for *all* of Scripture as is often the case in the Christian scriptures, especially in the writings of Paul (who was also an expert in "the Law" in the narrower sense).

185. Van Til, *Defense of the Faith*, 77. Emphasis added.

> And God is able to make all grace [every favor and earthly blessing] come in abundance to you, so that you may always [under all circumstances, regardless of the need] have complete sufficiency in everything [being completely self-sufficient in Him], and have an abundance for every good work and act of charity.

Here the Greek word αὐτάρκειαν (*autarkian*) is used for "complete sufficiency" from which the English word *autarky* (self-governing, self-sufficient) is directly associated. The Greek of the verse and those following are particularly emphatic regarding the *overflowing* abundance of a believer to be a blessing to those around them. Of course, and this is recognized in the Amplified Text, the self-sufficiency or autonomy of the believer is not a self-sufficiency originating with their humanity but in their contact with the divine nature.

The conception of "autonomy" that we are criticizing is the sense of where it is conceived that humanity was "coming of age" and rejecting external sources of coercive authority, particularly as manifested in the Catholic hegemony and then the Protestant hegemonies that replaced, or at times, worked adjacent to them.[186] It might also be expressed in the naturalistic and scientistic philosophies we have considered that explicitly and completely, as a matter of methodology, rejected the noumenal, elevating the power of an independently functioning reason as the final criteria of action and the judge of knowledge, even if this resulted in a skeptical conclusion and its own diminution. Similarly, a religious expression of the autonomous attitude was seen post the legitimate rejection of the coercive power of the Catholic Church by the "stepchildren" of the Reformers or the "radical Reformation"; some Anabaptist sects were particularly antinomian and moved to extreme positions rejecting *all* civic authority.[187] Many "anabaptists," including the Pietists, deemphasized objective scripture that was seen to legitimize the coercive authorities, preferring the "inner light" and subjective criteria. Kant, being from a Pietist background, would have been exposed to this non-dogmatic conception of Christianity and we can understand his complex attitude to religion

---

186. Notwithstanding, it is easy to be overly judgmental regarding the attitude of Luther, Calvin, and some of the Reformed fathers to the "radical" Reformation. They felt that the progress of the Reformation was disrupted by the popular agitation associated with some of the radical groups which gave the papist kings excuse to attack the Reformed communities. With the eventual attempted insurrection at Munster violently crushed, it seemed their caution was warranted.

187. See Verduin, *Reformers and Their Stepchildren*.

A CHRISTIAN CONCEPTION OF PHILOSOPHY

more easily with that knowledge.[188] So, our sense of "autonomy," and indeed the general Van Tillian sense of the term, is when reason is employed independently of any scriptural reference or accountability to God, rather than challenging the moral culpability of a person. Our introductory remarks at the start of this work emphasized this was the sense understood with respect to the Greek thinkers who had discovered "humanism."

Thus, the theonomical perspective that emphasizes the interpretation of scripture as a whole in search of ethical principles is not analogous to the primitive fundamentalism of the 1920s and 1930s which was often characterized by "proof texting" and anti-intellectualism.[189] For the Puritans, and modern theonomists would concur, theonomy meant taking God's laws and statutes as normative though that did *not* mean without interpretation; sometimes a law specific to the cultural situation of ancient Israel illustrated a more general principle, and that principle was what was sought after.[190] As is well known to students of American history, the "Puritan Canopy" was a reflection of the New England Puritans' desire to construct a society based on what they had found in the scriptures by their covenantal compacts between and within families at the foundation of their settlements:

> Puritan theologians assumed there was a given (rather than a constructed) character to human nature, the world, and God's way of reaching out to the world. *They took for granted that the central religious task was to orient the self to the prerogatives of God as those prerogatives had been revealed in Scripture.*[191]

However, the canopy had begun to fragment by the 1750s, ironically under the stress of the Great Awakening centered around Jonathan Edwards's "subtle and most able restatement of [the] inherited Calvinist convictions."[192] Edwards was a revivalist in the literal sense of the word: he was seeking to revive that which, like Eli the high priest during the time of King Saul, had become old, fat and blind in its old age. However,

---

188. Kant, *Religion*, was his most mature piece of moral philosophy. It is of interest that he submitted the work via the theology faculty in case it needed to be "censored" for impiety.

189. See Macneil, "Scripture and the Post-Darwinian Controversy."

190. It is thus not merely a form of crude Divine Command Theory that some twentieth-century Christian ethicists such as Wolfhart Pannenberg found "so unpersuasive today."

191. Noll, *America's God*, 21. Emphasis added.

192. Noll, *America's God*, 25.

his ecclesiological innovations of prohibiting the openly unregenerate from partaking of the Lord's Supper[193] and his growing doubts over the theological validity of a localized covenant as envisaged by the New England Puritan orthodoxy and social organization, had in them the seeds of a New Evangelicalism which grew in freshly ploughed Arminian soil on the new frontiers. Additionally, however unintentionally or indirectly, Edwards's work opened the door to political republicanism; Noll sees in this the transition: "move from theology to politics, and intellectual leadership . . . from the clergy to men of state."[194]

Nevertheless, the influence of the biblical narratives and more specifically the Law of God remained strong and basic in the American Christian consciousness[195] and provided inspiration for the wave of "Arminian" revivalists during the nineteenth century. Finney was to write:

> In studying elementary law, I found the old authors frequently quoting the Scriptures and referring especially to the Mosaic Law as authority for many of the great principles of common law. This excited my curiosity so much that I purchased a Bible, the first I had ever owned. Whenever I found a reference to the Bible made by the law authors, I turned to the passage and consulted it in its connection.[196]

Finney's theology was rich and deep and it is a gross simplification to simply designate him as the archetypal modern Arminian evangelical.[197] Finney was committed to the Law of God, was both a political and

---

193. This was in reaction to the admission to the Lord's Supper those from covenant families just on that basis even though they had a lifestyle that showed no interest in piety or the things of God. See Macneil, "Jonathan Edwards and the Destruction."

194. Noll, *America's God*, 50.

195. Noll has an appendix in which he addresses the issue of the historiography of the "Christian Republicanism" with regard to the founding of the United States. The issue of the role and the measure of influence of Christian thinking is a highly contested arena, often dominated by the political interests of the parties. His point is that Christian apologists tend to overplay or give exclusive place to the role of biblical thought, and secular authorities try to downplay or eliminate its influence. In many ways the debate is more acrimonious and more intense than it was when Noll wrote, particularly in the wake of the Trump era when President Trump held the door open to Christians in a manner not known since the era of Lincoln or Washington. A notable recent contribution to the debate based on validating contested historical accounts against the primary sources is Barton and Barton, *American Story*.

196. Finney, *Autobiography of Charles G. Finney*, 8.

197. Finney, *Life and Works of Charles Finney*, vol. 1. This collection includes work on systematic theology, revivalism, autobiography, sermons, and Christian ethics.

a religious reformer, and was far more similar in his broad social and political program to his near contemporary and Presbyterian founder of Westminster Theology Seminary, J. Gresham Machen, than to the fundamentalist evangelicals that from the 1870s onward were emerging as a response to theological liberalism.[198] Like Finney, Machen was heavily socially and politically involved, emphasizing the imperative of biblical law as the foundation for ethics:

> Men are wondering today what is wrong with the world. They are conscious they are standing over some terrible abyss. Awful ebullitions rise from that abyss. We have lost the sense of the security of our western civilization. Men are wondering what is wrong. It is perfectly clear what is wrong. The law of God has been torn up . . . and the result is appearing with ever greater clearness. When will the law be rediscovered?[199]

In summary, the point I make here is that to the time of Machen there was a clear and enduring commitment to the Law of God as the basis for Christian ethics. An abandonment of the Law of God as the basis for Christian ethics has been an anomalous interlude in the history of the Church corrected by its restatement in Van Tillian thought and applied practically by his early interpreters such as Rushdoony and Bahnsen, which then fed into the wider Reconstructionist movement. However, with this application, there was an important dimension added to the term which we will examine in the next section.

3.4.4 Modern Theonomy

As noted above, modern theonomy was primarily the work of two men[200] in applying Van Tillian thought to first the socio-political sphere and then more broadly.[201] Bahnsen was to reflect on this seminal work:

---

198. For example, owing to Machen's stringent defense of the Bible he is sometimes misidentified by critics (e.g., Barr, *Fundamentalism*, 165) as a "fundamentalist" or a "conservative evangelical," but early fundamentalists were often obscurantist and advocated withdrawal from mainstream culture and academia. See Macneil, "Fundamentals and Fundamentalism."

199. Machen, *Education, Christianity, and the State*, 41–42.

200. A concise summary is found in Bahnsen, "Theonomic Position." See Macneil, "Theonomy in Christian Ethics," for further links.

201. See North et al., *Foundations*.

Theonomy in Christian Ethics argued that God's word is authoritative over all areas of life (the premise of a Christian world-and-life view). It argued that within the Scriptures we should presume continuity between Old and New Testament moral principles and regulations until God's revelation tells us otherwise (the premise of covenant theology). It argued therefore that the Old Testament law continues to offer us an inspired and reliable model for civil justice or socio-political morality (a guide for public reform in our own day, even in the area of crime and punishment).[202]

There *should* have been nothing of especial novelty here, it being as Bahnsen put it "vanilla Reformed social theory"[203] and it might be characterized more formally within moral philosophy as a version of the ancient Divine Command Theory which considers morality as somehow dependent on God.[204] However, Rushdoony and Bahnsen formalized the general commitment of the Reformers into a *modern* socio-political program that became one of the major distinctives of that Reconstructionist movement that grew out of their work.[205] Their theology was rigorous and more consciously consistent with Reformed principles,[206] with the remnant of the neo-Thomistic positions founded on natural law theory purged, and where ethics is not merely theistic but is dependent *directly* on the Christian God as a reflection of his character, particularly his justice and his love.

That is, when we say that "God is good" we mean that in a specific *epistemologically self-conscious* manner. We are not embroiling ourselves in the Euthyphro dilemma by considering "goodness" as a standard that somehow God lives up to (and is therefore outside of God) and

---

202. Bahnsen, *No Other Standard*, 3–4.

203. The Puritan Westminster Confession is generally accepted as theonomical and as advocating civil society based on God's Law as revealed in both covenants. This is the argument presented in full by Bahnsen in *Theonomy in Christian Ethics*, 1–40.

204. Austin, "Divine Command Theory." But see also n. 190, n. 208.

205. A highly compressed summary of the emergence of the movement and the major personalities in it is found in North and DeMar, *Christian Reconstruction*, ix–xxi. Christian Reconstructionism was also the subject of my master's dissertation, *Dominion Theology*. There I argued (correctly, I maintain) for its orthodoxy.

206. In a personal exchange where I congratulated an academic theologian on his account of presuppositional apologetics, I was most surprised when he said, "I am no longer a presuppositionalist as classical (Calvinist) apologetics was so Thomist [so I have reverted to it]." Ironically, that Thomism was precisely the heart of Van Til's objection to Warfieldian (Old Princeton) apologetics.

undermines him as the foundation of moral action, but we immediately take the position God is the *origin* of goodness as he was also the origin of physical creation.[207] The "is" here is both the existential "is" and the predicative "is"; God is linguistically and logically unique in this respect and that is what modern theonomy recognizes.

Similarly, God acts *virtuously* because he is the origin of virtue and demonstrates virtue just because that is who he is and he acts completely in accord with his own Law, it being a codification of his character. The Euthyphro dilemma is a dilemma because one *considers* God to be charged with *obeying* his own commands as analogical to *our* act of obedience. That is, it fails to recognize the creature-Creator distinction for in contrast, there is no action of obedience required on God's part because to be obedient would suggest God has some sort of option to deny the perfect unity and balance of his own character. Alston makes this clear in a more formal fashion:

> A necessary condition of the truth that "S ought to do A" is at least the metaphysical possibility that S does not do A. On this view, moral obligations attach to all human beings, even those so saintly as to totally lack any tendency, in the ordinary sense of that term, to do other than what it is morally good to do. And no moral obligations attach to God, assuming, as we are here, that God is essentially perfectly good. *Thus divine commands can be constitutive of moral obligations for those beings who have them without it being the case that God's goodness consists in His obeying His own commands, or, indeed, consists in any relation whatsoever of God to His commands.*[208]

Fundamentally, in Van Tillian terms we dissolve the dilemma because we consider the ontological Trinity as our Foundation of Reality.[209]

---

207. The Hebrew word רֵאשִׁית (*re'shiyth*) refers to being first both in position and in temporality (time), similarly reflected in languages such as Gaelic where the word *taoiseach* has both the positional and the temporal sense (hence, the title of the Irish prime minister).

208. Alston, "Some Suggestions for Divine Command Theorists," 303–26. Emphasis added.

209. Bosserman in *The Trinity* provides us with a book length exposition of this complex but foundational aspect of Van Tillian thought. The pertinent level of the argument here is that *only* a Triune God guarantees the unity of thought and purpose, i.e., God is good *all* the time. Anything more than three persons could mean possible pairing to the exclusion of the others and a disunity in the composite personality of God. It is also interesting to consider that the psychologist Jung advocated a quaternity for this very purpose that the fourth element of "evil" would "complete" God whereas

Bosserman captures this thought by demonstrating how *abstracting our situation* from the metaphysical context leads us away from truth and into epistemological error and thus culpable ethical failure:

> Satan responds with a direct contradiction of God's claim, and the reasoning at work behind it is a rudimentary example of abstract thinking. If fruit is really good for food, then every particular piece of fruit may be enjoyed as food, and that is that. Any additional claim that it is also good, or perhaps better for the time being as an educational device, to be peered at, but not eaten, represents an obvious contradiction of the earlier, and of course, complete interpretation of the goodness of fruit. In fact, it can easily be discarded as a lie. Satan appealed to something good—the law of God—as a ground for disobeying the law of God (cf. Matt 4:1–11). But, in order to support his argument, Satan had to reinterpret God in light of it, casting Him as forbidding the tree out of a selfish desire to prevent Eve from attaining the sort of wisdom and maturity necessary for governing the creation.[210]

So, in summary, we see the importance of the normative scripturally based presuppositions that constitute our "worldview" rather than trying to abstractly theorize, analyze, or synthesize on an autonomous basis; our metaphysical commitment must be to the goodness of God and the knowledge provided for us by the scriptures. Our ethical orientation must be to theonomy, a commitment to the wisdom (understood as the ability to apply socio-politically our knowledge) revealed to us in the scriptures. Thus, we are now in a better position to understand the import of Paul's proposition, "Christ, in whom are hidden all the treasures of wisdom and knowledge."[211] In summary, it is *only* a Christian *worldview philosophy* that will be able to provide the ethical position fully consistent with the implications of the Christian metaphysics and with Christian epistemology. It is to that task we now turn in more detail.

---

it would do exactly the opposite; it would fragment the unity of the divine personality.

210. Bosserman, *Trinity*, 235–36.
211. Col 2:3 (NAS).

3.5 Christian "Worldview Philosophy"

3.5.1 Introduction

In summary of our argument so far, we have seen Plantinga argued as an analytic philosopher and presented an argument for the *rationality* of Christian belief. That is, Plantinga was not so much concerned with proving the *truth* of Christian belief (though he believes it *is* true and the *only* viable option) but rather to shut the mouths of those who would accuse Christians of irrationality. Plantinga frequently argues on his opponent's own terms and demonstrates the inadequacy of their arguments and how they claim more for their arguments than can be sustained.

We have then posited that Van Til's thought provides the bridge to prove the *truth* of Christianity. It is with bringing Van Til's thought to the fore that we are primarily concerned with in this section, but we unexpectedly find Plantinga an ally in that regard. The perceived difference between Van Til and Plantinga can be mitigated to a large degree and not seen as weakening either one, with both positions standing in support of distinctively Christian philosophy and in opposition to "classical" and "evidential" apologetics. That is, for *any* system of knowledge, we have already seen that Plantinga has taught us that the *justification* or *warrant* of the beliefs in question are a central concern. Plantinga became known for his analytic scrutiny[212] of issues in contemporary analytic philosophy on their own terms with no apologetic intent but is perhaps less well known for his positive and negative apologetic challenges to Christian philosophers; that is, to both present their own program *and* to demonstrate the inadequacies of the alternatives.[213]

That is, at this high level, both Van Til and Plantinga were methodologically equivalent—they wanted to expose the shortcomings of secular thought and present the only plausible alternative: *Christian* theism. However, when we stopped our program with Plantinga we found

---

212. A contemporary of Plantinga's recommended to the APA the term "alvinise" to describe a rigorous deconstruction of what appeared to be a simple problem into its complex parts! For example, the common philosophical proposition that "some *things* do not exist" was proved in a standard way by logicians by saying "Pegasus was a mystical beast from a fantasy, that proves there are some *things* that do not exist." Plantinga later rejected that view with great rigor by drilling down into what "thing" necessarily entails. Similarly, Kenny, *New History*, 796, pays homage to Plantinga for "unsolving" the "solved" philosophical problem (after Russell) of the ontological argument.

213. Plantinga, "Advice to Christian Philosophers," 296–315; afterword to Sennett, *Analytic Theist*, 353–58.

that there was nothing in his conception which implies there *should* be, logically or ethically, a *Christian* basis for philosophy, only that it is rationally defensible and *if* true, is a justified and warranted purveyor of knowledge.[214] We concluded that we needed to move in a progressively Van Tillian direction in order to anchor our beliefs not just as rational, defendable and warranted but also *necessarily* true, in a substantive and metaphysical sense.

His claim is thus stronger than Plantinga's or, as we have argued, it picks up where Plantinga leaves off to not just to give *sufficient* conditions for Christian epistemology but to establish the *necessity* of Christian epistemology. This strong claim is correspondingly more controversial, disputed and is what the epistemological self-consciousness project seeks to advance. It is evident that the very *nature* of Van Til's challenge to unbelievers and Christian philosophers makes his work far less palatable and less likely to be discussed in mainstream religious studies or philosophy of religion overviews, even within the Reformed community.[215] For Van Til, philosophical discussion was not merely abstract, therapeutic, pragmatic or elucidatory, it was also about *solving* problems and revealing to a sinful subject their sinfulness—this is an example of epistemological self-consciousness in the *most* basic and explicit sense. The apologetic task was a tool for bringing the hearer to epistemological self-consciousness as a *tool of evangelism*, which was also an expression of his passion and compassion.[216]

3.5.2 What Is "Christian Worldview" Philosophy?

As Butler noted,[217] the term "Christian worldview philosophy" was once almost patented by the Reformed Van Tillians but is now much more in the common parlance. This raises a semantic problem, as "Christian Worldview Philosophy," much like the designation "fundamentalist," has been used merely as an imprecise, pejorative term. For example, Robbins

---

214. Edgar and Oliphint, *Christian Apologetics*, 589. As Edgar and Oliphint note, this has been a controversial aspect of Plantinga's approach in Reformed circles.

215. Bartholomew and Goheen, *Christian Philosophy*.

216. Greg Bahnsen, a one-time student but later close friend of Van Til, recounts his visits to Van Til's home after his retirement and his habit of walking every day, "evangelizing" the nuns at the convent close to where he lived. He also sent open letters of "gospel hope" to various national leaders.

217. Butler, *On Plantinga*, MB209 ff.

in his rather ill-tempered exchange with Plantinga[218] directed the designation at any philosopher that might have the *audacity* to disagree with his appropriation of Rortian postmodern pragmatism into Christian ethics and his subsequent denial that a strong Christian philosophy was even possible. However, Plantinga in reply, although he did not use the term "worldview" himself, clarified and encapsulated the proper definition and use of the concept perfectly:

> First, Christian philosophers and Christian intellectuals generally must display more autonomy—more independence of the rest of the philosophical world. Second, Christian philosophers must display more integrity . . . in the sense of integral wholeness, or oneness, or unity, being all of one piece. . . . And necessary to these two is a third: Christian courage, or boldness, or strength, or perhaps Christian self-confidence.[219]

Similarly, in addressing the need for a distinctively Christian philosophy, he is more explicit still:

> According to the view of Christian philosophy I and others advocate, Christian philosophers should consider the whole range of problems from a Christian or theistic point of view; in trying to give philosophical account of some area or topic—freedom, for example, evil, or the nature of knowledge, or of counterfactuals, or of probability, she may perfectly properly appeal to what she knows or believes as a Christian. She is under no obligation to appeal only to beliefs shared by nearly what common sense and contemporary science dictate, for example. Nor is she obliged first to try to prove to the satisfaction of other philosophers Christianity is true before setting out on this enterprise of Christian philosophy. Instead, she is entirely within her rights in *starting from* her Christian understanding addressing the philosophical problems in question.[220]

In other words, Christian philosophy proceeds on its own terms and using its own presuppositions. Van Til would concur here but would also make the stronger point that this demonstrates there is no "neutral" ground between these positions.[221] Secular philosophy assumes the autonomy of

---

218. Plantinga, "On Christian Philosophy," 617–23; Plantinga cites Robbins extensively in this response.
219. Plantinga, "Advice to Christian Philosophers," 297.
220. Plantinga and Robbins, "On Christian Philosophy," 618. Emphasis original.
221. Bahnsen, *Van Til's Apologetic*, 640–41.

the human intellect and its ability to make ultimate rational judgments. Christian philosophy denies that right; our intellect and rationality are derivative and dependent for their operation on the Christian God.

3.5.3 The Requirement for a Worldview Transcendental

That is, in Van Tillian terms, our "worldview" governs the overall semantic content of our discourse; our theological views derived from scripture alone will govern the boundaries in which our philosophy is constructed, which must also find its referent in scripture. Thus, Van Til argues you *cannot* have a Christian worldview without simultaneously outlining *both* a theology and a philosophy; he often emphasized you cannot talk about the individual facts of the world until you nailed down a philosophy of facts and have decided what "a fact" *is*.[222] To repeat, there is no neutral ground shared with the unbeliever where we may meet and use some authority that we both accept to resolve our differences, without subverting the authority of scripture. He was a philosophical theologian even if he was reticent in admitting it, preferring to be considered a purveyor of scriptural truths with a call to conversion throughout his work:

> From reading your first pages you make me out to be a philosopher. Well, I guess I am one of sorts, but you put everything in a better perspective by pointing out that even [in] my philosophizing . . . I am trying to bring out that only the biblical answer to this problem is the true answer.[223]

Without the Van Tillian *transcendental* Christian presupposition that belief in God is rationally defensible and provable from the impossibility of the contrary, there can be *no* philosophy that is logically sound. On a purely descriptive basis, this incongruity is witnessed to no better than in the history of twentieth-century philosophy where the meaning and formulation of autonomous and Godless philosophy has been recapitulated again and again. The logical positivist Otto Neurath posited the modern predicament this way:

> There is *no way to establish fully secured, neat protocol statements as starting points of the sciences. There is no tabula rasa. We are like sailors who have to rebuild their ship on the open sea, without*

---

222. This issue is examined at great length with reference to Van Til's work contrasted with other apologetic methods by Bahnsen, *Van Til's Apologetic*, ch. 8.
223. Van Til, "Response to R. J. Rushdoony," 348.

A CHRISTIAN CONCEPTION OF PHILOSOPHY

ever being able to dismantle it in dry-dock and reconstruct it from its best components. Only metaphysics can disappear without a trace. Imprecise "verbal clusters" [*Ballungen*] are somehow always part of the ship. . . . A new ship grows out of the old one, step by step—and while they are still building, the sailors may already be thinking of a new structure, and they will not always agree with one another. The whole business will go on in a way that we cannot even anticipate today. *That is our fate.*[224]

Cat in explicating Neurath summarized his skeptical cul-de-sac thus:

He denied any value to philosophy over and above the pursuit of work on science, within science and for science. *And science was not logically fixed, securely founded on experience nor was it the purveyor of any System of knowledge.* Uncertainty, decision and cooperation were intrinsic to it. From this naturalistic, holistic and pragmatist viewpoint, philosophy investigates the conditions of the possibility of science as apparent in science itself.[225]

We discern that philosophy had been understood as washed up on the shores of what Schaeffer insightfully calls "anti-philosophy":

Thus, we are left with two antiphilosophies in the world today. One is existentialism, which is an antiphilosophy because it deals with the big questions but with no rationality. If we follow [the alternative] it defines words using reason, [but] finally language leads to neither values nor facts. Language leads to language, and that is all. *It is not only the certainty of values that is gone, but the certainty of knowing.*[226]

Schaeffer was not the most thorough or systematic of apologists, drawing criticism from friend and foe alike, but though he could be wrong or inaccurate in the *details*, both Bahnsen[227] and Packer[228] rec-

---

224. Neurath, "Protocol Statements," 91–99; emphasis added; Neurath, "Foundations of the Social Sciences," 47.

225. Cat, "Otto Neurath." Emphasis added.

226. Schaeffer, *He Is There*, 315. Emphasis added.

227. Bahnsen, *Presuppositional Apologetics*, 241–60. Bahnsen here performs a critique of Schaeffer in which he demonstrates Schaeffer was inconsistent and incoherent in the details of his apologetic while respecting his general accomplishments: "For the most part he has done a better job of relating biblical Christianity to the whole of life. . . . Though what he has to say has not been thorough in any one area, all of his works suggest valuable insights with which no substantial difference need be taken" (*Presuppositional Apologetics*, 241).

228. Packer, "Francis A. Schaeffer," xi–xiv.

ognized the profound insight of his "broad strokes" into the modern malaise, even if their own program was substantially different from his. In short, unless we want to join the anti-philosophers who can know nothing and cannot state the basis on which a Nazi concentration camp guard should be condemned,[229] there is, of necessity, a requirement to articulate a transcendental basis for all philosophy. We argue that the transcendent authority claims of scripture are *legitimate* as a basis for providing the foundation of the Christian claims of knowledge. More generally, as we proceed in our analysis, we are able to demonstrate that *any* alternative worldview either fails the coherency test, contradicting its own basic propositions, or is shown to be borrowing intellectual capital from the Christian worldview in order to facilitate the criticism of the Christian worldview. This was succinctly expressed in three words by Cornelius Van Til, "atheism presupposes theism,"[230] and our next section aims to bring out the distinctiveness of this presuppositional approach.

3.5.4 Evidentialism and Rationalism

Van Til was credited with the "reformation of Christian apologetics"[231] by articulating a means of defending the faith that remained consistent with the faith itself, while avoiding fideism on the one hand and rejecting the appeal to a common intellectual ground between the believer and the unbeliever on the other. He is generally accepted to have originated a distinctive apologetic method during his career.[232] Significantly, Van Til broke categorically with the evidentialism and rationalism of Enlightenment apologetics that had come to be identified with Protestant orthodoxy, even within the conservative schools.

Traditionally, this model of apologetics had come to treat theology as a "science"[233] and was concerned with the "facts" of apologetics,

---

229. The postmodern pragmatist Richard Rorty pointedly refused to do this in interviews with sympathetic interviewers: "moral condemnation is too easy here" (Rorty, *Take Care of Freedom*, 96–103). Blackburn, one of the fiercest critics of Rorty on ethical grounds, asserted (politely) this demonstrated moral bankruptcy, in Blackburn, *Ruling Passions* and *Truth*.

230. Bahnsen, *Van Til's Apologetic*, 128–29. According to Bahnsen, who was taught by Van Til, he would challenge his students to unpack this aphoristic triplet to demonstrate that they had mastered the basic features of his apologetic philosophy.

231. Bahnsen, "Socrates or Christ," 191–240.

232. Edgar, Introduction to *Introduction to Systematic Theology*, 3 ff.

233. For example, see chapter 1, "On Method," in Charles Hodge, *Systematic*

e.g., the unaided reason of a man or woman should be able to evaluate "evidences" for God's operation in the world and by the shared human rational process be convinced by argumentation to a place of belief, vis-à-vis the "theistic proofs." Such an approach was implicitly based on a natural theology, suggesting a common ground was available to believers and unbelievers.

In other words, on this view, also known as the classical or Princetonian view, as facts could be considered "objective reality," the existence of God was *objectively provable*, with "facts" shared qualitatively and quantitatively between men and men, and between men and God; their meaning is in themselves, they are "brute facts."[234] Thus, apologetic philosophy provided the intellectual foundation or "the facts of" systematic theology;[235] a person *must* be convinced by rational arguments before he has sufficient warrant or obligation to believe. The last great Princeton theologian, B. B. Warfield (1851–1921), argued against his peer, the great Dutch theologian Abraham Kuyper (1837–1920) (who had posited an antithesis between believer and non-believer resulting in two distinct sciences), that a person *could* start from an unbelieving, autonomous science and be convinced with rational argument to surrender to the "truth" of those arguments and *then* relinquish their intellectual autonomy.[236]

On Van Til's view, which at this level accepts the basic presupposition of Kuyper in direct contradiction to the Warfieldian school, systematic theology lays the intellectual foundation for apologetics. As we posited in the previous section, philosophy is built not just upon the scriptures but *with* the scriptures; it uses a different language than theology and might

---

Theology, first published 1845. The treatment of "theology as a science" suggests presuppositions based upon Enlightenment humanist thought rather than Reformation thought. Alister McGrath, *Passion for Truth*, engages in a lengthy analysis of the domination of Enlightenment thought within the Old Princeton, and Barr pours caustic, ill-tempered scorn on Warfield for the "architectonic confidence in reason" (Barr, *Fundamentalism*, 272).

234. Rushdoony, *Van Til and the Limits of Reason*, loc. 234.
235. Bahnsen, "Socrates or Christ," 191–240.
236. Bahnsen, *Van Til, B B Warfield, and Abraham Kuyper*. The interrelation between these men and how Van Til reconciled their apparently opposing positions with a novel synthesis is explored in detail in an accessible fashion. Most of the material in this presentation is also found in written form in Bahnsen's "Socrates or Christ." It is unclear whether the essay was updated in the later edition before Bahnsen's death in 1995; there are some indications the text as whole was updated for the reprinted edition.

engage a different audience, but it is not discontinuous with theology. Thus, Van Til asserted:

> Philosophy, as usually defined, deals with a theory of reality, with a theory of knowledge, and with a theory of ethics. That is to say, philosophies usually undertake to present a life-and-world view. They deal not only with that which man can directly experience by means of his senses but also . . . *with the presuppositions of experience* . . . . Christian theology deals not only with God; *it deals also with the world. It would be quite impossible then to state and vindicate a truly Christian theology without also stating and defending—be it in a broad outline only—a Christian philosophy.*[237]

To emphasize, Warfield had asserted the *exact* opposite—you establish the authority of the scriptures on a *common* rational basis with the unbeliever ("right reason") and that persuades the unbeliever to surrender their rational autonomy.

However, the implication of this position is that *any* type of *proven* discrepancy (or new research) might invalidate the entire corpus; "a proved error in Scripture contradicts not only our doctrine, but the Scripture claims and, therefore, its inspiration in making these claims,"[238] an inductive generalization which has at its heart a logical fallacy if for no other reason that it is an *inductive* generalization for which there can be no logical necessity.[239] However, that is a technical discussion, and there is a more basic, theological reason as to why the Warfieldian view is un-Christian which we shall examine next.

3.5.5 The Impossibility of "Right Reason" and "Common Ground"

Van Til's transcendental critique of Warfield and Kuyper and his resulting synthesis had the following key characteristics:

---

237. Van Til, *Christian Apologetics*, 55–56. Emphasis added.
238. Hodge and Warfield, "Inspiration," 245.
239. How Warfield attempted to avoid this critical weakness was by asserting it was not possible to prove any error was present in the autograph (because we did not have the autographs), it had been introduced in the copying process—a novel inversion of the text-critical principle. See Macneil, "Scripture and the Post-Darwinian Controversy," for a discussion.

a. He accepted Warfield's basic position that Christianity was *objectively* provable, and that people were not being rational when they rejected it.

b. He accepted Kuyper's basic position that the believers and unbelievers created two types of science because of their antithetical principles which produces two opposing theories of knowledge; the unbeliever was vain in their reasoning and was not able to understand the things of God's Spirit or his Word. The scripture had to be accepted with its self-attesting authority and a worldview was built upon it. There was no neutral, "common ground" on which both could meet and sort out their differences.

c. However, Kuyper's conclusion from his principle, that apologetic discussion between believers and unbelievers was therefore impossible because there were two, *different*, rationalities, was rejected by Van Til.[240]

d. He accepted with Warfield that Christianity was the *only* rational position (for to deny the Christian worldview would collapse into skepticism and irrationality) but he denied that Warfield was warranted to state that the *means* of attaining rational certainty was through the "right reason" of the unbelieving person. This was because this principle would have had the implication that "right reason" had to be satisfied at *any* point of objection in the future, the actions of Christ in scripture were only to be validated once "right reason" has been satisfied.

e. In contrast to Warfield, he insisted that it was the *impossibility* of right reason because of the sinfulness of the human condition that provided our strongest transcendental argument for the necessity of the self-attesting nature of the scriptures and the call to repentance within them. This reversed the inference of Kuyper; apologetic argument was not excluded but became necessary, the sinful person was incapable of right reason (of being rational) as long as they continued in their rebellion, they *destroyed* rationality.

f. He concluded then, by accepting both Warfield's and Kuyper's basic propositions but rejecting their conclusions as fallacious.

---

240. It should also be noted that though Kuyper *formally* rejected apologetics, he nevertheless, in practice, engaged in a rigorous defense, regeneration, and application of Christian thought to the wider culture as evidenced in his *Lectures* (1898).

Van Til's position was that the noetic effects of sin made Warfield's position untenable and inconsistent with Warfield's own Calvinistic theological work on the noetic consequences of sin. It also highlighted Kuyper's conclusion did not follow because *only* the Christian position could be considered fully rational, and any use of rational argument meant the unbeliever was importing assumptions possible only on the Christian worldview. In summary, Van Til is asserting that it was possible to be objectively certain of Christian claims (with Warfield, contra Kuyper) though this was only possible on a *transcendental* basis because believers and unbelievers create distinct sciences (contra Warfield with Kuyper).

Van Til thus offered the convincing proof that it was systematic theology that had to lay the foundations for philosophy and apologetic philosophy, "by asserting a separation between philosophy and theology, you are destroying the foundations of philosophy."[241] The natural person was not capable of applying their reason and climbing up to God; thus, Plantinga also: "it is hard to avoid the conclusion that natural theology does not provide a satisfactory answer to the question. . . . Is it rational to believe in God?"[242] The implications of Van Til and Plantinga here are that an evidential apologetic is methodologically deficient to resolve issues as to the status of theistic belief and the nature of God; the transcendental approach is the *only* one that remains. Thus, we can recognize that Roman Catholic and Arminian evidentialist apologetics, which assert there is a neutral, common ground where believer and unbeliever can meet, i.e., a zone free of theological or philosophical presuppositions, is untenable. We instead recognize that the impossibility of right reason and, as argued in previous sections, the theory-laden imperatives of a worldview would never permit an argument to be constructed that would satisfy both the atheological and the theological requirements for a common starting point.[243]

So, in summary, if we were to be asked, "Why do you feel no obligation to only appeal to beliefs shared by nearly what common sense and contemporary science dictate? Do you not understand that philosophy and theology deal with differentiated domains of reality?" We should no longer feel embarrassment if we have followed the arguments of this work into epistemological self-consciousness. The differentiation is a naturalist mist that evaporates as the sun rises. The very structure of the world and reality on the Christian worldview is assumed in the atheological

---

241. See Van Til, *Christian Apologetics* (2nd ed.), 56n1.
242. Plantinga, *God and Other Minds*.
243. Plantinga, *Knowledge and Christian Belief*, x.

questioning and renders the question incoherent by assuming a logical structure derived from a worldview it wants to refute. The "differentiated domains" are not *metaphysically* differentiated; they are different spheres of reality rightly considered as having their own modalities, but primarily merely functionally differentiated and linguistically separated for meaningful discourse.

3.5.6 Plantinga and Van Til on Apologetics—Contrast and Confluence

As we have noted in the introduction to this section, the strong claim of Van Til is made even more controversial because some Christian philosophers sympathetic to Plantinga have been extremely dismissive of Van Til. It should also be noted that Plantinga himself only mentions Van Til once in what is considered his most important apologetic work, and this is only to indicate the common parody of Van Til's epistemology that states "those that do not know God . . . don't really have any knowledge at all."[244] Yet this is not Van Til's point at all, and we can only assume Plantinga has not read Van Til in any depth (if at all). Van Til's point was that if the unbelievers lived *consistently* with their stated presuppositions, they could have no knowledge, but they *do not*, for they assume logic, causality, and coherence (however inconsistently) and borrow intellectual capital from the believer's Christian worldview to make sense of the world. Rather paradoxically, the context in which Plantinga quotes Van Til is in the course of making an argument that is substantially similar to Van Til's argument and the conclusion is *also* similar; we do not *know* as we ought, either things or ourselves without the foundation of a Christian worldview:

> But if we don't know there is such a person as God, we don't know the first thing (the most important thing) about ourselves, each other, and our world . . . because . . . the most important truths about us and them is that we have been created by the Lord and utterly depend upon him for our continued existence.[245]

We can mitigate the conflict further by recognizing that there could hardly be a greater contrast in their respective methods and their vocabulary which lends itself to the obfuscation of Van Til's views when approached with an analytical philosopher's perspective. On this basis,

---

244. Plantinga, *Warranted Christian Belief*, 217.
245. Plantinga, *Warranted Christian Belief*, 217.

some have even refused to recognize Van Til as a philosopher[246] with very little willingness to work through Van Til's language that is reminiscent of idealism. Van Til also writes on occasions where it is clear English was not his first language, was rather unsystematic in presentation,[247] and can assume a lot of philosophical knowledge in his readers which can make his presentations seem obscure or overly compact. As we have already noted, he also had a penchant for using terms which had a long history in philosophy but with a distinct sense that frequently caused misinterpretation of his views.[248] However, this hostility I believe obscures an otherwise great and neglected concord between the positions, and it is in the understanding and explication of their concord which helps us progress in epistemological self-consciousness.

Firstly, we have already seen a similar conception of the role and practice of philosophy that it should be *Christian* not just as some kind of end but in method and premise. Secondly, we have already seen how Plantinga had disarmed his *philosophical* opponents by considering their arguments and invalidating them on their own terms. Thirdly, Anderson makes the important assessment of the concord between their work while recognizing the distinctiveness, but he notes that it is in the transcendental direction of some of Plantinga's arguments where his apologetic force was greatest and where he approximates to the method of Van Til.[249] Consequently, we will concentrate increasingly from this point onward on the distinctiveness of Van Til's transcendental and presuppositional

---

246. William Lane Craig was a case in point. Anderson, "Cornelius Van Til and Plantinga," outlines this controversy. John Frame, a former student of Van Til, now full professor, took issue with Craig over that assertion and it is a strange one; Van Til was recognized as an exceptional student by the noted metaphysician A. A. Bowman (then professor of logic), who offered him a graduate scholarship at Princeton. He studied Christian philosophy under Jellema (as Plantinga did) and was awarded a PhD in philosophy.

247. That is, many of his works were broad in scope and intent giving the impression for the uninitiated that they lacked focus. There were some notable exceptions to this criticism, both of his works dealing with neo-orthodoxy (1946/1974) are recognized by friends and foes alike as systematic and rigorous critiques.

248. It was precisely these considerations that inspired Bahnsen to write his commentary and guide to Van Til; see *Van Til*, xvii ff. Butler, *Bahnsen*, gives firsthand testimony of conversations on this issue. The most explosive misinterpretation of Van Til was what he meant by "analogical reasoning"—for his detractors this was a retreat into irrationality; for Van Til it was a recognition of the qualitative difference in the quality of thinking between creator and creature. This was quite a different sense than how it had been previously used.

249. Anderson, "If Knowledge Then God," 25–27.

A CHRISTIAN CONCEPTION OF PHILOSOPHY

apologetic approach as integral to epistemological self-consciousness, only mentioning Plantinga in revision and where we notice a confluence or contrast between their views.

3.6 Summary and Conclusion

We began this chapter by considering the specifics of the philosophical categories we had established as the basis of our research in the previous chapters: metaphysics, epistemology, and ethics. First, we considered first metaphysics, the theory of reality, and noted how it had frequently become speculative, obscure, and distant from sensible accounts of the universe; we contrasted such accounts with the scientifically oriented metaphysics. We acknowledged that metaphysics was important to ground and give philosophy a context; we noted how significant intellectual movements had denigrated metaphysics to seek a scientific view of reality but had collapsed into a scientistic view, rarefying vast swathes of human experience as meaningless or in having emotive meaning only. We noted that the social consequence of the denial of meaning or purpose in the universe was that of social dissipation, eroticism, and nihilism; we noted it was "science" freed from metaphysical moorings that had provided the rationale for the totalitarian variations of Nazism and Communism, noting that naturalistic science could provide no critique of such brutality. We contrasted this with the experience of a survivor of Auschwitz who argued that a metaphysical awareness of one's purpose and value was the essence of being and becoming even when confronted with the worst of humanity and the worst of existence. We then concluded that metaphysics was essential in providing both an ethical and interpretative framework for science and by providing organizing categories and transcendentals for human experience generally.

We then examined epistemology as the theory of knowledge. We clarified our terminology around what we understand by "belief," "fact," "evidence," and "truth" as these are central to most theories of knowledge. We noted that both Quine and Kuhn as the most influential of the twentieth-century philosophers of science had argued for the theory-laden nature of these concepts that reflected an interconnected web, constituting a worldview concept. Such a concept becomes useful to us as the basis for a key element of our own epistemology, but we examined in some detail as to why their naturalism was untenable. It was demonstrated as self-vitiating as a theory of knowledge by considering its various dependencies on tautological evolutionary thought, physicalism, and induction. We noted their conclusions were relativistic, scientifically in the case of Quine and sociologically in the case of Kuhn because they lacked a metaphysical basis, and a skeptic could reject them as arbitrary. We then revisited this issue of skepticism and by identifying that skepticism was predominantly psychological in character, that permitted us to largely mute its central claims. We recognized we need to wait for a future chapter on transcendentalism to expunge it more fully at a logical level, but we introduced the transcendental *vocabulary* at the pertinent point which allowed us to map out the contours of our theory of knowledge as a practical imperative.

We examined why the Platonic Justified True Belief (JTB) thesis was inadequate as a theory of knowledge and how it must be supplemented and reconstituted using a concept named *warrant*. Whereas justification in the JTB thesis was internalistic, Plantinga argued that warrant was externalistic, derived from proper functioning faculties in a conducive epistemic environment, following a design plan, aimed at truth. By refining and improving upon the Reidian basis of this thought, he demonstrated convincingly that Christian knowledge claims will have warrant *if* they are true; but we noted that Plantinga considered it beyond the capability of philosophy to demonstrate that truth to the satisfaction of all parties. We noted that Plantinga, although providing a naturalistic account of warrant, admitted that only assuming the Christian metaphysic would validate the truth claim. In response, we then considered Butler's criticism of Plantinga's terminus as inadequate as a *Christian* theory of knowledge, concluding at best that it was theistic, and how he posits that we need to move beyond Plantinga's theory of knowledge into the theory outlined by Van Til to demonstrate that Christian knowledge claims are *necessarily* true. Yet, despite this final dissonance between the theories, we noted that to a large degree there was substantial agreement between the two, the apparent difference being mitigated to a large degree by the distinct aims and methodologies of the philosophers; Plantinga was an analyst dealing with detailed arguments and demonstrating the inadequacies of their logical underpinnings, while Van Til was a transcendentalist dealing with worldviews and general principles of coherence.

We noted that Van Til proposed the way forward was to consider the issues of factuality, evidence, warrant, and justification in a transcendental manner using a transcendent transcendental framework. Thus, we find

A CHRISTIAN CONCEPTION OF PHILOSOPHY

that both Van Til and Plantinga posit the essential and central role that the Christian conception of God must play in our epistemological self-consciousness, providing a context for those definitions that the skeptic could only refute by implicit self-contradiction. Both men could thus be seen as emphasizing the same metaphysical context and concluding that the failure of human thought was an ethical failure. We then considered more broadly the topic of ethics as a theory of value, focusing on the interconnections and interdependencies with our metaphysical and epistemological position. We noted the centrality of the scriptures and emphasized the commentary within the scriptures on the principles stated in the Commandments which provided an overall theonomical context for our worldview. The important conclusion was that theonomy remained of central importance as a basis for ethics in a Christian worldview.

We noted in our discussion of worldview that the Christian philosopher operated in a Christian context and was perfectly warranted in approaching philosophical issues from a Christian perspective rather than limited to using presuppositions that were universally shared by all or by nearly all involved in the debate. Both Van Til and Plantinga recognized the incommensurable nature of worldviews and that there is not *necessarily* neutral epistemological ground upon which we can meet opponents and engage in a Socratic dialogue. We found Van Til was far stronger than Plantinga here, asserting that transcendental logic *requires* the Christian worldview if human predication is to be intelligible at all; systematic theology had to lay the foundation for apologetic philosophy and not vice versa. This was understood as a restatement of the Augustinian assumption of the priority of faith in the faith-reason debate. We noted how Van Til's position was a synthesis between the Warfieldian and Kuyperian accounts, with him accepting their basic insights but rejecting their final conclusions as fallacious. It was possible to be objectively certain of Christian claims (with Warfield, contra Kuyper) though this was only possible on a transcendental basis because believers and unbelievers create distinct sciences (contra Warfield with Kuyper).

Thus, in the positive sense, we have argued in this chapter that Christian worldview philosophy *is* epistemologically self-conscious *by definition*. You cannot have a comprehensive knowledge of the world unless you can give a general account of the world both in terms of its objects, the relationships between them and the moral imperatives to which they are subject. There is an implicit coordination and interdependence between our metaphysics, our epistemology, and our ethics. This has been recognized within the secular academy by naturalists such as Quine and Kuhn who argued in the context of a holistic theory of nature. As Ó Murchadha also argues, anything short of a complete account *on its own terms* is no account at all because it defers in the final analysis to an external source of authority to validate it.[250] *Christian* worldview philosophy must be articulated and defended in a manner consistent with the presuppositions of Christianity conceived of as its normative, scriptural tenets.

Both Plantinga and Van Til agree that *unless* philosophy is done on a Christian basis, it ceases to be authentic or coherent because it can give no rational justification for its own foundation; that is, its *worldview* is transcendentally the foundation for its coherence. Thus, in the next three chapters we examine in more detail the transcendentalist basis of a truly Christian philosophy by considering transcendentalism in general, identifying how Christian presuppositions shape a distinctively Christian transcendentalism, and then give precise expression to the Van Tillian transcendental argument for God.

250. Ó Murchadha, *Phenomenology of Christian Life*, preface.

4

Beyond Anti-Philosophy to Transcendentalism

4.1 Transcendentalism—First Remarks

WE SEEM TO BE confronted with a most basic philosophical problem that has become increasingly into focus whether we approach the problem from a naturalist direction as in Quine and Kuhn or seek an authentically Christian philosophy through Plantinga and Van Til. It appears we can only cogently argue when we posit a worldview or, following Wittgenstein, a distinct "form of life"[1] which defines our terms and gives us semantic content. However, therein lies the philosophical problems, "on its own terms" or a "form of life" have been attacked as synonyms for "circular" reasoning or "fideism"[2] when applied to religious or spiritual

---

1. This is one of the most famous of the themes that emerges in Wittgenstein's *Philosophical Investigations*. It is often mistaken for cultural relativism in that it is taken to argue for the circumscription of a community based on shared linguistic use and convention. Similarly, it is often appropriated by postmodernists to deny the possibility of objective reference. However, in my view, these are appropriations of Wittgenstein's work in support of their own programs rather than it being something argued for by Wittgenstein himself, illustrated in that there was an enormous debate over the "meaning" of what he was in fact arguing (or describing), particularly in light of Kripke's interpretation in *Naming and Necessity*. This matter arises again in our future discussion. See McGinn, *Wittgenstein*, for a short, accessible, and well received introduction to the *Investigations*. See also Macneil, "Wittgenstein," for a broader discussion of Wittgenstein and religious language.

2. Fideism can be broadly conceived of in two main ways: either that subjective

thought. Part of the task of this chapter is to understand this charge of circularity and to refute it. Similarly, we will assert that circularity does not imply relativism for a correctly articulated Christian philosophy.

That is, both these objections are shown to evaporate as problems when circularity is correctly understood. First, we understand that all *argumentation* is circular because it is assuming that rationality itself is *rational* (or reasonable); it cannot *proceed* on any other basis. That is, there is a *transcendental* assumption about the nature of reason which we must implicitly acknowledge to engage in debate, and we must consequently make this explicit by giving a basic articulation and defense of rationality and the necessity of the transcendental framework if we are to salvage rationality from postmodern relativism.

Our transcendental vision of reason is most immediately associated with Kant and his *Critique of Pure Reason*, where he posits as *transcendental* that which makes possible, or which must be assumed when we claim knowledge of objects. While we reject the details of his solution[3] and deny that his transcendental deduction deduced sufficient transcendental principles,[4] we concur with his asking of that question. Our major task will be to map out the character of reason, the transcendental category and defend this conception to provide the groundwork for its application in our particular Christian context.

---

experience rather than objective reason justifies religious belief (or even denies rational expression is possible in principle); or that a belief can only be understood within a believing community that uses language in a particular way and shares a form of life. The former might be considered characteristic of the Kierkegaardian "leap of faith" and the latter as the basis for the famous dispute in the philosophy of religion between Wittgensteinian and Christian thinker D. Z. Phillips and atheist Kai Nielsen found in *Wittgensteinian Fideism*. Phillips disagreed strongly with Plantinga (and Van Til) on the nature of Christian philosophy (see Phillips, "Advice"), arguing there *was* a philosophical mode of thought available to *all* philosophers.

3. It is worth noting that for Kant, a *transcendental* argument *always* terminated in a category of the understanding. This is not necessarily the case with modern transcendental arguments and was the subject of an ill-tempered debate; see §6.3.4.

4. A humorous meme exemplifies this well. Hume: *science is just a habit of the mind, there is no causal necessity.* Kant: *I can save science and causality, it is a habit of the mind, we necessarily think in the way we do* (Bahnsen, *History of Philosophy*, tape 29). Much ink has been spilled over whether Kant did in fact answer Hume and, besides that, what precisely Kant meant on his own terms. Plantinga, "On Christian Scholarship," noted that the polyvalency of Kant was "part of his charm." Similarly, Scruton, in *Kant*, notes he "took sides" in his discussion in response to the opacity of Kant.

4.2 Transcendentalism and Skepticism

Transcendentalism has a most unusual and welcome side-effect for our war against skepticism. Consider one who *argues* as a thorough-going Humean skeptic argues that we can have no reasonable basis for reason and therefore we have no obligation to behave reasonably. By doing a transcendental critique we can dismiss this argument as incoherent because on its own basis there can be no basis for drawing that conclusion, i.e., it is assuming to be correct by the action of arguing what it is trying to show *by* the argument to be false. This was the radical approach of neo-Kantian Strawson in the early 1960s who revived interest in the nature of transcendental arguments and what could be proved with them. Their most attractive feature to philosophers at that time was this potential to be skepticism refuting in a post-positivistic climate that was antagonistic to the possibility of strong knowledge claims.

As an illustrative example, Wittgenstein *argued* and argued *transcendentally* against the possibility of a "Private Language" *because* he argued that "language" *always* assumes a communal context.[5] This is one of the clearest examples of the form and promise of the transcendental mode of argument where you move from a premise that is commonly accepted (even by the skeptic) to the oftentimes fiercely disputed general principle that rests behind it (or better, that is logically necessary to it) and that you want to establish (contra the skeptic). In this case, we also get a sense of the broad character and scope of the conclusion, it is a *general* principle rather than a logical deduction, an inductive or abductive inference of the same basic character as the premise(s). This is another distinctive of the truly transcendental argument, it is a principle with broad application to the world and its conclusion is categorically distinct from its premises.[6]

---

5. It was notable, owing to Wittgenstein's phenomenological, anti-theoretical approach to philosophy, that in this section of the *Investigations* he proceeded to *argue* and presented a complex, transcendental argument. However, not all have been impressed by it; Plantinga describes it as "weak" and in a new preface to his *God and Other Minds* notes that he would now spend much less time defending himself against Wittgensteinian criticisms. In this era of artificial languages (particularly computer programming languages) we might see Plantinga's point; though we should also recognize that these languages are very different from spoken languages, which is what Wittgenstein had in mind.

6. There are arguments which are said to take the "form" of a transcendental argument but are not full transcendental arguments; see §7.3.3.

There is much more to be said regarding transcendentalism but for our purposes now it enables us to *prima facie* posit that reason *is* reasonable and we can in principle offer some basic analysis and defense of reason, rationality, and some further mitigations of the skeptical challenge. This is pertinent for us as it helps us to appreciate how it is both possible to understand alleged worldviews or "forms of life" on their own terms yet subject them to transcendental critique to evaluate them for coherence and correspondence. This is our defense against relativism, we acknowledge their "circularity" and any transcendental claims to be justifying human predication as *prima facie* legitimate, while subsequently subjecting them to an internal critique on their own terms and judging them to be illegitimate as truly transcendental.

4.3 Practical and Theoretical Reason

Most obviously, we understand that the concept of reason itself is only made cogent by having a commitment to it both in its theoretical and practical operations.[7] In broad strokes, "theoretical" reasoning is what we employ when we are dealing with reason as a tool of analysis and theorizing; "practical" reasoning is dealing with moral reasoning, i.e., deciding between right and wrong. At this point, by considering the integral role of the whole of reason with respect to life and living, we are fully confronted with its role as fundamental and basic to existing and living in the world; this surely arrests the skeptical challenge to the epistemological legitimacy and importance of a non-skeptical orientation to reason.[8]

That is, we are positing rationality (acting in accordance with reason) is an inevitable and an ethically commendable state of affairs; it is to be *preferred* over the irrational and the immoral. Ethical theorists such as Baier (who during the 1960s was influential in arresting the slide into relativism in moral philosophy[9]) and Blackburn in the postmodern epoch[10] offer a vigorous account of rationality and argue passionately

---

7. See Baier, *Rational*, ch. 1, for an explanation of the terms "theoretical" and "practical" reasoning.

8. We might still argue about its metaphysical status—there is a difference to what our theory says about the world (noting Quine's "any of various") and the way the world *is*, but we must defer that question to later sections.

9. Baier, *Rational* and *Moral* are generally considered landmarks in moral philosophy.

10. Blackburn, *Ruling Passions*. Blackburn was known for his direct confrontation

BEYOND ANTI-PHILOSOPHY TO TRANSCENDENTALISM

that there are such a thing as moral truths, which are what we *ought* to do as rational beings. This is often cogent writing in response to the denial of the possibility of moral knowledge and so should be welcomed. However, we have reason to be concerned. Baier and Blackburn after a lifetime of reflection give us these defenses of rationality and ethical imperatives respectively:

> "What are the capacities, powers, and abilities involved in having reason, in being a rational being?" The answer is that we cannot (at least, as yet) say, in any physiological, or other precise empirical terminology, wherein that capacity consists... full rationality consists in the ability to perform the various activities of reason, involving the use of the various appropriate types of reasons in accordance with the relevant procedures of reasoning.[11]

> Systemisation should stop in theory just as it does in proper living. So what we need is not elaborate codifications and deductions.... Persons on different mountains need not perturb us ... unless they can show that they are where we ought to be. But to show that they must do some ethics.... That is how it is, and how it must be.[12]

Both of these passages seem to have linguistic scaffolding that is relying on what they were trying to argue that is narrow enough to make us consider whether there are logical fallacies at the center of these conceptions. The definitions are in terms of related words—rather like looking in a dictionary to find a definition of science as "that which follows the scientific method," and the next question is naturally, "What is the scientific method?"; you then look at the definition of scientific method and find "the method that is in accordance with science." At best, we have a "miserable tautology" and at worst we are logically fallacious.

However, being charitable, we *want* to agree with Blackburn against the postmodern relativist, and with Baier we *want* to believe there is a singular moral point of view and we want to legitimately maintain with Blackburn that a concentration camp guard who tortures *is* culpable.[13]

---

with the postmodern pragmatism and ethical relativism argued by Richard Rorty and is considered to have made a substantial contribution to practical, i.e., ethical reasoning.

11. Baier, *Rational*, 53.

12. Blackburn, *Ruling Passions*, 310.

13. As mentioned previously, Blackburn had taken great exception to Rorty's equivocation on this point and, while respecting Rorty's erudition, offers a full-bodied, meticulous critique. Apart from when Blackburn encounters religious thought, he is

Both recognize there is "something" we want to recognize as reason and rationality, but their circularity still makes us instinctively uneasy, because their naturalist conceptions fail to offer an objective grounding. When pushed at this point of ambiguity they have no authority claim but convention or some other social basis as a grounding, and that is precisely the point at issue for the postmodern skeptic: "morality is socially constructed, and I reject the tyranny of its totalizing metanarrative!" The skeptic can sneer thus, and the relativist retains a smug sense of satisfaction.

However, there is not necessarily a need to construe this terminus as destructively circular and then re-surrender to skeptical doubt. Rather we remind ourselves of the impossibility of a neutral vantage point to view our problem that we considered in the previous chapter, and we must recognize that there are limits to where the theorizing can take us before we are making a commitment that might fail the rigors of an alleged "neutral" standard to judge against. In fact, we can see that this claim to "neutrality" is now seen to be completely empty; at a certain level in our reasoning claims, what we might call *ultimate authority*, we (and our opponent) are assuming the authority of what we are arguing for as we argue for it, so there is no external, neutral ground upon which we can meet; that is, we have begun to argue by presupposition and *transcendentally*, whether well or poorly. This is another characteristic that Kant considered unique to the transcendental mode of argument: *it makes possible its own proof.*

Thus, the transcendental approach, in important aspects, is a general epistemological and methodological position, not a specifically Christian one. Both Quine and Neurath[14] wanted to appeal to the "whole of science" as the ultimate authority (or transcendental) and did not consider it *destructively* circular, though they openly acknowledged its circularity. Thus, *we* should be well within our epistemic rights to legitimately adopt a similar framework and claim equal philosophical respectability. Except,

---

painfully meticulous and fair in his argument; with religious thought he inexplicably seems to jettison his careful and considered method.

14. Neurath's conception of knowledge was far more dynamic and fluid (as seen in his famous raft metaphor) than many of his positivist peers and is perhaps best considered as a weaker, mitigated skeptical view when compared to Schlick. In his later period especially, he did not believe in a normative conception of science based on a set of "true" propositions as was favored by many positivists. He was much more akin to the pragmatist or instrumentalist, "solve our problems" approach to science. Consequently, his conception of science is rather a rarefied one, which is why we have favored Quine in our discussion, who though an empiricist was a sophisticated one and was not a positivist.

as noted in our earliest analysis, our definition of "science" is comprehensive and our belief in a natural law is not an aggregation of brute fact with the passing of time but reflects the providence of God. We posit a *transcendent* transcendental of the triune God that rationally justifies these transcendentals of nature. Let us examine this issue more closely and see how this analogous approach is justified in principle and practice.

4.4 Worldviews and Ultimate Authority

We have already encountered in our previous discussion at various points the philosopher Quine who was one of the most influential of the "scientific" philosophers of the second half of the twentieth century, famous first for his refutation of logical positivism and then for the construction of a rigorous naturalism that favored a behavioristic interpretation of the knowledge construction process. In formulating his philosophy, Quine summarized his methodology thus: "the answer to any scientific question must come from within science itself—it is the whole of science that is constitutive of knowledge."[15] However, imagine repositing the proposition thus: "the answer to any question regarding the status of Christian belief must be answered from within the revelation of the scriptures—it is the whole of scripture and only scripture that is constitutive of Christian knowledge." Now, to assert the latter would immediately raise fierce accusations of "circularity" and "question begging," not least from within the evidentialist Christian theological community and open derision from the secular "scientific" community.[16]

However, we have already seen that Quine recognized the *circularity* of his position but was unfazed by it—it was a *necessary* interpretative principle of his naturalistic worldview: *if* his proposition regarding the whole of science was correct, the answer *must*, necessarily, be from within science.[17] It is functioning as a *transcendental* in the sense it is making

---

15. Quine, *Theories and Things*, 21.

16. As perhaps found in Richard Dawkins's *A Scientist's Case Against God*, an edited version of his speech at the Edinburgh International Science Festival on April 15, 1992, published in *The Independent*, April 20, 1992.

17. It is also worth noting that Quine's conception of "science" was broad. He attaches scientific status to any statement that makes a contribution, no matter how slight, to a theory that can be tested through prediction; see Quine, *Pursuit of Truth*, 20. This correlates well with the argument I presented earlier that the distance between science and philosophy, philosophy and theology, narrows (if it can be said to exist at all) on close inspection.

possible the objects of knowledge.[18] Thus, for Quine it was appropriate to naturalize *philosophy* by making it contiguous with science and thus amenable to a naturalization of first ontology, then epistemology, and finally ethics.[19] The scope of his principle really was the entire account of reality interpreted within the interlocking presuppositions that formed his worldview:

> All ascription of reality must come from within one's theory of the world; it is incoherent otherwise.... Truth is immanent, and there is no higher. We must speak from within a theory, albeit any of various.[20]

For example, Quine in response to a critical essay over normative ethical judgments asserted:

> Naturalization of epistemology does not jettison the normative and settle for the *indiscriminate* description of ongoing procedures ... normative epistemology is a branch of engineering. It is the technology of truth-seeking.[21]

There could be no more a consistent naturalist than Quine to ascribe moral questions as a matter of *engineering*,[22] yet the question remains how he decided what is "indiscriminate" in ethical reasoning. Quine's answer was that the normative was a description of what was with respect to some "terminal condition" and offers the solution to the normative ethical problem as requiring "[viewing the terminal condition] as aimed at reward in heaven."[23] We can hear the hallelujah chorus as all the Christians say "Amen"! Of course, he is stating this not by way of a newly found religious commitment because of the relentless march

---

18. It is another matter as to whether that claim could be *sustained* under critique; our position will be that the only transcendental claim that can be sustained will be the Christian transcendental claim.

19. Two of the most famous essays are "Ontological Relativity" and "Epistemology Naturalized," both in Quine, *Ontological Relativity*, and a third, "On What There Is," originally published in 1948 with minor modifications to the version published in *From a Logical Point of View*. Quine wrote very little on ethics, following broadly the contours of Schlick, *Problems of Ethics*, in his "On the Nature of Moral Values." The latter is interesting for the interaction of White and Quine's response in the same volume.

20. Quine, *Theories and Things*, 21.

21. In response to White, "Normative Ethics, Normative Epistemology," 664-65. Emphasis added.

22. This is reminiscent in some respects of the "moral calculus" of Jeremy Bentham (1748-1832); see Macneil, "Moral Calculus."

23. In response to White, "Normative Ethics, Normative Epistemology," 665.

BEYOND ANTI-PHILOSOPHY TO TRANSCENDENTALISM

of apologetic logic, but as *a* possible solution to the normativity problem in ethics which he is effectively asserting will yield no solution by the same process we decide on "normativity" in the other parts of nature. Thus, it is difficult to see how a thoroughgoing naturalism can ever be anything more than arbitrary in any criterion it furnishes to *judge* an ongoing procedure of life, for that very act of judging (as Quine's final words of response demonstrated) imports in non-natural conceptions.

Yet Quine goes even further for us in providing the criteria for validating a particular view of the world:

> What if, happily and unbeknownst, we have achieved a theory that is conformable to every possible observation, past and future? In what sense could the world then be said to deviate from what the theory claims? Clearly in none . . . [our theory demands] only that it be structured [to assure us what] to expect.[24]

This is his characteristic recourse to the legitimacy of theories on the basis of their empirical equivalence regardless of their ultimate truth value[25] (though, importantly, Quine maintained there *was* such a state as *true*), but in context Quine is concerned in making both ontological and epistemological (and by implication ethical) claims. Eyebrows might certainly be raised accusing Quine of the latter, and he indeed calls it "unaccustomed territory"[26] but it is noteworthy that like Blackburn he does not endorse a neutral pluralism in the public square:

> The *proper* counsel is not one of pluralistic tolerance. One's disapproval of gratuitous torture, for example, easily withstands one's failure to make a causal reduction, and so be it. We can still call the good good and the bad bad, and hope.[27]

Thus, when Van Til takes his ultimate authority as scripture, arguing that the answer to any problem must be found from within the worldview ascribed by scripture, he argues essentially in a methodologically manner analogous to Quine. Similarly, when Van Til asserts that

---

24. Quine, *Theories and Things*, 22.

25. See Churchland and Hooker, *Images of Science*, for the substance of this debate, focused on the "constructive empiricism" of Bas C. van Fraassen. He authors a lengthy reply to ten critical essays.

26. Quine, *Theories and Things*, preface.

27. Quine, "On the Nature of Moral Values," 64–65, emphasis added; see also White's review and Quine's reply for an indication that he recognized an "ultimacy" for moral judgments that sat legitimately apart from scientific objectivity.

there are no such things as brute, uninterpreted facts,[28] he is perfectly within his Quinean granted epistemic rights; he is merely articulating his theory of the world: "Factuality like gravitation and electric charge, is internal to our theory of nature."[29] Similarly, we can with Van Til, assert our ontological, epistemological, and ethical claims and be perfectly confident that our theory of the world corresponds and coheres with reality as we perceive and conceive of it. We are merely articulating our view of the world and find that we too can call the "good good and the bad bad."

However, where Quine stumbles over moral commitments as matters of blind hope in Darwinian chance we differ, in that because we have the transcendental of a transcendent God, we have a normative basis which we claim as *objective*—where objective is posited as in concordance with this mind of God. The challenge in our following sections will be to substantiate that claim and demonstrate that our transcendental is the only valid one that facilitates a coherent worldview.

4.5 All Reasoning Is "Circular Reasoning" but Not All Reasoning Is "Viciously Circular"

So, in summary of the argument above, no one informed enough to understand Quine's argument would accuse him of being logically fallacious, drawing a conclusion for a syllogistic argument while assuming the conclusion in a premise, i.e., *viciously circular*, but his reasoning *is*, nevertheless, clearly, and undeniably circular. Similarly, our main philosophical protagonists beyond myself in this work, Van Til and Plantinga, too are "circular" in their argumentation, but they need not hang their heads in shame; we cannot escape it. Plantinga's "circular argument" is the wide circle of the cogency and legitimate rationality of Christian belief:

> Even if Christian believers are *justified* in their beliefs, they might still be *irrational*.... A belief is rational if it is produced by cognitive faculties that are functioning properly and successfully

---

28. Van Til, *Defense of the Faith*, 18–19, 19n78, 160. Oliphint's editorial note on 19 is significant; Van Til did not mean some kind of Kuhnian or Rortian relativism where "everything is under a description" but rather that without the Christian "interpretation" of a fact, it is a "mute" fact—it can say nothing. However, in light of Quine's conception of "factuality" as worldview dependent, I do consider there is still sufficient contact with the Rortian or Kuhnian sense that the *worldview* gives the fact its interpretation. It is just for Rorty or Kuhn that the worldview was subjective, conventional, and arbitrary; for us, we can claim objectivity—harmony with the mind of God.

29. Quine, *Theories and Things*, 23.

aimed at truth.... Now warrant, the property enough of which distinguishes knowledge from mere true belief, is a property or quantity had by a belief if and only if ... that belief is produced by cognitive faculties functioning properly in a congenial epistemic environment according to a design plan successfully aimed at truth.... [T]he real question ... is whether Christian belief does or can have warrant.[30]

For Plantinga, the warrant accumulates on the basis of an interpretation of Calvin's concept of the *sensus divinitatis*, the part of the human cognitive makeup that recognizes "God" when it encounters him in the world.[31] As we worked through in a previous chapter, Plantinga has modified rationality from classical foundationalism, recasting it using a thoroughly strengthened form of Reidian foundationalism and it is *this* specific conception of rationality (his circle) that he seeks to validate, and which serves to authenticate the biblical Christian worldview.[32]

In contrast, Van Til's circle used the idioms of idealism and explicitly addresses the charge of circularity, at once admitting to it and qualifying how it should be understood, i.e., not as an elementary logical fallacy. He spoke of "spiral" reasoning and "implicating" oneself deeper into a system at each iteration assuming what was posited:

> Who wishes to make such a simple blunder in elementary logic, as to say that we believe something to be true because it is in the Bible? Our answer to this is briefly that we prefer to reason in a circle to not reasoning at all. *Or we may call it spiral reasoning.* We must go round and round a thing to see more of its dimensions.... Unless we are larger than God we cannot reason about him in any other way, than by a transcendental or circular argument.[33]

---

30. Plantinga, *Knowledge and Christian Belief*, 46.

31. Plantinga argues this concept is also found in Aquinas, Augustine, and the biblical epistles of Paul. He thus refers to it as the "Extended A/C model."

32. This becomes increasingly clear as one progresses through the chapters of *Knowledge and Christian Belief*. Chapters 5 and 6 tie his apologetic tightly to Calvin and Edwards; so, although he is often criticized as having departed from classical or orthodox "Reformed" dogmatics, he defends himself with the primary sources of scripture, Calvin, and other Reformed heroes such as Edwards. The material in these chapters I consider the most apologetic and effective of Plantinga's work I have read. It has a nourishing spiritual richness to it, as William J. Abraham (Perkins School of Theology) also notes on the back cover.

33. Bahnsen, *Van Til's Apologetic*, 518–19; 518nn121–22. The main text is Van Til's; n121 was a footnote added by Van Til; n122 was an explanatory note added by Bahnsen.

Thus, "circularity" might simply be taken to mean *consistency* and *coherence* of any rational system *as a whole*; if our circles are "broad," we can withstand the circularity charge without so much as a blush.

4.6 A Form of Life

Our conclusion above seems to involve a paradox. As we noted in Quine, he merely recommended "any theory from various," which if we did not know better from our previous examination of his position, would seem to imply relativism on his part. However, something different is being argued here: relativism argues for an absolute equivalency of competing epistemologies, but Quine still believed there was immanent truth to be had; he just recognized that incommensurate theories might nevertheless be empirically equivalent in under-attested conditions. As data accumulates the efficacy of one or both rival theories could be compromised, and a new one needs to emerge.[34]

So, although we can dismiss the charge of relativism, he can *never* give us an objective basis for his commitment because his naturalism constrains him that one is not possible.[35] It would also seem that although he repudiates relativism, the cash value of his position becomes that of the relativist; we might say he was *operationally* relativist. It seems the real difference between the Quinean naturalist, and the relativist seems to be one of philosophical temper; one is a physicalist, the other is a philologist and never the twain shall meet except to throw missiles across the epistemological barricade, but they end up on the same battlefield, nevertheless. The intelligent relativist, appropriating Wittgenstein, argues that it is indeed impossible to judge a "form of life," a composite of metaphysical, epistemological, and ethical positions, i.e., a *worldview* with a specific linguistic expression that can only be understood from within that community. Although one might "speak" with the same words and signs, it is in the living of life and the *use* of the words in the context of that community which give it meaning.[36] This is indeed a powerful argument, but it must be

---

34. In this sense, he is close to the position of Neurath's sailors, where the raft must be rebuilt at sea because there is no dry-docking capability.
35. Quine, "Response to Morton White," 664.
36. Richter, "Wittgenstein," §5.

recognized that Wittgenstein was *also* a man of principle and values,[37] and he believed that one *could* and *should* be a "decent human being."[38]

"Decent" implies a value judgment and an appropriate framework. He certainly did not advocate a life without principles though it is undeniable that his work has frequently been used by those who have favored a postmodern, relativistic, or pragmatic philosophy and who view morality as simply "socially constructed."[39] Such a reading of Wittgenstein, though popular, is difficult to sustain on close examination as it seems to misconstrue Wittgenstein as somehow "theorizing" about "forms of life," rather than just describing them and analyzing them to understand them. If there was anything that Wittgenstein rejected, it was "theorizing" in the traditional philosophical sense. However, what Wittgenstein *might* have properly asserted as a theoretical aspect of language is that it had a *public* context and he then proceeded to argue *transcendentally* to demonstrate the necessity. For example, his famous "Private Language" argument from the *Investigations* is sometimes viewed as a highly complex transcendental argument where he seeks to establish the impossibility of a private language and in doing so refute *solipsism* (the denial of the existence of other minds). Such is the complexity of the argument, there are rival schools of interpretation of it.[40]

For our purposes, Plantinga, interestingly, describes this argument as "weak." His first major book asserted that the status of the justification of other minds and of arguments for theistic belief were of equivalent logical quality.[41] So, *the believer could not be considered irrational* in believing *if* it was rational to believe in other minds, which he believed could also not be proved but was clearly considered "rational." What Plantinga was perhaps admitting here was that if Wittgenstein's transcendental argument has succeeded, *his* was the argument that was weak. However,

---

37. See, for example, Engelmann, *Memoir*; Wittgenstein, *Culture and Values*.

38. Engelmann, *Memoir*, 11, letter 12.

39. The "socially constructed" thesis is associated with the ground-breaking work of Berger and Luckmann, *Social Construction of Reality*. However, what is notable in their account is the complete *omission* of any direct discussion of ethics or morality (even the index has no entry for either). They also made it plain in their opening remarks that they were using a weakened sense of the word "knowledge" that certainly indicates an enormous red flag for the critical reader regarding their overall thesis; it should certainly be pushed to provide an epistemological account of its presuppositions.

40. Richter, "Wittgenstein," §6.

41. Plantinga, *God and Other Minds*. The original edition appeared in 1967 and was reissued with a new preface in 1990.

in line with Richter's assessment that "Ordinary Language Philosophy" (inspired by this mode of interpreting Wittgenstein) had fallen "out of favor," Plantinga downgraded the relevance and applicability of Wittgenstein's argument for the rationality of religious belief in the new preface published twenty-three years later.[42]

However, Plantinga's sophisticated skeptical approach in that work was also considered controversial by some such that in responding to the criticism of it and the developing his own thought, he progressively built on the rejection of the classical foundationalism of this early work. He refined and improved it over the succeeding decades, until the RE project[43] with Wolterstorff, Alstom, and others gave the arguments a much stronger form and stronger still in his *Warrant* trilogy.[44] In that form there are elements of Plantinga that most certainly resonate with the epistemic rights of a community to proceed to believe without a common evidential basis with their critics.

Thus, both Wittgenstein and Plantinga are seen to agree on the grounding of meaning as something more complex than empirical considerations and local to a community whose use of the language gave meaning to the discourse. Plantinga was even considered as offering a "transcendental defense" against naturalism by Craig, but this claim is at best an inference characterizing his philosophical project *as a whole*, rather than explicitly articulated in his work.[45]

---

42. See the new preface to the 1990 edition, where he states he was responding to the Wittgensteinian arguments at many places in the book when he originally wrote it.

43. See Macneil, "Van Til and Plantinga," for more background.

44. Everitt, *Non-Existence*, 30, gives a useful summary of the RE literature and the ensuing debate which has remained robust within the philosophy of religion. However, Everitt never engages with Plantinga's strengthening of the position after the 1980s, despite referring to the existence of that literature in the Further Reading section with which he closed out the chapter. Plantinga himself believed he had further developed his position through the *Warrant* trilogy (1992–2000) and published a compressed version of the final argument in 2015, which has a significantly more ecumenical feel and less of the "Reformed" moniker, though Plantinga himself asserts that the "Reformed" prefix was never intended to imply criticism of RC epistemology, perhaps understandable with his joining the great Catholic institution of Notre Dame.

45. This point is made in Collett, "Van Til," n42. Craig made this claim in "Classical Apologist's Response," 233. "Classical apologetics" in this sense refers to the Old Princeton approach of the late nineteenth century and Warfieldian era of Princeton (cf. Aquinas's "classical arguments"; Craig was following the expansion of the term to include evidentialism; see §1.3.2), which is continued in some of the more conservative Reformed seminaries. "New" Princeton has a far more liberal, ecumenical theology and thus its apologetics are markedly weaker.

4.7 The Necessity of a Transcendental Defense

Thus, as unexpected as it may be, we are seeing that a transcendental defense of Christian belief and a transcendental critique of the non-Christian worldview are the only ways of assessing the competing truth claims. Otherwise, it seems a matter of preference whether we pick Quine or Van Til. Thus, we will consider the critique in the next section and the defense in more detail here. Van Til argues for not just a transcendental justification for our reason but for *worldview* apologetics with a *transcendent* transcendental first principle. In this way he circumvents the self-vitiating naturalism of Quine and can move beyond the relativism of a neo-Wittgensteinian without the religious fideism.[46]

Van Til argues that God is the necessary, metaphysical bridge in our belief structure (Plantinga uses the term "noetic structure") that allows us to move to certainty, that the thoughtful ethical naturalism of a Blackburn we noted desires but can never get us to. We might even pull in Descartes as a supporting witness who, at this level, recognized absolute claims of knowledge need a transcendent basis: "[the atheist, strictly speaking] cannot have systematic knowledge unless he has been created by the true God, a God who has no intention to deceive."[47] Similarly, in the words of Williams, "we may feel happier to live without foundations of knowledge [but Descartes did not]"[48] and it is well to remember the first division in Descartes's notebook was "the fear of the Lord is the beginning of wisdom"[49] which is the very foundation of Van Til's (and Plantinga's) epistemological methodology.

However, we, of course, have just entered inadvertently into the controversy of Descartes's religious commitment or the lack thereof and need to be careful to represent Descartes accurately. Schouls argued that the sacred-secular dichotomy in his methodology permitted an apologetic interpretation equally suited for atheism as to theism.[50] The atheist Cartesian can in thought maintain a *hypothesis* of a perfect deceiver but if it was a perfect deceiver then by Descartes's rule the perfect deceiver must exist and would be God because God alone has necessary existence. However, the concept of God is then self-contradictory because Descartes

---

46. This was a debate captured in Nielsen and Phillips, *Wittgensteinian Fideism?*
47. Descartes, *Meditations*, 99–104.
48. Descartes, *Meditations*, xvi (Bernard Williams's "Introductory Essay").
49. Prov 9:10 (KJV).
50. Schouls, *Descartes*, 60–63, n60.

himself asserted that "the will to deceive is undoubtedly evidence of malice or weakness, and so cannot apply to God,"[51] and the atheist Cartesian following Descartes's own rules can safely assert God cannot exist and can trust his reason with no fear of contradiction. Descartes himself seemed to hold the door open to the ultimate autonomy of the human will because of the innate freedom of it even when confronted with an all-powerful deceiver:

> But meanwhile whoever turns out to have created us, and even should he prove to be all-powerful and deceitful, we still experience a freedom through which we may abstain from accepting true and indisputable those things of which we have not certain knowledge, and thus obviate our ever being deceived.[52]

Thus, we must acknowledge that Descartes, despite his pious language and form in the dedication to the *Meditations* wants to prove "philosophically rather than theologically" and to appeal to the power of "natural reason,"[53] though he would surely retort he was surely defensibly Thomistic in that assumption. Nevertheless, we might thus caution ourselves from too readily appropriating Descartes who was ever mindful of the fate of Galileo—his choice to live in Holland was in his own words an act of self-preservation—he is almost universally acknowledged to have been the beginning of modern philosophy and perhaps to have shown God the epistemological exit door, at least as far as philosophy is concerned. Even accepting his proof, he was philosophically defending a generic theism rather than a specifically Christian conception that we are seeking to develop. However, on balance, I am prepared to give Descartes the benefit of the doubt[54] and to accept that he does offer *something* important apologetically when he recognized a divine guarantee for knowledge was the only guarantee there could be. It certainly had a transcendental feel when he emphatically assigned *necessary* existence to God alone and considered the *cogito* as an intuited logical unit rather than as a syllogism.[55] We might fault him in how he worked his program out, but he had some important insights. Nevertheless, Van Til found his

---

51. Cottingham, Stoothoff, and Murdoch, *Philosophical Writings of Descartes*, 2:37.

52. Cottingham, Stoothoff, and Murdoch, *Philosophical Writings of Descartes*, 2:194.

53. Descartes, *Meditations*, 8.

54. See Macneil, *Descartes*, for a fuller discussion.

55. Cottingham, Stoothoff, and Murdoch, *Philosophical Writings of Descartes*, 2:36.

BEYOND ANTI-PHILOSOPHY TO TRANSCENDENTALISM

approach inadequate in providing a true transcendental for knowledge, arguing that even if we accept the *cogito* its scope is parochial[56] and with that assessment we are obliged to concur.

More specifically, Van Til rejected the egocentricity and the anthropocentricity of the Cartesian program because it began with the self and moved out from the self to prove God. Rather, we must start with God's self-revelation to us, specifically in the scriptures and what they speak to us metaphysically, epistemologically, and ethically. This might be "circular" reasoning, but we have already seen it is not the vicious, logically fallacious circularity when our premise includes or assumes our conclusion. It is rather a *transcendental*. That is, when we talk of "circular" reasoning we are demonstrating that we are dealing with the ultimate or top-level authority claims for the *justification* of our reasoning. If a claim has "ultimate" status in our noetic structures, there is no external proof available, and we cannot help but employ it while arguing for its legitimacy. Only transcendental forms of argument have the unique feature that they provide the very grounds for their own legitimacy and conclude with a *transcendental*, or precondition for their intelligibility. As Van Til put it:

> At the outset it ought to be clearly observed that every system of thought necessarily has a *certain method* of its own. Usually this fact is overlooked. It is taken for granted that everybody begins in the same way with an examination of the facts, and that differences between systems come only as a *result* . . . this is not actually the case. It could not actually be the case with a Christian. His fundamental and determining fact is the fact of God's existence. That is his final conclusion. But that must also be his starting point. *If the Christian is right in his final conclusion about God, then he would not even get in touch with any fact unless it were through the medium of God.*[57]

There is a remarkable amount of foundational epistemology packed into this paragraph. When it comes to our top-level or ultimate authority claims for the legitimacy of our worldview, it can *only* be justified in terms of itself; that is, transcendentally.

---

56. Bahnsen while a student of Van Til indicates he would frequently characterize Descartes's *cogito* as "a rock in a bottomless ocean," emphasizing its narrow achievement, even if we accept it. (Bahsen, *Van Til's Apologetic*, 509–10). We examine why such a parochial argument fails the transcendental designation in §7.

57. Van Til, "Revelational Epistemology," 170. Emphasis added.

4.8 The Transcendental Mode of Criticism

How then are we to evaluate a "form of life" or a worldview? The only method available to us is to examine their *content* for coherence and logical consistency *on their own terms* by engaging in a transcendental critique. We must immediately recognize that there can only be one, true transcendental; there may be attempts at arguing that a non-Christian worldview is transcendental, but the argument always fails, sometimes without too much effort, on close examination. For example, in an impressive *tour de force* Van Tillian Bahnsen dismisses Islam, Buddhism, Hinduism, and naturalism on their own terms from their own writings while simultaneously conceding that *if*, for example, Islam or any other worldview claims it *is* the Word of God, it *should* have been taken on its own authority.

This is an important part of the concept of transcendental critique—just because something *claims* to be a transcendental, it does not mean that it *succeeds* in being so. An empiricist might want to claim that his empiricism is a transcendental principle of nature. However, we find that the "verification principle" at its center is arbitrary and self-refuting.[58] We cannot go out into nature and observe the verification principle; it is rather a metaphysical dogma. Similarly, a rationalist might want to claim transcendentally that logic provides an *a priori* basis for science, but different logicians argue over what counts as logic. Quine's critique of Carnap's analytic-synthetic distinction was one of the most devastating attacks on the logic of empiricism. Quine also denied that modal logic (the logic of necessity) was possible because it relied on intension and essences (Quine labeled this "Aristotelian essentialism"). However, in response, Plantinga's *Nature of Necessity* contained a technical appendix dealing specifically with Quine's objection and concurs with it but rejects the implications Quine drew from the rejection—we thus conclude logicians argue with each other over the "nature" of logic and it certainly does not self-evidently provide its own foundation and thus demonstrate a transcendental character. Only a Christian with a transcendental basis for logic in the mind of the Christian God,[59] whose triune nature resolves

---

58. Baird, "Transcendental Arguments," has suggested that the verification principle might be understood in a transcendental fashion. This seems to me equivalent to suggesting the principle is analytic. Baird began from a Christian premise and sought to dissolve Stroud's objections to transcendental arguments which have dominated the debate over them; see §7.

59. The prologue of John and John's repeated use of the loaded term *logos* is a

the tension between the "One and the Many," of particular and kind, can sustain the claim to a genuine transcendental.

4.9 Summary and Conclusion

In this chapter we have introduced transcendental reasoning. We had arrived at a philosophical impasse by considering the work of Quine and Kuhn which seemed to imply a relativistic terminus and where ethical commitments were readily characterized as Wittgensteinian fideism or with a purely voluntaristic, subjective basis. That is, there was a "form of life," and rationality might be defined and expressed within a theory, but that theory was just one of many possible, "empirically adequate" theories of the world. Transcendentalism offered us a mode of reasoning that moved beyond this terminus. We examined that it was first associated with the philosophy of Kant, who defined as transcendental those principles that must be assumed to make *any* knowledge of objects possible.

This immediately served to provide us with the dictum that reasoning is implicitly circular, when we reason about reason, we are assuming the rationality of reason. Thus, we were able to discern that there is a categorical difference between the fallacy of circular reasoning where the premise in a syllogistic construction assumes the conclusion and the overall circularity of a theory of nature. We understood that the nature of transcendental reasoning was categorically distinct from inductive, deductive, or abductive reasoning and deals with conclusions which are principles with broad application to the world. We understood how the skeptical terminus was then rendered incoherent; we would have needed to have employed the cognitive processes to have arrived at the conclusion that the cognitive processes are inadequate.

Thus, by establishing a prima facie basis for reasoning we could examine something of the taxonomy of reason. We examined the main divisions of reasoning, the practical and the theoretical; the theoretical mode of reason is that which allows us to analyze and posit about our

---

compelling argument regarding the foundations of logic which space does not permit us to examine further other than to note its importance as an issue of apologetic dispute here. Butler, *Biblical Presuppositional Apologetics*, addresses this contention in Clark's *Logic* by noting that the Greeks had other words that they used at the time John was writing that would have been much closer to our use of the word "logic"; it was not until around the fourth century that logic would have been the preferred meaning. Clark was a competent logician though, and this work is worth reading as an introductory work from a Christian perspective on that basis.

world, and the practical deals with our theory of value, both aesthetic and ethical. We concluded that we could not live in the world without reason and that being reasonable was ethically commendable. However, we noted that some ethical theorists, while passionately recognizing the value of practical reason, struggled to define it in terms that were not tightly circular. In other words, they struggled to find a basis for reason that was adequately transcendental rather than voluntaristic.

We probed that it was possible to move past this terminus by considering that an ultimate authority is what we assume transcendentally in all our reasoning. It is our transcendental that makes possible the grounds for its own proof and thus its own ethical commitments. We understood that part of the strategy of assessing the rival worldviews was to examine their internal relations on their own terms, if elements of the worldview are shown to be incoherent on analysis, their arguments are flawed, and they do not warrant the label "transcendental." We used the terms "presuppositional" and "worldview" to describe our transcendental method, recognizing that there is never a neutral place to start our reasoning from and to build our science upon. We bolstered our account by considering our position was analogous to the holism argued by Quine where he had argued it was in assuming a theory of the world that we would always speak, and that all our reasoning about the world must assume that theory.

We also examined that Quine had recognized the place of normative ethical values and commitments, rejecting the scientistic assumptions of the positivists; there was no mere pluralistic tolerance, and gratuitous torture was wrong regardless of the adequacy of the theoretical account of it. We noted Wittgenstein also argued that there was something that constituted a "decent" human being and thus the characterizations of his philosophy as relativistic were faulty in this important ethical respect; he was also seen to employ transcendental modes of argument in his account of language as requiring a public context, further buttressing our account of the legitimacy of the mode of reasoning. However, we equally recognized the weakness of these accounts: Quine's account of moral commitments and his ethical theory was easily characterized as arbitrary, his worldview relying on a Darwinian conception of chance; Wittgenstein arguing meaning was tied with use is similarly problematic as a general theory for intercommunal relations, easily represented as supporting relativism.

We argued that only a transcendent transcendental would more adequately address the charge of arbitrariness. We examined that both Van Til and Plantinga had epistemologies that, though radically different in detail, relied on a transcendent transcendental assumption and that established both the consistency and coherence of their Christian worldviews. We also noted that Descartes can be interpreted in a transcendental fashion when he argues that systematic knowledge was not possible for an atheist. We noted the ambiguity in Descartes and that Van Til asserted that the *cogito* was not an adequate transcendental principle for knowledge because it defended a generic theism. It was also noted that the *cogito* could be conceived of in a fashion that supported atheism and was too narrow in scope to be considered a genuine transcendental. We also noted a fundamental weakness in Descartes's epistemological conception which moved outward from the self to God and then the natural world. We argued we must begin with God's self-revelation as a transcendental and build our metaphysics, epistemology, and ethics from the written Word of God. This established a very important principle; we can judge between rival transcendental claims by examining them on their own terms; just because we have a "form of life" that does not make it immune from critique.

Thus, our next task is the proof that *only* the Christian transcendental has sufficient coherence without an elaborate hermeneutic to reconcile its problems.[60] What we will see is unique about Van Til's use of transcendental argumentation is that it is not seeking to do a piecemeal refutation of a specific fact in or about nature but rather establish a principle by which the non-Christian worldview (in all its sub-genii) as a whole *and* as a unit can be judged illegitimate and self-refuting. Thus,

---

60. This is not to deny the importance of hermeneutics to Christian thought or of philosophical hermeneutics more generally. Our consideration of the problem of circularity is also known as the "hermeneutic circle"—the problem of circularity *is* a problem of hermeneutics as are preunderstanding we bring to a text, presupposition, and the role of the transcendental. Thiselton's *Hermeneutics* is probably the definitive graduate text on the subject. The 2012 twentieth anniversary edition of his *New Horizons in Hermeneutics* was also a substantive milestone in the subject, a masterful exposition noted for its engagement with and critique of postmodernism; postmodernism which was highly influential during the period he originally wrote it, and many Christians felt that "making room for the sacred" in postmodernism meant making room for them. However, this was a kindergarten mistake, and Thiselton offers a substantial critique of the limitations of postmodernism "that most Christians do not realize" (*Hermeneutics*, 327–49). I would also be amiss if I did not note his *Two Horizons*, originally his PhD dissertation, described by the eminent Professor J. B. Torrance as "one of the most competent dissertations I have ever read" and which established his reputation.

any specific fact of nature should be able to be taken and only made *intelligible* by assuming the Christian transcendental.

5

The Christian Presupposition

5.1 The Christian Transcendental as the Only True Transcendental

IN THE PREVIOUS SECTION we argued for the validity and indeed the necessity of a transcendental mode of argument. Now let us consider the Christian claim to be the only possible transcendental more fully. Firstly, it is important to note a critical feature of Van Til's transcendentalism: Van Til collapses the distinction between non-Christian worldviews as simply one of emphasis, rather than substantive difference. Thus, our previous discussion of worldviews and "forms of life" undergoes a grand synthesis or rarefaction in Van Til to simply the *Christian* worldview and the *non*-Christian worldview. Now where the non-Christian viewpoint is *religious*, it is seen to collapse into:

a. Either a heretical form of Christianity, heretical in the sense it asserts a verbal revelation from an absolute God who has given us an absolute scripture. That is, it is aping the Christian worldview in some way, and we posit that because it does not maintain Christianity as a unit, it collapses into incoherence.

b. Irrationality or fideism, as in Hinduism, Buddhism, or so-called primitive religions or New Age[1] spiritualities.

---

1. Most practitioners familiar with Hindu meditation and transcendental meditation would consider so-called New Age spiritual practices and experiences identical.

The fundamental conception that Van Til believes establishes the unity of the varieties of non-Christian thought is the "univocal"[2] and autonomousnature of their thought. That is, the mind and intellect of humanity is deemed sufficient apart from God to explain and correctly understand reality.[3] However, Van Til asserts like Kant that *natural* arguments can only ever establish a God which is a part of nature.[4] Thus, it is only on the basis of a *transcendent* transcendental of the Trinity both immanent and transcendent that allows our transcendental to offer the possibility of coherence and diversity, necessity and contingency by providing a metaphysical bridge between nature and supernature.

That is, the cornerstone of the Christian presupposition is the ontological Trinity—the Christian resolves the tension between immanence and transcendence[5] by the Holy Spirit from God coming to dwell *in* the temple of our bodies revealing God to us but preserving God's personal autonomy and the things which belong to him alone: "The secret things belong to the LORD our God, but the things revealed belong to us and to our sons forever, that we may observe all the words of this law."[6] For the Judeo-Christian[7] tradition, God has committed to the reliability of natural law until the end of this age; there is both determinism and contingency perfectly resolved in his universe:

Many "New Age" groups have as their head a guru as in Hinduism, often from a Hindu nation. Just as Buddhism is considered a localization of a form of Hinduism with the same basic perspective, "New Age" is a Westernized version of Hinduism that might also import a lot of Western psychology and life-coaching to offer an eclectic spirituality.

2. "Univocal" is used by Van Til in the sense that there is no Creator-creature distinction recognized in the *quality* (not just the *quantity*) of the reasoning. Van Til asserted that our reasoning should be *analogical* in the sense we are reinterpreting experience in terms of the guidance of God's revelation. As "analogy" is used elsewhere in analytic philosophy with a very different meaning, this led to a frequent misunderstanding of what Van Til meant when he asserted we reasoned *analogously* to God.

3. Van Til, *Systematic Theology*, 178–82.

4. As an ethical analogue, Moore called it the naturalistic fallacy to move from what ought to be the case to what *is* the case.

5. I would argue this is recognized in Islam but only resolved on a non-rational basis as an issue of faith; see Macneil, "Applying the Epistemological."

6. Deut 29:29 (NAS).

7. Butler, *Biblical Presuppositional Apologetics*, objects to this term because modern Judaism is Talmudic rather than Abrahamic and so there is no "Judeo-Christian" tradition. However, there is still an idiomatic use of this term which I would argue makes sense while accepting Butler's criticism of it.

THE CHRISTIAN PRESUPPOSITION

> But I, the LORD, make the following promise: I have made a covenant governing the coming of day and night. I have established the fixed laws governing heaven and earth.[8]
> I call heaven and earth to witness against you today, that I have set before you life and death, the blessing and the curse. So *choose* life *in order that* you may live, you and your descendants.[9]

It is this metaphysic which is implicitly assumed when *anyone* wants to argue *logically* but wants to allow for contingency.

5.2 Contingency and Predestination

Yet, contingency can be a difficult subject for Christians and a source of great disagreement. One of the great divisions in Protestantism is the measure to which a person's will is "free."[10] However, we can reconcile the tension by some biblical exegesis. In Acts 13:46–48 we see the passive voice of the Greek verb[11] in v. 48 emphasizing the "appointing" was by God to eternal life of the Gentiles but contrasted with the rebellion, i.e., the exercising of their wills against God, of the Jews in v. 46:

> And Paul and Barnabas spoke out boldly and said, "It was necessary that the word of God should be spoken to you first; since you repudiate it, and judge yourselves unworthy of eternal life, behold, we are turning to the Gentiles. 47 For thus the Lord has commanded us, 'I have placed You as a light for the Gentiles,

---

8. Jer 33:25 (NET); Gen 8:22 (NAS).

9. Deut 30:19 (NAS). Emphasis added. It is of note here that the Greek Septuagint translation of this verse uses the "hina–subjunctive" clause to emphasize the result of the choosing.

10. This also has an enormous intersection with the "problem of evil" where the presence of evil in the world is defended on the basis of God creating free creatures. This is often seen to mitigate the logical force of the traditional argument from evil where it was viewed as contradictory that an omnipotent God who is also wholly good would permit evil to exist. There is much more to the argument, stated fully by Plantinga, *Nature of Necessity*, and in a more accessible form in *God, Freedom and Evil*. Hick, *Evil*, gives historical coverage of this subject and provides a helpful precis of Plantinga (and other logicians) in the final chapter. Van Inwagen, *Christian Faith*, edited a volume that indicated none of the fire had gone out of the debate. However, the issue with evil is not so much *logical* (Plantinga dealt with this in 1974), but *psychological*, a point also made by Bahnsen. Plantinga has described it as the most difficult of problems facing the Christian theist and contributed an essay, "O Felix Culpa," to Van Inwagen that is undoubtedly an impressive development of his earlier work dealing with the logic, anchored in Calvinism.

11. τεταγμένοι—verb participle perfect passive nominative masculine plural.

That You should bring salvation to the end of the earth.'" 48 And when the Gentiles heard this, they *began* rejoicing and glorifying the word of the Lord; and as many as had been appointed to eternal life believed.

This is all in the context of them rejecting the gospel of salvation which God was offering (and seemingly refused on their own terms). This would seem to be confirmed in 1 Tim 2:3-4:

> Such prayer for all is good and welcomed before God our Savior, since he wants all people to be saved and to come to a knowledge of the truth.[12]

Thus, the language of these verses, regardless of the complexities of the debate around free will, demonstrates that predestination and free will are not mutually exclusive in the logic of God. The implication of this is that a will can be free but is never autonomous: "The spirit of man is the lamp of the LORD, Searching all the innermost parts of his being."[13]

---

12. Calvin in his *Commentary*, loc. 12685, understands this verse differently as referring to the *kinds* of men, i.e., kings, princes, governors. His commentary is very interesting on this point because he emphasizes the proper relationship of the believers with the authorities (we will consider this in more detail in §7) as Calvin, like Paul would have also been writing in the context of political tyranny. The French refugees in Geneva had suffered at the hands of those same kings, princes, and rulers. He also had in mind the extreme position of the "radical Reformation" who had rejected all human authority (e.g., the Anabaptists), providing justification for heavy political action against the Reformers by the monarchs and the Catholics.

There is undoubtedly considerable force to this interpretation and truth in it, but the verse *also* sits adjacent to an unambiguous generalizing statement (v. 5) and the continuing argument regarding the salvation of the Gentiles. Consequently, its interpretation is highly disputed and subject to the hermeneutic you bring to the verse and your basic Calvinist or Arminian commitment in theology. It is undoubtedly clear that "election" is taught within the Christian scriptures, e.g., Rom 9–11 presents a difficult and full argument, as well as within the Hebrew scriptures. However, it is equally clear that the gospel is to be preached to *all* nations and it is the power of God to the salvation of *all* who believe. That the gospel is preached is perhaps the most important aspect to root our thinking—Whitfield was a Calvinist who viewed his preaching as finding the elect; Wesley, his partner and associate, was Arminian.

The real challenge for Christian praxis is the so-called hyper-Calvinism that asserts people will be saved whether or not they are preached to (for God has individually decided the fate of each person); or which concludes the whole missionary movement is unnecessary because God will save them anyway (as the young William Carey, the founder of the Baptist Missionary Society, found out in the 1790s when he was told to "sit down" by his elders for "God will save those men if he chooses to" [my paraphrase]). These are extremely important issues that I can only consider, except for political ethics, outside of this book.

13. Prov 20:27 (NAS).

That is, the individual person is never separated from access by their creator and never lives independent of their creator, they rather "suppress the truth in unrighteousness."[14] Van Til thus contrasted philosophical physical, causal determinism with divine sovereignty,[15] with the former a derivative of the latter, not an absolute property.

In essence, when he speaks of the logic of God as the "absolute conditioner," he understands creation as exhausting absolute novelty within the Trinity, so the one and the many are *correlative* in the Trinity; this means an absolute God and an absolute scripture. In terms of logical necessity then, the wills of persons or the principles of the natural world do not operate outside of this realm independently in absolute freedom, for it would make both God and scripture subject to the wills of men:

> A God who cannot control history because of countless men with wills not fully dependent on his own can only make salvation a bare "possibility." Christ might have died in vain. Being "free" all men might refuse to exercise their supposedly "God-given-freedom" . . . God's plan, to call out a people for himself, might never have been realized [it] distorts the doctrine of Scripture itself by finding the ultimate exegetical tool in the subjective experience of human freedom and by denying to Scripture and the Holy Spirit the power, the authority, and necessity of invading the souls of men.[16]

That is, the transcendental status of logic is only supported in the Christian conception because it is not immanent to the creation but in the transcendent Trinity.[17] It is thus the only possible *true* transcendental or the only possible basis for the *a priori* that is not vulnerable to the claim of arbitrariness.

---

14. Rom 1:18 (NAS).

15. Van Til, "My Credo," 16.

16. Van Til, "My Credo," 9.

17. This was also the point of disagreement between the *later* Dooyeweerd and Van Til (who had been greatly encouraged in his own transcendental critique reading the early Dooyeweerd) captured in the essays and the rejoinder in Geehan, *Jerusalem and Athens*, 74–128. This was by far the longest and most detailed response written by Van Til in the volume. Contrast this also with the Islamic view that Allah is not bound to the creation and is free to act in any way at any time to affect that creation, i.e., it is antithetical to the conception of a natural law guaranteed by God's character.

5.3 General Revelation and Special Revelation

The Christian conception is also unique in that right at the beginning of Hebrew scripture, God himself states that he made humanity in "his image." Though there is a qualitative difference between creature and creator, the apostle Paul reflecting on our status as creatures states we *immanently know* God through the faculty called *conscience* but proceed to make the *conscious choice* to suppress our knowledge of him. That is, there is a *general revelation* of God to all humanity, and it is this general revelation through the operations of conscience that makes all accountable to God:

> For not the hearers of the Law are just before God, but the doers of the Law will be justified. For when Gentiles who do not have the Law do instinctively the things of the Law, these, not having the Law, are a law to themselves, in that they show the work of the Law written in their hearts, their *conscience bearing witness*, and their thoughts alternately accusing or else defending them.[18]

That is, the Christian God does not separate himself from creation or position himself above or outside the universe but is intimately involved in maintaining it:

> He is the image of the invisible God, the firstborn of all creation. For by Him all things were created, both in the heavens and on earth, visible and invisible, whether thrones or dominions or rulers or authorities—all things have been created through Him and for Him. *He is before all things, and in Him all things hold together.*[19]

Truth is thus always available to humanity because reality itself is evidence for God's providence and common grace.[20] This concept of *natural revelation* is distinct from *natural theology*—we are not arguing that nature

---

18. Rom 2:13–15 (NAU). Emphasis added.
19. Col 1:15–17 (NAU). Emphasis added.
20. This is a major article of Reformed faith and has been particularly controversial in the last two centuries. Van Til, *Common Grace*, was an extremely important milestone in the debate. It concerns the degree to which the "[appreciation of] the good and the beautiful that God has given to sinful men [while maintaining] the seriousness of sin and the rights of the natural" (*Common Grace*, 21). Kuyper's "Common Grace in Science" was also considered a major milestone on which Van Til reflects and develops in his own views.

itself or an intimate knowledge of nature can lead us to a true knowledge of God. Plantinga thus explicates this classical Reformed position:

> This natural knowledge of God is not arrived at by inference or argument (for example the famous theistic proofs of natural theology) but in a much more immediate way. The deliverances of the *sensus divinitatis* are not quick inferences.... It is rather that [on] perception ... these beliefs just arise within us. They *arise* in these circumstances; *they are not conclusions from them.*[21]

That is, it is only the special revelation of the scriptures that can bring one to regeneration, but natural revelation can confirm what special revelation teaches.[22] Sin is said to obscure the clarity of revelation, but it cannot expunge it, a person must actively, and thus *culpably*, suppress the knowledge of God that general revelation brings them.[23] It is this culpable suppression that renders all, regardless of their religious commitment, guilty before God.

5.4 Common Grace, Pluralism, and Epistemological Self-Consciousness

The arguments we have presented above were necessarily dealing with Christian philosophy to buttress our transcendental claims regarding our epistemological self-consciousness. However, they have general application to the process of legitimizing philosophizing for in lieu of common grace and general revelation one should indeed expect an energetic if not fierce debate and exchange of views over the *details* of how one might demonstrate what is "right" or "correct" or is "consistent with science" for components X, Y, and Z of its worldview. We would also expect without

---

21. Plantinga, *Knowledge and Christian Belief*, 35. Emphasis original.

22. This is a specifically Reformed, Protestant conception of the relation between special revelation and natural revelation. The RC view is far more amenable to the possibility of a natural theology. Some modern protestant thinkers such as Richard Swinburne also argue for natural theology—Plantinga, *Law*, credits Swinburne with advancing natural theology further than it has ever been advanced, softening his own, earlier, categorical rejection of natural theology and the "classical" arguments for God's existence (teleological and cosmological). However, though now acknowledging those arguments as having *some* value, Plantinga advanced very different arguments, mentioning them only in passing.

23. As Plantinga notes, this concept is embryonic in Aquinas but explicit in Calvin, which is why he calls his own model the "Extended A/C" model, *Knowledge and Christian Belief*, 31.

prejudice or obscurantism historical research and scientific investigations to evaluate historical or scientific claims with theological dimensions, e.g., the age of the earth or creation science[24] claims, Mohammed's response to North African Christian apostasy[25] and his early attempt to appear as a prophet to the Jews.[26]

More broadly, then, these specific investigations serve to defuse uncritical religious and cultural *pluralism* as a coherent option. For example, such discussions might help us to understand Islam, from a Judeo-Christian perspective, as a heretical version of the Judeo-Christian conception of God—a God who is personal and who has given a verbal revelation of himself. For the Islamic scholar, Deut 18:18 refers to Mohammed, and for the Christian it was fulfilled in Jesus; there is no hermeneutical resolution of these two positions; they are mutually exclusive; they state and believe the data differently.[27] As we have already seen, we

---

24. By the "Creation Science" movement we are referring specifically to what might be called "seven-day creationism" which is vulnerable to severe criticism as neither properly creationist, scientific, or Christian; see Butler, *Philosophy of Science*, MB107–MB110, for an in-depth discussion of issues surrounding an important legal case over claims it was a legitimate scientific position. Additionally, strongly connected, but distinct, to the movement is what might be called the Intelligent Design (ID) movement which Plantinga was frequently conceived of as lending support to because of his critique of naturalistic science.

However, his position is distinctly more nuanced as witnessed in this reply to protagonist Michael Ruse: "Like any Christian (and indeed any theist), I believe that the world has been created by God, and hence 'intelligently designed.' The hallmark of intelligent design, however, is the claim that this can be shown scientifically; I'm dubious about that." See Ruse, "Alvin Plantinga," and Plantinga, *Conflict*, 225–64. Plantinga in his "design discourse," cf. "design argument," employs an argument analogous to that covered previously in this chapter regarding the distinction between natural theology and natural revelation: we *perceive* design immediately when we *see* it; we do not *reason* to it.

25. It is of considerable historical interest that various protestant groups in Spain lived alongside Muslim settlements in peace because they both rejected the idolatry of the papal church. The genocide directed against the Moor civilization by the Roman Catholic church was equally aimed at the protestant Christians, unfortunately just one such episode in its bloody history.

26. Certain polyvalent qur'anic texts when Mohammed was said to be seeking a unity among the theistic faiths belonged to this early period. However, the condition of this conciliation was a recognition of himself as presenting a renewed and unadulterated revelation. When they refused to recognize him, texts were added on which the jihadists base their practice of evangelism by the sword.

27. Although some might wish to assert the "spirit which animated Jesus now animates Mohammed" (as "Elijah" was equated with John the Baptist by Jesus in Matt 17:10–13). Similarly, some New Age doctrines abstracted "Christ consciousness" from Christ but *also* from Christian doctrine. This is because any dogmatic corpus of

encounter the data in a theory-laden fashion and interpret it according to that theory of the world and only an internal transcendental critique will invalidate an incorrect view.

Now we want to immediately qualify this. We recognize, with Kuyper, the concept of "common grace," the legitimacy of the modal spheres of human life.[28] We are not trying to impose or legitimize a particular religious hegemony. Yet, we are *challenging* those positions to be epistemologically self-conscious with a view to legitimizing the Christian one as their assumed basis. Some arguments *are* better than others; there are not just a plurality of "arguments" or "accounts" which are decided on some subjective, preferential basis. That is, just because a worldview (let us say, pluralist option "A") claims to be right about X, Y, and Z or can offer an "empirically sufficient" account or justification for a proposition (as in the rival conceptions of Deut 18:18), it does not mean that the system it claims to represent is coherent unless we accept the principle of induction which we cannot admit as a *logical* principle *unless* it be accepted that the same God is guaranteeing the inductive principle. That is, the overall coherence of the system can thus only be established on a *transcendental* basis. The *only* conception of a God that does not change and who guarantees the order of nature (allowing us to admit induction among other logical constructs), or who makes immutable promises regarding the future, *is* the Judeo-Christian conception of God.

To illustrate this bold proposition, in a personal conversation I had about Islamic metaphysics, it was put this way to me: "if Allah wills a square to be a circle tomorrow, it would be." Similarly, that logic explains why in 2015, 2,400 zealous pilgrims to the Hajj perished, according to the Saudis, simply because "Allah willed it"[29] rather than the desperately poor logistical management of the Saudis themselves, reported by those on the ground at the time who survived it. Or the Islamic belief that the prayers of those on earth could evict someone previously admitted to paradise or vice versa—someone in "hell" could be promoted to paradise. These admit a principle of "indeterminacy" that is fundamentally

---

scripture would have been considered a situational, culturally conditioned manifestation at a particular point in time that certainly has no normative force, i.e., bearing some affinities with postmodern hermeneutics. The essence of this approach is syncretistic and in attempting to honor all faiths, it ends up elevating a pluralistic (and, in our milieu, *secular*) replacement "faith" of "tolerance for all" with equal dogmatism, and thus, offensive to all *orthodox* expressions of faith.

28. Kuyper, "Sphere Sovereignty," 461–90.
29. Langewiesche, "10-Minute Mecca Stampede That Made History."

contra Judeo-Christian metaphysics and does not align with the Judeo-Christian conception of the nature of God or how he determined history should flow according to prior commitments in the scriptures. This is another reason why we assert that the transcendental for the intelligibility of reality can only be the *Christian* transcendental.

5.5 Sovereignty, Indeterminacy, and Natural Law

However, it must be immediately admitted that the issue of God's freedom to act, the freedom of his will and the corollary challenge of the freedom of creation, has played a significant role in Christian philosophy and arguably a pivotal role in the formation of the self, and thus the philosophizing self, in modernity.[30] It is significant that these issues in a secularized context are still live issues as we discovered when we considered the behaviorist denies freedom of the will in the name of the determinism of human behavior. We are thus limited in our ambition here as to what degree we can do justice to this dilemma, but we can certainly propose an understanding consistent with our overall thesis.

The drift from the teleological synthesis of Aristotelian and Christian concepts to naturalism was a long, slow track in its entirety encompassing many centuries and many different thinkers, but in the twenty-five years from Aquinas to Scotus, there was a major shift. Aquinas was one of the first to grant a realm in which the created, although enveloped by a wider conception of the will and purposes of God, could maintain an operation essentially independent of God, the first strong articulation of a realm of natural law that could be studied in a non-teleological fashion. Then Duns Scotus (ca. 1265–1308) was one of the first to articulate what was known as *Voluntarism* that developed the concept of will beyond Aquinas's expression of it as linked in a constitutive manner with reason and ascribed it a far broader and important role both in God and the creation. For example, "God *could* create in a human mind a conviction of the presence of an individual entity without that entity being present" but this was with the qualification "God only acts in with his orderly power, power guided by wisdom."[31] Scotus, who prefigured Descartes

---

30. This, and the subsequent improvement in the section, again owes a debt to the commentary of Professor Ó Murchadha. The wider issues of the tensions of the philosophical self, faith, reason, and grace with the emergence of modernity are clearly and cogently argued by him in his *Modern Self*.

31. Kenny, *New History*, 324. Emphasis added.

THE CHRISTIAN PRESUPPOSITION

in this respect, then relied on the goodness of God to not deliberately deceive to mitigate a descent into radical skepticism and contingency regarding the real.

However, the *potential* for epistemological anarchy and ethical skepticism was clearly evident in Scotus, "God was free, for instance, to dispense with or cancel many of the moral precepts commonly believed to belong to the natural law."[32] Nevertheless, such a radical antinomian position was not in fact actualized until the era of liberal Protestantism many centuries later, perhaps mitigated in the Catholic philosophical succession by an intellectual context that still believed God was essential in some respect to epistemology. Thus, his chronological successor Ockham, less innovative but perhaps more famous,[33] emphasized that God was free to the point of non-contradiction, though we will reference a critique of this shortly that tends to obviate its significance as a meaningful limit on divine freedom. He offered a forceful, but by no means a conclusive,[34] criticism of Scotus's reconciliation of freedom and necessity which concluded at a radical contingency in the will of God for individual entities. This was a radical break from a unity of a teleological account of nature as a whole, but the philosophical implications of such radical contingency offended Ockham's desire to orthodoxy, and as he could not resolve the tensions, he ended by advocating what Kenny characterized as the "dead end" of devout fideism and a philosophical agnosticism.[35] In other words, he was not prepared to follow the implications of his philosophizing, though he was to set the stage for those who were. Ockham opened the door to a standalone study of nature and others were prepared to go where he was not, where the concept of being was no longer univocal and thus directly dependent on God's being but merely of individual objects in a relation to his will.

Consequently, it should be of no surprise that in some parts of the Roman Catholic church history and implicit in some streams of Protestant post-Reformational thought there was not a problem with the

---

32. Kenny, *New History*, 324.

33. "Ockham's razor" asserts that confronted with two empirically adequate explanations a preference should be given to the one that dispenses with unnecessary entities. It is a powerful principle but Kenny, *New History*, 326, notes that Ockham's razor was probably never spoken by Ockham!

34. It was not "conclusive" in the sense he accepted that Scotus had saved contingency, but this was insufficient to justify God's foreknowledge of the same contingent events. He offered no account to connect these two.

35. Kenny, *New History*, 493.

indeterminacy permitted in the Islamic view of reality; some liberal conceptions viewing it as a convergence in thought between the two theisms, indicative of a common root and the same God. I have personally heard a sermon where a Christian minister said that the Christian God could arbitrarily change reality (as Allah above is said to) and whole denominations have practiced "purgatory"[36] where the believers on earth can make intercession or give gifts that enable the departed to gain entrance into heaven from an intermediate place of waiting (a place of their "purging" considered to be sins that are not punishable by eternal torment). This would also seem to approximate closely to the Islamic view that prayers on earth can demote from or promote to heaven, especially when "naturalized" to their monetary equivalents on earth.

This was the notorious practice in medieval Christianity but in its original form was not simply a papist innovation for disreputable money-making purposes. The origin of purgatory specifically stretches to the earliest millennial doctrine of the early Jewish converts and the early Christians giving it an extremely early date, where it was viewed it as a spiritual discipline of "preparation" or purification for the Second Resurrection at the end of that period. Thus, some caution must be taken where Edwards, a modern liberal scholar, identifies it as a Roman Catholic medieval innovation,[37] but what perhaps should be said was that during this period it was *elevated* to a core doctrine of "pastoral" praxis of traveling clergy in contrast to an ascetic spiritual discipline; in losing that mystical context, it was then consolidated and given a perverted form for those disreputable money-raising purposes. It would thus be a category mistake to take purgatory as evidence of indeterminacy as rationally or theologically justified in the Christian worldview.

Perhaps of greater significance for us in our discussion here where we are arguing as those broadly Augustinian, was that it was also arguably seen in post-Reformational Protestant disputes between Arminians and Calvinists regarding the freedom and status of the will. Calvinists were viewed as emphasizing divine sovereignty which would then minimize a meaningful conception of freedom for creation. However, as

---

36. See Foakes-Jackson, *History*, 176–77. Although old, this was a "standard" history popular through to the 1960s in evangelical and Pentecostal Bible colleges, written at a time just prior to the great battles with liberalism. The author was a Church of England canon as well as a fellow of an Oxford college, despite only having the bachelor of divinity degree, perhaps an interesting reflection on the higher quality of degrees in previous ages.

37. Edwards, *Christianity*, 155.

mentioned previously, the contribution of Scotus here and the details of the response of his successors such as Ockham is particularly significant for us to frame our interpretation. Kenny goes as far to argue that:

> Many of his [Scotus's] philosophical innovations came to be accepted as unquestioned principles by thinkers in later generations who had never read a word of his works. . . . The Reformation debates between Luther and Calvin and their Catholic adversaries took place against a backcloth of fundamentally Scotist assumptions.[38]

Perhaps the most important of Scotus's innovations in diffusing our dilemma was his *compatibilism* where he resolved, in Kenny's view with lasting effectiveness,[39] that freedom and determinism were not philosophically incompatible. He posed the question thus: "God believes I will sit tomorrow; but it is possible that I will not sit tomorrow; therefore God can be mistaken," but since God cannot be mistaken, the argument seems to show it is not possible for me to do anything other than what God has foreseen I will in fact do. For Scotus, this dilemma was employing the schema if p and q entail r, then p and possibly q entail possibly r. Scotus resolves the dilemma by demonstrating the schema as faulty; Kenny provides a modernized version of his argument:

> Suppose there are two suitcases A and B, each of which I can carry. But suppose further that I am carrying my suitcase A. In these circumstances, to carry your suitcase B would be to carry A and B, which is beyond my strength. "I am carrying A and I am carrying B" obviously entails "I am carrying A and B." But "I am carrying A" and "I can carry B" do not between them entail "I can carry A and B."[40]

Thus, Scotus asserts on this basis that human freedom is compatible with divine decrees; they are not the contradictory opposites they would appear to be. He says God foresees future events by being aware of his own intentions and future events are contingent rather than necessary because there was nothing necessary in God's decrees about the world.

---

38. Kenny, *New History*, 324.

39. Kenny, *New History*, 491. In the discussion of Scotus's compatibilism, I follow his discussion. This is derivative from Scotus's own discussion found in *Lect*. 17. 509. However, it is unclear which of Scotus's works this refers to though he gives a full bibliography of those works.

40. Kenny, *New History*, 491.

If we consider freedom as the opposite of necessity,⁴¹ then the actions within the creation are free. As we noted above, Ockham and many others since have not been fully persuaded but the issue does seem to be migrated into the degree of *voluntariness*; voluntariness is not a sufficient condition for freedom, yet it is an essential prerequisite, but an action may be voluntary without being free.

Thus, we should now be in the position to appreciate the philosophical significance of the important theological qualification conspicuous in Van Tillian thought that the will remains free but was not autonomous; the influence of Scotus's compatibilism is clearly seen here, and he wants to address Ockham's reticence. For Van Til, the will of the individual was free, but not *independent* from the Creator; human thought was not considered novel but derivative in character. The artist who paints or the musician who plays is only doing so because they are interpreting what God has already placed in Creation and this maintains sufficient basis for God's foreknowledge. So, even if there is not a radical novelty in their artistic "creations," their arts are free and voluntary because there was nothing necessary in that creative act; an artist may choose to create a work of art or not to create a work of art but whatever is instantiated would be present in the foreknowledge of God. Van Til is thus sensitive to maintaining both the freedom of God and humanity, while maintaining the sovereignty of God. Arminianism, in contrast, was far stronger in asserting the genuine independence of the human will and a realm in which humanity have a being outside of the Creator. Thus, I have heard extreme contingency and indeterminacy argued in Arminian and charismatic circles and the position remains highly influential in evidential apologetics.⁴² The criticism of the latter is thus that the question of God is conducted in terms of probabilities rather than certainties, which as we have made repeatedly clear is unacceptable in terms of our thesis.

However, there is a more general hermeneutical circle at work here that should also be considered. Scotus did an admirable work in advancing the discussion, but Ockham got stuck with fideism in trying to follow

---

41. Kenny, *New History*, 666.

42. This has much to do with the conscious return to neo-Thomism within the Reformed community, even Reformed seminaries. In a personal communication with Professor Clary of Colorado Christian University, he indicated he was no longer a Van Tillian presuppositionalist because the Reformed tradition on a proper reading was "Thomist." However, as Professor Ó Murchadha has pointed out to me, this designation itself needs careful qualification and one "needs to distinguish between Aquinas and a certain kind of [neo-]Thomism."

the argument where it seemed to lead. This is because, when we assert what is *possible*, this too begs the question:

> It is today more evident than ever before that it is exactly on these most fundamental matters, such as possibility and probability, that there is the greatest difference of opinion between theists and antitheists.... Non-believers have false assumptions about their musts.[43]

In other words, the category of possibility is enveloped by God and not vice versa. I maintain views which assert a radical contingency either in natural processes or as expressions of the omnipotence of God are *unbiblical*, at best *ignorant* of what the normative standards of scripture give. The omnipotence of God is not violated by God's own choice to limit his freedom of action and he frequently in scripture "swears by himself" that we can have confidence in what he says. The paradox of contingency, sovereignty, and natural law resolves itself if we admit the premise that the God of the Judeo-Christian view has freely bound himself to his Word with its written commitment to a natural order and he will not break it:

> For when God made the promise to Abraham, since He could swear by no one greater, *He swore by Himself*, saying, "I will surely bless you, and I will surely multiply you." And thus, having patiently waited, he obtained the promise. For men swear by one greater than themselves, and with them an oath given as confirmation is an end of every dispute. In the same way God, desiring even more to show to the heirs of the promise the unchangeableness of His purpose, *interposed with an oath, in order that by two unchangeable things, in which it is impossible for God to lie*, we may have strong encouragement, we who have fled for refuge in laying hold of the hope set before us.[44]

We find further support in a pattern of God "swearing by His own name":

> "I solemnly swear by my own name," decrees the LORD.[45]

> But listen to what the LORD has to say, all you people of Judah who are living in the land of Egypt. The LORD says, "I hereby swear by my own great name that none of the people of Judah

---

43. These are chained quotes from Van Til in Bahnsen, *Van Til's Apologetic*, 281 ff., in the context of a discussion of this issue.
44. Heb 6:13–18 (NAS). Emphasis added.
45. Gen 22:16 NAS).

who are living anywhere in Egypt will ever again invoke my name in their oaths!"[46]

By "name" we understand that Hebrew idiom was emphasizing something about the fundamental existential nature and ethical character of God. God binds himself in *covenant* both to creation generally and secondly to his Israel first as a geographical area, later as a multiracial and multinational body known as his *ekklēsia*[47] or "church." One of the first arrests to the chaos imminent to creation after the figure of the fall was the *covenant* of God to maintain order in creation; certain cycles of the Earth were not arbitrary but would be a feature as long as the Earth remained:

> And the LORD smelled the soothing aroma and said to himself, "I will never again curse the ground because of humankind, even though the inclination of their minds is evil from childhood on. I will never again destroy everything that lives, as I have just done. While the earth continues to exist, planting time and harvest, cold and heat, summer and winter, and day and night will not cease."[48]

The significance of this passage is that God is not merely limiting his action to the law of contradiction which as Ó Murchadha noted was an "arbitrary stipulation"[49] but as an ethical act of the creator with regard to the creation. Thus, we have no imperative to follow what Louis Dupré had called the collapse in the belief in a rational quality of nature; there

---

46. Jer 44:26 (NAS).

47. The Greek word ἐκκλησία (*ekklēsia*, Strong's #1577) was originally a term applied to a governmental assembly in Greek city states. The etymology of the word reflects that meaning: the preposition *ek* refers to a moving or calling out of a general body; *klesia* was a calling, so we have a "calling out" to a governmental vocation. It was an apparently anachronistic use of the term by Jesus (Matt 16:18); its sense had been greatly weakened to mean little more than an association by that period, but the context makes it clear he was referring to this original sense of the word. Jesus' resurrection of the word ἀγαπᾷς (*agapaō*) as a more objective and stronger sense of "love" is another example of this renewal of the sense of a word that had almost disappeared from common parlance. It is vividly seen in the closing narrative of John where the difference between *phileo* and *agape* is played on with intense dramatic effect in the conversation between Jesus and Peter; Jesus interrogates Peter twice with *agape*, Peter replies with *phileo*, and in the third instance Jesus uses *phileo* but then makes clear to Peter the difference between the two. I respectively disagree with the NET translation notes in this respect, who argue that the scholarly consensus of the twentieth century is that there is no significance of the variation of the verbs.

48. Gen 8:21–22 (NET).

49. Ó Murchadha, *Modern Self*, 52.

remains a *logos, the* Logos, for us. While we might concur with Ockham that our primary relation is not to be found in the relations of this world but in terms of the will of God, we deny that those relations are unimportant and that the will is inscrutable in its entirety.

In contrast, God created us for his good pleasure[50] but also divided Adam that he might not be alone, i.e., "all one," that his sufficiency was not to be found in an autonomous self; it is in Adam's relation to Adam, the male to the female in the world and of the world, that elucidates what modernity wanted to call the "dark" God.[51] The natural order was to reveal what inscripturation was to interpret properly for us and fulfilled in the "Word becoming flesh." When Jesus describes himself as "the Truth" it provides us with an anchor, and it makes the will of God known and arrests the disordered contingency of the world; one lives not "by bread alone" but "by every word that proceeds from the mouth of God."[52] This is a relational, experiential matter with both rational and spiritual dimensions. Our work here seeks to validate that union but is focusing on the recovery and exposition of the rational dimension. Jesus as "the Truth," *the* Word of God, demonstrates to us the correct use both of scripture and the communion with the Spirit of God, the paraclete[53] that leads us into all truth by bearing witness to the truth.[54] The rational dimension is instantiated in a specific commitment to what we would call metaphysical laws of nature:

> But I, the LORD, make the following promise: I have made a covenant governing the coming of day and night. I have established the fixed laws governing heaven and earth.[55]

---

50. Col 1:15–23.
51. Ó Murchadha, *Modern Self*, 55.
52. Matt 4:4; Luke 4:4. This is a quote by Jesus of Deut 8:3.
53. The Greek word παράκλητος (*paraklētos*, Strong's #3875) has been rendered Comforter, Helper, Teacher, Intercessor, and Advocate in Bible versions, the latter three being more forensic and preferred in more modern translations to the first two, which in modern English are much weaker in their sense. The context seems to demand this stronger, forensic sense of the word, especially in John 14:26, 15:26.
54. John 15:26 (NET). As Jesus is "the Truth" so the Spirit is the Spirit of Truth (or the truthful Spirit, the Spirit from the realm of the Truth—all possible renderings of the Greek genitive). There is a marvelous theological richness to John's language in chapters 14–17, which are perhaps some of those most profound and intimate passages within the Christian scriptures.
55. Jer 33:25 (NET).

Thus, in summary, as my rhetorical point, I would rather critically label Voluntaristic Nominalism as Islamic Christianity to make the point that it is closer in its theology to Islam than Christianity; only in Islam is divine freedom unrestrained as a matter of doctrine. In Islam contingency is banished and that banishment is expressed in whatever has happened or will happen is "Allah's will" with the absurd practical consequences we noted at the end of the previous section. This is without prejudice in acknowledging the prevalence of a similar view across a wide spectrum of Christianity and it being highly influential in both Catholic and Protestant positions.

Yet finally, my principal objection to an unrestrained divine omnipotence is an ethical one: I do not believe it is a biblically supportable position, and it is a mistaken position born out of the pressures and tensions with the emergence of modernity as cogently examined and expertly explicated in the account of Ó Murchadha, which we have made reference to in ordering our own thoughts. Part of the service Van Til offered was what Bahnsen called the "Reformation of Christian Apologetics"[56] in arguing for a defense of the faith which rejected both the synthesis of Aristotle and Christianity in Aquinas and the irrationality of voluntarism by a secularization of Ockham in evidentialism. Though Scotus allows us to glimpse a reconciliation of freedom and determinism, the hermeneutical circle prevents any general resolution that would satisfy all objections. Our philosophical point then becomes it is only a Christian conception of Christianity that has any claim as the transcendental of rationality, and it is only by referring to scripture that we can resolve the philosophical tension.

5.6 Biblical Presuppositionalism

As indicated, space will not permit us to argue the details sketched above in any more depth, most certainly because of the theological nature and the range of the rebuttals and replies they warrant, but it does permit us to strengthen our main *philosophical* point of method. *If* we are asserting the *necessary* truth of the Christian worldview, that the Christian worldview provides the foundation for the intelligibility for *all* propositional claims, *then* we can see that only by the *borrowing* from this worldview can the claims advanced by any variant of the contra worldview be *understood*. A non-believer cannot argue with us until they have accepted, perhaps

---

56. Bahnsen, "Socrates or Christ," 191–240.

implicitly and unconsciously, the Judeo-Christian metaphysics with both its determinacy and contingency, logic, the possibility of language and the guarantees of certain knowledge that the Christian metaphysics enables.[57]

That is, the transcendental mode of reasoning, or the more exact synonym indicating Van Til's particular Christian form of transcendentalism, *reasoning by biblical presupposition*, is the precondition for intelligibility. The challenge is then to understand correctly how the term "presupposition" is being used by Van Til as failing to recognize the transcendental context merely places Christianity as one competing *a priori* against any other.[58] Further, a failure to recognize the distinct sense in which Van Til is using the term confuses Van Tillian presuppositionalism with other forms of "presuppositionalism" that were contemporary to his[59] and frequently appear lumped together with him in the literature. For example, the Clarkian use of the term, which viewed presuppositions in an axiomatic or geometric fashion, i.e., not subject to proof,[60] means something entirely different to Van Til's use of the term presupposition subject to a transcendental proof. Similarly, Schaeffer and Carnell[61] understood "pre-

---

57. This is what Van Til labeled as the "unbelieving believer," one who has persuaded themselves they do not believe and yet they live their life on assumptions only supported outside their worldview. This concept Van Til described as "difficult" owing to the implied paradox, and he struggled to express it clearly. It was left to Bahnsen, *Conditional Resolution*, to present this concept in a philosophically rigorous manner.

58. Montgomery, "Once Upon an A Priori," 380–92. Van Til's lengthy rejoinder (392–403) was written to correct this misunderstanding, though Montgomery continued to push this interpretation of Van Til throughout his career.

59. It is an interesting question as to how great Van Til's influence was on these men. Carnell and Schaeffer had both studied under Van Til, although Schaeffer never acknowledged his influence and Carnell only mentioned Van Til once in a footnote in his own major apologetic work, *Apologetics*.

60. Clark, *Three Types*. Clark was a logical foundationalist early in his career but in this work (his last major work), he finally argues for fideism.

61. Carnell was the professor of apologetics at Fuller Theological Seminary, one of the great fundamentalist seminaries created by the second wave of fundamentalists in 1947. The story of Fuller is told in Marsden, *Reforming Fundamentalism*; these were not as anti-intellectual, obscurantist, or isolationist as had characterized some of the first wave. However, they were certainly not Calvinistic in any respect other than favoring the same linguistic constructions, e.g., inerrancy, scriptural authority, etc. (contra Packer's apology at the end of his *"Fundamentalism,"* 173, which *had* equated it with Reformed Christianity), and they favored rigorously evidentialist apologetics. Carnell recognized the need to engage with conventional intellectual thought which he felt was "existential." He was thus more than happy to import in some Kierkegaardian conceptions into his thought as well as the post-positivistic emphasis on empirical methods.

supposition" as the statement of a scientific hypothesis and let the one with the best correspondence to the court of reality emerge victorious:

> Good philosophers are those who can construct systematically consistent systems of meaning.... This conclusion establishes the *possibility* of Christianity as an answer to life's dilemma. Careful investigation of it as a system might establish its *actuality*.[62]

> The fact of these data makes the postulation of God's existence both scientifically and rationally satisfying.... It is likewise good science to declare for faith in the existence of God. The mark of an acceptable hypothesis is its ability to explain the facts as we experience them.... Is it not good science to postulate the existence of God to account for known data in human experience?[63]

> The Bible claims itself to be a propositional truth.... Therefore it is open to discussion and verification.[64]

All these examples are radically distinct from Van Til's sense of the term "presupposition." The formulations are second-order derivations from what Van Til considers as the presupposition of these presuppositional positions, or the *transcendental* that makes it possible to *support* these formulations; or, remembering Kant's definition, what is assumed for *any* knowledge. To emphasize, Van Til *does* consider his presuppositions as subject to an indirect proof from the impossibility of the contrary, i.e., a transcendental proof. For example, in reply to an evidentialist "assault" from apologist Dr. Clark Pinnock,[65] Van Til in his rejoinder pinpoints the transcendental, biblical presuppositional nature, i.e., *Christian* nature, epistemologically self-conscious, logically coherent nature of his position:

> You are quite right in saying of me, "he believes he can *begin* with God and Christianity without first consulting objective reality." This is the heart of the matter. *If I were to attempt to know what "objective reality" was, apart from the all-embracing message of God as Christ speaking in Scripture, I would deny . . . all that it means to be a "Christian."*[66]

---

62. Carnell, *Apologetics*, 97.
63. Carnell, *Philosophy of the Christian Religion*, 270 ff.
64. The expanded version of this material is found in Schaeffer, *God Who Is There*, 129–50.
65. Pinnock, "Philosophy of Christian Evidences," 420–25.
66. Geehan, *Jerusalem and Athens*, 426 (Van Til's response to Pinnock). Emphasis added.

The glaring mistake Pinnock makes is he assumes "objective reality" is a set of brute facts that are exempt from interpretation or any type of theoretical description, an astonishingly naïve position. It is the *mode* of reasoning and proof which is at issue here, rather than the nature of the premise.

We recognize the categorical distinctiveness of the transcendental mode of reasoning while stipulating only the transcendent ontological Trinity permits a truly transcendental and coherent philosophy to emerge. This was a radical departure from historic apologetic approaches, and we might say, a radical rediscovery of biblical method, most certainly true to the precursors found in the work of the Reformers and specifically in Calvin:

> Mingled vanity and pride appear in this, that when miserable men do seek after God, instead of ascending higher than themselves as they ought to do, *they measure him* by their own carnal stupidity, and neglecting solid inquiry, fly off to indulge their curiosity in vain speculation. Hence, *they do not conceive of him in the character in which he is manifested, but imagine him to be whatever their own rashness has devised.*[67]

A recurring theme in Calvin is that a failure to honor the word of God *on its own terms*, what we are calling a transcendental, presuppositional, and epistemologically self-consciousness manner, leads to what the apostle Paul called "philosophy that is vain and deceitful"[68] which should be contrasted with Calvin's positing of a Christian philosophy:

> It is the duty of those who have received from God . . . to guide and assist them in *finding the sum of what God has been pleased*

---

67. Calvin, *Institutes* 1.4.1. Emphasis added.

68. Col 2:8, my translation, as also seen for example in the NET. The NET notes are helpful here: "The Greek reads *tēs philosophias kai kenēs apatēs*. The two nouns *philosophias* and *kenēs* are joined by one article and probably form a hendiadys. Thus, the second noun was taken as modifying the first." That is, the emphasis is on qualifying "philosophy" as of the "vain and deceitful" type, not "philosophy and vain deceit" as rendered by some translations (e.g., KJV, NAS) which would suggest the illegitimacy of philosophy generally (hence, the hostility of many fundamentalists and charismatics to it, with this being the "proof text"). It is true there might be other grammatical constructions that could have been used here that would not have been so ambiguous when translating into English, but this is Greek idiom. The extended second clause of the verse (introduced by the *kata* preposition followed by the *accusative* case) strongly suggests an amplification of what a "vain and deceitful" philosophy would be: "according to human traditions and the elemental spirits of the world, and not according to Christ," which most translations *do* unambiguously agree on.

to teach us in his word. Now, this cannot be better done in writing than by treating in succession of the principal matters which are comprised in Christian philosophy.[69]

Thus, we now have all the parts of our philosophical toolbox ready to be combined into a Transcendental Argument for God. We need to summarize, formalize, and clarify our salient points but we are now in the position to demonstrate the power and application of epistemological self-consciousness.

5.7 Summary and Conclusion

We began this section by identifying that Van Til's transcendentalism collapses the difference between non-Christian worldviews as simply a difference of emphasis rather than a substantive difference. He made the distinction between competing non-Christian worldviews a dichotomy between religious worldviews that patterned themselves after Christianity, relying to some degree on Christian patterns of thought and irrational or fideist conceptions. We recognized that in Van Til there is a qualitative as well as a quantitative distinction maintained between Creature and Creation; a worldview is considered "univocal" when it refuses to recognize this distinction and exalts human conceptions, or the human intellect as considered able to operate independently from God. To this end, we saw that Van Til recognized the Kantian distinction that a natural theology can only ever establish a naturalized God; in order for there to be a bridge between nature and supernature there must be a transcendent Trinitarian conception for our transcendental that can at once unite mind and world, universal and particular; at once immanent and transcendent. The Holy Spirit unites with the spirit of the individual believer, but God's autonomy is also protected in the other personalities of the Godhead. We also established the principle that the Trinitarian concept allows determinism and contingency to be reconciled in the will of God; God guarantees through his covenant the "Laws of Nature" and indicates his will is that humanity might choose freely.

We recognized that sovereignty, contingency, and predestination have been difficult subjects for Christians seeking a coherent account;

---

69. Calvin, in the French preface added to the French version of the *Institutes* published in Geneva. Emphasis added. Calvin had originally published in Latin (which was considered the "international" language of the academy) and then published in French as the influence of the Reformation grew.

yet, by considering the scriptural narrative we concluded that predestination and free will are not mutually exclusive in the logic of God. To accept that the natural world operates in a realm of absolute freedom would make both God and scripture subject to the wills of men; rather, the transcendental status and character of logic is derivative from the very nature of God and makes possible the only conception of the *a priori* that is not vulnerable to the claim of arbitrariness. We noted that the apostle Paul asserts all humanity immanently know God but decide to suppress the truth because of their unrighteousness and rebellion, and they are thus culpable irrespective of their confession or understanding of faith. In this conclusion is the recognition of the distinction between natural *revelation* and natural *theology*, the latter untenable but the former universal to all; natural revelation can *confirm* what the special revelation of scripture teaches, but natural revelation cannot lead to the knowledge of God revealed only by the special revelation of the scriptures.

We confirmed that there is a legitimate place for detailed evidential or scientific research regarding the metaphysical claims that might be found in scripture or to assess the historicity of biblical claims. We understood such investigations can help to diffuse pluralism rather than establish it; we are granting a legitimacy to the modal sphere of human life and are rejecting a religious hegemony, though maintaining the ethical mandate of the Church to ensure research recognizes the transcendental assumptions of its methods as gaining legitimacy and coherency only on the basis of the existence of the Christian God for only that specific conception of God that guarantees determinism in nature while maintaining the freedom of individual men. We traced the relations through Aquinas to Scotus, who maintained a compatibility between freedom and divine decrees, to Ockham which would give way to a fully independent realm of nature and a fideist commitment; to the Augustinian position in both Reformed and modern Catholicism which maintained that nature and providential grace are not separate. We concluded that Van Til is Augustinian in this very important manner, for he maintained a human will was free but was never autonomous, and human thought was not novel but was derivative; we asserted that the category of possibility is enveloped by God and not vice versa. God conditions what is possible. Thus, a discourse that does not recognize this view of possibility invalidates itself for the paradox of contingency, sovereignty, and natural law only resolves itself if we admit the premise that the God of the Judeo-Christian view has freely bound himself to his Word.

We thus concluded the necessity of biblical presuppositionalism in establishing that only the Christian worldview, its metaphysical relations, epistemological assertions, and its ethical principles unveiled in the narrative of the scriptures, provides the transcendental foundation for *all* intelligibility. It is a general condition for the intelligibility of any discourse. We understood that it is important to understand presuppositionalism in Van Til's sense; there were presuppositionalists that operated on axiomatic or hypothetical assumptions, and which fail to provide a transcendental terminus, dealing only with probabilities, rather than certainties. In contrast, Van Til's view was characterized as providing the transcendental that makes possible the transcendental principles assumed in science and logic, managing to succeed where Kant failed with his categories of the understanding. With this confidence in the transcendental basis of our method established, we now want to formalize it and then apply it to the central question of our thesis, whether there is an objective proof for the existence of God and the moral imperative for a Christian philosophy.

6

The Transcendental Argument for God (TAG)

6.1 Introduction

IN THIS SECTION, WE formalize our work of the previous two chapters with transcendental reasoning and demonstrate how Van Til presented his argument designed to demonstrate the existence of God as objectively provable.

- a. We consider the distinctive logical form.
- b. We examine the historical pedigree of the form.
- c. We formalize the other distinctives of the mode of reasoning.
- d. We consider the controversies surrounding the conceptual and ontological necessity of the argument form.
- e. We present Van Til's proof and consider the criticisms of it and the possible mitigations in recent work.

6.2 Logical Form and Overview

To formalize the argument of the previous two chapters, the general *logical* form[1] of the transcendental argument is this:

> *Assume X*   X is accepted by all participants in the argument, even a local skeptic.
>
> *Demonstrate* that X presupposes Y (often through a *reductio absurdum* or the *impossibility of the contrary*).
>
> Y is the controversial or contested proposition.

We should immediately recognize that certain forms of global skepticism might not be prepared to accept X or later reject it if they are required to accept Y, but their skepticism is then held to be *incoherent* (they are rejecting a *necessary precondition* of formulating their skeptical argument) and there is no argument to be had. We wish to engage with those who consider it is possible to argue in a constructive and philosophical manner, to first understand and then make progress toward philosophical solutions to philosophical problems.

Transcendental argumentation stretches all the way back in Western philosophy to Aristotle where he argues transcendentally for the law of non-contradiction.[2] Aristotle's point was simple—if you argue *against* logic, you are *assuming* logic in making an argument against logic and your challenge is incoherent. Bahnsen puts the promise of the form rather less arcanely, if you want to be in the "reason giving game," you must play by the rules of that game—if you *deny* reason as reasonable, there is no need to listen to you as all your own utterances must be irrelevant in their unreasonableness by your *own* standards. If you believe you *can* demand an answer, you have entered the game, the *rules apply* and those rules *disqualify* you[3]—you are of necessity operating on my presuppositions regarding reason whether or not you accept that you are, it is a logical prerequisite of us engaging in any discussion.[4]

---

1. Stern and Cheng, "Transcendental Arguments," § 2.2.

2. Aristotle, *Metaphysics* 1005 b35–1006 a28. Competent editions of Aristotle's work (e.g., as listed in the bibliography) will have references to the positions within the original manuscripts to which these numbers refer.

3. Wittgenstein in his *Investigations* has much to say regarding the role of "rules" in philosophical discussion. In the revised fourth edition the index entry for "rules" is exceptional as is the indexing of the volume generally.

4. Bahnsen, *Four Types of Proof*.

THE TRANSCENDENTAL ARGUMENT FOR GOD (TAG)

A similar argument may be had to those worldviews that offer a mitigated account of reason or ascribe it a subsidiary role. To the *degree* that the role and power of reason is mitigated in those systems is the *degree* to which we need not be bound by their conclusions. While we are not so foolish as to claim an "absolute" power of reason in the human subject, we are claiming an absolute *principle* of reasonableness capable of being understood by the human subject, that is, the transcendent transcendental of God himself revealed to us within scripture. That provides us the confidence that we have access to the Truth, both in a metaphysical, experiential sense encompassing our religious experience and the epistemological sense for living in the world, recognizing these two are intimately and unavoidably involved in one another. For the latter, epistemological sense, that is reflected and made evident in our derivative reasonings which may legitimately be subject to detailed exposition, refinement, or falsification. We can be certain with regard to the metaphysical status of Truth—it exists—but fallible in our understanding and application of it.

As mentioned in our previous review, this "skepticism refuting" potential of transcendental argumentation has been what, in the modern debate,[5] has generated the most interest in them. That the skeptic somehow wins despite all our attempts at providing grounds for reason is what Kant, the most famous exponent of the argument form, finds principally objectionable as found in his famous footnote:

> It remains a scandal to philosophy, and to human reason in general, that we should have to accept the existence of things outside us (from which we derive the whole material for our knowledge, even for that of our inner sense) merely *on trust*, and have no satisfactory proof with which to counter any opponent who chooses to doubt it.[6]

For many philosophers who believe in discourse and discussion as a means and an end, that progress is possible with philosophical problems, skepticism is a most unsatisfactory terminus.[7] It was on this basis that we asserted a *prima facie* case for the value and distinctiveness of transcendental reasoning.

---

5. Generally accepted to have begun with the publication of Strawson's *Individuals*, from which time they became a "prominent fixture in contemporary philosophy" (Butler, "Transcendental Argument for God's Existence," 90).

6. Kant, *Critique of Pure Reason*, Bxl (footnote). Emphasis original.

7. Körner, *Fundamental Questions*, xi.

6.3 The Distinctiveness of Transcendental Reasoning

6.3.1 The Conclusion Is a *Transcendental*

One of the distinctives of transcendental argumentation is that the conclusion of a transcendental argument is not a conclusion about a specific fact of reality but rather a *transcendental*, that which is assumed to make the argument or the interpretation and evaluation of any other fact of reality intelligible at all:

> [Transcendental argumentation] would serve . . . to purge . . . our reason [and] would guard reason against errors. I call all knowledge transcendental which deals not so much with objects as with our manner of knowing objects insofar as this manner is to be possible *a priori*.[8]

The same does not apply for inductive, abductive, or deductive reasoning—the conclusions of the individual arguments do not form a category in themselves; they are just said to indicate some fact (in the case of deductive arguments), the best explanation (in the case of abductive arguments) or a generalized principle from experience (in the case of inductive arguments) about nature. It is a given of the deductive or inductive argument that the conclusions are derivative in character, whereas with a transcendental argument, premise and conclusion are involved in one another:

> [The transcendental argument] has the peculiar property that it renders its own proof namely, experience, first of all possible, and that it has always to be presupposed in experience.[9]

6.3.2 All Reasoning Is Circular Reasoning

We can expand our previous concluding sentence into a principle—the very act of reasoning must assume that reason is itself *reasonable*, i.e., that there is a rational basis for reason. As we argued previously, when understood in this way, *any* rational argument is circular. Rather ironically, it may be precisely this implicit circularity that an informed skeptic wishes to establish in their argumentation, but transcendental reasoning

---

8. Kant, *Critique of Pure Reason*, A11–12.
9. Kant, *Critique of Pure Reason*, A737|B765.

THE TRANSCENDENTAL ARGUMENT FOR GOD (TAG)

renders this a *non sequitur*. Transcendental reasoning alone seeks to mute the skeptic on this point by demonstrating that the attempting of a skeptical argument is incoherent because it is assuming the coherence of reason while arguing there can be no basis for its coherence.

6.3.3 The Scope of the Argument

The *scope* of the argument is another important principle in establishing the distinctive character of transcendental arguments. Some simple or trivial formulations with a limited scope might have the formal structure of a transcendental argument (we might call it a transcendentally framed *statement*) and be amenable to *rhetorical (re-)phrasing* as inductive or deductive constructions but these are then seen to not fulfill the full criteria of being a transcendental *argument*.[10] That is, the *scope* of the argument is determinative in whether an argument is to be considered as *truly* transcendental. The broader the scope of the terms and the implications of the conclusion, the more authentically transcendental it is. Only when understood in this way as arguments of broad scope yielding a conclusion which is a transcendental itself, are such arguments a distinct category from inductive, deductive, pragmatic, or abductive argument.

So, for example, P. F. Strawson's famous transcendental argument in *Individuals* seeks to establish that *conceptually* we assume the persistence of objects in a spatial-temporal relation:

> There is no doubt that we have the idea of a single spatio-temporal system of material things; the idea of every material thing at any time being spatially related, in various ways at various times, to every other at every time. There is no doubt at all that this *is* our conceptual scheme. Now I say that a *condition* of our having this conceptual scheme is the unquestioning acceptance of particular-identity in at least some cases of non-continuous observation.[11]

The argument is *not* that in any *individual* case we guarantee the persistence of the objects when they are unperceived—it is perfectly possible that someone wishing to refute the thesis arranges for the swapping of items in a room with similar ones while we sleep. It is rather that the *general principle* of the *conceptual* persistence of distinct objects over

---

10. Bahnsen, *Van Til's Apologetic*, 500.
11. Strawson, *Individuals*, 35.

time while unperceived *must* be assumed by the skeptic who seeks to frame an argument that denies the persistence of unperceived objects. It is not for us to argue here whether Strawson was successful, but merely to point out this argument is designed to establish our conceptual belief that objects continue to exist over time, a non-specific, generally applicable conclusion.

This would be in contrast to the "polar case" arguments associated with Austin, Ryle, and others, in what is sometimes called the "Oxford School"[12] of Ordinary Language philosophy. Butler summarizes this well:

> [Transcendental Arguments] should not be confused with paradigm-case and/or polar concept arguments. . . . For while these types of arguments share a similar form with TAs, they differ greatly in the type of conclusion that is inferred. . . . A brief comparison should bring out this distinction. Austin argues that the skeptic's appeal to illusion does not work because the term "illusion" makes sense only in a context of having some real things to compare with it and thus everything could not be an illusion (or better put, it makes no sense to say everything is an illusion).

Now, we can immediately recognize the "transcendental" form, in that Austin was arguing the concept of illusion assumes the "real"; we would be tempted to say the "'real" is a transcendental for "illusion." However, the conclusion is parochial, narrow, and does not significantly hinder the skeptic. Butler continues:

> Assuming this argument works, the conclusion in somewhat parochial: it defeats only one particular skeptical challenge. The skeptic, though, can simply propose to toss away both words and offer a fresh challenge. A TA aims at something more cosmopolitan . . . the difference between a TA and a polar concept argument is one of scope; the latter asks what are the necessary preconditions for the intelligible use of a small set of terms, the former is concerned with the use of a much larger set.[13]

Thus, to further clarify this, if we were to be asking within what epistemological or metaphysical context does speaking about both "real" or "illusion" make sense or is intelligible, e.g., we are concluding that there is a world of external objects, identifying something about the nature of

---

12. However, Austin undoubtedly interacted with Wittgenstein's use of transcendental logic. For an introduction to the Oxford "ordinary language" school, see Longworth, "John Langshaw Austin."

13. Butler, "Transcendental Arguments for God's Existence," 92.

our mind and its relation to objects and identifying significant features of the mechanisms of perception; then we are arguing about fundamentals and preconditions of intelligibility that have a broad applicability. *We could thus be sure we are dealing with a transcendental argument rather than just an argument of an analogous form.*

Hence, in summary, we are establishing that the transcendental argument not only has a logical structure but has a specific kind of *semantic* content. Of course, it would not be difficult to imagine cases which fall between the polar case and the transcendental proper, but that there *is* a distinction is what is necessary for our purposes. When we consider Van Til's argument specifically, we should immediately recognize them as not just logically transcendental in form but semantically sufficient in content.

6.3.4 The Kant Controversy

Considering our definitional tension above, it is mindful that we do not get distracted by further pseudo-definitional controversies. Firstly, it is correct that the "modern" transcendental argument is properly to be interpreted as broadening the Kantian designation. The broadening of the scope is most clearly seen in the light of the modern debate which was initiated by P. F. Strawson's *Individuals* and *The Bounds of Sense*. Strawson was a *neo*-Kantian and modified Kant's transcendentalism to "avoid the [problematic] doctrines of transcendental psychology"[14] and to purposefully avoid the problematic category of the *synthetic a priori*.

However, some such as Hintikka directly challenged Strawson on this point (and the many others who were philosophically provoked by Strawson's posit), that their approach was not transcendental in the Kantian sense for:

> The references to the "psychological apparatus" which recent writers on transcendental arguments tend to dismiss as inessential are in fact close to the very gist of the Kantian arguments.[15]

That is, as Hintikka correctly noted, Kant reserved the term "transcendental" for the *specific* arguments that demonstrated how the mind imposed its categories, its sensibilities, and its understanding on the objects of experience, that is, the process of the mind "constructing

---

14. Strawson, *Bounds of Sense*, 97.
15. Hintikka, "Transcendental Arguments," 276.

knowledge" from phenomenal experience and giving it order, thus making that experience possible. He thus felt Strawson, Stroud, and "recent literature" had misunderstood the essence of the Kantian transcendental argument. However, the attack seems muddled as Hintikka then goes on to describe a feature of the "authentic" transcendental argument:

> The conclusion (the possibility of certain conceptual practices) is arrived at by reasoning which itself relies on these practices. The conclusion makes possible the very argument by means of which it is established. [In this] we seem to have in it a much better example of what would be a transcendental argument in a genuinely Kantian sense.[16]

This, of course, is *precisely* the essence of what Strawson, Stroud, and the "others" assumed in their arguments. For Strawson, the skeptic is disarmed because the skeptical conclusion can only be arrived at by reasoning that relies on a non-skeptical transcendental premise. While conceding to Hintikka that there is indeed a difference in the sense Kant understood the term, it is possible to put the dispute to rest, at least in the sense of anything philosophically important, by considering that the very same logical form of argument that bear the modern nomenclature of transcendental argument *are* Kantian arguments in the sense he employed them in the *Critique* (in the "second analogy" in the Refutation of Idealism). The most we need concede is that Kant reserved the term *transcendental* argument for arguments regarding the categories, the *neo*-Kantian does not and need not. It should also be noted that Aristotle argued transcendentally in this broader sense for the law of excluded middle, so the form has a long pedigree independent of the modern debate.

So, in summary, although there is an important technical sense in which modern transcendental arguments are distinct from Kantian transcendental arguments, just as modern neo-Darwinian arguments are distinct from Darwin's arguments,[17] it can be said that modern tran-

---

16. Hintikka, "Transcendental Arguments," 278.

17. In fact, modern "Darwinian" arguments are predicated on a different basis all together. "Natural selection" is not *the* mechanism for evolutionary change, and the radically different "Darwinian" models proposed to replace it proved an explosive debate between the rival evolutionist camps; see Sterelny, *Dawkins vs. Gould*.

THE TRANSCENDENTAL ARGUMENT FOR GOD (TAG)

scendental arguments, be they from Strawson, Wittgenstein,[18] Lewis,[19] or Van Til,[20] are still "transcendental" when understood in an analogous and widened sense in the context of Kant's critiques as a whole.[21]

6.3.5 Option "A" and Option "B" Transcendental Arguments

The most famous response to Strawson's seminal use of transcendental argumentation was that of Stroud.[22] In it he argued that the most transcendental arguments can do is to prove the necessity of certain *concepts* for our understanding of the world (option "A" arguments); it does not mean that the world is *actually* that way (option "B" arguments). That is, there is no ontological necessity associated with the transcendental argument that terminates at A. Stroud went on to argue that for transcendental arguments to bridge the gap to B, they would need to import in a form of verification principle which thus renders the transcendental move redundant. With verificationism dead and buried[23] fifteen years prior with Quine's critique of it, Stroud concluded the arguments were of no value in telling us the way the world *really* is, and the metaphysical skeptic remains undefeated, though perhaps with a far weaker justification for their skepticism.

However, although Stroud's arguments were insightful, he seemed to misunderstand that Strawson was *not* making an ontological claim. Strawson did not abandon transcendental argumentation in the wake of Stroud. In fact, he believed Stroud had radically misinterpreted what he himself was claiming for transcendental arguments. His interest was to

---

18. Wittgenstein's "Private Language" argument in the *Investigations*, 243–315, is perhaps the most complex example of a transcendental argument in the modern era. Rival schools of interpretation post-Kripke's appropriation of it developed. The basic transcendental concept is clear though: language is public by nature and exists in a communal form of life, therefore a "private" language known only to an individual is not possible.

19. Lewis's arguments in *Miracles* against naturalism are transcendental. He argues (as does Plantinga after him) that if naturalism is true, then it refutes itself.

20. We examine Van Til's distinctive form of transcendentalism, "Presuppositionalism," shortly.

21. Schaper and Vossenkuhl, *Reading Kant*, 56.

22. Stroud, "Transcendental Arguments," 241–56.

23. Some like Michael Martin attempted to resurrect the corpse as late as 1999. We will also consider an interesting variation on justifying the verification principle unrelated to this classical conception of verificationism.

demonstrate the interconnectedness of concepts as part of a "descriptive (as opposed to validatory or revisionary) metaphysics."[24] He was notably unmoved by the persistence of skeptical doubt:

> The point has been, not to offer a rational justification of the belief in external objects and other minds or of the practice of induction, but to represent skeptical arguments and rational counter-arguments as equally idle—not senseless, but idle—since what we have here are *original, natural, inescapable commitments which we neither choose nor could give up*. The further such commitment which I now suggest we should acknowledge is the commitment to belief in the reality and determinateness of the past.[25]

Here I would assert Strawson is making a conceptual version of Moore's appealing to what is *obvious* to *my* perception I am perfectly justified in believing in preference to *your* skeptical doubt, with no accommodation to the skeptic; viewing such doubt as "idle" and the evidentialist argument as equally idle.[26] Just as Wittgenstein considered the proposition "my name is Ludwig Wittgenstein" as certain but ungrounded, so Strawson (and Moore) view the skeptical question. That is, it does no *useful* work for us in relating to and living in the world, a view which we have seen finds resonance in Blackburn and Plantinga.

6.4 Van Til's Transcendentalism

6.4.1 Presuppositional Apologetics

In simple terms, Van Til's transcendentalism is captured in his famous aphorism, "atheism *presupposes* theism." Now the "presupposes" here is not merely a psychological or perceptual claim (an option "A" argument) but one which deals with the way the world really is (an option "B" argument). For Van Til, the transcendental argument is elevated to the worldview level, the whole account of nature and of supernature is laid as the bounds of the argument and the transcendental principle is deduced as the transcendent Trinity. Thus, the challenges of diversity and unity, of the one and the many, the particular and the universal are reconciled:

---

24. Strawson, *Scepticism and Naturalism*, 23.
25. Strawson, *Scepticism and Naturalism*, 27–28. Emphasis added.
26. Moore would have had no such reticence in describing it as "senseless."

THE TRANSCENDENTAL ARGUMENT FOR GOD (TAG)

> The presuppositional challenge to the unbeliever is guided by the premise that only the Christian worldview provides the philosophical preconditions necessary for man's reasoning and knowledge *in any field whatever*. This is what is meant by a "transcendental" defense of Christianity.... From beginning to end, man's reasoning about anything whatever (even reasoning about reasoning itself) is unintelligible or incoherent *unless the truth of the Christian scriptures is presupposed.*[27]

Now this means for Van Til, that Stroud's criticism of the option "B" argument loses its teeth. The Christian worldview explicitly connects the world as perceived with the world as it really is. The scriptures provide the mandate for a regularity of nature (thus validating inductive science), the *logos* for deductive and logical certainty and a pragmatic imperative for the solving human problems. Plantinga expresses this elegantly:

> *If we don't know that there is such a person as God,* we don't know the first thing (the most important thing) about ourselves, each other, and our world ... the most important truths about us and them is that we have been created by the Lord and utterly depend on him for our continued existence ... **we don't grasp the significance** of ... human phenomena ... science, art, music, philosophy.[28]

6.4.2 From Probability to Certainty

Van Til argued that the alternative models of reason, the inductive, deductive, abductive, pragmatic, and positivistic in all their variations and inflections, resolve to probabilities rather than certainty. He held that the challenge of Hume's deconstruction of empiricism and his denial of causality forever remained an asymptotic limiting concept to secular reasoning and permitted irrefutable skeptical doubt. Only with the help of the TAG can this be defeated, and the alternative modes of reasoning legitimized.

This is an important principle to understand, we are seeking to validate *all* forms of reason. Certain modes of reasoning are more suited to different problems than other kinds of reasoning, e.g., we can never reason deductively to answer the question whether it is raining (though

---

27. Bahnsen, *Van Til's Apologetic*, 5–6. Emphasis added.
28. Plantinga, *Warranted Christian Belief*, 217. Emphasis added.

we could argue inductively based on air pressure, windspeed, humidity etc.), it must be settled with an empirical operation.

6.4.3 Indirect Argumentation

When we have an argument over any feature of nature and share common presuppositions then appeal can be made to the legitimizing authority to resolve a dispute. For example, two botanists in a dispute over a particular genus can refer to their common taxonomical authority, follow an agreed procedure, and settle the dispute. This is an example of a *direct* argument where the facts can be established because there is a common *philosophy of facts* between the parties. However, when common presuppositions are not shared, i.e., our accounts of nature are different, when our "conceptual schemes" or "worldviews" are in conflict, our philosophy of facts differ; when there are competing *a priori* conceptions or "incommensurate paradigms,"[29] then it is not possible to settle the argument directly.

Some believe that there is some kind of philosophical stand-off in this situation and that no reasoning is possible between the competing parties. We saw what Wittgenstein called a "form of life" and the language game can only be understood from within that community. Each community is self-validating, and neither can dismiss the other. Van Til was frequently accused[30] by critics of this position which might also be called fideism.[31] However, such a criticism of Van Til totally misconstrues the transcendental nature of his reasoning. Transcendental reasoning allows for the assessment of the truth claim of a worldview by subjecting the opposing positions to an internal critique on their *own* terms and/or demonstrating the impossibility of the contrary view to the Christian view.

As we have seen, with Van Tillian logic, there are only two worldviews—the *Christian* and the *non*-Christian. The *Christian* worldview starts from the presupposition of the transcendent God who reveals himself in the scriptures with the mind of the human subject derivative in its reasoning and subject to divine authority and sanction. The *non*-Christian worldview asserts the autonomy of human thought. Thus, although there are apparently incommensurate non-Christian worldviews,

29. This phrase is particularly associated with post-Kuhnian discourse. We will consider Kuhn in much more detail later.

30. Montgomery, "Once Upon an A Priori," 380–403.

31. More specifically *Wittgensteinian* fideism; see Nielsen and Phillips, *Wittgensteinian Fideism?*

THE TRANSCENDENTAL ARGUMENT FOR GOD (TAG)

they are variations on the same basic presupposition of the autonomous status of the human mind as ultimate authority—seen most obviously in the varieties of naturalism.

It is not possible to settle the differences between worldview directly but by arguing that denying the Christian presupposition renders any *other* account of reality unintelligible, it refutes the non-Christian worldview in *all* its inflections. We are not arguing directly over some "fact" of nature but indirectly regarding the very structure of the thought that renders it intelligible. The unique logical structure of transcendental argument is that we can start with p or $\sim p$ (where p is any fact of the universe as a premise) and demonstrate the transcendental necessity of our presupposition. This is not the case with inductive or deductive arguments: you refute a premise, it invalidates the conclusion. Kant implies this when he asserts the transcendental makes possible the ground for its own proof and is assumed as we are arguing for that very same transcendental.

What makes Van Tillian argument distinctive is that he broadens the transcendental argument to not just a conceptual scheme, but the *worldview* level. The argument is simple, *only* the Christian *worldview* makes human predication possible. For Van Til, human *predication*[32] is concrete and not abstract reasoning,[33] by which we mean the mind of God establishes the coherence between and the correspondence with the facts of the world. This sets it apart from the transcendental deductions of the categories of understanding in Kant,[34] the *cogito* of Descartes[35] or the modalism of Dooyeweerd.[36] Van Til maintains that their critiques fail because they seek only to establish transcendentally a principle, but a further transcendental proof would then be required to *ground* the transcendentals themselves.[37] In essence, Van Til starts his transcendental

---

32. "Predication" was a term still in common use in philosophy during the 1930s when Van Til was working out his theory. To predicate means simply to ascribe a property to an object, e.g., "redness," "roundness," "physical," "mental," etc.

33. Bahnsen, *Van Til's Apologetic*, 461–530.

34. Bahnsen, *Van Til's Apologetic*, 508. There are many places in Van Til where he deals directly with Kant. Van Til accepted that the transcendental *program* of Kant was appropriate but completely repudiated the autonomous presumption of Kant.

35. Bahnsen, *Van Til's Apologetic*, 509, 510n90.

36. Bahnsen, *Van Til's Apologetic*, 48 ff.

37. This is the essence of Van Til's treatment of Descartes. He said the *cogito* failed as a transcendental because it does not prove anything beyond that thinking is occurring; it *assumes* the further ground necessary for its own validation rather than proving an external world, as such it was like "a rock in a bottomless ocean."

reasoning with God, God does not earn his place at the philosophical table after the autonomous mind of humanity has validated the legitimacy of his presence.

6.5 The Criticisms of TAG

6.5.1 Global Criticisms of Transcendentalism

It would be amiss of us to ignore the controversial history of modern transcendentalism before we consider the possible criticisms of TAG specifically, for TAG is a specialization of the category. If the category is unsafe, then TAG is moot. It is not our intention here to rehearse these arguments in their agonizing detail, but rather to offer a high-level survey that demonstrates the plausibility of the category can be maintained despite these criticisms.[38] The justification for such a brief examination is threefold in addition to the obvious one of our limited space:

a. Van Tillian transcendentalism as presented above offers a very clear argument, the force of which it is not difficult to appreciate. Criticisms of TAG are often more specific to TAG rather than the general criticisms of transcendentalism.

b. Much of the dispute over transcendentalism appears linguistic rather than substantive.

c. Others have made it the central focus of their advanced studies[39] and we have the benefit of summarizing the main conclusions of their work.

The most trenchant criticisms were found in Gram's paper where he denied the category in its entirety.[40] However, he received a strong response from Hintikka who was keen to clarify what precisely a transcendental argument was as some confusion[41] had arisen in the literature as

---

38. Emphasis here on the *agonizing*. As Quine noted in his *Theories and Things*, it can be difficult to make sense of transcendentalism, especially when we deal with some post-Heideggerian writing.

39. For example, Baird, "Transcendental Arguments," provides the most thorough review, reassessment, and extension of transcendental arguments that I know of.

40. Gram, "Transcendental Arguments," 15–26.

41. As we have noted previously, Hintikka was keen to draw a distinction between Kantian transcendental arguments and arguments like those of Strawson that were claiming to be transcendental. This might be technically correct, but it simply indicates

THE TRANSCENDENTAL ARGUMENT FOR GOD (TAG)

reflected in Gram's "paradigm case"[42] in that paper. He then "corrected" Gram in the most explicit way by re-positing the "proper" category in its pure Kantian sense, receiving equally vigorous ripostes from Gram.[43] Leaving out the details,[44] it would seem Hintikka *had* established criteria sufficiently persuasive against the transcendental skepticism of Gram which would arguably distinguish a space for a transcendental *method*,[45] if not the category.

However, alongside this vexed technical dispute there were notable philosophers such as Grayling and McDowell[46] making influential and extensive use of a transcendental approach and as Butler notes, Frege, Wittgenstein, Davidson, Putnam, and Searle had all employed the mode of argumentation.[47] It would thus seem the ground is firm enough beneath transcendental arguments that we can acknowledge them as valid;

---

the bounds of the definition had widened; it cannot be denied that Strawson was a neo-Kantian.

42. Hintikka, "Transcendental Arguments," 274–81.

43. Gram, "Must We Revisit Transcendental Arguments?," 235–48.

44. There was a *technical* and somewhat ill-tempered debate between the two men that ran for at least five years, with Gram in the final paper adopting a very different strategy, ceding a small amount of ground to Hintikka (perhaps making room for a method that might be "transcendental," while simultaneously refusing to admit the category). Other exchanges involving Gram and Hintikka on unrelated matters seemed equally tense; both were Finnish and so there may have been a cultural angle to their exchanges that has not been sufficiently appreciated.

45. The technical issues might be distilled thus: transcendental arguments are *a priori* arguments, and they are deductive arguments. We already have *a priori* and deductive arguments as categories, *why* are we positing another category?

46. McDowell's *Mind and World* and a successor volume, *Having the World in View*, are examples of modern post-Kantian transcendentalism. McDowell was noted for importing "continental" philosophy into analytic philosophy, and the density (or enigma) of his prose at times is reminiscent of Continental writers though he was startlingly well received in analytic circles (according to the back cover of *World in View*). Speaking as one analytically minded, "Continental" transcendentalism can make one empathize quickly with Quine's observation regarding transcendentalism, "as much as I can make sense of it." With Quine, I find it opaque, difficult to understand, and even harder to apply, but that could equally be a failure on my part to give sufficient attention to understanding the Continental mode of thought. Interestingly, it seems Strawson runs against the grain of this movement despite being the best-known transcendentalist of the generation (see Han-Pile, "Early Heidegger's Appropriation," n17) and gains clarity and understandableness as a consequence. Ó Murchadha, *Phenomenology*, does a far better job of applying this mode of thought in a Christian context, which makes my point—it is the Christian context that validates the transcendentals and transcendentalism generally.

47. Butler, "Transcendental Argument for God's Existence," 101.

the specific issues of dispute are more related to the domain of their application rather than a foundational invalidation. Further, as I noted it introducing this section, it is *not* unclear as to what the Van Tillian transcendental argument claims, even if it is denied that it is an effective argument. It should be immediately admitted that Van Til's argument is breathtaking in its ambition and perspicuous in its simplicity.[48] It is an eminently accessible statement of revolutionary apologetic principles, but as Butler notes, "He was content to present the argument in broad strokes and leave the details aside ... he left the detailed work to his followers."[49] Inevitably, the brevity of presentation, the revolutionary character, and his lack of a defense meant the attacks levied against it were many and furious from his opponents.[50] It is to them we turn and assess whether the argument can withstand them.

6.5.2 The Nature of TAG

One criticism, particularly associated with "Van Tillian" John Frame,[51] is that TAG is not a unique argument form, rather it is merely a rhetorical

---

48. The fullest statement of his argument runs to just 633 words and was originally found in Van Til, "Survey of Christian Epistemology" (1969), now in *Defense of the Faith*, 204–5. The brevity, of course, is not necessarily a weakness as this means the basic thrust of the argument can be understood by the young student as well as the tenured professor of fifty years, but Van Til left it to his immediate disciples to develop and strengthen the argument.

49. Butler, "Transcendental Argument for God's Existence," 76.

50. Van Til's most influential work, *Defense of the Faith*, was first published in 1955 and went through three editions to 1967. He was made emeritus in 1972 at over seventy years of age, so it can be seen this work was extremely important in the latter stages of his career. Large sections of the work are responses to criticisms from both within and without the Reformed community, which tends to obscure the coherence of the presentation of his views; this is why Bahnsen created his commentary, *Van Til's Apologetic*, pulling together and systematizing Van Til from this and other sources. Van Til certainly considered Bahnsen as the authority on his position.

51. Frame, *Apologetics*, 73–94. Some of Frame's less sympathetic critics like to call him a "soft" Van Tillian. Butler, recognized as a "strong" Van Tillian, does argue Frame has "fundamentally departed" from Van Til in some respects while acknowledging Frame as one who has made use of and developed other aspects of Van Til's thought. It should be noted that Frame personally knew Van Til and testifies that Van Til encouraged him as an advocate for his thought. It should also be noted that Frame, alongside Bahnsen, is one of the few who have attempted a systematic overview of Van Til's thought, and his work was generally well received in Reformed circles closest to Van Til.

Frame's greatest difficulty was with respect to transcendental arguments as a distinct argument form. Bahnsen's *Answer to Frame* was a direct challenge to Frame's

THE TRANSCENDENTAL ARGUMENT FOR GOD (TAG)

method[52] and can be reduced to the more traditional arguments for God's existence as found in Aquinas, particularly the cosmological and teleological arguments which argue from design and causality to God.[53] However, there is a basic misunderstanding demonstrated by Frame here. The unbeliever has no right to even formulate the concept of *causality* in the autonomous fashion that the traditional arguments employ. Van Til's position is that the concept of causality would not be intelligible as a standalone concept without the ontological Trinity to provide the transcendent basis of the transcendental. As Butler notes:

> [Traditional cosmological arguments assume] that the non-believer is perfectly justified in believing in causation and/or using the concept of causation. Indeed, it assumes that human experience and understanding in general and causation in particular are perfectly intelligible outside the Christian worldview.[54]

In contrast, a *transcendental* argument demonstrates the necessity of the concept by the impossibility of the opposite, not by a direct inference about cause itself, as seen in the traditional arguments. At best, the traditional argument might be seen *within the believing community* as concluding that God is the *transcendent* cause of the universe, but equally for the unbeliever it might just demonstrate some "transcendental" that fits into a deterministic view of "nature." Thus, this is very different from proving the existence of God is *transcendentally* necessary, the ground for all being and for the intelligibility of nature[55] and thus Frame's contention is unsound.

---

interpretation on this key point of difference, made even more notable in that Frame was in the audience for one of the four lectures and Bahnsen was presenting his lecture *to* Frame's class. Butler was also in attendance. There is an interesting exchange at the end of the presentation in which Frame was present, but in later work it seems Frame *does* acknowledge the strength of Bahnsen's counterarguments and accepts the legitimacy of the transcendental argument.

52. We might be tempted to argue here that this is a theological version of Gram's assault as he too argued it was merely a "method." However, anyone reading Gram and Frame would have to concede they are proceeding on a totally dissimilar basis. Frame, in broad outline (with the qualification in the previous note), accepts Van Til's analysis.

53. Frame goes as far to argue that Aquinas was formulating his arguments *assuming* the Christian worldview and therefore the Christian worldview was the transcendental for Aquinas. However, remarkable as Aquinas was, it was in his appropriation and application of *Aristotle* that provides the conceptual background to his work.

54. Butler, "Transcendental Argument for God's Existence," 80.

55. It is also worth noting, as both Butler and Plantinga do, that the traditional causal arguments are *poor* arguments that have been "sliced and diced" since Hume

6.5.3 The Uniqueness Proof

By this, what is meant is that Christianity might be proved by TAG as being a *sufficient* condition to satisfy the premise of human experience and intelligibility of that experience, but it has not been demonstrated that it is a *necessary* one. Most commonly, this is asserted that there may be a worldview "X" that may or may not have been discovered that might also provide the conditions of intelligibility. Thus, it can *never* be established that Christianity is the *only* instantiation fulfilling the premises or that it will remain so.

This contention, however, misunderstands the nature of transcendental proof which is not localized to a particular worldview. From the point of view of TAG internally, this is not problematic as for TAG there are only two possible worldviews, the Christian or the non-Christian. If *any* non-Christian view is refuted, then *all* are refuted, and the Christian is by default correct (what is termed a disjunctive syllogism).

6.5.4 The Mere Sufficiency of the Christian Worldview

This is really a special case of the previous objection. If the critic asserts, we have a simple disjunction (A or B or ... N), it no longer holds that given ~B (or ~C ... ~N) we have A. Any of the alternatives will present a sufficient worldview, including the Christian one, but not a *necessary* one. However, as with the "uniqueness" objection, this misses the crucial issue regarding transcendental argumentation. It is not arguing about refuting a specific instantiation of the class "non-Christian worldview" but rather the conceptual validity of the non-Christian worldview *type* that provides the template for that class.[56]

---

and Kant took issue with them. Russell gave a second coat of derision in the twentieth century. Whereas the ontological argument has managed a better defense in Plantinga, he hardly gives it a ringing endorsement even though he presents a "triumphant" version of it (Plantinga, *God, Freedom and Evil*, 75–111), stating it fails as a piece of natural theology even if it can be proved as sound in form. It is of note he spends only seven pages on both the teleological and cosmological arguments before dismissing them as logically inadequate, going as far as to call the cosmological argument "outrageous."

56. This might be more understandable to those (like me) with a background in programming in object-oriented languages such as C++ and C#. The programmer defines a "type" which will have properties and other characteristics; this defines the basic behavior and data for a "class" (a program element template). Other types can "inherit" this type and sub or superclass its data or behavior, but it will always be based on the base *type* and will be constrained in its operations by that type. It does not matter how

THE TRANSCENDENTAL ARGUMENT FOR GOD (TAG)

That is, there really *are* only two possible worldviews, and to refute one variation of the non-Christian worldview is to refute them all because the presuppositions are common even if the details are different. Even the radical relativist who appeals that there *could* be a possible world or conceptual scheme so different from our own which will *someday* satisfy the criteria for intelligibility can be answered. Donald Davidson in an epoch-making paper[57] demonstrated that it makes no *sense* to talk about a conceptual scheme *different* from our own; to be *recognized* as a conceptual scheme *is* to be part of our conceptual scheme.

This we must recognize as an *epistemological* point though, as Christians we understand that God's conceptual scheme *is* different from our own.[58] There may be other conceptual schemes, it is just we can have no knowledge regarding them unless that knowledge is provided providentially and intersects with our own conceptual scheme. This objection thus migrates into how the gap between conceptual necessity and ontological necessity is bridged, which we will consider shortly.

6.5.5 The "Fristianity" Objection

In this case, the Christian worldview is modified on one single point, or an adjunct or revision is made and a new religion, "Fristianity" we will call it, is born with its unique theology. This is another special case of the uniqueness objection that argues that the objection is not just conceivable but *instantiated* in the denominational variations among Christian believers. Now, as Butler notes, this objection is unproblematic in the case of the modification of the major doctrines of Christianity. This is because the major doctrines of Christianity are a unified whole, a transcendental unity guaranteed by a transcendent triune Being. You cannot modify one, e.g., turning the Trinity into a Quadrinity[59] or collapsing it

---

many variations with dramatically different behavior there might be, there will always be some fundamental characteristic inherited from that base class.

57. Davidson, "On the Very Idea of a Conceptual Scheme," 183–98.

58. "'For My thoughts are not your thoughts, Neither are your ways My ways,' declares the LORD. 'For as the heavens are higher than the earth, So are My ways higher than your ways, And My thoughts than your thoughts'" (Isa 55:8–9 NAS).

59. The founder of "analytic psychology" (in contrast with the rival *psychoanalysis*), and onetime collaborator with Freud, Carl Jung, did exactly that. He argued that evil must be integrated in the godhead to ensure the goodness of God was properly balanced, i.e., that God was psychologically stable and whole. His "Dream" (of God the Phallus born from below) and the mystical "Day Vision" (where God on his throne

into a unity,[60] without changing its very nature. However, what if we just change one detail, or issue some counterfactual challenge, e.g., regarding the canonicity of certain books? Now, this is easily countered because the change is not a *relevant* change to the worldview, some Christian communities indeed maintain a genuine Christian commitment with differences to their canons.

However, more fundamentally as a basic feature of a Christian philosophy, the Christian "conceptual scheme" is a *subset* of the "Christian worldview." The Christian experience shares a phenomenology that supports a cultural diversity, for the scriptures were presented by God to humanity as narrative (rather than as a systematic theology). There is freedom and liberty to express the creativity of God that allows for contingency, choice, and variety. The Christian community was maintained for centuries when people were unable to read or when the papists controlled society and the Church. It was not merely a conceptual scheme but a rich phenomenology of Christian life.[61] In contrast, all that the Christian worldview need posit in conceptual and theological terms is the salvation of humanity through the substitutionary work of Christ, which is the call for all to repent and to be reconciled to God.

6.5.6 From Conceptual Necessity to Ontological Necessity

Of all the objections to TAG, this objection is the most serious and draws its strength from the very nature of transcendental arguments. As Butler notes there is a paucity of response in the positive literature regarding TAG to this objection. Stroud[62] was the most famous expositor of this criticism:

---

defecates on the Basel cathedral) demonstrates to Jung that God was showing him He could be both good and bad; "Jung experiences show the rebirth of a God in the underworld and the destruction of the old religious dispensations of a God above moral reproach" (from a slide by my psychology of religion teacher, an expert Jungian scholar, Prof. Lucy Huskinson). Of course, and this is very evident in Jung's other work, this took inspiration from Taoism and certain forms of Buddhism (Jung used mandalas as symbols of four-dimensional wholeness).

60. This is evident in the "biblical cults" of Jehovah's Witnesses, Mormons, Christadelphians, Christian Science, etc., which inevitably evolve an entirely different system of theology that becomes antithetical to orthodox Christian thought, despite claiming allegiance and faithfulness to the same scripture.

61. Ó Murchadha, *Phenomenology*, undertakes an extremely ambitious account of this within the Continental school of thought but manages to maintain a perspicuity of language which, with some work and patience on the part of the reader, makes it a rewarding and enriching read both on a spiritual and a philosophical level.

62. See also §6.3.5 where we discussed the context of Stroud's criticism in more detail.

THE TRANSCENDENTAL ARGUMENT FOR GOD (TAG)

> The conditions for anything's making sense would have to be strong enough to include *not only* our beliefs about what is the case, but *also* the possibility of *our knowing whether those beliefs are true*. . . . But to prove this would be to prove some version of the verification principle, and then the skeptic will have been directly and conclusively refuted.[63]

In other words, this is the connection of how we must conceive of the world with the way the world really is. There is a clear distinction between perceiving the world a certain way and the way the world really is.[64] Stroud asserted that the transcendental method had to import in some form of verification principle to bridge that gap, but if that were the case, the transcendental argument is redundant. This is because the verification principle immediately draws that connection. However, we have already seen that the verification principle is self-refuting; it is not established based on empirical evidence but is a rational, metaphysical premise, and following Quine, dogmatically assumed within the empiricist mode of thought.

Thus, Butler notes, "all that is proven [by TAG if the objection stands] is that in order to be rational, we must believe that God exists" which is conceptually different than proving God *actually* exists.[65] Now, of course, if we were simply concerned with apologetics, the *rational defense* of Christianity against its detractors, we might consider the apologetic task complete and the criticism irrelevant. Butler thus continues:

> This defense carries a great deal of force. It effectively undermines the unbeliever's ability to rationally reject the Christian faith. But notice that this defense construes TAG not so much as a proof for God's existence but, rather, as a proof for the necessity of believing the Christian worldview.

Butler's next remarks are telling for they are exactly where Plantinga left off and that would imply Van Til and Plantinga have the same terminus:

> The problem with this . . . is that although Christianity may be the necessary precondition for experience, it does not follow from this that Christianity *is true*.[66]

---

63. Stroud, "Transcendental Arguments," 256. Emphasis added.
64. The preponderance of "Flat Earth" theorists armed with their empirical analysis and their two hundred proofs why the Earth is flat should make this clear, lest we doubt!
65. Butler, "Transcendental Argument for God's Existence," 121.
66. Butler, "Transcendental Argument for God's Existence," 89. Emphasis added.

We remember that Plantinga believed it to it be true and maximally so but noted he was speaking personally and did not believe philosophy had the tools to establish its truth.[67] Our very justification for moving to a Van Tillian conception was to demonstrate its truth *could* be established transcendentally. Without this connection, the skeptic might be perfectly happy to assert that they accept an amoral and irrational world without essences or metanarratives, and our previous discussion of postmodernism demonstrated there were plenty that are now content to be paralogical and consider reality a random, disconnected multiverse. We would have then catastrophically failed in the epistemologically self-consciousness project. Now Butler can only make a theological move at this point to propose a resolution to this issue. He proposes that TAG as presented in our analysis thus far has been equated with "conceptual scheme." This, he contends is a serious error as:

> Christianity provides us with a detailed metaphysical, epistemological, and ethical system. The foundation of this system is an *absolute personal God*. . . . This God is . . . a speaking God who reveals truths to us about Himself and the world.[68]

Now, we might be uncomfortable with this move as it would seem to be begging the question for the non-Christian, but it is certainly a reasonable one for the Christian. We have already established that ultimate authorities *will* beg the question. We understand that God has given us perception and faculties that teach us about the way the world is and how it works. We accept the testimony of scripture and its normative statements. However, I would argue that Butler's terminus here is then effectively equivalent to Plantinga's, and we have made recourse to a Christian version of reliabilism.

However, before we cede this an issue of faith and capitulate afresh to what Kant called the scandal of philosophy, Baird offered a resolution that does not require a theological move but was based on a philosophical disarming of the Stroudian critique. Recollect that Stroud asserted the primary problem was bridging the gap between concept and reality, for a transcendental argument to do so would require the reliance on or the importing of the verificationist premise. Baird argues[69] that McDow-

---

67. He finishes both Plantinga, *Warranted Christian Belief*, and the abbreviated summary, *Knowledge and Christian Belief*, with this thought.

68. Butler, "Transcendental Argument for God's Existence," 123.

69. Baird, "Transcendental Arguments," 126–77.

ell in his *Mind and World* constructed a transcendental argument that justifies the verificationist principle. McDowell was looking to complete the Kantian task and was arguing what the presuppositions of empirical experience and objectivity must be, and he is alleged to have established it transcendentally. Leaving out the details, it certainly seems a fair reading of McDowell that he has a principal aim of collapsing the distance between mind and world to justify empirical experience, and in doing so the verificationist principle is no longer seen as self-refuting.[70]

Baird also notes that a worldview is assessed not just on coherence of conceptual scheme but on pragmatic criteria as to how well our theory works in the world; or *why* some approaches work better than others. This bridge between pragmatic utility and truth is not dismissed as unimportant as in pragmatism but is seen to be the domain of metaphysics. Self-evidentially, for the believer, this correlates to the wider components of the Christian worldview that complete this connection. Thus, if Baird is correct, we can indeed make the connection between concept and world in a rather unexpected manner. In the strong philosophical sense, the separation between mind and world evaporates[71] and in the "weaker" (but equally significant) theological sense, the Christian metaphysic is validated and indeed mandated.

6.6 Summary and Conclusion

In this chapter we were interested in a formal understanding of the transcendental mode of argumentation as it had become of central importance to the arguments we were making through this work. By improving our formal understanding of the category, we could then go onto to consider its applicability more precisely and then consider more effectively the criticisms which have been leveled against it. We understood first that it had a distinctive logical form which has a long history in Western philosophy from Aristotle and has been of particular interest to those philosophers dealing with the problem of skepticism; the transcendentalist argues that the skeptic's challenge is incoherent because they are assuming in the logic of their skeptical challenge what they seeking to dismiss. We noted that

---

70. He bolsters this claim by citing historical work by Genova, "Transcendental Form" and "Good Transcendental Arguments," and Stine, "Transcendental Arguments," as a support to the transcendental derivation of the verificationist principle.

71. We might be reminded of the conclusion of Schlick in repudiating classical Kantian dogma of the mind imposing its form on reality.

in the modern period, Kant in the eighteenth century and Strawson in the twentieth century understood the category in terms of demonstrating the necessity of certain conceptual constructions that framed our understanding of the world which could not legitimately be denied.

We noted that for Kant a transcendental argument was concerned with how it was possible *a priori* to have a knowledge of any object and to build a *synthetic a priori* understanding and description of the phenomenal world, rather than with merely a purely empirical or rational account of it. The conclusion of a transcendental argument is thus not a particular fact about reality or a generalized principle from experience but a concept. We found that one of the distinguishing features is that necessarily the premise and conclusion are involved in one another; there is a conceptual difference between the fallacy of circularity and the circularity implicit when arguing transcendentally, to argue regarding ultimate authorities must necessarily imply their use for there can be no reference to an external authority as that would then be more ultimate.

In this respect, we needed to draw a distinction between transcendentally framed statements, which some have argued might be recast as either inductive or deductive arguments and might thus be conceived as of denying the legitimacy of the transcendental category more generally, and the transcendental argument. We demonstrated that the transcendental argument has a non-parochial conclusion; it is broad principle whereas a polar case argument might be mitigated in a purely linguistic manner by picking a new word; the transcendental argument would rather seek to explicate just what is required or is assumed that rends the linguistic couplet coherent and intelligible. We could thus conclude that the transcendental argument does not have a logical form alone but a particular type of semantic content; this distinction is necessary to understand Van Til's appropriation and use of transcendental argumentation.

Further, owing to the force of the historical controversy in the post-WWII period when philosophers such as Wittgenstein and Strawson had begun making use of transcendental argumentation, we noted the dispute among the neo-Kantians regarding the propriety of using the designation outside the strict Kantian sense. We concluded that there was nothing of philosophical importance in the dispute, noting that the central conception of what was required to make reasoning intelligible was preserved in the modern understanding; we noted that it was commonplace for categories to expand from their original meanings even to cases where the new meaning was in near contradiction to the original meaning, citing the substantive differences between classical and Neo-Darwinism. We concluded that because Kant did indeed employ an identical argument form to the modern form in the Second Refutation of Idealism, the most that could be claimed was a degree of confusion in the modern literature as for what context Kant had reserved the term "transcendental"; most precisely, modern transcendental arguments were Kantian arguments but not Kantian *transcendental* arguments.

Accepting the broadened sense, we then examined the most important distinction in the classes of transcendental arguments, that between the option "A" and the option "B" designations. Option "A" arguments are said to demonstrate merely the necessity of certain concepts for our understanding of the world; option "B" arguments were said to have had ontological force; they are not merely describing how we need to think about the world but are arguing that the world is necessarily what the argument demonstrates. We examined Stroud's claim that transcendental arguments can never bridge the gap to ontological claims without importing in a verification principle which would then have rendered the transcendental move moot. We concluded that Stroud seemed to have misunderstood Strawson on this point for Strawson was interested in descriptive metaphysics and was not making an ontological claim; he had asserted that arguments and counterarguments regarding *necessary* commitments did no useful philosophical work for us; commitments can be certain but ungrounded.

We then proceeded to examine Van Til's variation of transcendentalism known as presuppositional apologetics. Van Til avoided the Stroudian dilemma by using the concept of the Christian worldview which explicitly connected our concepts about the world with the way the world really is. He argued that reasoning necessarily assumes the truth of the Christian worldview for intelligibility and coherence and that inductive science is validated because within our worldview God's providence guarantees the principle, escaping the skepticism of Hume regarding reason. We fully recognized that alternative worldviews have an implicit circularity and can only be judged for transcendental coherence by undergoing an internal critique; that is, their claims are tested on their own terms. We found that this avoided the accusation of fideism for Van Til as only a single view, the Christian worldview, maintained its claims on a rational basis without incoherence; only in the Christian worldview, where the transcendent Trinity provides the basis for transcendental logic, are the transcendental principles themselves grounded, otherwise the principles would be arbitrary and defeasible. We noted that Van Til asserted the unifying feature among disparate and incommensurable non-Christian worldviews was their assertion of their intellectual self-sufficiency, the autonomy of the human mind as the final judge and arbiter. This distinguished the transcendentalism of Van Til from that of Kant, Descartes, and Dooyeweerd.

We then examined the general criticisms of transcendentalism which had come to focus in the lengthy and intense debate between Hintikka and Gram; we concluded that Hintikka had established the legitimacy of methodological transcendentalism, even if the category was vulnerable to criticisms. We noted that Grayling, McDowell, Frege, Wittgenstein, Davidson, Putnam, and Searle had all made use of transcendental argumentation despite the denial of its legitimacy; we thus concluded that it has sufficient cogency as a philosophical method. We then proceeded to examine the specific criticisms leveled against Van Tillian transcendentalism which were judged on most occasions to be erroneous because of an inadequate understanding of the nature of the transcendental claim as having a distinct, categorical nature; we made use of our previous work which demonstrated that rhetorical rephrasing in inductive or deductive terms was only possible for arguments that were not sufficiently broad to be considered transcendental arguments as opposed to transcendentally framed statements.

Other criticisms failed to appreciate the disjunctive nature of the Van Tillian claim that there are only two worldviews, the Christian and the non-Christian; in refuting any one claim within any non-Christian worldview, all are refuted. We noted that Davidson's argument regarding the impossibility of being able to recognize a conceptual scheme different from our own was basic in this regard with the important qualification that Davidson's point was strictly epistemological; there might indeed be different conceptual schemes, but we would not be able to recognize them. We then examined one of the more theological criticisms that attempted to assert we could keep the substance of the Christian worldview but only change it on a single point; however, we noted that the core and basic Christian beliefs were a unified whole and a transcendental unity, and you could not change one without changing the essence of the position.

Lastly, we considered the most challenging objection to the transcendental thesis, that of bridging the gap between conceptual necessity and ontological necessity; there is a clear philosophical distinction between perceiving or conceptualizing the world in a particular way and

THE TRANSCENDENTAL ARGUMENT FOR GOD (TAG)

the world really being that way. Unless that gap can be bridged, we noted that the most that could be claimed was that TAG established the necessity of believing the Christian worldview to make reality intelligible but not that belief in the Christian God was logically necessary for intelligibility. Stroud argued that this could only be bridged by a verification principle which would then invalidate the argument as we had previously concluded that a verificationist principle can never justify itself on its own criteria.

We noted that Butler obviated this objection by asserting that TAG had been misconstrued as a conceptual scheme, rather than as a worldview which had built-in ontological commitments, thus circumventing the abstract objection. We considered this a satisfactory terminus for the Christian but argued further that McDowell's justification of the verification principle on a transcendental basis might also mute Stroud's objection, lending greater force to the proof for non-believers; we also found that others argued that, because some approaches to the world work better than others, this implies metaphysical analysis, and conclusions were possible. Thus, as our aim was to establish not just the probability of the Christian worldview but the necessity of it, we have arguably found a transcendental formulation which demonstrates how this gap can be plausibly bridged.

7

The Philosophy of Christian Involvement

7.1 Overview and Prerequisites

THE AIM OF THIS chapter is to build a case for a revival of the position that champions active political and wider cultural involvement, attempting to prove not just the divine prerogative of our involvement, but what the governing principles of our involvement should be. We then examine what is the locus of the problem for Christians: the role and interpretation of Rom 13. We asserted at the beginning of our study that unless philosophy is transformative, it has failed in its purpose and so this section is not an addendum to our study of epistemological self-consciousness but a central part of it. We have already learned that arguments as epistemologically self-conscious Christians *must* be done on a scriptural basis at *every* step:

> [Christian philosophy] must always be based on an accurate interpretation of the teaching of the Scriptures. For some . . . there is a danger they may derive their knowledge more from [secular, unbelieving] philosophy than from a careful study of the Scriptures. They tend to extract just a certain number of great principles from the Bible and from there on they more or less forget the Bible and work the application out for themselves. . . . True theology should always be based upon a careful and accurate exegesis and exposition and understanding of the

Scriptures . . . we do not derive any theological principle from one scriptural statement only.[1]

Thus, we are in complete agreement with the *sense*[2] of what Lloyd-Jones asserts: disputes of praxis need to be resolved by exegeting the objective text of scripture rather than just preferring one version of subjectivity over another and then tagging on a few scriptures we used to validate our argument otherwise constructed from outside of scripture.

This is the governing principle for the simple reason that these matters at hand are needing to be settled because they are serious enough and are recognized as just not matters of preference where we accept Christian freedom and liberty which would admit of a range of positions.[3] We are assuming that the questions before us are of the type that can, to a large degree, be settled. The issues are foundational where we should be able to arrive at what the scriptural position is that is arguably binding in its essentials on all believers. They are not trivial issues of individual conscience (though we will recognize the important place of conscience) but admit of both philosophical and theological reflection and study.

7.2 The Imperative for a Political Ethic

7.2.1 Is Political Involvement Legitimate?

A question that could be in some minds and which concerned me greatly a few years ago as I became frustrated with what I considered insipid

---

1. Lloyd-Jones, *Exposition of Chapter 13*, 16–17.

2. While Lloyd-Jones maintains a strong distinction between philosophy and theology, which we have argued against, he does so in a way we can clearly understand with a clear rhetorical sense; I have supplied the understood sense with my amplifications in the brackets. As Calvin tells us, our aim is a *philosophy* constructed from scripture, while most describe his works as works of theology. In the *Institutes* Calvin frequently uses the Latin and French equivalent words for "philosophy" in both positive and negative senses, drawing a similar distinction as Lloyd-Jones does in rhetorical passages, often prefixing it with "profane." The Latin "profane" explicitly carried the sense of "outside [pro-] or before the temple [-phane]," of heretical and godless thought. He clearly talks about "constructing a Christian philosophy" (*Institutes*, introductory prefix to the French edition) close to the head of the work. This is the sense in which this book has argued that philosophy should be conceived in this manner. Thus, I have no problem with the contextual interchange of the words "theology" or "philosophy," and it is a practice I shall follow occasionally in this chapter.

3. This is discussed in magisterial fashion in Lloyd-Jones, *Exposition of Chapter 14*; see 1 Cor 1:12; Rom 14:1–23. His multivolume commentary on Romans was one of the notable achievements of twentieth-century Christian scholarship.

evangelical theology regarding our political and cultural positions is whether it is right for Christians to be involved *at all* in the wider cultural or political processes. Are we not rather to be engaged in loading up the "[Noah's] Ark of the Church" before we are removed either by the Rapture or the Second Coming? A famous radio preacher during the 1940s put it this way: "you do not polish brass on a sinking ship,"[4] and he spoke for two generations of Fundamentalists.

Thankfully, I believe it is straightforward to answer this question biblically as the apostle Paul had to write very early on in the life of the church to prevent people leaving their employment to wait for the coming of the Lord,[5] despite that the Second Coming was considered imminent even by himself.[6] For even while having this eschatological conviction, he at times insisted both that believers should work and on his political and civil rights as a Roman citizen.[7] He had no problem addressing Agrippa in a political context and eventually appealing to Caesar to prevent his undoubted martyrdom at the hands of the Jews.[8] That is, we do not cease to have rights, a political relationship, and a responsibility to our nation because we have joined the kingdom of God. Lloyd-Jones summarized it this way: "our citizenship is in heaven does not mean we do not stop being citizens [on earth] in contrast to various movements within the Church. Thus, we should [remain] involved in politics."[9]

One of the biggest problems in some "Christian" countries during the twentieth century which had almost continual revival for fifty to sixty years is the prevalence of economic, social, and moral corruption in their societies. In some countries of Central and South Africa which now have over 90 percent Christian populations, they are known for their mass poverty, corruption, and a lack of basic infrastructure despite being some

---

4. Quoted in Rushdoony, *God's Plan for Victory*, loc. 175.

5. 1 and 2 Thessalonians. The injunction "if one does not work, one does not eat" was made in the eschatological context within these letters.

6. 1 Cor 7:26 ff.

7. Acts 22:25; Acts 16:37.

8. Paul was certainly prepared to die for the gospel (and he did) but seems to have had a much bigger problem with rank injustice among those that considered themselves just and civilized (Acts 25:16). Additionally, like Jesus, he took the greatest exception to hypocrisy, particularly the religious hypocrisy (Acts 23:3) of "the Jews." Like the Johannine use of the term, "the Jews" here refers to the Jewish authorities that were an unhealthy political-religious hybrid, and it is not used as an ethnic slur. The authorities were the chief adversaries of both Jesus and Paul in their ministries.

9. Lloyd-Jones, *Exposition of Chapter 13*, 17.

of the richest countries in terms of their natural resources. However, far more dramatically and with much more polemical force for our purposes here, Cope vividly describes how the most "Christianized" city in the US (the most "Christianized" nation in the world) failed to show any difference in many of the basic social indices that would make it a "good" place to live[10] in direct contradiction to the regenerating narrative of the evangelical churches.

In my view, and I believe it to be self-evident, this demonstrates a total failure of this form of "revivalism" to reform their societies by failing to reform the political and social dimensions of society.[11] Our political philosophy is a "fake" gospel if it does not change the social and political character of the nations in which it is applied. Without such a political philosophy, we are just surrendering cultural real estate to secularism and humanism and failing in our primary objective of "discipling all nations."[12] Thus, what is argued in this chapter is a rejection in principle of any withdrawal from the marketplace as advocated in some Christian convocations in lieu of reflections on the Trump era[13] and the building of the case for an informed, increased involvement and commitment to see reform in the political realm.

7.2.2 One Further Possibility—Political Neutrality

It must be recognized that there has been a flurry of thought, scholarly and otherwise, in Christian circles on this issue triggered by the "Trump Problem."[14] In one relatively recent convocation on political theology in which I was an invited participant, the discussion proper began by presenting an argument based on cultural relativism, the thrust of which

---

10. Cope, *Old Testament Template*, 21–27.

11. "Revivalism" in the modern sense is a term most associated with the ministry of Charles Finney (1792–1875). However, as noted earlier in the thesis and expanded upon in my *Dominion Theology*, I demonstrate how he was extremely active in the political, educational, and wider cultural spheres. He did not limit himself to "spiritual matters" as was to become the habit of some of his imitators in the evangelical and Fundamentalist movements of the nineteenth and twentieth centuries, most of whom believed any such engagement was a "distraction" from the real task of saving souls.

12. Matt 28:19–20 (NAS).

13. Brown, *Evangelicals at the Crossroads*. Brown distills the issues down exceptionally well here; he has an earned doctorate (and it shows), as well as a substantial standing in the evangelical world.

14. For my extended use of this term, see Macneil, "Politics," appendix A.

was that our reading of scripture is never neutral but colored by our cultural glasses. The application of this was then that politically, we had been unable to see that we had fallen in love with democracy[15] and our way of doing things to the degree we had entered an inappropriate "syncretism" of our understanding of scripture with the understanding of the political arena and, consequently, had incorrectly formed alliances or loyalties with particular politicians or parties.[16] Our closeness to particular ideologies[17] had meant we were no longer capable of understanding God's perspective and articulating a Christian political philosophy. The rest of the discussion was to present a "corrected" political theology that would restore to us this function.

In brief, the principal feature of the position being advocated was a type of political agnosticism and detachment from the workings of the political world. That is, God is indifferent to our political systems, and we should be too other than to trust he puts in the leaders *he* wants to fulfill his Kingdom purposes.[18] Now, despite its initial plausibility to us an argument, we must always remember that philosophically *any* argument based on asserting relativism and insurmountable cultural prejudice must *exempt itself* from its own analysis to have anything coherent to say because otherwise, it too becomes just another culturally conditioned narrative, nothing more than a possibility in the sea of competing possibilities; as the meme goes, the argument "all judgments are relative" is rightly footnoted "*except* this one."

The very fact I am asserting we are suffering from cultural prejudice and zero objectivity in reading scripture is asserting that I can stand outside of that prejudice and culture and make that assertion. If that is the case, then I have just refuted my own argument which is my point about relativism above—the presenter proceeding to give us a political

---

15. In Macneil, "Politics," I discuss how the argument was made that democracy or republicanism is no more God-ordained than say, despotism or some other form of totalitarianism. Even the Nazis could be commended for "keeping order" if the alternative was violent anarchy. We *might* be prepared to countenance the last proposition, but we should remember the Nazis were voted *in*, but then they made very sure they could not get voted *out*.

16. In this case, Trump.

17. In this case, Republicanism and/or political conservatism.

18. This "Kingdom" language might seem a strange idiom to those outside of modern charismatic and Pentecostal Christianity. In brief, Jesus = King, dom = his domain, which includes the church but also his providential rule as "King of kings, Lord of lords" (Dan 2:37; Rev 19:16 [NAS]), which is explicitly dealing with the civil and political authorities.

theology on their own analysis will be just as full of inescapable presuppositions and cultural prejudice; granted, they will be different ones but present, nevertheless. Thus, I believe such an argument (the details of which I examined in far more detail here[19]), is an illegitimate and a retrograde step; the Church has never improved a society by withdrawing from it but when it was fully engaged in it.[20]

7.2.3 The Lack of a Shared Cultural Reference

The principal qualification for epistemological self-consciousness to be important in this reformation results because of the collapse of a shared value base of Judeo-Christian origin in our wider culture, even if it was grudgingly maintained.[21] Indeed, at the present time, the very *negation* of those standards is considered praiseworthy and righteous.[22] Similarly, recent history has witnessed some watersheds in Christian culture that mandate a reexamination of Christian political philosophy. First, the polarizing influence of the Trump presidency demonstrated the antithetical and incoherent positions that were held by Christians regarding his first term as president. Second, the political tyranny of the COVID-era policies and the almost universal capitulation of the churches to what we will argue was the illegitimate use of authority by the national and international governments.

---

19. Macneil, "Politics," §2.
20. As I also argued in Macneil, *Dominion Theology*, §3 ff.
21. I would say it arguably existed through to the mid-1980s, perhaps to the end of the Thatcher era in the UK (which itself finally petered out after a long, slow decline in 1990). The "sexual revolution" that began in the second half of the 1980s on the Left (when I was a member of various far-Left groups and witnessed it firsthand) legitimized (culturally, at least) cultural ideologies with violently anti-Christian premises, which were a wedge to evict the ghost of Christianity from the public square.

However, even during the subsequent Blair era in the UK (both Labor leaders John Smith and Tony Blair were active members of the Christian Socialist Movement), certain moral matters were "banned" (unofficially) from journalists' questions despite being newly "fashionable" for the radical (or liberal) Left. A journalist who referred directly to the homosexuality of certain Cabinet members would no longer be "invited" to briefings. The US situation is more complex in regard of "shared values," but it should be noted that Barack Obama publicly defended that marriage was for heterosexuals as late as 2008 to get the black evangelical vote.

22. See for example, Macneil, "Censorship"; Francis, "Cancelling Christians."

7.2.4 The Importance of Our History

A shocking discovery for many is that this is not the first time in Christian history that this subject has taken on an elevated importance:

> One of the most foolish aspects of modern life is the tendency to assume that all that has happened in the past is quite irrelevant and unimportant and that nobody knew anything until this present generation came.[23]

Thus, this means a good look at Christian history to understand the different views of the Christian understanding of and involvement in the political process. We would all benefit from a good history lesson and learn from our past. We are not called to make an idol of the past or to canonize tradition, and we are called to "forget those things [the excrement of religion] behind us"[24] but that is something very different from ignoring the lessons of our history.

7.3 The Role of Epistemological Self-Consciousness and Two Basic Principles

7.3.1 Are We Called to Defend Truth?

Another strong statement during the convocation was made that, as a matter of principle, "we are not called to defend truth but relationships." This takes some unpacking to counter its undoubted intuitive appeal and surface profundity; it has the distinctively pragmatic, postmodern, and Rortian flavor—we are to value the subjective relations and operations rather than being concerned about grasping that elusive nettle of "truth" and "being right."[25] Certainly, we can all accept that truth might be progressive for us and as a pluralistic form of life we do not need total agreement among ourselves to value each other's views and perspectives. In that respect, we can "defend" our relationships from unnecessary angst, particularly from those outside. However, in the name of epistemological

---

23. Lloyd-Jones, *Exposition of Chapter 13*, 135.

24. Paul refers to "dung" in his famous "forgetting the past and pressing to the future" passage of Phil 3 which, contextually, dealt with his previous life in Judaism. The word he specifically uses in 3:8 was what we would call a "swear word"; it was only used in vulgar conversation.

25. One of Rorty's famous quips was "take care of freedom and truth will take care of itself."

self-consciousness, I am constrained to immediately question the proposition that we are not called primarily to defend "truth" in preference to "relationships," even more so when the leader of our religion claimed the title of "the Truth."[26]

As with many things postmodern it is difficult to locate precisely what is meant by "relationships" here, but our early fathers of the faith really had to work hard in sorting out our basic theology in the midst of both internal schism and external philosophy. Perhaps more compelling from a pure exegetical perspective, our New Testament pattern demonstrates a radical stand for "(T)ruth" in the ministries of Jesus and Paul, and explosive confrontations to wit. Thus, despite being a painful and sometimes explosive process, the results of say the Council of Chalcedon or the Council of Nicaea are still with us. This is even more the case with the forensic logic of Wycliffe, Huss, Luther, and Calvin in challenging papal dogma with scriptural precedent that began the Reformation. The strength that came from taking a position and then defending it was of benefit to not just the Church but the entire social and economic order. The Reformation broke the hold of Aristotelian metaphysics and made possible the scientific revolution.[27] In this sense, epistemological self-consciousness is a recovery of what has been lost, rather than some radically novel innovation.

In summary then, although there are matters of subjective preference over which we do not divide there is solid, objective ground on which most evangelical Christians should stand if they are thinking clearly. The testimony of scripture for us *is* normative, and we are called to be intelligently "dogmatic" in the face of challenge. If we are not defending truth, then apologetics is redundant, and our faith is arbitrary. However, we have argued in our previous sections that Christianity is *objectively* defendable and presentable in such a way the unbeliever *understands* the challenge intellectually that is given to them. Only the spirit of God *saves* people, but Peter addresses us that we should be ready to give an *apologia*. An *apologia* is not simply a testimony, but a *reasoned*

---

26. John 14:6 (NET): Jesus replied, "I am the way, and the truth, and the life. No one comes to the Father except through me."

27. The lack of progress in science was a notable feature of the medieval period until the Reformation, despite major advances in other areas of culture (progress in medicine was perhaps the exception). This issue is examined comprehensively in Butler, *Philosophy of Science*.

defense of our faith, a defense by which we defend the truth.[28] Thus, this must also include a defense of a set of political principles.

7.3.2 The Response of Epistemological Self-Consciousness in Brief

Thus, regarding our project, both as issues of philosophy, theology, and methodology, we should be promoting political involvement of believers at every level of the political State to restrain the evil direction in which our political states are going.[29] We might formally agree that under *certain* sets of circumstances, partnership with politics is a form of idolatry, for it *is* God that raises up those he chooses and casts down others[30] and who are we to question God?[31] However, that does *not* mean that partnership with politics is *always* idolatry or that we should *always* accept powerlessness rather than influence if we are not to make immediate nonsense of "making disciples of all nations" and the "kingdom coming on Earth as it is in heaven."[32] Again, this would seem self-evident that the kingdom does not come independent of the political realm: you cannot have kingdom standards in social and political matters without those who can understand and implement them in positions of power and influence.[33] In other words, the argument needs to be had not only about the legitimacy of certain principles but also in the details of working them out.

---

28. ἀπολογία: defense; as a legal technical term, a speech in defense of oneself; *reply, verbal defense* (2 Tim 4:16); BDAG emphasizes this is a *speech* in defense; it is reasoned, rather than inspirational or preached.

29. This position, I believe, represents an orthodox Christian perspective. Granted, some might see our moral condition as the most enlightened or advanced that it has ever been and that our governments served with distinction in keeping us safe during COVID while simultaneously respecting law, life, and liberty.

30. Dan 4:17 (NET); Rom 9:17 (NAS).

31. See Rom 9. In my view, chapters 9, 10, and 11 of Romans contain some of the most complex and challenging logic of the Christian scriptures.

32. Matt 28:18–20; Matt 6:10 (NAS).

33. Some mystical iterations of Christian belief might dare to assert this as I touch on in *Dominion Theology*. This is normally rooted in a controlling catastrophic pessimism regarding the human condition. In certain Gnostic heresies this might also be the case; imported into this view was the Platonic conception of the inferiority, even the evil character of the physical.

7.3.3 The Domains of Study

Thus, epistemological self-consciousness warrants a strong, positive statement of scriptural principles. There is a lot of theological and philosophical complexity in such an important subject, so it requires us to cover a lot of philosophical ground by considering at a most basic level what the Bible tells us:

a. About the relationship of ourselves as *individual* members of the body of Christ (the Church) to the political State.

b. Of the relationship of the *institution* of the Church to the *institution* of the political State.[34]

When we get those basics right, we can establish the necessary principles to both answer the questions and evaluate to what degree what was presented to us is scriptural, complete, and defensible. The evaluation is only ever against scripture and scripture alone.[35]

7.3.4 Our Civic Responsibility—Recovering It Through Dominion Theology

For those of us who are children of the Reformers, the sacred-secular distinction *should* be an untenable dichotomy that we should not accept, because it is certainly not a biblical one—there is *no* secular for the believer. If we do not argue on such a basis, we have already surrendered the ground to the secular-humanist opponents of Christianity. As we have argued repeatedly through this work, our position should be rather at its *foundation* a distinctively *Christian* one, perhaps captured perfectly by Abraham Kuyper in an 1880 speech as he opened the university which he had founded:

---

34. We are all members of the body of Christ, what Luther called the "priesthood of all believers." However, this is conceptually and practically distinct from those who work full time *in* the church as a ministerial calling. We tend to be very loose in our use of the term "church"; see Cope, *Old Testament Template*, 103–12.

35. Care should be taken here not to misinterpret this as to say any source of theology outside scripture is illegitimate, otherwise all the philosopher or theologian could do was to copy out scripture. It is rather that the rooting and grounding of our philosophy is in scripture and hermeneutically in scripture as a whole.

> There is not a square inch in the whole domain of our human existence over which Christ, who is sovereign over all, does not cry: "Mine!"[36]

For Kuyper, there was no sacred or secular; *all* was sacred:

> Whatever man may stand, whatever he may do, to whatever he may apply his hand—in agriculture, in commerce, and in industry, or his mind, in the world of art, and science—he is, in whatsoever it may be, constantly standing before the face of God. He is employed in the service of his God. He has strictly to obey his God. And above all, he has to aim at the glory of his God.[37]

This emphasis is also found in J. Gresham Machen who, like Kuyper, was concerned with the whole of culture and the transformational power of the gospel. Machen was the founder of Westminster Theological Seminary in 1929 after the split with Princeton caused by the removal of the commitment to orthodox Christian theology as a requirement for ministers to graduate from the seminary. He was a passionate believer in the reformation of *all* culture by ensuring there could be Christian education at all levels rather than a centralized, State-controlled education.[38] This was his first-hand response to the noted anti-intellectualism, obscurantism, and narrow evangelistic focus of the emerging Fundamentalist movement of the time.

Unlike the Fundamentalists, Machen had not just defended scripture, but the *entire* Christian worldview, against Liberalism and was concerned with the regeneration of *all* of culture.[39] That is, despite this

---

36. Kuyper, "Sphere Sovereignty," 488.

37. Kuyper, *Lectures on Calvinism*, 45.

38. Machen, *Education, Christianity and the State*. This was a collection of his speeches and essays, as well as an account of the founding principles of Westminster.

39. Machen, *Christianity and Liberalism*, 1–13. This introductory section is invaluable reading as a restatement of a Christian conception of culture and immediately engages with the necessity of warfare in the cultural realm and specifically with socialistic political philosophies. It must be remembered Machen had witnessed the Russian revolution a mere five years to publishing this work and the greatest intellectuals of America like John Dewey, who were laying the foundations of the "Progressive" movement that was to incubate American socialism. It is arguable that the baby has *just* been born; it is only in the Trump era that American politicians in the *mainstream* Democratic Party and in the *mainstream* media were happy to campaign under the banner of "socialism," despite Marxism, in the guise of "critical theory," having been well established in the academy since the 1960s.

His "Christianity and Culture" address, which is the first part of this collection, was originally entitled "The Scientific Preparation of the Minister" and was delivered

nominal thematic agreement with Fundamentalism regarding the status of scripture, Machen was really the precursor of the modern Dominion Theology movement whose central theological distinctive was to become the entire reformation of culture.[40] It is a theological position that has no reticence in taking political positions based on his understanding of the *implications* of scripture. Machen was aggressive in his statement of the need to battle in the realm of intellectual ideas, believing correctly, that it was ideas which would come to dominate the political direction of a nation:

> We may preach with all the fervor of a reformer and yet succeed only in winning a straggler here and there, if we permit the whole collective thought of the nation or of the world to be controlled by ideas which, by the resistless force of logic, prevent Christianity from being regarded as anything more than a harmless delusion.[41]

Thus, through some noted professors of WTS such as Cornelius Van Til and a second generation of students such as Greg Bahnsen (both of whom should be familiar names from earlier in this work), his cultural philosophy became foundational for the Presbyterian Dominion Theology movement that emerged into public view in the early 1970s with Rushdoony's *Institutes of Biblical Law*.[42] Within five years, by the time Rushdoony sponsored the publication of Bahnsen's *Theonomy*,[43] it had begun to assert itself strongly as a controversial school of Reformed theology. However, as we noted previously, it is only controversial to those who have forgotten that theonomy was central to the Reformed position

---

on Sept. 20, 1912, at the opening of the one hundred and first session of Princeton Theological Seminary. This at once shows how basic in his thinking was his concern to engage and transform *all* of culture and how this eventually motivated him to break with Princeton and found Westminster Theological Seminary (WTS) and the Orthodox Presbyterian Church (OPC).

40. When Machen founded WTS, his first professor of apologetics (who was to remain over forty years in that post) was Cornelius Van Til, whose work featured predominantly in earlier chapters of this book. Rousas Rushdoony (who had written the earliest summary of Van Til, *By What Standard?*) was the man most responsible for developing the perspective in a sociological direction which became known as "dominion theology" or "Christian Reconstructionism"; see Macneil, *Dominion Theology*, §§4.5–5.4.

41. Machen, *Christianity and Liberalism*, 6.

42. Rushdoony, *Institutes of Biblical Law*.

43. Bahnsen, *Theonomy in Christian Ethics*.

and was the dominant influence in the Puritan confessions.[44] The intellectual climate of Christian thought had become so dominated by the import of the *autonomous* mindset of non-Christian philosophy that it ceased to be authentically Christian. Our work is, in many ways, a restatement of these principles in a novel context.

7.3.5 The Theonomic Imperative

Thus, in vanilla Reformed social theory, theonomy (the "Law of God") is contrasted with "autonomy" (being the law to myself). Cope captures something for us that must be fundamental to our political philosophy:

> The law given to Moses [is] to disciple the newly free nation of Israel. God begins to speak for himself and gives *clear, concise,* and very *specific* instruction for how to achieve justice in a community.[45]

We will all stand before the judgment seats of both the Father and the Son to give account according to the moral and social principles of this same Law. Though we may have cultural idiosyncrasies, and we may need to probe beneath the application to find the principle, God's Word is not rendered null and void by our culture. Again, Cope clarifies this for us while fully admitting our responsibility for establishing the application of the Law in our culture:

> Remember that the truths of the Bible are told primarily in story form. We study the history and the context, but we will never be in the same circumstances as Moses and Israel, so their application will not necessarily work for us. The *principles*, however, are God's truth and are applicable in new and dynamic ways in any age, any set of circumstances in any nation.[46]

Importantly, for the postmodern apologist, those "new and dynamic ways" do not extend to contradicting the explicit outworking of those principles in the nation of Israel that are given, as the apostle Paul

---

44. It was rather the position arguably of Augustine and given its systematic expression by Calvin. It was developed by his successor Beza, by Bullinger, our own John Knox, and then the Puritan movement of the 1640s, from which modern Reformed theology owes most.
45. Cope, *God and Political Justice*, loc. 231. Emphasis added.
46. Cope, *Old Testament Template*, 62. Emphasis added.

tells us, "for teaching, for reproof, for correction, for training."[47] Now, and this is my main philosophical point, you cannot be "corrected or reproved" in just any type of fashion; there must be *objective* standards of correction or reproof. It can only be *just* if it applies equally to all in morally equivalent circumstances.[48] It is God who defines the "morally significant" components of our reasoning through his Law—polygamy becomes no more acceptable to us, even if it is culturally normal for us. To argue otherwise, is simply the Christian form of cultural relativism and needs to be dismissed as such.

To take a much more politically significant specific example, we can consider the social gospel movement, even the more "evangelical" version of it associated with evangelicals such as Ron Sider. It is often stated by apologists for that movement that God "told us 'Not to steal'" but "did not define 'stealing' for us." This is an outright fallacy, as we have chapter upon chapter within Exodus, Leviticus, Numbers, and the restatement in Deuteronomy that establishes the principle of private property, your right to it, and that stealing is the illegitimate violation of those property rights. It further gives a penal code and authorizes the punishment of thieves; but equally, not all theft is treated as criminal—there are extenuating circumstances—but *all* theft is defined as sin and retribution is *always* made.[49] As Cope argues, they are "dynamic" in the sense we do not talk about boundary markers and oxen when we talk about property rights, but it will apply to our cars and tax systems. This is not to deny that there are not places of ambiguity or of great challenge as to how we are to understand and apply God's Word, but it becomes very clear whether our cultural practices measure up to his Law or not in many cases because of the fruit that they bear.

---

47. 2 Tim 3:16 (NAS).

48. Even Sartre accepted this piece of moral reasoning. He framed it in terms of a man having to choose between fighting in the Spanish civil war and taking care of his sick mother. *Whatever he chose, he would choose for all men*. It is a misnomer to think existentialism equates with a lack of binding or universal ethics. One of Plantinga's earliest papers ("Existentialist's Ethics") discusses existentialism and ethics.

49. That is, there is a civic sanction associated with it. One example in scripture is associated with the stealing of a small amount of fruit; restitution is made but there is no further punishment. In other cases, there is a fine, compensation and restitution. It is an oft neglected feature of the Law code in the Hebrew scriptures that it encourages intelligent discrimination of the nature of a misdemeanor or a crime.

7.4 Theocracy or Representative Government

Some vocal critics of Dominion Theology argued it was urging the creation of a theocracy, where society is subject to the direct rule of the Creator.[50] However, such a view is a puerile distortion of the position and scripture itself mandates a theocracy *only* for the nation of Israel.[51] It is of note that even for the ancient Israelites, the LORD instructed them to choose the wise among them to "govern themselves" with the Law giving clear instructions for representative government and what we would call "checks and balances":

> You shall select out of all the people able men who fear God, men of truth, those who hate dishonest gain; and you shall place *these* over them *as* leaders of thousands, of hundreds, of fifties and of tens. Let them judge the people at all times; and let it be that every major dispute they will bring to you, but every minor dispute they themselves will judge.[52]

This, of course, is the precise reason why the American founders adopted the model of representative government they did.[53] In practical terms, this side of omniscience, there are limits to what statecraft can accomplish. Politics is not messianic, or Jesus would have perhaps started a political party or conquered the Roman Empire.[54] We must make a clear distinction between what an individual Christian as a member of the State can do and what the Church *as an institution* can do. The *individual* Christian can be a politician, and the Church should be clear in its statement of principles over a political matter:

---

50. Martin, "Righteous Revolution."

51. On a practical note, we would do well to seek such a society, but it would be introduced based on consensus, not imposition. It is of note that George Washington, the first American president, made such a proclamation based on consensus of the Congress.

52. Exod 18:21–22 (NAU).

53. This story is vividly told in Barton and Barton, *American Story*, which is notable for its use and enumeration of primary sources. The scholarly standard for early American religious thought is Noll, *America's God*.

54. One stream of Jewish messianic thought had precisely this expectation, one which was evident even in his disciples (Acts 1:6). There was great disillusionment with Jesus for his political "weakness"; after welcoming him into Jerusalem, they were happy to shout "crucify him" a week later.

THE PHILOSOPHY OF CHRISTIAN INVOLVEMENT

> The church keeps to the realm of principles and not detailed programmes. She does not, as it were, enter into the arena either through preaching politics, or by sitting in the House of Lords.
>
> The business of the individual members of the church to work out these principles, *in detail*, for every aspect of life. Christians must not confine their Christianity to their own personal lives and piety and their own acts of worship. Christianity takes up the whole person. If men and women really believe the gospel, it must govern the whole of their outlook and thinking.[55]

There are thus some principles of involvement emerging here, not for theocracy but for participation and representative government:

1. The *Church* is not to be involved in the details of a political program but is to teach principles.
2. The *individual* Christian is at liberty to be involved to whatever depth is necessary to ensure that the "powers that be" are "influenced in the right direction. It is their duty to do this, and they must not abdicate from their responsibility."[56]

So, in summary, we can accept with Lloyd-Jones and with Cope that a "perfect" society is not possible on Earth but that does not mean we cannot have the expectation of a better one more in line with the principles of the Kingdom this side of any return of the Lord; we can accept that a complete reformation is only possible with the personal presence of Jesus, yet it *is* possible for us to be his government now because that is what *he* tells us in the "Great Commission":

> Then Jesus came up and said to them, "All authority in heaven and on earth has been given to me. Therefore go and make disciples of all nations, baptizing them in the name of the Father and the Son and the Holy Spirit, teaching them to obey everything I have commanded you. And remember, I am with you always, to the end of the age."

The imperative verb here is the *making disciples* rather than the teaching or the baptizing; the discipling or *Christianizing* of our society, or our reformation, salting, or whatever word we want to use, is what is commanded and expected.[57]

---

55. Lloyd-Jones, *Exposition of Chapter 13*, 159. Emphasis added.
56. Lloyd-Jones, *Exposition of Chapter 13*, 159.
57. The NET Bible exegetical note is informative here: "'Go . . . baptize . . . teach' are

7.5 Understanding Romans 13

7.5.1 Overview

Few passages of scripture have created as much controversy as Rom 13 owing to the chronic lack of understanding of it in the modern Christian consciousness despite there being substantive studies available. During the COVID lockdowns, an uncritical use of the passage was made to justify the unconditional surrender of religious freedom and civil liberty by the vast majority of Christian leaders. Unfortunately, this demonstrates a complete ignorance of the passage and demonizes all those over the centuries who found within the scriptures a mandate for social reform, civil disobedience, and political revolution. It would indeed be perverse to rebuke a Luther, the abolitionist movement on both sides of the Atlantic, the American independence movement, or the apartheid activists within the South African church for a refusal to submit to the governing authorities.[58]

However, Rom 13 does require interpretation and contextualization to counter what some have argued is the plain sense of the text. That said, it is not my intention to do a verse-by-verse exegesis as this has been authoritatively and competently completed by Lloyd-Jones, taking him 162 pages, which we cannot afford here.[59] That said, I incorporate most of his arguments in the following section and modify them as necessary with my own revisions as we draw conclusions from our present context. The early Christians needed the apostolic input of Rom 13, 1 Tim 2, and in 1 Pet 2 because the believers needed to know how to respond to pagan rulers who were often extremely hostile to the point of persecution and execution.[60]

We will only consider Rom 13 extensively in this section because it is the locus of most discussion among believers regarding the relationship of the individual Christian to the State and of the institution of the

---

participles modifying the imperative verb 'make disciples.' According to *ExSyn** 645 the first participle (πορευθέντες, *poreuthentes*, 'Go') fits the typical structural pattern for the attendant circumstance participle (aorist participle preceding aorist main verb, with the mood of the main verb usually imperative or indicative) and thus picks up the mood (imperative in this case) from the main verb (μαθητεύσατε, *matheteusate*, 'make disciples')." *Here they are referring to Wallace, *Exegetical Syntax of the New Testament*.

58. In the dying days of apartheid, it was common for government ministers to quote Rom 13 to the dissident church centered around Archbishop Tutu.

59. Lloyd-Jones, *Exposition of Chapter 13*, 1–162.

60. I deal with this passage more fully in Macneil, "Should I Obey My Government."

Church to the State. First Peter 2 is very much a recapitulation of the Pauline teaching; we know Peter clearly took direction from Paul and considered his works scriptural (2 Pet 3:15) and we only mention it here in passing as this is a good reason to highlight this specific feature of Peter's view. First Timothy 2 has the primary subject of intercession for those in authority that the social conditions of effective evangelism might be possible and will not be considered further here other than to emphasize such intercession was expected by Paul to create those conditions. We are not to hide in our Christian ghettoes watching the reign of the antichrist and waiting for the rapture.

7.5.2 The Context of Romans 13

It must be remembered that this section does not exist in isolation from the sections around it. This is important because some commentators seem to think it is an intrusion or clumsy insertion of thought. Yet this is a new subsection in the section that began with chapter 12—the application of the doctrine laid down in the first eight chapters.[61] The great emphasis of chapter 12 is that of "living peaceably with other people." Chapter 13 is thus perfectly in position, "[Government enables us] to live peaceably with one another, to maintain order, to avoid disorder."[62] The "vengeance of God" mentioned in 12 would then arguably be part of the function of the State and its laws. So, the first great conclusion we can draw from Rom 13 is the legitimacy of the State *in principle* as against those who reject all the institutions of men as fallen and illegitimate.[63]

---

61. Chapters 9, 10, and 11 form a self-contained pericope on the problem of the Jews and their relationship to the gospel. There are still important principles in these passages, but the chapters are strongly focused on the Jews.

62. Lloyd-Jones, *Exposition of Chapter 13*, 2.

63. This was one of Calvin's strongest criticisms of the Anabaptist post-Reformation movement (sometimes called the "radical Reformation"), which came progressively to reject all forms of human authority. The seeds of messianic Nazism and Communism are sometimes argued to have originated in their theology, which justified violence against all non-believers (where the non-believer was widely conceived)—they were celebrated by the Deutsche Demokratische Republik (particularly Thomas Müntzer) in the twentieth century for the attempt to create a commune in Munster in 1534. However, the experience of Munster moderated their politics such that the Amish, Mennonites, even Quakers and Baptists all lay claim to some kind of heritage from the Anabaptists. In an important sense, all these groups *were* social radicals but became committed to a *demonstration* rather than an *imposition* of Christianity. See Verduin, *Reformers and Their Stepchildren*, for a historical review from within the Reformed community but with sufficient chronological distance to present a well-balanced view.

God has instituted it that the conditions of social peace might exist for the benefit of all:

> I urge, then, first of all, that requests, prayers, intercession and thanksgiving be made for everyone—for kings and all those in authority, that we may live peaceful and quiet lives in all godliness and holiness. This is good, and pleases God our Savior.[64]

However, and I believe this is where many formulations regarding our rights, relationships, and responsibilities are at their weakest, based on this foundational principle, it then becomes much too easy to give the State much *too much* authority over the Church and the individual believer, to the degree that all the believer is entitled to is a weak, passive resistance, or martyrdom. In contrast, we will find as we work through the chapter that there is a justification for a Christian taking part in a revolution to overthrow a corrupt government.

7.5.3 Obedience and Submission Are Different Concepts

So, let us consider the first verse of Rom 13:

> Let every person be subject to the governing authorities for there is no authority except from God and those that exist are appointed by God. Therefore whoever resists the authority resists what God has appointed, and those who resist will incur judgement.

Thus, it is straightforward to understand why many teach an unconditional obedience to the State. This is reinforced by some commentators who note that the term translated "be subject" was originally a military term meaning "to rank under" but this is one of those occasions where we need to understand the semantics of the word have moved far beyond its original meaning as witnessed in the Greek literature of that era of what the Bible is an integral part. By overstressing the etymology, extremely severe interpretations of this passage that would admit no conditions for civil disobedience. As Lloyd-Jones explains, there are three other Greek words in common use during that period would convey far more strongly the concept of "obedience" if that was what Paul had wanted to communicate. We must understand that "be subject to" does

---

64. 1 Tim 2:1 (NAS).

not simply mean "be obedient to" though the Greek verb in the middle voice was sometimes used with this meaning.[65]

Thus, continuing our analysis, *subjection* implies a *reasoned* choice. For example, Eph 5:21 states "*submitting* yourselves one to another in the fear of God" and it should also be clear that in this case there is clearly a logical difference between subjection and obedience. Both parties cannot simultaneously *obey* one another if a difference arises but they can respectfully resolve their differences by having a mental posture or attitude of *submission*. To not recognize this is to make this and other examples[66] of the usage of the word logically contradictory. Thus, Lloyd-Jones argues the context demands "making room for" or "preferring out of respect" as appropriate renderings.

7.5.4 The Boundaries of Christian Resistance

So, a minister of the State demands respect unconditionally only with regard to respect for their office and conversely, the ruler *must* behave in an honorable and just manner before the people because that is the terms of their ordination before God, "He means the powers that are governing [well] and maintaining law and order."[67] Thus, it is pointedly *not* proven that every occupant of the office "has been ordained by God" and thus we are not morally obligated to immediately obey them if they are *not* governing well. Particularly, we need to ask what we are to do with rulers who abuse their position or are tyrannical. We need only think of Nero using burning Christians coated in tar to light his feasts or of a Hitler orchestrating the Holocaust.

This can be made clearer by an analogy. If our nation was attacked or was in imminent danger of being attacked, most of us would consider it perfectly just to sign up to fight if we were asked to, in addition to

---

65. To emphasize our main point here regarding the semantics of the word, BDAG, the academic standard reference work for the Greek language of this period, does not offer the meaning "obey," listing only the passive and active voice (BDAG, ὑποτασσω). *Vine's Expository Dictionary* (another standard work) lists "obey" as a possible but minor inflection in the passive or middle voice, noting the military origin of the word (Vine's, "Subject, Subjection"). The Strong's number is 5293 and Strong lists "obey" as a possibility for the middle voice. Pertinently, the "middle" voice (often reflexive in nuance) was dying out during this period of the Greek language adding to the improbability this was the sense intended.

66. Col 3:18; 1 Pet 3:1, 5.

67. Lloyd-Jones, *Exposition of Chapter 13*, 23.

whatever diplomatic response there might be. We might even end up fighting for our nation and killing people of another nation to preserve our freedom. We would consider this self-defense, and it seems a concept well founded in the Hebrew scripture. There was no scriptural mandate for a standing army in Israel but there were certainly borders and there were arrangements made for tribes to join with one another for national defense and settling disputes militarily if diplomacy failed.[68]

Thus, we should at least be able to ask the question, If those that attack us just happen to be members of our own nation and those in authority over us, should we not too have a right to self-defense? The logic of the Second Amendment of the American Constitution was based on just that type of reasoning. The colonists and settlers had come from nations all over the Old World where the monarchs and priests systematically oppressed the people and, in some eras, the people were systematically tortured and killed in the most brutal and public fashion often at the behest of the papal hegemony that used the army of the Holy Roman Emperor.[69] They came in search of religious freedom and political liberty. This is why Lloyd-Jones, who was something of an expert on the Puritanism of the early colonists, was able to write:

> Surely, as Christians, we are entitled to argue that if a state, a king, an emperor, a governor, a dictator or anybody else becomes tyrannical, then this state is violating the law of its own being and constitution as laid down in Romans 13:2.[70]

That is, the State was instituted, as 1 Tim 2:2 states, to ensure "we may lead a peaceful [tranquil] and quiet life in all godliness and dignity" (NET). Thus, he continues:

> The moment . . . the State turns itself into a master and into a tyrant, it is disobeying the Law of God that brought it into being and it must itself be punished; and the form the punishment

---

68. Deut 20:10ff.; Josh 4:12; Num 32:6–25.

69. The "Holy Roman Emperor" was a title bequeathed by the pope on one of the monarchs of Europe once the papacy had established its domination (ca. AD 600). This then made that monarch's military resources available to the pope for dealing with "heresy" in any nation rebelling against his authority. The monarchs were normally feuding with one another as well as trying to weaken the authority of the pope over their nations. This was why some of the monarchs were sympathetic to the proto-reformers such as Wycliffe and Huss who vigorously asserted the political autonomy of nations and the superiority of the civil authorities over the Church within the national boundaries.

70. Lloyd-Jones, *Exposition of Chapter 13*, 46; Lloyd-Jones, *Puritans*.

takes is that the government is *thrown out* and replaced by one that is prepared to abide by the teaching of Romans 13:1–7.[71]

This statement begs the question, "What does 'thrown out' mean?" Are we permitted to fight, with arms (as the American founders felt it necessary to mandate) to evict a tyrannical government? We have already seen the inadequacy of the unconditional submission position and we can see that our options are much greater than simply a passive resistance, but just what *are* the limits of our resistance?

7.5.5 Christians Can Be Revolutionaries

The "just war" is defined as an extension of the duty of a magistrate to "restrain evil" and it is exactly this moral imperative to "restrain evil" that allows "[a Christian] to take part in a rebellion to change your government."[72] Whether that evil is internal or external to a nation, it is not an option for us to ignore it. Such an action is the "last resort" as is going to war; but as it was necessary to go to war against a Hitler, a Mussolini, or a Stalin, for the purposes of restraining their evil, so it is necessary to resist the evil of our own leaders.

Indeed, this is not unusual in the history of the Protestant Church and was a feature of the movement around Puritan Oliver Cromwell (the English Civil War) that spawned egalitarian groups such as the Levellers and the Diggers who prefigured many of the policies which became associated with the later labor and trade union movements.[73] Christians were very active in these movements and the Workers Educational Association (WEA), a Christian wing of the Working Men's Club movement (that was founded to promote literacy among working people) still exists in the UK today in accord with its original mission, while the WMCs are rather tatty, low-end social clubs.

Now, it is also important to recognize that there are degrees of resistance between non-resistance and a full-blown rebellion that we can exercise. We start with dialogue and our elected representatives, but we cannot allow ourselves to be neutered when our representatives cease

---

71. Lloyd-Jones, *Exposition of Chapter 13*, 46. Emphasis added.

72. Lloyd-Jones, *Exposition of Chapter 13*, 69.

73. The history around these groups and their relationship to Cromwell is contested history and all did not go well, but there was a strong element of novel Christian political thinking in all these groups.

to represent us. We can protest, we can boycott, and we can take collective action both as individuals and as collections of congregations to try and ensure social or political change; though with congregational action there are specific issues which we do need to consider if we are not to confuse the individual and Church institutional positions in relation to government. However, in cases where oppressive government tyranny is directed at the congregation *as a whole*, e.g., in the banning of public worship (as happened during COVID), the congregation should be able to respond collectively.

Now, I hope it is understood that I am not asserting we are immediately revolutionaries, it is just we need to understand we *can* be in the extreme. We can agree as Lloyd-Jones puts it "Christians should always be the best citizens in the country" and "good and peaceable"[74] in their basic attitudes. We have an ethical obligation to be the best citizens we can be *and* to be the most cooperative with the authorities over us as we can morally be. Even Stalin began to lessen the persecution of Christians because of the reputation for them being the best workers.[75] Christians, by default, *are* on the side of law and order because they understand that sin has produced lawlessness among men and that lawlessness needs the sword of the State to restrain it; this is also why Paul makes the statement it is an "issue of conscience" (v. 5) that we submit and even to *pay taxes* to ensure the smooth operation of the State. However, Lloyd-Jones strongly and immediately qualifies this general orientation to the State after establishing it as a basic principle with this statement:

> There is a limit beyond which it [the submission to the State and its enactments] is not true. It is quite clear in the scriptures that *if the State should ever come between me and my relationship to God*, then I *must* not obey it.[76]

During the COVID-19 pandemic we have just suffered, this limit was undeniably violated throughout Europe as congregations were prohibited from congregational worship and our almost universal failure to resist has cost us enormous space in the public sphere. Where there

---

74. Lloyd-Jones, *Exposition of Chapter 13*, 51.

75. This is a well-known paradox, even in today's Russia, where specific Christian ministries have access to and favor with the highest levels of the Russian government (I personally know of two) because of their reputation for honor and ethical conduct. Similarly, in some Islamic countries, Christians have access to TV stations because they are honorable and pay their bills on time.

76. Lloyd-Jones, *Exposition of Chapter 13*, 52. Emphasis added.

was or is substantive resistance, as was the case with the River Church in Tampa, Florida, and in some of the other US states where governors rejected federal mandates, the contrast could not be greater—they had full liberty to meet for worship, and citizens can trade freely with one another rather than lose their businesses and become reliant on federal welfare. This is also why the book of Acts provides the narratives for us of the conflict between the early church and the "authorities" that we might know there is no unconditional moral mandate to obey our governing authorities.[77]

7.6 Final Words

In this chapter we have sketched how we apply the basic principles of epistemological self-consciousness to our political philosophy; specifically we established the principle of involvement and that it should be an involvement that is not passive or neutral. We asserted that it is an anomalous distinctive of twentieth-century evangelicalism to separate from wider political and cultural involvement. The Reformed Church has had a history of political involvement since the days of Luther and Calvin, through to modern figures such as Machen and revivalists such as Finney.

We noted that for as long as there has been a Christian Church, there has been political opposition to it as witnessed in the biblical narratives of Acts in which there are recorded accounts of conflict. We then dealt specifically with the contemporary difficult issue of Rom 13 noting that because the biblical narratives record conflicts with the authorities for us, a simple, surface reading of Rom 13 is insufficient. We also rejected that the correct Christian position was one of agnosticism to the political environment, as 1 Tim 2 implies prayer for a social environment

---

77. Some might object that it was the religious authorities they came into conflict with, but Roman history does tell us that the Romans were shrewd enough to allow a degree of autonomy to their colonies in the sense they could keep their own civil law if they recognized the supreme jurisdiction of Rome. In the Donatist controversy in the early church of North Africa, this was as simple as throwing some incense on the fire once a year. We can glean this from the gospels and Acts where the governors would rather the Jews "judge according to their law" (Acts 18:15; Acts 24:6) than get involved in such civil disputes. It was why Pilate was just plain reluctant to get involved in the trial of Jesus and refused to judge as justice demanded but rather in accord with what he perceived as public opinion.

conducive to the preaching of the gospel which is correlative to a pluralistic political context.

We considered in some detail the account of Rom 13 provided by the finest evangelical expositor of the twentieth century, Dr. Martyn Lloyd-Jones. He drew the distinction between "honor," "submission" and "obedience" in considering the original Greek syntax and semantics of the passage. His central posit was that a State invalidates itself when it behaves in a tyrannical manner and when it intrudes into matters over which it has no jurisdiction, particularly in matters of religious practice and liberty. Only when the State is the minister of God to bring order and punish moral evil is obedience to the State required. We found that Lloyd-Jones even argued that revolutionary activity by believers was permissible as the act of ejecting an immoral or tyrannical State that had delegitimized itself. He argued further that the individual Christian is perfectly at liberty to be involved to any degree in political activity but the domain of the institution of the Church was separate to the political institutions; its role was to be the moral guardian that would speak into these institutions rather than to be directly involved in the institutions of government, e.g., bishops sitting in the House of Lords.

We broadly agreed with his position but noted that he was writing during a time when the Judeo-Christian position was generally accepted in all major political parties. Our qualification was that this is no longer the case, and the Church needed to expose the morally degenerate nature of "secular" politics and to support those parties which support ethical positions more in line with the gospel. This implied a greater level of involvement of the institution of the Church in political life and its explicit support of parties or policies. We maintain with Lloyd-George that the Church as an institution was not to argue for a theocracy which was reserved for ancient Israel alone, but it was to argue for a theonomical political position, seeing the principles of jurisprudence and government as immutable principles. God, in his Law, not only provides us with Commandments as top-level principles but works out the application in detail in the succeeding narratives.

In general, then, we were to defend Truth rather than to cede to postmodern subjectivity or cultural relativism, noting that the Reformation and councils of the Church established these as prerequisites for culture. A strong view of Truth also ushered in the scientific revolution. We concluded that we cannot have kingdom standards in social and political matters without those who can understand and implement them in positions of power and influence. In other words, the argument needs to be had not only about the legitimacy of certain principles but also in the details of working them out.[78]

---

78. There is far more to be said on the details of this involvement; see Macneil, "Politics."

8

Final Conclusion

8.1 Summary

OUR WORK HAS BEEN bold in presenting to us an outline of a vision of Christian philosophy. We examined the skeptical challenge and one of our most important conclusions was that it could be mitigated by understanding it was predominantly a *psychological* position rather than being a *logical necessity*. Skepticism or a general epistemological timidity was not an option for the epistemologically self-conscious. Similarly, we critiqued the role of science as the dominant cultural narrative, concluding there should be no special privileging of science above other cultural narratives. We then considered a critique of the wider conception of reason and rationality, positing it was defensible if and only if, the context was Christian. We then made extensive use of Plantinga who enabled us to arrive convincingly at the *reasonableness* of Christian belief as an epistemic option but found we needed to engage with Van Tillian thought to arrive at a proof of the necessity of Christian belief to be able to defend any claim to a fully rational philosophy.

To that end, we found that we needed to move beyond traditional deductive or inductive arguments, and into transcendental modes of reasoning. We examined the notion in general and the specific Van Tillian version of it identifying a set of objections and noting all but one could be robustly answered in a straightforward and convincing manner. We examined the final objection and noted that the previous attempt of

Butler to answer this objection relied on a theological move that while permissible was not wholly satisfactory. We examined another possible solution which relied on further analysis of the nature of transcendental argument and found a plausible solution to the final objection. With the necessity of Christian belief established, we then probed the relevance of our program for Christian political philosophy which had proved radically ineffective in countering the recent tyranny of government. We concluded that Christian involvement was mandated by epistemological self-consciousness owing to our conception stated at the beginning of our work that philosophy should be transformative.

8.2 Specific Conclusions

8.2.1 Overcoming Skepticism

The basic philosophical problem that stands most aggressively opposed to us was that of skepticism, but we found that on analysis, skepticism itself was multifaceted. We examined the skeptical challenge, understanding that philosophy asked questions and sometimes those questions originated in doubt and skepticism, we considered Descartes as the archetypal example of this mode of skepticism. This, in itself, was unobjectionable—we might call it methodological skepticism—but when accepted as a general epistemological principle, as found in Hume, it proved utterly destructive of human understanding and importantly for our project, undermined any possibility of a universal, moral knowledge. We concluded such metaphysical skepticism could be mitigated by understanding it was predominantly a chosen, voluntaristic *psychological* disposition as opposed to being a logical necessity.

That is, skepticism in the global sense is incoherent: if we *really* could know nothing, we could *never express* that we could know nothing. Thus, the tragic terminus of Hume as he sought to take empiricism seriously was precisely that, he could not even find an ego that was the recipient of experience; even his position that he was just a "bundle" of perceptions was illegitimate on his own terms, as "bundle" already assumes a non-empirical unifying concept. Wanting to mitigate this catastrophic conclusion regarding human rationality, we saw that Kant, with his division of nature into the phenomenal and the noumenal, was the first to answer Hume with the conception of transcendentals: those things which are assumed to make the knowledge of objects possible at all. For Kant this was a psychological apparatus, and his categories were those we must necessarily take to the world, with the traditional interpretation of Kant being that he was metaphysically agnostic regarding the noumenal, and we cannot know the world as it really is.

Thus, with Kant we found there was a skeptical pivot in Western philosophy. Some retreated into the intuition or mysticism as encountering reality as it is "in itself," accepting the legitimacy and indeed preferring the noumenal; knowledge gaining is at least in part and when pushed to the extreme, fundamentally irrational. Others denied the noumena and asserted phenomena is all we have, who we traced as the naturalistic movements of the twentieth century sometimes elaborate and intricate in their details but fundamentally without a foundation for their reasoning. What we witnessed with the liberalism of a Schleiermacher was a demythologizing of a religious worldview to arrive at an ethic which suggested Christian virtues, which might also be, for a Schopenhauer, considered the virtues of other "holy men and women" of any religion, or of all. Yet, it was denied an authoritative, epistemological basis. Thus, the next step was to abandon such "bourgeois sentimentality" and to embrace the opposing "scientific" materialist view impregnated with a Hegelian assumption of the relentless march of history to its glorious confirmation of Ultimate Spirit.

We concluded we do not need to argue over the legitimacy of the materialist philosophies; the millions dead through Marxism and Fascism are a testimony to their failure. In contrast, we understand why Kant still wanted to posit concepts such as God as existing in the noumenal realm as necessary for practical reason, the phenomenal realm providing limiting boundaries for the faculty of scientific reasoning. This is a supremely important explication of philosophy that Kant gives us here and it confirms that at the root of our philosophy is an *ethical* assumption and that flows from our metaphysics and structures our epistemology. So, our practical ethical and political philosophy was argued to be by necessity theonomic, with the scriptures providing a resource of narrative that allowed us to generate a set of political principles consistent with the faith. Our conclusion was not that of a religious hegemony but an endorsement of the sphere sovereignty of neo-Calvinism found first in Kuyper which rejected theocratic or ecclesiastical government but maintained the moral imperative of the Church to speak to each sphere regarding important ethical dimensions in research or technology. Thus, one of our most important conclusions was our argument for a taxonomy of philosophy that denies metaphysical skepticism and maintains a tripartite basis and a Christian metaphysical basis, that is articulated in our broader worldview as our imperative in the face of the failure of the non-Christian constructions.

8.2.2 Philosophy and Science

Philosophy we now understand as correlated with the whole of human knowledge, a synonym of science. We discovered from considering the work of Plantinga that methodological naturalism could not be founded upon a commitment to philosophical naturalism but only on a supernaturalistic metaphysics. Philosophical naturalism, so characteristic of modern empirical science, was demonstrated as being self-vitiating. To deconstruct and challenge this pattern of reasoning as the model of all rationality, we gave substantial space to a discussion of the status and the nature of science in the wake of this discussion of Darwinism. Darwin himself had recognized what Plantinga called "Darwin's doubt": if all we have is nature, why should we believe in what nature says? If naturalism was true, there would be no way of expressing that it was in fact true; there would be no non-arbitrary starting point. Thus, we discovered that there is no solid edifice of "science" but that there are many different sciences and many incommensurate modes of what are said to be "science." Carnap, Popper, Quine, and Kuhn bear testimony to radically different conceptions of "science." Thus, one of our most useful conclusions is to debunk science as somehow the arbiter of all rationality or the foundation upon which a worldview is built, science is rather a function, a derivative of the worldview context in which it is established.

So, we considered for example, after the rise and fall of philosophical positivism, our age has been characterized by an equation of *methodological* naturalism with science, or a science that proceeds on the basis that there is no such being as God or the supernatural. This has proved to be a powerful, pragmatic mode of progressing the sciences, particularly those which we have later leveraged for technology and industrial progress; perhaps less so with the softer, social sciences but an emphasis on the tangible "cash value" of an idea is a powerful tool for judging its efficacy, and the fruits of modernity have brought the potential, if not the actuality, for the great improvement of the conditions of living on the planet. Life on Earth today is very different than little over a century ago.

We also examined the central role of evolutionary thought in modern science. We understood that there was a tautological dependency that was repeatedly appealed to that undergirded so many sciences; a trait "X" present is deemed to be present because it offered evolutionary advantage, but that is simply to state what is there, is there. We have no explanation as to *why* it should have been of advantage. In the post-positivist naturalism of Quine and his disciples, this is expressed as an unargued behaviorism. We found that in the debate between the evolutionary schools of Dawkins and Gould, evolutionary thought was not an evidentially based science but a set of conflicting metaphysical dogmas upon which many divergent sciences were built. This is a powerful instrument in countering the tyranny of the sciences and its arguments against the Christian worldview.

We also examined the influence of physicalism in science, the belief that all non-physical processes, specifically those that are considered "mental" in character, are ultimately reducible to physical processes. This, again, was exposed as unargued dogma supported only by a clique of physicists and naturalists who were attempting to work out the implications of their naturalism. We also considered the importance of concepts of randomness and chance, especially as found in the new era of quantum physics. Much use had been made of the apparent lack of objectivity regarding the quantum world as justifying a lack of objectivity generally in the world, which was then seen to provide justification for a subjective and/or a skeptical philosophical position generally. However, we found that among some of the most senior mathematical physicists, there was an argument that quantum physics was failing to offer *any* coherent account of the physical world. Thus, far from establishing an imperative of rationality, it served to undermine any claim for science to be offering a rational account.

It was also seen to be a serious category mistake to attempt to use quantum physics as a general hermeneutical principle for reality as random and chaotic; it is rather that quantum effects are seen as explanatory in edge-case or anomalous data events. As Christians we can have confidence in the commitment of God to there being principles or laws of nature that are maintained by his commitment to them "as long as the Earth remains" (Gen 8:22) which also provides a guarantee for the inductive logic at the heart of many physical sciences. Philosophers of science have historically failed to satisfactorily give an account of induction, and the sciences have proceeded using the principle as an unargued dogma. The awareness of the weakness of inductive logic was one of the drivers for the many different iterations of scientific philosophy in the twentieth century, none of which could provide a rigorous account.

So, in summary, without an answer to the "*why* should science be successful" question, science becomes value-agnostic, and history has taught us it then becomes a tool of the totalitarian. If we refuse to sidestep the philosophical question, we concluded from Plantinga that methodological naturalism could have warrant only when grounded in supernaturalistic metaphysics which we might also correlate with the principles of common grace and general revelation that we found were central to Van Tillian accounts. Science, when honestly executed, that is, executed with Christian metaphysical presuppositions, implicit or explicit, works because it really does tell us something about the way the world is. That is, we asserted a *realistic* conclusion, that it is plausible that the world really is the way a holistic science finds it to be because scripture gives us confidence in a logos that permeates all of creation.

Scripture communicates to us that we can expect laws, principles, and the inductive method to tell us something about the way the world is. Thus, we concurred with some of the major philosophers of the twentieth century such as Wittgenstein, Kuhn, and Quine, that holism, or a view of nature as a self-referential unity, is fundamental for us and that should be the definition of science. While rejecting *their* metaphysics, we would concur that our empirical experience is always theory laden; there is no neutral place from which we sit outside of our worldview to judge the world. Thus, we can conclude it is perfectly legitimate for us to sit within our worldview and that is a place of substantial confidence for us as Christian philosophers.

8.2.3 Christianity, Religious Experience, and Apologetic Philosophy

It is not pretended that this work presents the only vision of Christian philosophy that is possible and indeed, much of the outworking of this project has intersected sympathetically or critically with other, sometimes incommensurable, visions and versions of Christian philosophy. The desire was to do justice to the diversity of perspectives and deeply held convictions among different Christian communities in responding to the scriptural injunction to defend the faith; or simply, even the basic Christian spiritual instinct to testify to others regarding the positive message and effects of the gospel. A distinctive of historical Christianity has been the outward looking nature of the faith; it evangelizes (clearly believing it has a message worth hearing) and seeks to be of service to both its nation and the wider interests of humanity in living at peace with one another. Thus, we needed to recognize the diversity of the objective and subjective orientations within apologetics, which in turn were reflections on and sometimes Christian responses to the cultural milieu in which the Christian communities found themselves.

However, the historical and orthodox Christian faith, in all its inflections and traditions, has always had those who believed that there was an intellectual challenge implicit in the message of the scriptures which had reached a loud crescendo in the person and words of Jesus of Nazareth. Taken at face value, the words of Jesus demanded of us a personal response and a choice to take up our own cross of Calvary with its implicit ridicule, pain, and shame but also the crucifixion of the flesh and the receiving of a new nature born of the Spirit of God. The greatest apostle of the Christian faith, St. Paul, in the magisterial letters we now call the book of Romans and the book of Hebrews, should also be recognized as presenting some of the finest intellectual defenses of those words and some of the finest diagnoses of the defective psychology of the human condition which was later to prove so influential on Augustine as he agonized over stealing pears that he did not even like; for him he stole because he *wanted* to steal and that "*wanting* to steal" was the problem of fallen humanity that Christian philosophy must answer and which Paul had first addressed.

We thus chose to use the Van Tillian term "epistemological self-consciousness" as it encapsulated well the central proposition of this work that the conception of an authentic Christian philosophy must be able to articulate and defend its position in a manner *consistent* with the philosophical presuppositions and praxis or phenomenology of the Christian faith. In conducting the research for this work, it became evident that within Christian apologetic philosophy, this would often be considered an extreme position. Modern apologetics, particularly in the Anglo-American Protestant tradition since the establishment of the great American colleges in the Colonies, had favored philosophical traditions drawing from commonsense realism, empiricism and evidentialism, responding to an increasingly naturalistic conception of science and rationality more generally. It became overwhelmingly dominated by a perception that there was somewhere a neutral, common ground upon which we could meet and then resolve the differences on the basis of a common rationality.

The Christian "worldview" was then simply a "conceptual scheme" which one was free to accept or reject as one weighed the evidence for and against; the Christian praxis was steadily divorced from its reasons. We found that the greatest challenge to this form of apologetics came with the publication of Darwin's thesis. On the basis of empirical observations and common sense, Darwin proposed a naturalistic rationale that contradicted the Christian metaphysics. This led to the rise of liberalism and other forms of subjective apologetics because the evidence which seemed to demand a verdict, the scientific account, the commonsense account, *refuted* the traditional religious account. The great Protestant universities, built on a foundation that believed the faith it defended was a rational faith, seemed compelled to abandon their traditional positions, in some cases ceding first to Unitarianism (as in Harvard and Yale) and others secularized completely; the only evidence they were once Christian institutions would be in their insignia and motto (as in Columbia University, New York).

This was clearly an affront to orthodox Christian praxis and spirituality, and we cannot ignore these spiritual dimensions in the name of philosophical or academic respectability and acceptability, or it has then compromised itself. Thus, through this work, our conception of the Christian "worldview" was developed into a far stronger conception than a "conceptual scheme"; it has fundamental ontological, epistemological, and ethical commitments. We argued that the traditional problem of the circularity problem between metaphysics and epistemology are resolved in the Christian commitments, given full expression in the inscripturation process. The transcendental of a God both transcendent and immanent, present in Spirit but dwelling in eternity, as reconciling the "universal" and the "particular," is able to substantively ground philosophy. Though some reticence to the Trinitarian concept as foundational to Christian philosophy has to be recognized because it is argued as an intellectual innovation in the early centuries of the Church, such reticence was not compelling for us.

We concluded that transcendental logic makes it tenable that even accepting a conclusion was an inference from scripture, assuming a pattern of reasoning we were seeking to establish, that this would not be problematic for us. Transcendental reasoning concludes that this circularity is not objectionable as reasoning assuming ultimate authorities could not proceed in any other manner. Another important conclusion for us was that we are able to strengthen our confidence in reason by considering that one of the principles we recognized as present in Van Til in which he agreed with the great neo-Calvinist Kuyper, and which can be traced directly to both Calvin and recognized in seminal form in Augustine and thus present in some streams of Catholicism also, was that to the degree even the rebellious honor the image of God within their intellect, they will produce *genuine* science. That is, there is no requirement that knowledge only originates with the regenerate and truth can be appreciated and valued wherever it is found.

This established an important and pluralistic conclusion, but equally this is not to assert that sin has no noetic effects or to deny the wider Christian and scriptural imperative of salvation. One of Van Til's sharpest arguments we considered in this work was in the reconciliation of the opposing positions of Warfield and Kuyper, where his apologetic asserts that the full rational autonomy claimed by Warfield for the unbeliever is impossible without faith; faith must be the foundation for claims to rationality and not vice versa. He departed fundamentally from Kant in this respect also; Kant would argue, in some ways echoing Descartes's confidence in an unadulterated access to internal mental states, that rational autonomy was a prerequisite of being able to submit to the moral law of God. In contrast, Van Til's important conclusion was that special and general revelation dovetail together; the scriptures at once sort out our thinking and renew our mind but the operation of salvific grace is a prerequisite of receiving that renewal through the scriptures.

In that sense we might also agree that the scriptures give an account for what is already present, but they also bring to the present what is not yet present. Without the scriptures there can be no renewing of the mind, and it is always a commitment to the propositional challenge of a heart believing and the mouth confessing that distinguishes the regenerate from the unregenerate. That is, there are no "anonymous Christians,"[1] though there might be many of different faiths that would readily believe the Christian message on the basis of the general consciousness of God within their own conscience that the scriptures also recognize in Rom 2,

---

1. Although not considered in the body of the thesis, the concept of an anonymous Christian was associated most directly with Jesuit theologian Karl Rahner (1904–84). It is easy to mischaracterize Rahner as merely arguing for universalism and "all will be saved" but this would be a straw man misrepresentation; as with much Catholic theology, it requires detailed study to be properly understood before criticism. It is far more nuanced than the popular parody.

FINAL CONCLUSION

which is why there is a mandate to preach to all nations in Rom 10. This is what I believe Paul meant in Romans when the Gentiles are a law to themselves when they have responded to the immanent knowledge of God by the virtue of being human (Rom 2:14–15). Thus, importantly, and significantly, if a philosophy has a conclusion or a principle that is in harmony with scripture, whether consciously or unconsciously, reason has behaved in a non-autonomous manner, irrespective of any conscious religious commitment. We must recognize in conclusion that our conception of "autonomous reason" must be understood in a specific, theory-laden manner distinct from the Kantian sense; the regenerate in spirit are not necessarily regenerate in mind. The former might be considered to be of punctiliar aspect (the logic of salvation expressed in Rom 10:8–9); the latter of the continual present aspect, the discipline of the Christian life.

Thus, because of this overlap there is still the interesting discussion possible at this point that because we know the truth of the Christian worldview in a transcendental sense, we then make scripture incidental. However, the Christian worldview emphasizes the importance of regeneration through baptism, living a life of repentance and of the supreme importance the "renewing of the mind" (Rom 12:2; 2 Cor 10:4–6). This "renewal" is both a rational operation and a spiritual one, but these are an integrated, irreducible parts of a whole. When Jesus talked about "rivers of living water *flowing*" out of the "innermost being" (John 7:37–38), we have a figure of a noetic renewal. Similarly, when Paul spoke of "pulling down strongholds" (2 Cor 10:4) he was not talking about supernatural structures in the heavenly realms[2] but a conscious, epistemological methodology where every thought and intent of the heart is tested against the scripture: we "*tear down* arguments" (v. 4 NET) that are "raised up against the knowledge of [from] God"[3] and "we take every thought captive to make it obey Christ."[4] Thus, we can formally agree scripture is

---

2. I was repeatedly taught over the years that "strongholds" were spiritual kingdoms that dominated the natural world. Such a conception is arguably the subject of Eph 6:12 ff. and a repeated motif throughout the book of Daniel, particularly in those narratives where Daniel specifically is being shown visions in the heavenly realm. However, the context of 2 Cor 10 is clear and is talking about patterns of thought and the discipline of testing them for coherence with and correspondence to the Christian worldview.

3. 2 Cor 10:5 (NET) with my amplification. Here I believe it is appropriate to consider the genitive in the ablative sense.

4. Here the translators of the NET consider the genitive clause as having an

accounting for what is already present and its purpose is to sort out our thinking, but scripture is never merely incidental to the Christian life but central to it.

This was also why we needed in this work to distinguish between representing Christianity merely as a "conceptual scheme" and emphasizing it as a "worldview." However, because of its wider appropriation within non-Augustinian Christian philosophy, we discovered that even the concept of "worldview" has been misunderstood in purely rational terms as a more elaborate conceptual map attempting to present a more full-bodied and coherent conception of what it means to be a Christian; that is, an improved or more rigorous conceptual scheme. We have seen that because modern literature has tended to conflate conceptual scheme and worldview, with philosophers preferring the former and theologians the latter, the critical difference between the two has been sublimated to the detriment of genuine spirituality. This is why the challenge of Jesus was most forcefully made with his identification as "I am the way, and the truth, and the life. No one comes to the Father except through me" (John 14:6). The key word here is the "comes": this is not just a one-time salvation event but a lifestyle of communion with the Father; this is the emphasis of the narrative of the entire chapter. Thus, one of our strongest conclusions must be the importance of engaging in worldview apologetics but not merely in the formal sense that has characterized much of Augustinian apologetics, both in the Reformed and Catholic traditions, but also to give attention to the phenomenology and the spirituality of Christian life. This was perhaps a contra-intuitive conclusion for us to reach in a thesis concerned primarily with a rational defense of the faith.

In summary, we should conclude there are different senses of knowledge that must be recognized, and we can have knowledge about God and from God, *without* having a saving knowledge of God and a communion with God. We might indeed formally acknowledge that there is a transcendental sense in which the Christian conceptual scheme is assumed by all, or better that the Christian conceptual scheme provides all with the basis for whatever intelligibility there is in a worldview, which is one of our primary claims argued within this work. Yet, the full Christian worldview, or a completed knowledge of God, is only known when salvation has been received, knowing God through the salvific exchange of an

---

objective sense with Christ as the object. Many other translations stay neutral and render it simply as "every thought captive to the obedience of Christ," which is rather clumsy English and does not help to make the intended sense clear.

individual's belief and confession as a matter of volition. This still raises some difficult issues regarding those who are disadvantaged through physical or mental disease or dysfunction, but this would rather appear to be an issue of Christian praxis and the ministry of the Church in the world, where healing and deliverance were considered as part of the ministry to people suffering in that way, rather than epistemology. Some of the intellectual paradoxes for Christians perhaps result from Christians not behaving as they were instructed to do so from within the Gospel scriptures and the book of Acts.

8.2.4 Transcendentalism and TAG

One of the important questions we asked philosophically was, Are all my answers private answers, or is there a public, objective world which we all can reach? Following neo-Kantian Strawson, our beliefs in the regularities of nature were *transcendentally* necessary, they were not reasoned to in an inductive or deductive sense, they were commitments we did not choose, and it was idle (in the sense of doing no useful work) to reason either in confirmation or disconfirmation. We can certainly agree with Strawson, but his conclusions are piecemeal and parochial; by considering a broader critique of the wider conception of reason and rationality which can only be grounded for us normatively from scripture, we found transcendentalism was defensible if and only if, the context was Christian. This helped us establish further that our philosophical choices are at base *ethical*; these are *choices* that we make.

To proceed we needed to find a transcendental that justified these transcendentals which we posited as the triune, transcendent God unique to Christianity. This was a strong claim and not without problematics, our central pivot being a perception regarding the division of reason between an autonomous reason that proceeds on a basis independent of a reference to scripture; and a reason that proceeds recognizing scripture as providing its foundation. We can recognize, formally, that an autonomy of reason would seem to be a prerequisite for one to *freely* submit to God's Law; it would need to be *our* choice to be a moral choice, and, on that basis, God would be just in his judgment of us. However, we concluded that non-Christian logic had already invaded our thinking here; both Van Til and Plantinga recognized that sin has noetic effects, and we should argue that it is God's grace that is a *prerequisite* of even our being able to make that free choice, let alone fully appreciate the moral quality of that choice as a Creator would demand of it.

This would seem to be the implication of John 6:44, that the prerogative is God's choice and not ours; the Greek verb used in this verse where most English versions use "draw" is better translated "drag." This is why we needed to consider at length what we called the Christian Presupposition, which was our complex mix of theological and philosophical variables to map what Van Til called "analogical thinking" by which he did not mean, as his critics wrongly represented him as saying, that our thinking gives us an analogy of God or the world (for we really do know God and the world) but in the sense that how a creature knows as contrasted with how the Creator knows. There is a qualitative difference between when we know an object and God's knowledge of it, for God *knowing* it makes it what it is: God's knowledge is *constitutive* in this regard; ours remains derivative. The autonomous reason for Van Til is defined as that which considers itself constitutive or definitive, even if definitively skeptical; reason properly employed as a tool defers to the authority of scripture.

Thus, we should conclude that our final definition of autonomous reason we have developed is that which judges not just on the basis of right/wrong and truth/falsehood but on the basis that it operates outside the constraints of scripture that delineate its legitimate operation. Illegitimate operations are an abstract mode of reasoning, rightly described by scripture as "vain and deceitful" (Col 2:8), considered an operation defining its own content and context. If a philosophy has a principle or a conclusion and it is oppositional to scripture, this vanity is self-evident; however, even a skeptical conclusion that wishes to suspend judgment, has taken an autonomous posture if scripture speaks on that matter. So, for example, we considered that even asking the question "Does God exist?" imports in a conception of reason that is vainly autonomous, for it assumed that possibility is more ultimate than God himself; rather, possibility is what it is because God exists.

Thus, it is not merely a general orientation of reason, though that is a helpful beginning point, but also a criterion of evaluation of individual acts of reason. Scripture in its narrative speaks to the whole of human life. That is why we asserted a Christian and a non-Christian worldview rather than "worldviews"; they have a unity at a base level. Nevertheless, there is a sense in which our wills and our choices are always our own and our conscience, as Paul notes, is always standing ready to accuse us but can be suppressed in unrighteousness (Rom 1:18). We want to formally agree with Kant that a prerequisite of freedom is the autonomy of the individual but that will only be a result of grace. Kant was insufficiently rigorous to recognize that a conscience can be "seared" (1 Tim 4:2) such that it is no longer capable of recognizing right or wrong, truth and falsehood as God would define it; but that it would be functioning in defining its own versions of right and wrong. It is equally autonomous if it denies in skepticism we can know right or wrong.

We then made extensive use of Plantinga who enabled us to arrive convincingly at the *reasonableness* of Christian belief as an epistemic option. Once classical foundationalism was shown to be untenable, it allowed us to establish that it is perfectly legitimate for a Christian community to decide which beliefs were basic for itself. The essence of Plantinga's position was to provide a notion of *warrant* which was established on an externalistic basis, in contrast to the internalism of evidentialism that derives from its classical foundationalist basis. This thus provided us with the conclusion that an apologetic defense needed to proceed on a similar basis. Plantinga's final form of reliabilism posited that warranted belief originates in cognitive faculties that are functioning properly, in a suitable environment, according to a design plan successfully aimed at producing true beliefs. This we understood as a fortified version of Reidian commonsense realism, addressing at great length the inadequacies of the commonsense concept in contrast to the naïve, evidentialist appropriation of Reid.

However, we noted that Plantinga himself had the final position that he did not believe it was philosophically possible to *prove* that God existed, using premises that would be accepted by all or even nearly all; though he did, importantly, assert that the arguments were as *strong as philosophical arguments could be*, giving substantive *de jure* grounds for Christian belief. Thus, it was necessary for us to posit and evaluate Van Til's contention that only with a *transcendental* argument would it be possible to proceed any further to offer a proof for the *de facto* necessity of the Christian worldview and to be able to defend any claim to a fully rational philosophy. The potential for the transcendental argument to proceed from a necessary conceptual logical premise which establishes a necessary reliance on a contested conceptual logical claim, provided the basis for our application of the method.

Our final argument in this mode was thus simple and elegant: the Christian worldview provides the intelligibility for all predications; that is, in attempting to argue against the Christian worldview, the worldview must be assumed. This was much like Aristotle's first recorded use of a transcendental argument to justify logic; in attempting to deny logic he argued you were employing it. This long pedigree of the argument form and its recent use in the work of Frege, Wittgenstein, Searle, Strawson, and others served to establish its legitimacy in the face of criticisms. We identified a set of objections and noted that all but one could be robustly answered in a straightforward and convincing manner once the transcendental nature of the argument was properly understood. We examined the final objection that was considered the strongest objection associated with the famous criticism of Stroud against Strawson that asserted that the most a transcendental argument could accomplish was to demonstrate the conceptual necessity to view the world in a particular way, it did not establish the ontological necessity.

That is, the implication being that the most the TAG could accomplish was to demonstrate the *conceptual* necessity of belief in the Christian God to be *fully rational*; it did not establish that the Christian God did, in fact, exist. While we might consider the TAG as in actuality accomplishing the narrow apologetic task of providing a rational defense of Christianity, the thorough going skeptic is still left with a final, admittedly desperate out, and they could assert that they were prepared to accept the explicit irrationality of the world and live believing that attempts to describe the universe in rational terms were illegitimate and arbitrary. This paralogical position has an undeniable cultural presence; that is, in some respects we noted it was distinctive of the postmodern mood, as well as a position in the skeptical conclusions of some analytical philosophers.

Thus, we felt compelled to engage further to see if it was possible to strengthen the argument. The attempt of Van Tillian Butler to answer this objection relied on a theological move regarding the distinction between conceptual scheme and worldview that while permissible and legitimate, was not wholly satisfactory for us. We examined another possible solution which relied on further analysis of the nature of transcendental argument and found a plausible solution to the final objection that relied on research from several recent philosophers that argued that the verification principle was capable of a transcendental justification, most famously as employed by McDowell in his *Mind and World*. This work was notable as being considered acceptable to the analytic philosophical tradition while employing modes of thought more readily associated with the Continental tradition. It was thus considered to have considerable weight as a solution. With such a justification, it is no longer the self-refuting principle of empiricism but provided the necessary bridge between the way the world is and how it is conceived to be. However, we learned from our analysis that the transcendental principle cannot stand alone, it needs the transcendent transcendental of the Trinity to provide the ontological bridge, to render coherent the derivative transcendentals.

With the necessity of Christian belief established, we then probed further the relevance of our program for Christian political philosophy. We noted that philosophical categories were articulated with ethical assumptions and that metaphysics and epistemological categories were interdependent. Considering them as abstract categories could never resolve this circularity. Only by considering scripture as encapsulating unifying principles could we establish a substantive basis, and we concluded that Christian involvement was mandated on a *theonomical* basis. The narratives of scripture provide the raw material from which principles were both stated and explicated in their application. We recognize that while our cultural situation is different than ancient Israel and the outworking of those principles would be different, they were nevertheless still legitimate principles for us today. The ethical problems of humanity might be nuanced by our technological context but remain those explored in scripture. Thus, epistemological self-consciousness concludes that our conception stated at the beginning of our thesis, that philosophy should be transformative, was legitimate and has been defended successfully.

8.3 The Contribution of Our Thesis as Original Research

8.3.1 As Augustinian Apologetics

In the introductory sections we argued that we were approaching the subject of philosophy in what was considered the Augustinian tradition. This asserts that faith should provide the foundation for reason in contrast to the (neo-)Thomist position that reason should be preferred if there was a conflict between the two or if knowledge was possible to humanity by either route. We built on the work of the Dutch Reformed tradition which itself relied on the Calvinistic Reformers and thus Augustine. However, it was an unexpected discovery during the research regarding the nuances of Thomist thought and the important developments of Augustinian thought by those considered formally as Thomists. It was initially envisaged that it would have been primarily by considering the contribution of Reformed thinkers that we would have presented a conception of Christian philosophy that we have argued is faithful to that which is implicit in the scriptures. We discovered that the Catholic contribution to Augustinian thought should not be underestimated.

That is, internal High Church politics has obfuscated the philosophical contribution of those within Catholicism which sought to return to a more rigorous Augustinianism. As an example, we saw that Leo XIII in 1879 had issued a papal bull that made it mandatory for Catholic institutions to teach Aquinas as the "only right [philosopher]." This has not been remitted and so philosophers within the Catholic communion that wish to innovate needed to tie their work to Aquinas in some way, either as demonstrating that previous interpretations of Aquinas were erroneous or that they were clarifying or developing his thought. Even in the twentieth century, Catholic theologians and philosophers have suffered censure for their straying from orthodoxy, including Henri Lubac whom we featured as a modern Augustinian within the Catholic communion that we would certainly want to include within those seeking an authentic defense of the Christian worldview and faith.[5]

That is, we have discovered a common foundation for those who believe that Christianity should be defended in a manner consistent with the faith outside the denominational constraints. At the same time, we have drawn a clear distinction between apologetic traditions that proceeded on a classical foundationalist basis such as evidentialism and "classical" neo-Thomist apologetics which used teleological and cosmological arguments. We demonstrated the philosophical inadequacy of this methodology even though it had been employed and is still employed in defending the faith. Our important distinction was that such arguments were useful *within* the faith but not as logical proofs. We did this by explicating the incommensurable nature of the epistemological assumptions at the basis of these views with the Christian worldview.

---

5. As these theologians and philosophers are often within a school or community, this censure meant that they are unable to teach or publish until the censure is remitted or overruled by a new pope (as was the case with Lubac). Of course, censure for unorthodoxy is also common (and can be uglier) within the Reformed communion and normally erupts to scandal in the more evangelical and charismatic churches. The latter tend to favor a decentralized model of government that can fail to arrest aberrations both of doctrine and behavior before they become scandalous.

8.3.2 In Opposition to Scientism

We presented an analysis that demonstrated that philosophy in the nineteenth century had become dominated by the liberalism and naturalism in response to the crisis precipitated by the Darwinian conception of humanity. We articulated the failure of the naturalistic philosophy that flowed from this position and debunked our dominant cultural narrative of science as somehow implicitly naturalistic and authoritative whenever it comes into conflict with the Christian worldview. We stood in direct opposition to the view that elevated scientific questions as the *only* questions worth asking by exposing the fallacious verificationism and question-begging at the heart of that view.

Further, by considering the best science had to offer in evolutionary thought and in quantum physics, we demonstrated the epistemological inadequacy of the various naturalisms, and the various category mistakes made in attempting to generalize "chance" as a metaphysical principle. In particular, by exposing that one of the most senior mathematical physicists alive today believed that quantum physics was failing to offer *any* meaningful description of reality, we can conclude epistemic authority and right to our own position as achieving much more.

8.3.3 As Synthesis of Van Til and Plantinga

We noted that a revival in Christian philosophy occurred in Calvin College in the 1930s onward as Jellema inspired the two philosophers who articulated the need for a distinctively Christian philosophy most strongly. Both claimed to be articulating a *Christian* philosophy rather than just being philosophy by those who identified as philosophers who were Christians. One was rigorously analytic in their approach, and one had employed the language and methods of idealism. These two philosophers were Alvin Plantinga and Cornelius Van Til.

Although both men had very similar aims and had considerable overlap in their careers and had been taught in the same institution by the same professor that had profoundly influenced them both, there was no direct interchange between them and there was only a single reference to Van Til in Plantinga's entire corpus and none to Plantinga in Van Til's corpus. We noted that the Christian analytic tradition that experienced a renaissance primarily because of the influence of Plantinga had senior members who were extremely dismissive of Van Til with some refusing even to acknowledge him as a philosopher.

While there had been notable attempts by Anderson and Oliphint[6] to correct some of the misunderstandings and to demonstrate linkages between their work, we have endeavored to demonstrate more fully that these distinct streams are not in an adversarial mode but should be considered as complimentary because they both articulated very similar presuppositions. We identified considerable overlooked linkages between their epistemologies, and our key innovation was to dovetail the two together to strengthen the argument for a distinctively Christian philosophy that not only argued for the rationality of the position but provided an argument for the necessity of the Christian worldview as a prerequisite of rationality. We found that there was considerably more in common between the positions than was previously accepted; this was partially explained by linguistic issues, with Van Til's philosophical training belonging to a generation that favored idealism, whereas Plantinga was rigorously analytic in his approach.

We discovered that Van Tillians can readily endorse and use Plantinga's critiques of foundationalism and naturalism, and can benefit from his discussion of evidence, internalism, reliabilism, and externalism in fortifying their own position. We also emphasized that Van Til's position had been importantly misrepresented and misjudged by his analytic critics as suggested by Plantinga's single reference to him, though the reference might more charitably be considered as targeting the inelegant use some of Van Til's disciples had made of his work. The characterization of Van Til's work as asserting that "unbelievers could not know anything" was unequivocally incorrect because it omitted the second part of his quote "if they were consistent with their epistemological presuppositions";[7] central to Van Til's apologetic was rather that unbe-

---

6. Scott Oliphint is professor of apologetics and systematic theology at Westminster Theological Seminary, the institution at which Van Til spent virtually all his career. He is known as a Van Tillian, though perhaps quietly and uncontroversially so, and has been involved in editing and introductory sections to the new editions of Van Til, also writing an interesting foreword to Bosserman, *Paradox*, who explicated the doctrine and role of the Trinity in Van Tillian thought. I have not directly considered the work of Oliphint in this book with respect to Plantinga, as this seems to be a minor aspect of his work though he did offer a lucid introductory commentary to a section on Plantinga in his apologetic reader, *Christian Apologetics*. In contrast, Anderson was one of the first scholars who explicitly grasped this nettle and from whom I benefited in discussing issues surrounding the links between their work.

7. Plantinga, *Warranted Christian Belief*, 217; Bahnsen, *Van Til's Apologetic*, 420–21.

lievers were not consistent and that was a point of contact with them, allowing reasoning with them.

This was his novel appropriation and reconciliation of the rival conceptions of Kuyper and Warfield regarding apologetic philosophy; he accepted their basic premises but considered their conclusions as fallacious. We found that because of Van Til's agreement with Warfield that Christianity was objectively provable, his position was precisely the opposite to the fideism that some of his critics accuse him of. Indeed, his position was an important innovation from the fideist terminus of others in the Dutch Reformed Church such as Kuyper, who strongly asserted the incommensurable nature of believing and unbelieving "science" (which for Kuyper, as for us, encompassed the whole of human knowledge) and the impossibility of reconciling them; Kuyper was one of the finest expositors of a Calvinism fit for modernity and in opposition to modernism.

Part of the genius of Van Til was his reconciliation and synthesis of apparently contradictory positions to create a far more robust and philosophically rigorous and coherent apologetic. However, and in contrast to Plantinga, his influence has been far more muted, and his work rarely considered outside of narrow Reformed circles and even within those narrow boundaries, controversially so. This we suggested was perhaps best explained by the lack of the propagation of his work in the wider literature, his long tenure at a single institution, and his routine publishing in the in-house journals, which has meant his work has not been generally considered even within the Christian philosophical circles.

Thus, it is hoped that this work succeeds in commending the work of Van Til to those interested in Christian philosophy who would otherwise only encounter an inaccurate caricature of his work and that it goes some way to repairing his reputation in the eyes of those familiar with the work of Plantinga. They are flip sides of the same philosophical project which is to articulate a Christian philosophy consistent with the faith itself, rather than based on epistemologies borrowed from the non-Christian world. As was noted by the analytical Christian philosopher Craig, the positions had a surprising degree of convergence as Plantinga's philosophy might also be perceived of moving in a transcendental direction.

8.4 The Wider Relevance of the Research

8.4.1 As Van Tillian Scholarship

As a more general elaboration as the point above, it was striking to me during the research as to how sparsely Van Til's work was even acknowledged in Christian philosophy. Whereas Plantinga gets good coverage, perhaps reflecting his status not just in Christian philosophy but as a former president of the APA and a recipient of the Templeton Prize in 2017, Van Til seldom gets mentioned. Even in introductory works on philosophy by Christians that include most major philosophical figures from ancient Greece onward, he is conspicuously absent.[8] Now this might uncharitably be explained in that Van Til's work was of insufficient quality to merit serious consideration, but this claim does not stand up to scrutiny as we have repeatedly demonstrated through this work. Most notably in that respect, the famous Princeton metaphysician A. A. Bowman had recognized Van Til as having exceptional skill in metaphysical analysis and had offered Van Til a fellowship which allowed him to complete his doctoral work. Similarly, it is of note that even some of Van Til's fiercest critics complemented Van Til on his analysis and exposure of neo-Orthodoxy, being the first within the wider evangelical community to explicate it as a departure from orthodox Christianity.

We concluded it was thus incoherent for the students of those same critics to later accuse him of being neo-Orthodox, and it demonstrated no understanding of Van Til's transcendentalism. Similarly, Van Til was also readily misunderstood because he was trained within the framework of idealist philosophy whereas most of the development in Christian philosophy in the twentieth century was more in line with the analytical mode of thought. Rather, we should conclude that one of the challenges with Van Tillian scholarship has been reflected in that Van Til had an enormous corpus of class syllabi, articles, and reviews but perhaps only a single book[9] which would be considered a synoptic summary of his position. Although he had three major books published during his lifetime,

---

8. The notable exception is Frame in his *History*. This perhaps should not be surprising as Frame was a student of Van Til and became, with Bahnsen, one of the most influential expositors of his thought. However, other students of Van Til who went on to become influential apologists relegated him to a single footnote (Carnell) or omitted to mention him entirely (Schaeffer).

9. Van Til, *Defense of the Faith*.

two of those dealt specifically with neo-Orthodoxy as heterodox rather than his overall apologetic system.

This clearly indicated that there has been a lack of understanding of Van Til, even among those closest to him in claiming the Reformed moniker. It was only after Van Til passed that some of his disciples attempted to systematize his work and present the revolutionary nature of his thought. We discovered that the most effective account was found in Bahnsen,[10] which is recognized as Bahnsen's *magnum opus* in which he demonstrates the profound and systematic nature of Van Til's thought while recognizing the density of Van Til's prose and his sometimes-clumsy English idiom, being at least partially explained because English was his second language. However, Bahnsen's exposition of Van Til extends to eight hundred pages and many of those are packed with footnotes; it is a challenging read. Thus, in such a work as presented here, where we employed an analytic framework but managed to integrate Van Tillian transcendental logic to move from a discussion of probabilities to certainties when discussing the existence of God and the rational justification of Christian belief, it is hoped that the power of his method has been made available to a new generation of analytically minded apologists. Our philosophical preferences and prejudices should not prevent us from recognizing that Van Til belonged to a tradition of uncompromising believers such as Tertullian, Augustine, Luther, Calvin, Warfield, and Kuyper who not only clearly recognized the antithesis between believer and unbeliever but understood that a distinctively Christian philosophy of life was to be worked out from the scriptures.

8.4.2 For Christian Ethics

We recognized that the questions of ethics are sometimes phrased in terms of "how should we then live?" I first engaged seriously with the concept of a distinctively Christian ethical position during my master's studies which itself had resulted from a frustration with the insipid political philosophy I was encountering as a believer. Thus, one of the foundational principles we posited at the beginning of this thesis was the belief that philosophy should be transformational, and we have worked at establishing that position. While I experienced some pushback on that assertion when writing and being examined on this work, it remains to

---

10. Bahnsen, *Van Til's Apologetic*.

me a self-evident principle. The culture and society we have *now* has developed from philosophies *first* articulated in an academy, which are often then admittedly bastardized but are then pushed into popular culture by public intellectuals with a transformative agenda.

The thesis of this work was a call back for believers to understand their faith extends to every part of their life and that they are to "occupy till [He] comes" (Luke 19:13); that is, do the business of life, do politics, do sociology, do psychology, and do philosophy, to manage every compartment or sphere of creation.[11] When we recognize that each worldview operates on circular assumptions, we understand that there is no tyranny of science or secularism that should intimidate us but that we can stand on our own intellectual feet without the aid of epistemological crutches borrowed from oppositional forms of life. With transcendental logic, we have a tool with which we can evaluate oppositional forms of life for coherence and correspondence on their own terms. That is, this work endeavors to give the Christian the self-confidence to defend their faith robustly that they can stand in the face of the severest critic, be they the atheistic scientist, a thoroughgoing skeptic, or a mystic. As my background is in the sciences and engineering, I specifically gave attention to naturalistic science, both evolutionary science and physics, to demonstrate that neither give a coherent or convincing account that provides an epistemic mandate to prefer and defer to them.

Thus, our final confidence should be that we have a rational defense of the faith, and we have established that the scriptures are trustworthy in asserting that we are capable of a rational defense of our faith should any demand it of us (1 Pet 3:15). I personally hope to have stirred the confidence in the post-Reformational view of the world and faith. The world-changing nature of the Reformation resulted from its worldview; it was an entire philosophy of life rather than a piecemeal call to revivalism or evangelism while the rest of culture atrophied in striking contrast to the evangelical and fundamentalist world of the late nineteenth century to

---

11. πραγματεύσασθε, verb imperative aorist middle 2nd person plural from πραγματεύομαι. This verb has the literal meaning "to trade, to do business." It occurs only in this verse in the New Testament and so lacks an extended semantic context; many dominion theologians like to interpret it as we would describe an "occupying army" but that would be an unsafe inference. Neither BDAG or Vine admit any possibility of it meaning anything other than to do business; it certainly has no history in the Greek language of this figurative meaning. However, its situational context certainly implies that Jesus is not talking just about the narrow action of trading but the responsible execution of the *occupations* of living.

the early 1970s (see the next section). Things are slightly better now, but the emphasis is on the "slight." It is hoped we have part of the antidote to the aggressive evangelism of the liberals that seek to establish that "good is evil and evil is good" (Isa 5:20); that we have an equally robust belief in the good and have provided a philosophically satisfying exposition of it.

8.4.3 As Political Philosophy

There was an undeniable crisis in Christian political philosophy in the opening decades of the twentieth century. There had been an all-out confrontation with the theological liberalism of Schleiermacher and the political Liberalism that was correlative with it. With the Scopes trial regarding the teaching of scientific evolutionism, there was a substantial cultural and academic challenge to the religious narratives and the Fundamentalist response was to withdraw into a cultural ghetto for almost half a century. Similarly, the Reformed world fragmented into orthodox and liberal wings. It was only to be with the Reconstructionist movement of the 1970s that emerged as a sociological application of Van Tillianism, that the legitimacy of evangelical Christianity to engage in the wider cultural debates and the political sphere was once more legitimized.[12] However, although the influence of this movement was substantive with significant sister movements or individuals adopting the program while avoiding the controversy associated with its Reformed emphases and the label "Dominion Theology," an articulation of a coherent political philosophy within the charismatic and prophetic movements has been virtually non-existent.

Thus, with our attention to the critical contemporary context of the post-pandemic environment and the challenge of the Trump era, we have helpfully focused on some of the key basic principles and imperatives for reestablishing the principles for involvement. We have, as part of a wider philosophical vision, directly challenged the insipid political agnosticism that has been argued by some influential figures within the charismatic and prophetic movements.[13] We have forcefully argued for both an in-

---

12. I discussed this historical background, the emergence, influence, and legacy of the Reconstructionist movement in *Dominion Theology*.

13. In "Politics," I dealt with the subject of politics and involvement more generally considering the defeat of Donald Trump, who had held the door open to evangelical Christians for involvement in government unlike any previous president since Washington and Lincoln. The controversy caused within the evangelical and prophetic

dividual responsibility and an institutional involvement, recognizing the different dynamics of both and making the important distinction between the unique theocratic application of divine principles in ancient Israel and the application of those same principles in modern representative models of government. We argued that the principles of governance in scripture were representative rather than monarchical and thus we should value our republican and democratic models of government. We have emphasized, remembering the dictum of Kuyper who rejected the secular-religious dichotomy, that our Christian life is an integrated whole and that includes our political relationships.

8.5 Limitations to This Research

The latter stages of the creation of this work inevitably highlighted its shortcomings, especially in the eyes of those most qualified to pass judgment. While a major attempt was made to address these criticisms and improve the quality of the work, which I believe was largely successful, some of these bear rehearsing as they are pertinent and salient to the wider project.[14] This work was presenting a vision of Christian philosophy, and it was attempting to do so in as broad a manner as possible, acknowledging as many features as possible of the philosophical landscape. This was primarily to indicate our awareness of these schools and the potential for their criticisms of the views presented here and to highlight what were believed to be fundamental weaknesses in their positions.

However, this broad vista has meant that insufficient detail has perhaps been given to those perspectives and the criticisms I have made are then vulnerable themselves to invalidation. This is particularly the case with philosophies that might be identified as within the Continental

---

movements by his defeat was unparalleled with many calling for a withdrawal from political involvement as a reaction. Some of these calls were crude, others were argued with far more care. As a respectful and thorough response to these calls for withdrawal by someone who was mentoring me directly in the prophetic, I attempted to deal with the broader issues of involvement in a systematic and theological manner, examining the history of the church and the interpretation of Rom 13 which is the locus around which most discussion among Christians has revolved.

14. As I noted in the preface, this book was based on my PhD thesis. The external examiner made the following comment in response to the corrections in lieu of the criticisms the examiners had raised after the viva: "Let me add that Mr. Macneil should be commended for the diligence and care he took in responding to the reports of the examiners. In my estimation, he has done so in an exemplary manner and I am very happy now to approve the thesis."

school such as existentialism and phenomenology, as well as what might be called "postmodern" philosophy. Similarly, sections which discuss Islam, Judaism, Buddhism, and Hinduism would require a greater depth to fully do them justice.[15] So, in summary, there remains a large corpus of extant literature, both religious and philosophical, which would need to be discussed to strengthen our claims regarding the transcendental claim that Christianity provides the basis for all "predication."

It was also noted by one reviewer that philosophies which deny reason a strong role regarding right/wrong and truth/falsehood (that is, have a weaker conception of reason) are less vulnerable to Van Til's central claim that it is the autonomy of reason which unifies non-Christian views and thus it does not follow that *only* the Christian view is coherent. While this criticism was addressed to a degree in later drafts and more attention was given to religious experience and subjective aspects of epistemology, there is still more to be done in clarifying precisely what is understood to be "autonomous reasoning." I believe it is particularly helpful in this regard that we formulate our understanding of autonomous reasoning as "abstract" reasoning, an operation without Christian content or context. Our strongest claim was that reasoning can *never* proceed *coherently* on that basis but collapses into irrationality. We must always remember our worldview context and further work should be done in this regard.

The most important limitation which was highlighted on review, and which I addressed at some length in the later drafts, was the role of religious experience and its relationship to epistemological self-consciousness; that is, the wider conception of knowledge construction that might be considered intuitive or direct. In some senses, the rational defense of Christianity might be considered illegitimate in principle (as argued by Kierkegaard) or must be heavily qualified as to what it seeks to achieve (the competency of reason). I acknowledged that it is certainly the case that rational argument did not *directly* lead to my own conversion but equally I do believe rational argument helped me toward conversion and has most certainly helped to *keep* me converted in the sense of maintaining my Christianity as front and center of my life, rather than relegated to some personal, private "experience" inadequate as a philosophy of public life. Further development of this theme would certainly

---

15. However, in all cases I have judged these discussions as nevertheless useful and these can be found online at Macneil, "PhD Appendices."

benefit the overall conception of Christian philosophy. It is hoped to consider this more in future development of this work.

Thus, on a conservative assessment of the thesis presented here, rather than establishing our argument in its entirety, the most we can claim is to have taken several very important steps toward the aim of presenting an objective proof of the necessity of the Christian worldview. We would need to carefully consider the Continental tradition and offer a fuller account of the autonomy of reason. Yet, our achievements are substantial, in addressing skepticism, the tyranny of science, the rationality of the Christian worldview, setting the necessity of a transcendental context for the defense of the faith, and in setting forth the TAG itself and answering its common criticisms.

Finally, it is also important to recognize the distinction between proof and persuasion when judging the efficacy of this work. Of course, a rigorous proof is instinctively thought of as being persuasive, but part of our thesis has been to argue that presuppositions, prejudices, psychological factors, sociological conditions, personal experience, and our spirituality all have a bearing on what we *finally* decide to believe. As Wittgenstein discovered at the end of his *Tractatus*, the answers to what was *really* important to life seemed to lie outside of expressible language; Lyotard would also regard the philosophic enterprise as trying to bring the inexpressible to expression. So, although we have wanted to convey confidence and certainty through the reasonings of our work here, we cannot claim infallibility, but we can hope to have made a substantive contribution to the issues explored.

8.6 Recommendation for Further Research

In examining and evaluating the challenges to the TAG, the greatest difficulty, first articulated by Stroud, was in the move from *conceptual* necessity to *ontological* necessity. Our final solution was a semi-novel one based on the application of an argument which established what we required as a by-product of a complex transcendental argument made by McDowell on what makes empirical knowledge possible, rather than arguing for our position directly. What is particularly interesting surrounding the literature for McDowell is that though his work was welcomed into analytic philosophy, it borrowed heavily from the Continental school with the result that even a Rorty would describe it as "cryptic." In a follow-up volume which was an exchange between McDowell and his peers,[16] it was evident as to how difficult it was to understand McDowell as he had intended. McDowell himself wrote a follow-up volume, *Having the World in View*, in which it is clear he borrows from both Hegel and Sellars to provide a novel synthesis of both traditions.

To my knowledge, though this was first advanced as a possible solution by Baird,[17] there has been no detailed criticism or analysis of this solution within the proponents of TAG. With the complexity and nuances within McDowell's work, with which he himself acknowledges he receives criticism from both sides of the philosophic divide, this is certainly an area that requires further examination and validation. If successful, it would certainly strengthen the claims of TAG as offering a more generally acceptable proof for not just the conceptual necessity of the Christian God as the prerequisite of rationality but the ontological necessity also.

---

16. Smith, *Reading McDowell*.
17. Baird, "Transcendental Arguments."

Bibliography

Aland, K., and B. Aland. *The Text of the New Testament*. Translated by E. F. Rhodes. Grand Rapids: Eerdmans, 1995.
Alston, W. P. *Perceiving God*. Ithaca, NY: Cornell University Press, 1993.
———. "Some Suggestions for Divine Command Theorists." In *Christian Theism and the Problems of Philosophy*, edited by M. Beaty, 303–26. Notre Dame, IN: University of Notre Dame Press, 1990.
American Humanist Association. "Humanist Manifesto I." 1973. https://americanhumanist.org/what-is-humanism/manifesto1/.
Anderson, J. N. "Cornelius Van Til and Alvin Plantinga: A Brief Comparison." 2002. https://www.proginosko.com/docs/cvt_ap_comp.html.
———. "If Knowledge Then God: The Epistemological Theistic Arguments of Plantinga and Van Til." *Calvin Theological Journal* 40.1 (2005) 49–75.
Aristotle. *The Complete Works of Aristotle*. Vol. 1. Edited by J. Barnes. Rev. Oxford translation ed. Princeton: Princeton University Press, 1984.
———. *The Nicomachean Ethics*. Edited by L. Brown. Translated by D. Ross. Oxford: Oxford University Press, 2009.
Aquinas, Thomas. *Summa Contra Gentiles*. Translated and edited by J. Rickaby. E-edition. The Catholic Primer, 2005.
Aronson, R. "Albert Camus." *Stanford Encyclopedia of Philosophy*, last updated Dec. 13, 2021. https://plato.stanford.edu/entries/camus/.
Audi, R. *Epistemology: A Contemporary Introduction to the Theory of Knowledge*. 2nd ed. London: Routledge, 2003.
Austin, M. W. "Divine Command Theory." *Internet Encyclopedia of Philosophy*, n.d. https://iep.utm.edu/divine-command-theory/.
Ayer, A. Editor's introduction to *Logical Positivism*, edited by A. Ayer and P. Edwards, 3–30. New York: Free Press, 1966.
———. *Language, Truth, and Logic*. 2nd ed. New York: Dover, 1952.
———. *Wittgenstein*. Chicago: University of Chicago Press, 1985.
Bahnsen, G. *Always Ready: Directions for Defending the Faith*. Digital ed. Nacogdoches, TX: Covenant Media, 2011.
———. *Answer to Frame's Critique*. MP3. Nacogdoches, TX: Covenant Media Foundation, 1988.

———. *ASC3 Practical Apologetics*. MP3. Nacogdoches, TX: Covenant Media Foundation, 1993.
———. *By This Standard: The Authority of God's Law Today*. Powder Springs, GA: American Vision, 2008.
———. *A Conditional Resolution of the Apparent Paradox of Self Deception*. Los Angeles: University of Southern California, 1978.
———. *CVT and Gordon Clark*. MP3. Nacogdoches, TX: Covenant Tape Ministry, 1995.
———. *Evolution (Scientific and Theistic)*. MP3. Nacogdoches, TX: Covenant Media Foundation, 1992.
———. *Four Types of Proof*. Nacogdoches, TX: Covenant Media Foundation, 1995.
———. *History of Philosophy: Ancient, Renaissance and Modern*. MP3. Nacogdoches, TX: Covenant Tape Ministry, 1993.
———. *No Other Standard*. Tyler, TX: Institute for Christian Economics, 1991.
———. "Pragmatism, Prejudice and Presuppositionalism." In *Foundations of Christian Scholarship*, edited by G. North, 241–94. Vallecito, CA: Chalcedon, 2001.
———. *Presuppositional Apologetics: Stated and Defended*. Edited by J. McDurmon. Nacogdoches, TX: American Vision & Covenant Media, 2008.
———. "Socrates or Christ: The Reformation of Christian Apologetics." In *Foundations of Christian Scholarship*, edited by G. North, 191–240. Vallecito, CA: Ross House Books, 2001.
———. "The Theonomic Position." In *Four Views on the Reformation of Civil Government*, edited by J. H. White, 21–53. Phillipsburg, NJ: Presbyterian and Reformed, 1989.
———. *Theonomy in Christian Ethics*. Nacogdoches, TX: Covenant Media, 2002.
———. *Transcendental Argumentation Seminar ASV7*. MP3. Irving, CA: 1994.
———. *Van Til, B B Warfield and Abraham Kuyper*. MP3. Nacogdoches, TX: Covenant Media Foundation, 1994.
———. *Van Til's Apologetic: Readings and Analysis*. Phillipsburg, NJ: P&R, 1998.
Baier, K. *The Moral Point of View*. Abridged ed. New York: Random House, 1966.
———. *The Rational and the Moral Order: The Social Roots of Reason and Morality*. Chicago: Open Court, 1995.
Baird, B. N. "Transcendental Arguments and the Call of Metaphysics." PhD diss., University of Georgia Graduate School, 2003. https://getd.libs.uga.edu/pdfs/baird_bryan_n_200305_phd.pdf.
Barnes, J. *Early Greek Philosophy*. 2nd rev. ed. London: Penguin, 2001.
Barr, J. *Fundamentalism*. 2nd ed. London: SCM, 1984.
Bartholomew, C. G., and M. W. Goheen. *Christian Philosophy: A Systematic and Narrative Introduction*. Grand Rapids: Baker Academic, 2013.
Barton, D., and T. Barton. *The American Story: The Beginnings*. Kindle. Aledo, TX: Wallbuilders, 2020.
Bauer, W., W. F. Arndt, and F. W. Gingrich. *A Greek-English Lexicon of the New Testament and Other Early Christian Literature*. 4th rev. ed. Chicago: University of Chicago Press, 1952.
Berger, P., and T. Luckmann. *The Social Construction of Reality*. London: Penguin, 1991.
Berry, P. Introduction to *Shadow of Spirit: Postmodernism and Religion*, edited by P. Berry and A. Wernick, 1–10. London: Routledge, 1992.
Bertrand, R. *The Autobiography of Bertrand Russell*. London: George Allen and Unwin, 1969.

Bertrand Russell Society. "In This Issue." *Bertrand Russell Society Quarterly* (Nov. 2005–Feb. 2006). https://www.lehman.edu/faculty/rcarey/BRSQ/05nov.in_this_issue.htm.

Beversluis, J. "Surprised by Freud: A Critical Appraisal of A. N. Wilson's Biography of C. S. Lewis." *Christianity and Literature* 41.2 (1992) 179–95.

Blackburn, S. *Being Good: A Short Introduction to Ethics*. Kindle. New York: Oxford University Press, 2001.

———. *Ruling Passions: A Theory of Practical Reasoning*. Oxford: Clarendon, 1998.

———. *Truth: A Guide for the Perplexed*. Kindle. London: Penguin, 2006.

Bolos, A., and K. Scott. "Reformed Epistemology." *Internet Encyclopedia of Philosophy*, n.d. https://iep.utm.edu/ref-epis/.

Bosserman, B. *The Trinity and the Vindication of Christian Paradox: An Interpretation and Refinement of the Theological Apologetic of Cornelius Van Til*. Eugene, OR: Pickwick, 2014.

Bratt, J., ed. *Abraham Kuyper: A Centennial Reader*. Carlisle: Paternoster, 1998.

Brown, M. L. *Evangelicals at the Crossroads: Will We Pass the Trump Test?* Concord: Equal Time Books, 2020.

Burley, M. *Contemplating Religious Forms of Life: Wittgenstein and D. Z. Phillips*. New York: Continuum International, 2012.

Butler, M. *Bahnsen on Van Til*. MP3. Nacogdoches, TX: Covenant Media Foundation, 1997.

———. *Biblical Presuppositional Apologetics*. MP3. Nacogdoches, TX: Covenant Media Foundation, 1997.

———. *Modern Transcendental Arguments*. MP3. Nacogdoches, TX: Covenant Media Foundation, 1994.

———. *The Philosophy of Science*. MP3. Nacogdoches, TX: Covenant Media Foundation, 1995.

———. *On Plantinga: Religious Epistemology Seminar*. MP3. Nacogdoches, Texas, 1997.

———. "The Transcendental Argument for God's Existence." In *The Standard Bearer: A Festschrift for Greg Bahnsen*, edited by S. M. Schlissel, 65–124. Nacogdoches, TX: Covenant Media Foundation, 2001.

Calvin, J. *Calvin's Commentary on the Bible*. Kindle. Omaha, NE: Patristic, 2019.

———. *Institutes of the Christian Religion*. Translated by T. Norton. 1599 ed. Kindle. Fig Books, 2012.

Capra, F. *The Tao of Physics: An Exploration of the Parallels Between Modern Physics and Eastern Mysticism*. 35th anniversary ed. Boston: Shambhala, 2010.

Carey, T. V. "Hypotheses Non Fingo." *Philosophy Now*, 2012. https://philosophynow.org/issues/88/Hypotheses_Non_Fingo.

Carnap, R. *An Introduction to the Philosophy of Science*. Edited by M. Gardner. Kindle. New York: Dover, 1995.

———. *The Logical Structure of the World and Pseudoproblems in Philosophy*. Translated by R. A. George. Peru, IL: Open Court, 2005.

Carnell, E. *An Introduction to Christian Apologetics*. Grand Rapids: Eerdmans, 1948.

———. *A Philosophy of the Christian Religion*. Eugene, OR: Wipf & Stock, 2007.

Cat, J. "Otto Neurath." *Stanford Encyclopedia of Philosophy*, last updated Aug. 28, 2019. https://plato.stanford.edu/archives/fall2021/entries/neurath/.

Chisholm, R. M. *The Problem of the Criterion*. Milwaukee: Marquette University Press, 1973.

———. *Theory of Knowledge*. Foundations of Philosophy. Harlow, UK: Prentice Hall, 1988.

Churchland, P. M., and C. A. Hooker, eds. *Images of Science: Essays on Realism, and Empiricism, with a Reply from Bas C. van Fraassen*. Chicago: University of Chicago Press, 1985.

Clark, G. H. *Historiography: Secular and Religious*. Edited by J. W. Robbins. 2nd ed. Jefferson, MD: Trinity Foundation, 1994.

———. *Logic*. 2nd ed. Jefferson, MD: Trinity Foundation, 1988.

———. *The Philosophy of Gordon H. Clark*. Edited by R. H. Nash. Philadelphia: Presbyterian and Reformed, 1968.

———. *Three Types of Religious Philosophy*. Jefferson, MD: Trinity Foundation, 1989.

Clifford, W. K., and W. James. *The Ethics of Belief and The Will to Believe*. eBook. Pantianos Classics, 1896.

Collett, D. D. "Van Til and Transcendental Argument Revisited." In *Speaking the Truth in Love: The Theology of John M. Frame*, 460–88. Phillipsburg, NJ: P&R, 2009.

Comte, A. *A General View of Positivism*. Edited by J. Bridges. Standard Ebooks, 2018.

Conant, J. "Freedom, Cruelty, and Truth: Rorty Versus Orwell." In *Rorty and His Critics*, edited by R. B. Brandom, 268–342. Oxford: Blackwell, 2001.

Cope, L. *God and Political Justice: A Study of Governance from Genesis to Revelation*. Kindle. Seattle: YWAM, 2015.

———. *The Old Testament Template*. 2nd ed. Seattle: YWAM, 2015.

Corner, E. "Evolution." In *Contemporary Botanical Thought*, edited by A. M. Macleod and L. Cobley, 95–113. Edinburgh: Oliver and Boyd, 1961.

Cottingham, J., R. Stoothoff, and D. Murdoch. *The Philosophical Writings of Descartes*. Vols. 1–3. New York: Cambridge University Press, 2008.

Cowan, S. B., and S. N. Gundry, eds. *Five Views on Apologetics*. Grand Rapids: Zondervan, 2000.

Craig, W. L. "A Classical Apologist's Response." In *Five Views on Apologetics*, edited by S. B. Cowan and S. N. Gundry, 232–35. Grand Rapids: Zondervan, 2000.

Crimmins, J. E. "Jeremy Bentham." *Stanford Encyclopedia of Philosophy*, last updated Dec. 8, 2021. https://plato.stanford.edu/entries/bentham/.

Darwin, C. *On the Origin of Species by Means of Natural Selection, or The Preservation of Favoured Races in the Struggle for Life*. Edited by O. Francis. London: Macmillan, 1859.

Davidson, D. "On the Very Idea of a Conceptual Scheme." In *Inquiries into Truth and Interpretation*, 183–98. Oxford: Oxford University Press, 2001.

Dawkins, R. *The Blind Watchmaker*. Oxford: Penguin, 2006.

———. *The God Delusion*. London: Black Swan, 2006.

De Lubac, H. *Augustinianism and Modern Theology*. New York: The Crossroad Company, 2000.

Dembski, W. A., and H. Allen Orr. "Darwin and Design—A Debate About the Latest Defense of Intelligent Design." *Boston Review*, Oct. 1, 2002. https://bostonreview.net/articles/william-dembski-h-allen-orr-darwin-and-design/.

Descartes, R. *A Discourse on the Method*. Edited by I. Maclean. Oxford: Oxford University Press, 2008.

---. *Meditations on First Philosophy (With Selections from the Objections and Replies)*. Edited by J. Cottingham and B. Williams. Cambridge: Cambridge University Press, 2009.

---. *Meditations and Other Metaphysical Writings*. Translated by M. Clarke. London: Penguin, 2003.

Dewey, J. *Democracy and Education*. Kindle. Jovian, 2016.

---. *The Public and Its Problems: An Essay in Political Inquiry*. Athens: Ohio University Press, 2016.

Diethe, C. *Nietzsche's Sister and the Will to Power: A Biography of Elisabeth Förster-Nietzsche*. International Nietzsche Studies. Champaign: University of Illinois Press, 2007.

Dobson, E., E. Hindson, and J. Falwell. *The Fundamentalist Phenomenon: The Resurgence of Conservative Christianity*. Grand Rapids: Baker, 1986.

Dodsworth, L. *A State of Fear: How the UK Government Weaponised Fear During the Covid-19 Pandemic*. Kindle. London: Pinter & Martin, 2021.

Dooyeweerd, H. "Cornelius Van Til and the Transcendental Critique of Theoretical Thought." In *Jerusalem and Athens: Critical Discussions on the Philosophy and Apologetics of Cornelius Van Til*, edited by E. Geehan, 74–89. Phillipsburg, NJ: Presbyterian and Reformed, 1980.

Dreher, R. *Live Not by Lies: A Manual For Christian Dissidents*. New York: Sentinel, 2020.

Dupré, L. Introduction to *Augustinianism and Modern Theology*, by H. de Lubac, i–xv. New York: The Crossroad Company, 2000.

Eddington, S. A. *The Nature of the Physical World*. Edited by T. Goodey. Corrected Kindle ed. Shizu Bito, 2014.

Edgar, W. Introduction to *An Introduction to Systematic Theology*, by C. Van Til, 1–10. 2nd ed. Phillipsburg, NJ: P&R, 2007.

Edgar, W., and K. S. Oliphint. *Christian Apologetics Past and Present: A Primary Source Reader*. Kindle. Wheaton, IL: Crossway, 2011.

Edwards, D. L. *Christianity: The First Two Thousand Years*. London: Cassell, 1998.

Engelmann, P. *Letters from Ludwig Wittgenstein, with A Memoir*. New York: Horizon, 1968.

Everitt, N. *The Non-Existence of God*. Abingdon: Routledge, 2004.

Faraday, M. "Experimental Researches in Electricity." *Philosophical Transactions of the Royal Society of London* (1832).

Farrell, B. "An Appraisal of Therapeutic Positivism (I)." *Mind* 55.217 (1946) 25–48.

---. "An Appraisal of Therapeutic Positivism (II)." *Mind* 55.218 (1946) 133–50.

Feyerabend, P. *Against Method*. 4th ed. London: Verso, 2010.

---. *Conquest of Abundance: A Tale of Abstraction Versus the Richness of Being*. Edited by B. Terpstra. Chicago: University of Chicago Press, 1999.

---. *Killing Time*. Chicago: University of Chicago Press, 1994.

---. "Notes on Relativism." In *Farewell to Reason*, 19–89. London: Verso, 1987.

---. "Postscript on Relativism." In *Against Method*, 283–87. London: Verso, 2010.

---. *Science in a Free Society*. London: Verso, 1978.

---. *The Tyranny of Science*. Cambridge: Polity Press, 2018.

Finney, C. G. *The Autobiography of Charles G. Finney: The Life Story of America's Greatest Evangelist—In His Own Words*. Edited by H. Wessel. Condensed Kindle ed. Bloomington, MN: Bethany House, 2012.

———. *The Life and Works of Charles Finney*. Vol. 1. Kindle. Classic Christian Ebooks, n.d.

———. *Memoirs of Revivals of Religion*. Kindle. Christian Classics Treasury, 2011.

Finney, P. C. *Seeing Beyond the Word: Visual Arts and the Calvinistic Tradition*. Grand Rapids: Eerdmans, 1999.

Fitelson, B., and E. Sober. "Plantinga's Probability Arguments Against Evolutionary Naturalism." *Pacific Philosophical Quarterly* 79.2 (1998) 115–29.

Flew, A. *There Is a God: How the World's Most Notorious Atheist Changed His Mind*. eBook. New York: HarperCollins, 2009.

Foakes-Jackson, F. J. *The History of the Christian Church: From the Earliest Times to the Death of Leo the Great AD 461*. London: Simpkin, Marshall, Hamilton Kent & Co, 1905.

Frame, J. *Apologetics: A Justification of Christian Belief*. Edited by J. E. Torres. 2nd ed. Phillipsburg, NJ: P&R, 2015.

———. *Cornelius Van Til: An Analysis of His Thought*. Phillipsburg, NJ: P&R, 2015.

———. *A History of Western Philosophy and Theology*. Phillipsburg, NJ: P&R, 2015.

Francis, Lizzie. "Cancelling Christians." *The Critic*, June 14, 2021. https://thecritic.co.uk/cancelling-christianity/.

Frankl, V. E. "Logotherapy in a Nutshell." In *Man's Search for Meaning*, 101–36. London: Random House, 2004.

———. *Man's Search for Meaning*. London: Random House, 2004.

Gabbay, D. M., P. Thagard, and J. Woods. General preface to *General Philosophy of Science: Focal Issues*, edited by T. Kuipers et al., v–vi. Amsterdam: Elsevier BV, 2007.

Geehan, E., ed. *Jerusalem and Athens: Critical Discussions on the Philosophy and Apologetics of Cornelius Van Til*. Phillipsburg, NJ: Presbyterian & Reformed, 1980.

Genova, A. C. "Good Transcendental Arguments." *Kant-Studien* 75 (1984) 469–95.

———. "Transcendental Form." *Southwestern Journal of Philosophy* 11 (1980) 25–34.

Gettier, E. "Is Justified True Belief Knowledge?" *Analysis* 23 (1963) 121–23.

Glattfelder, J. B. "Ontological Enigmas: What Is the True Nature of Reality?" In *Information—Consciousness—Reality*, 345–94. Switzerland: Springer-Cham, 2019. https://link.springer.com/chapter/10.1007/978-3-030-03633-1_10.

Glock, H. J. *What Is Analytic Philosophy?* Cambridge: Cambridge University Press, 2008.

Goff, P. "Did the Dying Stephen Hawking Really Mean to Strengthen the Case for God?" *Guardian*, May 7, 2018. https://www.theguardian.com/commentisfree/2018/may/07/stephen-hawking-god-multiverse-cosmology.

Gold, S. *I Do Not Consent: My Fight Against Medical Cancel Culture*. New York: Bombardier/Post Hill, 2020.

Goodman, N. *Fact, Fiction and Forecast*. New York: Bobbs-Merrill, 1973.

Goswami, A. *The Visionary Window: A Quantum Physicist's Guide to Enlightenment*. Wheaton, IL: Quest Books, 2000.

Gould, S. J. *The Mismeasure of Man*. Rev. and exp. ed. New York: Norton, 1996.

———. *Punctuated Equilibrium*. Cambridge, MA: Belknap, 2007.

———. *The Structure of Evolutionary Theory*. Cambridge, MA: Belknap, 2002.

Gram, G. M. "Must We Revisit Transcendental Arguments?" *Philosophical Studies: An International Journal for Philosophy in the Analytic Tradition* 31.4 (1977) 235–48.

———. "Transcendental Arguments." *Noûs* 5.1 (1971) 15–26.

Groothis, D., and J. F. Sennett. *In Defense of Natural Theology: A Post-Humean Assessment*. Leicester: IVP Academic, 2009.

Gross, N. "Richard Rorty: The Making of an American Philosopher." 2008. https://press.uchicago.edu/Misc/Chicago/309903.html.

Hahn, L. E., and P. A. Schilpp, eds. *The Philosophy of W. V. Quine*. La Salle, IL: Open Court, 1986.

Hannay, A. Introduction to *Fear and Trembling*, by S. Kierkegaard, 48–52. Translated by A. Hannay. Kindle. London: Penguin, 2003.

Hannon, M. "Skepticism, Fallibilism, and Rational Evaluation." In *Skeptical Invariantism Reconsidered*, edited by K. Wallbridge and C. Kyriacou, 172–94. Oxford: Routledge, 2021.

Han-Pile, B. "Early Heidegger's Appropriation of Kant." In *A Companion to Heidegger*, 80–101. New Jersey: Blackwell, 2005. https://repository.essex.ac.uk/16294/.

Hawking, S. *The Illustrated A Brief History of Time*. Rev. and updated ed. London: Bantam, 1996.

———. *The Illustrated Theory of Everything*. Special anniversary ed. Beverly Hills: Phoenix Books, 2006.

Hawking, S., and T. Hertog. "A Smooth Exit from Eternal Inflation?" *Journal of High Energy Physics* (2018) 147–60.

Hawking, S., and R. Penrose. *The Nature of Space and Time*. With a new afterword by the authors. Princeton: Princeton University Press, 2010.

Heidegger, M. *Being and Time [Sein und Zeit]*. Edited by D. J. Schmidt. Translated by J. Stambaugh. New York: SUNY, 2010.

———. *Poetry, Language, Thought*. Translated by A. Hofstadter. New York: Harper-Perennial, 1975.

Herrnstein, R. J., and C. Murray. *The Bell Curve: Intelligence and Class Structure in American Life*. New York: Free Press, 1994.

Hick, J. *Evil and the God of Love*. 2nd ed. London: Macmillan, 1977.

Hintikka, J. "Transcendental Arguments: Genuine and Spurious." *Noûs* 6.3 (1972) 274–81.

Hobbes, T. *Leviathan: The Matter, Form, and Power of a Commonwealth Ecclesiastical and Civil*. Digireads.com, 2014.

Hodge, A., and B. B. Warfield. "Inspiration." *Presbyterian Review* 2 (1881) 245.

Hodge, C. *Systematic Theology*. Edited by Edward N. Gross. Kindle. N.p.: Ravenio, 2014.

Holub, R. C. "Nietzsche and the Jewish Question." *New German Critique* 66 (1995) 94–121.

Hulse Kirby, S. "7 Persistent Myths About Henri de Lubac's Theology." *Church Life Journal*, Mar. 23, 2023. https://churchlifejournal.nd.edu/articles/seven-myths-about-henri-de-lubacs-theology/.

Hume, D. *Dialogues Concerning Natural Religion*. Edited by H. D. Aiken. New York: Hafner, 1948.

———. *Dialogues Concerning Natural Religion with Of the Immortality of the Soul, Of Suicide, Of Miracles*. Edited by R. H. Popkin. 2nd ed. Indianapolis: Hackett, 1998.

———. *A Treatise of Human Nature: Being an Attempt to Introduce the Experimental Method of Reasoning into Moral Subjects*. Edited by L. Selby-Bigge. Oxford: Oxford University Press, 1946.

Hume, D., and E. Steinberg. *An Enquiry Concerning Human Understanding*. 2nd annotated ed. Kindle. Indianapolis: Hackett, 1977.

Hummel, C. E. "The Faith Behind the Famous: Isaac Newton." *Christianity Today*, n.d. https://www.christianitytoday.com/history/issues/issue-30/faith-behind-famous-isaac-newton.html.
Huxley, A. *Ends and Means*. Collected ed. London: Chatto & Windus, 1946.
Huxley, J. *Evolution: The Modern Synthesis*. Cambridge, MA: MIT Press, 2010.
Irvine, A. D. "Bertrand Russell." *Stanford Encyclopedia of Philosophy*, last updated May 27, 2020. https://plato.stanford.edu/archives/spr2022/entries/russell/.
James, W. *The Varieties of Religious Experience: A Study in Human Nature*. New York: Penguin, 1985.
Jeffrey, R. *Probability and the Art of Judgment*. Cambridge: Cambridge University Press, 1992.
Jeffreys, D. S. "How Reformed Is Reformed Epistemology? Alvin Plantinga and Calvin's 'Sensus Divinitus.'" *Religious Studies* 33.4 (1997) 419–31.
Jeffries, S. "Beautiful Minds." *Guardian*, Nov. 3, 2003. https://www.theguardian.com/media/2003/nov/03/broadcasting.artsandhumanities.
———. "Richard Rorty: The Man Who Killed Truth." Directed by Carole Lochhead. Aired on BBC 4, Nov. 7, 2003.
Johnson, P. *Intellectuals*. eBook. London: Phoenix, 2013.
Kant, I. *Critique of Practical Reason*. Translated by M. Gregor and A. Reath. Rev. ed. Cambridge: Cambridge University Press, 2015.
———. *Critique of Pure Reason*. Edited by M. Weigelt. Translated by M. Müller. 2nd ed. London: Penguin, 2007.
———. *Opus postumum*. Edited by E. Förster. Translated by M. Rosen. Cambridge: Cambridge University Press, 1995.
———. *Prolegomena to Any Future Metaphysics*. Edited by G. Hatfield. Rev. ed. eBook. Cambridge: Cambridge University Press, 2004.
———. *Religion Within the Limits of Reason Alone*. Edited by T. M. Greene. Translated by H. H. Hudson. New York: Harper Torchbooks, 1960.
Kennedy, J. "Kurt Gödel." *Stanford Encyclopedia of Philosophy*, last updated Dec. 11, 2015. https://plato.stanford.edu/archives/win2020/entries/goedel.
Kenny, A. *A New History of Western Philosophy*. 1 vol. Oxford: Oxford University Press, 2012.
Kierkegaard, S. *The Kierkegaard Collection*. Kindle. Blackmore Dennett, 2019.
———. "Postscript: The End or the Beginning." In *Papers and Journals*, edited by A. Hannay, 649–57. London: Penguin Random House, 1996.
Knowing Allah. "Monotheism—One God." Jan. 23, 2010. https://knowingallah.com/en/articles/monotheism-one-god/.
———. "Transcendence (Rising Above)." Aug. 7, 2011. https://knowingallah.com/en/articles/6-transcendence-rising-above.
Körner, S. *Fundamental Questions in Philosophy*. London: Penguin, 1973.
———. *Kant*. London: Penguin, 1990.
Kuhn, T. S. *The Structure of Scientific Revolutions*. 4th ed. Chicago: University of Chicago Press, 2012.
Kuipers, T., et al., eds. *General Philosophy of Science: Focal Issues*. Handbook of the Philosophy of Science. Amsterdam: Elsevier BV, 2007.
Kuyper, A. "Common Grace in Science." In *Abraham Kuyper: A Centennial Reader*, edited by J. D. Bratt, 441–60. Carlisle: Paternoster, 1998.

———. *Encyclopedia of Sacred Theology: Its Principles*. Translated by R. J. Hendrik de Vries. New York: Charles Scribner's Sons, 1898.

———. "Evolution." In *Abraham Kuyper: A Centennial Reader*, edited by J. D. Bratt, 403–40. Carlisle: Paternoster, 1998.

———. *Lectures on Calvinism*. Kindle. Princeton: L P Stone Foundation, 1898.

———. "Sphere Sovereignty." In *Abraham Kuyper: A Centennial Reader*, edited by J. D. Bratt, 461–90. Cambridge: Paternoster, 1998.

Ladyman, J. "Ontological, Epistemological and Methodological Positions." In *General Philosophy of Science: Focal Issues*, edited by T. Kuipers et al., 303–76. Amsterdam: Elsevier BV, 2007.

Lakatos, I., and P. Feyerabend. *For and Against Method*. Chicago: University of Chicago, 2010.

Langewiesche, W. "The 10-Minute Mecca Stampede That Made History." *Vanity Fair*, Jan. 9, 2018. https://www.vanityfair.com/news/2018/01/the-mecca-stampede-that-made-history-hajj.

Lawson-Tancred, H. Introduction to *Aristotle, The Metaphysics*, translated by H. Lawson-Tancred, loc. 158. Kindle. London: Penguin, 1998.

Lewis, C. S. *God in the Dock: Essays on Theology and Ethics*. Edited by W. Hooper. Grand Rapids: Eerdmans, 1970.

———. *Miracles: A Preliminary Study*. eBook. London: HarperCollins, 2015.

———. *That Hideous Strength*. London: HarperCollins, 2005.

Lloyd-Jones, D. M. *The Puritans: Their Origins and Successors*. Edinburgh: Banner of Truth Trust, 1996.

———. *Romans: Exposition of Chapter 14:1–7 Liberty and Conscience*. Edinburgh: Banner of Truth Trust, 2017.

———. *Romans: Exposition of Chapter 13*. Edinburgh: Banner of Truth Trust, 2015.

———. *What Is an Evangelical?* Edinburgh: Banner of Truth Trust, 1992.

Longworth, G. "John Langshaw Austin." *Stanford Encyclopedia of Philosophy*, last updated June 30, 2021. https://plato.stanford.edu/entries/austin-jl/.

Lyotard, J. F. *The Postmodern Condition: A Report on Knowledge*. Manchester: Manchester University Press, 1984.

Machen, J. G. *Christianity and Liberalism*. New ed. Grand Rapids: Eerdmans, 2009.

———. *Education, Christianity and the State*. Edited by J. Robbins. Hobbs, NM: Trinity Foundation, 1995.

Macneil, M. "Abraham Kuyper, Culture and Art." 2017. doi: 10.13140/RG.2.2.22706.50888/1.

———. "Applying the Epistemological Self Consciousness Transcendental Critique to Islam, Hinduism, and Buddhism." *Planet Macneil* (blog), June 29, 2023. https://planetmacneil.org/blog/applying-the-epistemological-self-consciousness-transcendental-critique-to-islam-hinduism-and-buddhism/.

———. *Are Science and Theology Competing Views of Reality?* BA thesis, Bangor University, North Wales, UK, 2011. doi: 10.13140/RG.2.2.17253.91369.

———. "Censorship—The New Normal." *Planet Macneil* (blog), Aug. 21, 2021. https://planetmacneil.org/blog/censorship-the-new-normal/.

———. "Christianity and Postmodernism." *Planet Macneil* (blog), Aug. 19, 2007. https://planetmacneil.org/blog/christianity-and-postmodernism/.

———. "Descartes Showed There Was No Need for God in Philosophy." *Planet Macneil* (blog), Jan. 27, 2014. https://planetmacneil.org/blog/descartes-showed-there-was-no-need-for-god-in-philosophy/.

———. *Dominion Theology: Its Origin, Development and Place in Christian Thinking*. MA thesis, Bangor University, North Wales, UK, 2016. doi: 10.13140/RG.2.2.10543.02722.

———. "Epistemological Self Consciousness." *Planet Macneil* (blog), Nov. 18, 2023. https://planetmacneil.org/blog/epistemological-self-consciousness/.

———. "Evolutionary Theory and Probability Theory." *Planet Macneil* (blog), Apr. 21, 2024. https://planetmacneil.org/blog/evolutionary-theory-and-probability-theory/.

———. "Fake (but Peer-Reviewed) Academic Papers Published by Fake (but Famous) Journals." *Planet Macneil* (blog), Sept. 24, 2023. https://planetmacneil.org/blog/fake-but-peer-reviewed-academic-papers-published-by-fake-but-famous-journals/.

———. "The Fideistic Leap." *Planet Macneil* (blog), June 29, 2023. https://planetmacneil.org/blog/the-fideistic-leap/.

———. "Feeling Good About Truth." 2019. doi: 10.13140/RG.2.2.18266.39362.

———. "The Fundamentals and Fundamentalism." *Planet Macneil* (blog), Apr. 25, 2024. https://planetmacneil.org/blog/the-fundamentals-and-fundamentalism/.

———. *The Great COVID Caper—Hoax or Greatest Public Health Emergency in Peacetime? A Dissertation on the COVID-19 Novel Coronavirus, Its Global Management and How To Survive the Next Pandemic*. 2020. doi: 10.13140/RG.2.2.14767.15528/2.

———. "Jonathan Edwards and the Destruction of the Puritan Canopy in Early US History." *Planet Macneil* (blog), Apr. 25, 2024. https://planetmacneil.org/blog/jonathan-edwards-and-the-destruction-of-the-puritan-canopy-in-early-us-history/.

———. "Kant, Rationalism, Empiricism, and the God Question." *Planet Macneil* (blog), Apr. 21, 2024. https://planetmacneil.org/blog/kant-rationalism-empiricism-and-the-god-question/.

———. "The Lewis and Anscombe Debate." *Planet Macneil* (blog), Apr. 22, 2024. https://planetmacneil.org/blog/the-lewis-and-anscombe-debate.

———. "Macneil's Guide for the Spiritually Perplexed." *Planet Macneil* (blog), Nov. 29, 2020. https://planetmacneil.org/blog/macneils-guide-for-the-spiritually-perplexed/.

———. "Moral Calculus." *Planet Macneil* (blog), Apr. 25, 2024. https://planetmacneil.org/blog/moral-calculus/.

———. "PhD Appendices." *Planet Macneil* (blog). https://planetmacneil.org/blog/category/thesis/phd-appendices/.

———. "Politics, Church and State in the Post-Trump Era." 2021. doi: 10.13140/RG.2.2.16282.16325.

———. "Richard Rorty's Iconoclastic Deconstruction of Philosophy." *Planet Macneil* (blog), June 29, 2023. https://planetmacneil.org/blog/richard-rortys-iconoclastic-deconstruction-of-philosophy/.

———. "Scripture and the Post-Darwinian Controversy." *Planet Macneil* (blog), June 14, 2015. https://planetmacneil.org/blog/scripture-and-the-post-darwinian-controversy/.

———. "Should I Obey My Government—Civil Disobedience in the COVID-Era." *Planet Macneil* (blog), Mar. 1, 2020. https://planetmacneil.org/blog/should-i-obey-my-government-civil-disobedience-in-the-covid-era/.

———. "Skinner's Utopia." *Planet Macneil* (blog), Apr. 25, 2024. https://planetmacneil.org/blog/skinners-utopia/.

———. "Theonomy in Christian Ethics." *Planet Macneil* (blog), Apr. 25, 2024. https://planetmacneil.org/blog/theonomy-in-christian-ethics/.

———. "Wittgenstein and Religious Language." *Planet Macneil* (blog), May 8, 2014. https://planetmacneil.org/blog/wittgenstein-and-religious-language/.

———. "Van Til and Plantinga, Comparison and Contrast." *Planet Macneil* (blog), June 29, 2023. https://planetmacneil.org/blog/van-til-and-plantinga-comparison-and-contrast/.

Mahner, M. "Demarcating Science from Non-Science." In *General Philosophy of Science: Focal Issues*, edited by T. Kuipers et al., 515–75. Amsterdam: Elsevier BV, 2007.

Mahon, Á. *The Ironist and the Romantic*. London: Bloomsbury Academic, 2014.

Marsden, G. *Reforming Fundamentalism: Fuller Seminary and the New Evangelicalism*. Grand Rapids: Eerdmans, 1988.

Martin, J. "The Righteous Revolution: Could There Be a Theocracy in America's Future?" *Pro-Separation of Church and State* (blog), 1996. http://prosocs.tripod.com/riterev.html.

Martin, M. *Atheism—A Philosophical Justification*. Philadelphia: Temple University Press, 1990.

McDowell, J. *Having the World in View*. Cambridge, MA: Harvard University Press, 2009.

———. *Mind and World*. Cambridge, MA: Harvard University Press, 1996.

McGinn, M. *Wittgenstein and the Philosophical Investigations*. London: Routledge, 2000.

McGrath, A. *Evangelicalism and the Future of Christianity*. Downers Grove, IL: InterVarsity, 1995.

———. *A Passion for Truth*. Leicester: Apollos, 1996.

Meinong, A. *Gesamtausgabe*. 1 vol. Edited by Rudolf Haller and Rudolf Kindinger. Graz: Akademische Druck- u. Verlagsanstalt 1978.

Mill, J. S. *On Liberty, Utilitarianism and Other Essays*. Edited by M. Philip and F. Rosen. New ed. Oxford: Oxford University Press, 2015.

Monk, R. "He Was the Most Revered Philosopher of His Era. So Why Did GE Moore Disappear from History?" *Prospect*, May 2020. https://www.prospectmagazine.co.uk/magazine/ge-moore-philosophy-books-analytic-ray-monk-biography.

———. *Ludwig Wittgenstein: The Duty of Genius*. London: Vintage, 1991.

Montgomery, J. W. "Once Upon an A Priori." In *Jerusalem and Athens: Critical Discussions on the Philosophy and Apologetics of Cornelius Van Til*, edited by E. Geehan, 380–403. Phillipsburg, NJ: Presbyterian & Reformed, 1980.

Moore, G. *Selected Writings*. Edited by T. Baldwin. Oxford: Routledge, 2006.

———. *Some Main Problems of Philosophy*. London: George Allen & Unwin, 2015.

Moorhead, P. S., and M. M. Kaplan, eds. *Mathematical Challenges to the Neo-Darwinian Interpretation of Evolution*. Philadelphia: Alan R. Liss, 1967.

Morning Star. "Full Marx: Is Marxism Scientific—And What Is Scientific Socialism?" Apr. 8, 2019. https://morningstaronline.co.uk/article/f/marxism-scientific-and-what-scientific-socialism.

Mumford, S. *Metaphysics: A Very Short Introduction*. Oxford: Oxford University Press, 2021.

Murdoch, I. *Metaphysics as a Guide to Morals*. London: Chatto & Windus, 1992.

Murdoch, I., and S. George. *Existentialists and Mystics*. Edited by P. Conradi. London: Penguin, 1999.

Nagel, J. *Knowledge: A Very Short Introduction*. Oxford: Oxford University Press, 2014.

Nash, R. B. "Gordon Clark's Theory of Knowledge." In *The Philosophy of Gordon H. Clark*, edited by R. B. Nash, 125–75. Philadelphia: Presbyterian & Reformed, 1968.

Neurath, O. "Foundations of the Social Sciences." In *International Encyclopedia of Unified Science*, 2:47. Chicago: University of Chicago Press, 1944.

———. "Protocol Statements." In *Philosophical Papers 1913–1946*, 91–99. Dordrecht: Reidel, 1983.

Nichols, R., and G. Yaffe. "Thomas Reid." *Stanford Encyclopedia of Philosophy*, last updated Sept. 23, 2014. https://plato.stanford.edu/archives/sum2021/entries/reid/.

Nielsen, K., and D. Z. Phillips. *Wittgensteinian Fideism?* London: SCM, 2005.

Noll, M. A. *America's God: From Jonathan Edwards to Abraham Lincoln*. New York: Oxford University Press, 2002.

North, G. "The Epistemological Crisis of American Universities." In *Foundations of Christian Scholarship*, 3–26. Vallecito, CA: Ross House Books, 2001.

North, G., and G. DeMar. *Christian Reconstruction: What It Is, What It Isn't*. Tyler, TX: Institute for Christian Economics, 1991.

North, G., et al. *Foundations of Christian Scholarship: Essays in the Van Til Perspective*. Vallecito, CA: Ross House Books, 2001.

Oberdan, T. "Moritz Schlick." *Stanford Encyclopedia of Philosophy*, last updated Oct. 13, 2017. https://plato.stanford.edu/entries/schlick/.

Okasha, S. *Philosophy of Science: A Very Short Introduction*. 2nd ed. Oxford: Oxford University Press, 2016.

Ó Murchadha, F. *The Formation of the Modern Self*. Kindle. London: Bloomsbury Academic, 2022.

———. *A Phenomenology of Christian Life*. Bloomington: Indiana University Press, 2013.

Otero, M. P. "Purposes of Reasoning and (a New Vindication of) Moore's Proof of an External World." *Synthese* (2013) 4181–200.

Packer, J. "Francis A. Schaeffer: The Man and His Vision." In *The Francis A. Schaeffer Trilogy: The Three Essential Books in One Volume*, xi–xiv. Leicester: InterVarsity, 1990.

———. *"Fundamentalism" and the Word of God*. Grand Rapids: Eerdmans, 2006.

Pawson, D. "HIS Return—IHOPKC May 2011." https://www.davidpawson.co.uk/search/?mediaID=3718&t=9.%20HIS%20Return%20-%20IHOPKC%20May%202011.

Penelhum, T. "Fideism." In *A Companion to Philosophy of Religion*, edited by P. L. Quinn and C. Taliaferro, 376–82. Malden, MA: Blackwell, 2007.

Penrose, R. *The Emperor's New Mind*. Oxford: Oxford University Press, 1989.

———. *The Road to Reality: A Complete Guide to the Laws of the Universe*. London: Vintage, 2005.

Phillips, D. "Advice to Philosophers Who Are Christians." In *Wittgenstein and Religion*, 220–36. Basingstoke: Macmillan, 1993.

———. *Wittgenstein and Religion*. Basingstoke: Macmillan, 1993.

Pinnock, C. H. "The Philosophy of Christian Evidences." In *Jerusalem and Athens: Critical Discussions on the Philosophy and Apologetics of Cornelius Van Til*, edited by E. Geehan, 420–25. Phillipsburg, NJ: Presbyterian & Reformed, 1980.

Plantinga, A. "Advice to Christian Philosophers." In *The Analytic Theist: An Alvin Plantinga Reader*, edited by J. F. Sennett, 296–315. Grand Rapids: Eerdmans, 1983.

———. Afterword to *The Analytic Theist: An Alvin Plantinga Reader*, edited by J. F. Sennett, 353–58. Grand Rapids: Eerdmans, 1998.

———. "Augustinian Christian Philosophy." *The Monist* 75.3 (1992) 291–320.

———. "A Defence of Religious Exclusivism." In *The Analytic Theist: An Alvin Plantinga Reader*, edited by J. F. Sennett, 187–210. Grand Rapids: Eerdmans, 1998.

———. "Dooyeweerd on Meaning and Being." *Reformed Journal* 8 (1958) 10–15.

———. "An Existentialist's Ethics." *Review of Metaphysics* 12 (1958) 235–56.

———. *God and Other Minds*. Ithaca, NY: Cornell University Press, 1990.

———. *God, Freedom and Evil*. Grand Rapids: Eerdmans, 1977.

———. *Knowledge and Christian Belief*. Grand Rapids: Eerdmans, 2015.

———. "Law, Cause and Occasionalism." In *Reason and Faith: Themes from Richard Swinburne*, edited by M. Bergmann and J. E. Brower, 126–44. Oxford: Oxford University Press, 2016.

———. *The Nature of Necessity*. Oxford: Clarendon, 1982.

———. "O Felix Culpa." In *Christian Faith and the Problem of Evil*, edited by P. van Inwagen, 1–25. Grand Rapids: Eerdmans, 2004.

———. "On Christian Philosophy (Responses and Rejoinders)." *Journal of the American Academy of Religion* 57.3 (1989) 617–23.

———. "On Christian Scholarship." Draft, n.d. http://veritas-ucsb.org/library/plantinga/ocs.html.

———. "On Christian Scholarship." In *The Challenge and Promise of a Catholic University*, edited by T. Hesburgh, 267–96. South Bend, IN: University of Notre Dame Press, 1994.

———. "Quine's Objection to Quantified Modal Logic." In *The Nature of Necessity*, 222–52. Oxford: Clarendon, 1982.

———. "Reformed Epistemology." In *A Companion to Philosophy of Religion*, edited by P. L. Quinn and C. Taliaferro, 383–92. Cambridge, MA: Blackwell, 1997.

———. "Self-Profile." In *Alvin Plantinga*, edited by J. E. Tomberlin and P. van Inwagen, 9–17. Profiles 5. Dordrecht: D. Reidel, 1985.

———. *Warrant: The Current Debate*. Oxford: Oxford University Press, 1993.

———. *Warrant and Proper Function*. New York: Oxford University Press, 1993.

———. *Warranted Christian Belief*. New York: Oxford University Press, 2000.

———. *Where the Conflict Really Lies: Science, Religion and Naturalism*. New York: Oxford University Press, 2011.

Pluckrose, H., and J. Lindsay. *Cynical Theories: How Activist Scholarship Made Everything About Race, Gender and Identity*. eBook. London: Macmillan, 2021.

Polkinghorne, J. *Quantum Physics and Theology: An Unexpected Kinship*. London: SPCK, 2007.

———. *The Quantum World*. London: Longman Group, 1984.

———. *Reason and Reality*. London: SPCK, 1991.

Popper, K. R. *Knowledge and the Body-Mind Problem*. London: Routledge, 1994.

———. *The Logic of Scientific Discovery*. London: Routledge, 2005.

———. *The Open Society and Its Enemies*. Abingdon: Routledge & Kegan Paul, 2011.

Psillos, S. "Past and Contemporary Perspectives on Explanation." In *General Philosophy of Science: Focal Issues*, edited by T. Kuipers et al., 97–174. Amsterdam: Elsevier BV, 2007.

Putnam, H. *Pragmatism*. Cambridge, MA: Blackwell, 1995.

Quine, W. V. "Autobiography of W. V. Quine." In *The Philosophy of W. V. Quine*, edited by L. E. Hahn and P. A. Schilpp, 1–46. La Salle, IL: Open Court, 1986.

———. "Epistemology Naturalized." In *Ontological Relativity and Other Essays*, 69–90. New York: Columbia University Press, 1969.

———. *From Stimulus to Science*. Cambridge, MA: Harvard University Press, 1995.

———. "On the Nature of Moral Values." In *Theories and Things*, 55–66. Cambridge, MA: Belknap, 1981.

———. *Ontological Relativity and Other Essays*. New York: Columbia University Press, 1969.

———. "On What There Is." In *From a Logical Point of View*, 1–19. Cambridge, MA: Harvard University Press, 1980.

———. *Pursuit of Truth*. Rev. ed. Cambridge, MA: Harvard University Press, 1992.

———. "Response to Morton White." In *The Philosophy of W. V. Quine*, edited by L. E. Hahn and P. A. Schilpp, 663–68. La Salle, IL: Open Court, 1986.

———. *The Roots of Reference*. La Salle, IL: Open Court, 1990.

———. *Theories and Things*. Cambridge, MA: Belknap, 1981.

———. "Two Dogmas of Empiricism." In *From a Logical Point of View*, 20–46. Cambridge, MA: Harvard University Press, 1980.

Quine, W., and J. Ullian. *The Web of Belief*. 2nd ed. New York: McGraw-Hill, 1978.

Quinn, P. L., and C. Taliaferro. *A Companion to Philosophy of Religion*. Oxford: Blackwell, 1999.

Ramberg, B., and S. Dieleman. "Richard Rorty." *Stanford Encyclopedia of Philosophy*, last updated Aug. 4, 2021. https://plato.stanford.edu/archives/fall2021/entries/rorty/.

Ramsey, I. T. *Christian Ethics and Contemporary Philosophy*. Edited by I. T. Ramsey. London: SCM, 1966.

Rauschenbusch, W. *Christianity and the Social Crisis in the 21st Century: The Classic That Woke Up the Church*. Edited by P. Raushenbush. Kindle. New York: HarperCollins, 2007.

———. *The Social Principles of Jesus*. Kindle. New York: The Woman's Press, 1916.

———. *A Theology for the Social Gospel*. Kindle. New York: Macmillan, 2017.

Rees, M. *Just Six Numbers*. London: Phoenix, 2015.

Reppert, V. *C. S. Lewis's Dangerous Idea*. Downers Grove, IL: InterVarsity, 2003.

Richter, D. J. "Wittgenstein, Ludwig." *Internet Encyclopedia of Philosophy*, n.d. https://iep.utm.edu/wittgens/.

Ritschl, A. *Three Essays*. Eugene, OR: Wipf & Stock, 2005.

Rivers, I., and Wykes, D. L. "Dissenting Academies." N.d. https://www.qmul.ac.uk/sed/religionandliterature/dissenting-academies/historical-information/academies/.

Rockefeller, S. C. *John Dewey: Religious Faith and Democratic Humanism*. New York: Columbia University Press, 1991.

Rodrigues, M. R., and J. J. O'Reilly. "Statistical Characterisation of the Response of a Volterra Non-Linearity to a Cyclo-Stationary Zero-Mean Gaussian Stochastic Process." Proceedings IEEE International Symposium on Information Theory, Lausanne, June 30–July 5, 2002. doi: 10.1109/ISIT.2002.1023280.

Rorty, R. Afterword to *Christianity and the Social Crisis in the 21st Century: The Classic That Woke Up the Church*, by W. Rauschenbusch, 347–50. Kindle. New York: HarperCollins, 2007.

———. *Consequences of Pragmatism*. Minneapolis: University of Minnesota Press, 2011.

———. *Contingency, Irony, and Solidarity*. Cambridge: Cambridge University Press, 1989.

———. *An Ethics for Today: Finding Common Ground Between Philosophy and Religion*. New York: Columbia University Press, 2011.

———. "Hilary Putnam and the Relativist Menace." In *Truth and Progress: Philosophical Papers*, 3:43–62. Cambridge: Cambridge University Press, 1999.

———. "The Last Intellectual in Europe: Orwell on Cruelty." In *Contingency, Irony, and Solidarity*, 169–98. Cambridge: Cambridge University Press, 1989.

———. *Philosophy and the Mirror of Nature*. Princeton: Princeton University Press, 2018.

———. *Philosophy and Social Hope*. Kindle. New York: Penguin Random House, 1999.

———. *Philosophy as Cultural Politics*. Vol. 4 of *Philosophical Papers*. Cambridge: Cambridge University Press, 2007.

———. *Rorty and His Critics*. Edited by R. B. Brandom. Oxford: Blackwell, 2001.

———. "The Philosopher as Expert." In *Philosophy and the Mirror of Nature*, 395–422. Princeton: Princeton University Press, 2018.

———. *Take Care of Freedom and Truth Will Take Care of Itself: Interviews with Richard Rorty*. Edited by E. Mendieta. Stanford: Stanford University Press, 2006.

Ruse, Michael. "Alvin Plantinga and Intelligent Design." *Chronicle of Higher Education*, Dec. 14, 2011. https://www.chronicle.com/blogs/brainstorm/alvin-plantinga-and-intelligent-design.

Rushdoony, R. J. *By What Standard?* Fairfax: Thoburn, 1974.

———. *Christianity and the State*. Kindle. Vallecito, CA: Chalcedon, 1986.

———. *God's Plan for Victory: The Meaning of Postmillennialism*. Vallecito, CA: Chalcedon, 1997.

———. *The Institutes of Biblical Law*. Phillipsburg, NJ: Presbyterian & Reformed, 1973.

———. *The Mythology of Science*. Vallecito, CA: Ross House Books, 2001.

———. *Van Til and the Limits of Reason*. Kindle. Vallecito, CA: Chalcedon, 2013.

Russell, B. *The Basic Writings of Bertrand Russell*. Edited by R. E. Egner and L. E. Denonn. Abingdon: Routledge, 2009.

———. *History of Western Philosophy*. 2nd ed. London: Routledge, 1991.

———. *Human Knowledge: Its Scope and Limits*. Oxford: Routledge, 1956.

———. "In Praise of Idleness." *Harper's*, Oct. 1932. https://harpers.org/archive/1932/10/in-praise-of-idleness/.

———. "Logical Positivism." In *Logic and Knowledge: Essays 1901–1950*, edited by R. C. Marsh, 365–82. London: George Allen & Unwin, 1991.

———. *Marriage and Morals*. London: George Allen and Unwin, 1929.

———. *My Philosophical Development*. London: Routledge, 1997.

———. *The Problems of Philosophy*. New York: Cosimo, 2007.

Sachs, J. "Aristotle: Ethics." *Internet Encyclopedia of Philosophy*, n.d. https://iep.utm.edu/aristotle-ethics/.

Sacks, B. "Jonathan Sacks and Richard Dawkins at BBC RE:Think Festival 12 September 2012." YouTube video, Sept. 14, 2012. https://www.youtube.com/watch?v=roFdPHdhgKQ.

Sainte-Beuvre, C. *Port Royal*. Paris: Robert Laffront, 2004.

Salazar, D. J. *A Comparative Analysis of the Philosophical Views of Alvin Plantinga and Cornelius Van Til: Metaphysics and Epistemology*. UMI Microform 1469022. Ann Arbor, MI: ProQuest, 2008.

Sample, I. "'We Are a Petri Dish': World Watches UK's Race Between Vaccine and Virus." *Guardian*, July 2, 2021. https://www.theguardian.com/world/2021/jul/02/we-are-a-petri-dish-world-watches-uks-race-between-vaccine-and-virus.

Sartre, J. P. *Words*. London: Penguin, 2000.

Schächter, J. Preface to *Letters from Ludwig Wittgenstein, with A Memoir*, by P. Engelmann, ix–x. New York: Horizon, 1967.

Schaeffer, F. A. *The God Who Is There*. In *The Francis A. Schaeffer Trilogy: The Three Essential Books in One Volume*, 1–206. Leicester: InterVarsity, 1990.

———. *He Is There and He Is Not Silent*. In *The Francis A. Schaeffer Trilogy: The Three Essential Books in One Volume*, 276–358. Leicester: InterVarsity, 1990.

Schaper, E., and W. Vossenkuhl, eds. *Reading Kant: Transcendental Arguments and Scepticism*. Oxford: Wiley-Blackwell, 1989.

Scharping, N. "What Stephen Hawking's Final Paper Says (And Doesn't Say)." *Astronomy*, Mar. 21, 2018. https://astronomy.com/news/2018/03/what-stephen-hawkings-final-paper-says-and-doesnt-say.

Schlick, M. *General Theory of Knowledge*. 2nd rev. ed. Repr., Peru, IL: Open Court, 2002.

———. *Problems of Ethics*. Translated by D. Rynin. New York: Prentice Hall, 1939.

Schouls, P. A. *Descartes and the Enlightenment*. Edinburgh: McGill-Queens, 1989.

Scruton, R. *Kant: A Very Short Introduction*. Oxford: Oxford University Press, 2001.

Sennett, J. F. "The Analytic Theist: An Appreciation." In *The Analytic Theist: An Alvin Plantinga Reader*, xi–xviii. Grand Rapids: Eerdmans.

———. *Modality, Probability and Rationality*. New York: Peter Lang, 1992.

Shea, W. M. "On John Dewey's Spiritual Life." *American Journal of Education* 101.1 (Nov. 1992) 71–81.

Shope, R. K. *The Analysis of Knowing: A Decade of Research*. Princeton: Princeton University Press, 1983.

Simon, B. *Being Good*. New York: Oxford University Press, 2001.

———. *What Future for Education?* Leicester: Laurence & Wishart, 1991.

Skinner, B. *Beyond Freedom and Dignity*. Harmondsworth: Penguin, 1976.

———. *Walden Two*. Indianapolis: Hackett, 2005.

Smith, N. E., ed. *Reading McDowell "On Mind and World."* London: Routledge, 2002.

Sookhdeo, P. *The New Civic Religion: Humanism and the Future of Christianity*. 2nd ed. McLean, VA: Isaac, 2016.

Sproul, R., J. Gerstner, and A. Lindsley. *Classical Apologetics*. Grand Rapids: Zondervan, 1984.

Stein, G. J. "Biological Science and the Roots of Nazism." *American Scientist* 76.1 (1988) 50–58.

Sterelny, K. *Dawkins vs. Gould: Survival of the Fittest*. New ed. Revolutions in Science. London: Icon, 2007.

Stern, R. and T. Cheng. "Transcendental Arguments" *Stanford Encyclopedia of Philosophy*, last updated July 7, 2023. https://plato.stanford.edu/archives/fall2023/entries/transcendental-arguments/.

Stine, W. "Transcendental Arguments." *Metaphilosophy* 3 (1972) 43–52.

Stout, J. "Rorty at Princeton." *New Literary History* 39.1 (2008) 29–33.
Strawson, P. *The Bounds of Sense*. London: Methuen & Co, 1966.
———. *Individuals: An Essay in Descriptive Metaphysics*. Oxford: Routledge, 1959.
———. *Scepticism and Naturalism*. Oxford: Routledge, 2008.
Stroud, B. "Transcendental Arguments." *Journal of Philosophy* 65 (1968) 241–56.
Swinburne, R. *The Existence of God*. 2nd ed. Oxford: Clarendon, 2011.
Taylor, R. *Metaphysics*. Englewood Cliffs, NJ: Prentice Hall, 1983.
Tertullian. *The Prescription Against Heretics*. In *The Complete Works of Tertullian*. Edited by Alexander Roberts, James Donaldson, and Arthur Cleveland Coxe. Kindle. 1885.
Thiering, B. *Jesus and the Riddle of the Dead Sea Scrolls*. San Francisco: Harper, 1992.
Thiselton, A. C. *Hermeneutics: An Introduction*. Grand Rapids: Eerdmans, 2009.
———. *New Horizons in Hermeneutics*. 20th anniversary ed. Grand Rapids: Zondervan, 2012.
———. *The Two Horizons: New Testament Hermeneutics and Philosophical Description*. Carlisle: Paternoster, 1980.
Thornton, S. P. "Solipsism and the Problem of Other Minds." *Internet Encyclopedia of Philosophy*, n.d. https://iep.utm.edu/solipsis/.
Time Archive. "Skinner's Utopia: Panacea, or Path." *Time*, Sept. 20, 1971.
Tolstoy, L. *The Gospel In Brief*. Edited by F. Flowers III. Translated by I. Hapgood. Lincoln: University of Nebraska Press, 1997.
Torrey, R., and A. Dixon, eds. *The Fundamentals: A Testimony to the Truth*. Repr., Grand Rapids: Baker, 2008.
Tuhovsky, I. *The Science of Interpersonal Relations*. CreateSpace, 2018.
Uebel, T. "The Vienna Circle." *Stanford Encyclopedia of Philosophy*, last updated Apr. 1, 2020. https://plato.stanford.edu/archives/fall2021/entries/vienna-circle/.
University of Cambridge. "The Darwin Correspondence Project." https://www.hps.cam.ac.uk/research/projects/darwin-correspondence.
Urmson, J. *Berkeley*. Oxford: Oxford University Press, 1985.
Van Fraassen, B. C. "Haldane on the Past and Future of Philosophy." *New Blackfriars* 80 (1999) 177–81.
———. "Naturalism in Epistemology." In *Scientism: The New Orthodoxy*, edited by R. N. Williams and D. N. Robinson, 63–96. New York: Bloomsbury, 2015.
Van Inwagen, P., ed. *Christian Faith and the Problem of Evil*. Grand Rapids: Eerdmans, 2004.
Van Til, C. *Christian Apologetics*. 2nd ed. Phillipsburg, NJ: P&R, 2003.
———. *Christianity and Barthianism*. Phillipsburg, NJ: Presbyterian & Reformed, 1974.
———. *Christian Theistic Ethics*. Phillipsburg, NJ: Presbyterian & Reformed, 1952.
———. *Common Grace and the Gospel*. 2nd ed. Phillipsburg, NJ: P&R, 2015.
———. *The Defense of the Faith*. Edited by K. S. Oliphint. 4th ed. Phillipsburg, NJ: P&R, 2008.
———. *An Introduction to Systematic Theology*. 2nd ed. Phillipsburg, NJ: P&R, 2007.
———. "My Credo." In *Jerusalem and Athens: Critical Discussions on the Philosophy and Apologetics of Cornelius Van Til*, edited by E. Geehan, 1–22. Phillipsburg, NJ: Presbyterian & Reformed, 1980.
———. *The New Modernism: An Appraisal of the Theology of Barth and Brunner*. Phillipsburg, NJ: Presbyterian & Reformed, 1946.

———. "Response to R. J. Rushdoony." In *Jerusalem and Athens: Critical Discussions on the Philosophy and Apologetics of Cornelius Van Til*, edited by E. Geehan, 348. Phillipsburg, NJ: Presbyterian & Reformed, 1980.

———. "Revelational Epistemology." In *Van Til's Apologetic: Readings and Analysis*, by G. Bahnsen, 165–86. Phillipsburg, NJ: P&R, 1998.

Verduin, L. *Reformers and Their Stepchildren—Fighting Amongst the Brothers*. Kindle. Grand Rapids: Baker Academic, 1980.

Vine, W., M. F. Unger, and W. J. White. *Vine's Complete Expository Dictionary of Old and New Testament Words*. Nashville: Thomas Nelson, 1996.

Wald, G. "The Origin of Life." *Scientific American* 191 (May 1954) 48.

Wallace, D. B. *Greek Grammar Beyond the Basics: An Exegetical Syntax of the New Testament*. Grand Rapids: Zondervan, 1996.

Wang, H. *Beyond Analytic Philosophy: Doing Justice to What We Know*. Cambridge, MA: Massachusetts Institute of Technology Press, 1986.

Watson, J. B. "Psychology as the Behaviorist Views It." *Psychological Review* 20.2 (1913) 158–77. doi: https://doi.org/10.1037/h0074428.

———. *Psychology from the Standpoint of a Behaviorist*. Forgotten Books, 2012.

Weisbord, A. "German National Socialism." https://www.marxists.org/archive/weisbord/conquest29.htm.

West, D. *Continental Philosophy*. 2nd ed. Cambridge: Polity Press, 2011.

Wheeler, M. "Martin Heidegger." *Stanford Encyclopedia of Philosophy*, Oct. 12, 2011. https://plato.stanford.edu/archives/win2024/entries/heidegger/.

White, M. "Normative Ethics, Normative Epistemology, and Quine's Holism." In *The Philosophy of W. V. Quine*, edited by L. E. Hahn and P. A. Schilpp, 649–68. La Salle, IL: Open Court, 1986.

Whitehead, A. N. *Process and Reality: Gifford Lectures 1927–28*. Edited by D. R. Griffin and D. W. Sherburne. Corrected ed. New York: Free Press, 1985.

Wilkinson, T. "The Multiverse Conundrum." *Philosophy Now*, 2012. https://philosophynow.org/issues/89/The_Multiverse_Conundrum.

Willard, D. *The Disappearance of Moral Knowledge*. Edited by S. L. Porter et al. New York: Routledge, 2018.

Williams, M. "Introduction to the 2009 Edition (In Memory of Richard Rorty, Teacher and Friend)." In *Philosophy and the Mirror of Nature*, by R. Rorty, xiii–xxix. Princeton: Princeton University Press, 2018.

Wittgenstein, L. *Culture and Value*. Edited by G. von Wright. Rev. ed. Oxford: Basil Blackwell, 2006.

———. *Lectures and Conversations on Aesthetics, Psychology and Religious Belief*. Oxford: Blackwell, 2007.

———. *Philosophische Untersuchungen—Philosophical Investigations*. Edited by P. Hacker et al. Translated by J. Schulte. Rev. 4th ed. Chichester: Blackwell, 2007.

———. *Tractatus Logico-Philosophicus*. New York: Cosimo Classics, 2007.

Zak, P. J. *The Moral Molecule*. London: Transworld, 2012.

Zuiddam, B. "Was Evolution Invented by Greek Philosophers?" *Journal of Creation* 32.1 (2018) 68–75.

Zukav, G. *The Dancing Wu Li Masters*. New York: HarperCollins, 2001.

Subject Index

a posteriori, 35, 163
a priori, 19, 65, 80, 117, 159, 163, 168,
    212, 221, 235, 239, 244, 252,
    255n45, 264
apologetics
    and systematic theology, 184
    and Van Til, 5–6
    Bahnsen vs Clark, 140
    Enlightenment, 184
    worldview, 34
Apologetics, 3–22, 37, 51, 53, 82n106,
    160, 166n167, 179, 183–88, 209,
    213, 218, 230, 234–38, 250–51,
    261, 265, 275, 300–304, 309–10
    Augustinian, 19
    evidential, classical, 4
    subjective, 8
argument
    against naturalism, 153
    Augustinian, 12, 19n54, 21–22, 61,
        103–5, 116–18, 193, 228, 239,
        304, 308, 309–10
    and Aquinas, 102–3, 239
    and reason, 105
    and Satan, 178
    and Wittgenstein, 206
    apologetic, 102
    atheological, 102
    Christian political, 268
    circular, 37, 134, 201
    cultural relativism, 195, 271–73
    ethical, 143
    evolutionary, 146–51

for Christian philosophy, 311–13
hypothesis of God, 150–51
in Calvin, 163
laws of logic, 18
logical positivism, 65–66
metaphilosophy, 295
naturalism, 89
probability, 150
quantum physics, 298
rational, 12–13, 113, 163–64, 184,
    187
reasoned, 8
secular vs Christian, 268
skeptical, 136, 143
Socratic, 6n12
transcendental, 111, 186–89, 195,
    294, 305, 241–67
Auschwitz, 125, 145, 191
autonomy, 5, 19, 48, 50, 56, 101, 113,
    171–73, 181, 185–86, 210, 218,
    238, 252, 266, 280, 288n69,
    291n77, 302, 305–7, 319–20

behaviorism. See psychology,
    behaviorism
belief, 1, 60–61, 79, 84, 95, 115, 129,
    154–66, 205, 276, 307–9, 314
    and concepts, 191, 249
    and Donald Davidson, 72
    and ethics, 166
    and foundationalism, 7

1

SUBJECT INDEX

belief *(cont.)*
  and Gettier, 154
  and natural law, 201
  and other minds, 59n18
  and Plantinga, 156
  and rationality, truth, 165
  and scientism, 68
  and skepticism, 73
  and Van Til, 209
  and volition, 129
  and warrant, 51, 154
  and worldview, 168
  Calvin, 130
  Christian, 1, 9, 51, 159, 201–4, 294, 314
  ethics, 316
  ethics of, 84
  evidentialism, 154
  evidentialism, theistic proofs, 184
  externalism, 156
  in an external world, 249
  in other minds, 114, 207
  internalism, 154
  internalism, externalism, 157
  Islamic, 224
  justification, 5
  knowledge, truth, 129
  natural law, 226
  physicalism, 151
  pragmatism, 85
  rational, 308–9
  reasonable, 294
  Reformed Epistemology, 61, 114
  Reidian reliabilism, 156
  reliabilism, realism, 156–57
  religious, 208
  sensus divinitatis, 159
  skepticism, 249–50
  subconscious, conscious, 129–30
  TAG, 241–67
  theistic, 188
  transcendentalism, 217
  truth, 91, 113–14
  unbelief, 4
  web of, Quine, 38
  will, 304–5

beliefs
  basic, 130, 307
  contingent, 155
  dogmatism, 139
  epistemic duties, 158
  Reformed Theology, 279
  transcendentalism, 143
  transcendentals, 128, 305
  truth, 180
  web of, 37
  web of, Quine, 117

causation, 36, 257

epistemology, 1; 128–66
  and science, 20–21, 23–24, 37, 42, 48, 50, 60–64, 75, 90, 91, 113, 123, 133–35 159n143, 169, 181, 191 201, 212
  and Gordon Clark, 139
  and justification, 154
  and Kant, 295–96
  and medieval Catholicism, 228
  and metaphysics, 58, 125, 300–301
  and ethics, 59
  and necessity, 180
  and Plantinga, 129
  and skepticism, 73
  and theonomy, 170
  and truth, 131–32
  Augustinian, 21
  Calvinistic, 162–63
  Christian, 164–66, 299–304, 319
  evidentialism, classical apologetics, 47
  evolutionary, 151–52
  fallibilism, 78–79, 91
  Gettier problems, 154
  holism, 109
  Hume, Kant, 75
  in classical Greece, 58
  Kuyper, 48–49
  naturalism, 127
  naturalized, 90, 119–22, 201
  physicalism, 151–53
  Quine, 27, 122–23
  neo-Platonism, 139
  Plato, Aristotle, 58

SUBJECT INDEX

psycholigized, 34
Reasonable Verisimilitude, 99
Reformed Epistemology, 61
transcendentalism, 8, 195, 215
Van Til, 134
Van Til vs. Plantinga, 188–91
within Philosophy, 59
ethics, 1, 13, 50, 125–27, 132, 141–46, 166–78, 184, 188, 191, 198–99, 202–3, 206, 214, 219–20, 280, 315
   aesthetics, 114
   and Arthur Schlipp, 83, 99, 109
   and Blackburn, 45, 113
   and John Dewey, 83n107, 84–86
   and logical positivism, 86–89
   and naturalism, 89–91
   and scripture, 6
   as philosophy, 59
   Christian, 1, 166–78
   descriptive, 115
   Kantian, 50–51
   political, 29–31, 41, 284–91
   practical, 50n142, 57, 214, 296
   Rortian, 113n210, 132
   ethical relativism, see relativism
   Wesleyan, 15, 15n41.
evidentialism, 7, 105, 154, 184–86, 300, 307

fact, 2, 35, 62, 88, 89n129, 106, 128, 128n37, 129–34, 137–38, 140, 148n97, 157, 168, 181, 191, 201–4, 211, 236, 244–47, 253, 307
fallibilism, 78–79, 84–85, 91–100, 109–11
   chance, 91, 112–13
   truth, 99

idealism, 19, 63, 68, 78n89, 79, 91, 135, 163, 190, 205, 311
intelligibility, 1, 2, 4, 60, 128, 211, 226, 234–35, 247, 257
   and apologetics, 5
   and presuppositionalism, 234–38
   and transcendentalism, 8, 112, 128, 143, 195–216, 225, 235, 241–67

and Van Til, 265
conceptual scheme, 245, 253, 304
TAG, 51, 256–57, 267
worldview, 307–8

Justified True Belief, 154–66

knowledge, 1–3, 8, 129–66
   a posteriori vs *a priori*, see a posteriori, a priori
   and Aquinas, 104
   and Augustine, 21–22
   and Calvin, 237
   and Descartes, 19, 45–46, 73, 75, 209, 215
   and faith, 308–9
   and Feyerabend, 28–29
   and Hume vs Kant, 75–78
   and Kierkegaard, 9–10
   and Kuyper, 313
   and logical positivism, 27, 63, 64n39
   and metaphysics, 113
   and Neurath, 182–83
   and Plantinga, 22, 162–79
   and Quine, 38, 122–23
   and religious experience, 8–13
   and Rorty, 112
   and Schlick, 31–32, 86
   and science, 38, 22–28, see also science
   and scripture, 13–17
   and secular reason, 171
   and skepticism, see skepticism
   and Socrates, 168
   and Strawson, 86
   and Thomas Reid, 156
   and Van Til, 188–89;
   certainty, 23, 56, 80, 142, 234
   chance, 90
   Christian, 83, 159–60, 184
   Clark's dogmatism, 139
   cogito, 73n70, 210
   conceptual schemes, 259
   conditions of, 20
   design-plan, 158
   different senses of, 45–46
   domains of, 48
   doubt, 73, 209

knowledge *(cont.)*
   empirical, 5
   empiricist, 32, 66
   evangelicalism, 108
   externalism, 157
   fallibilism, see fallibilism
   from God, 303
   general revelation, 222–23
   Hebrew and Greek conceptions of, 41–42
   Hebrew words for, 46
   human, 1, 33n96, 48, 75
   immanent, of God, 133
   internalism, 307
   language game, 10, 64
   modal spheres, 225
   moral, see moral knowledge
   naturalistic, see naturalism
   noetic effects of sin, 6, 301
   noumenal, 77, 295
   objective, 8
   objective proof, 165
   of God, 223
   of particulars, see a posteriori
   Plato, Aristotle, 56–57
   pluralism, 161
   postmodernism, see postmodernism
   pragmatic, 84–86
   presuppositionalism, 8, 234–38
   reasonable verisimilitude (RV), 99
   religious experience, 299
   sense, see *a posteriori*
   sensus divinitatis, see *sensus divinitatis*
   special revelation, 222
   synonyms of, 35–38
   synthetic a priori, 65n42, 247, 264
   theory of, see epistemology
   transcendental, 2, 195–240
   transcendentals, 111, 128
   uncertainty, 112
   worldviews, 201–4

language game, 8, 10, 38, 64n38, 119, 252
logos, 16–17, 48, 56, 145, 212n59, 233, 251, 299, cf. logic, 139n72

metaphysics, 1, 33, 50, 58, 59, 61, 62–64, 66–67, 72, 75–76, 81, 87–88, 118–28, 158, 170, 191, 297, 308
   and Aldous Huxley, 124
   and Aristotle, 242
   and Chisholm, 134
   and C.S. Lewis, 153
   and Kant, 296
   and Karl Popper, 33
   and Otto Neurath, 182
   and Plantinga, 153
   and skepticism, ethics of, 136
   and Strawson, 123n12, 265
   and Taylor, 123n12
   and The Reformation, 275
   and Van Til, 133–35
   Darwinism, see naturalism
   descriptive, 122, 265
   epistemology, interdependence with, 134
   evolutionary, Quinean, 27;
   holism, in Quine, Kuhn, 192
   Islamic, 221n17, 224
   Judeo-Christian, 226, 234
   Logical Positivism, 66
   materialism, empiricism, 135
   naturalism, see naturalism
   religious, 120–21
   science, see science
   speculative, 120
   supernaturalistic, 61, 159, 29
   theonomy, ethics, 170
   transcendentals, 125, 128
   Vienna Circle, 30
Moral Knowledge, 167–69
multiverse, 91–99
mysticism, 8, 78, 100n171, 108, 116, 296

naturalism, 22–25, 48, 56–58, 66–69, 89–91, 102–8, 113–27, 145–58, 190–212, 226–39, 297–99
natural law, 3, 56, 77, 94, 104, 176, 201, 218, 226
natural theology, 94–95, 103, 222
nature, 1–3, 212, 251
   and Aquinas, 102–5
   and ethics, 89–91, 203
   and God, 3, 224n24, 297–98

and grace, 105
and Heraclitus, 56
and Kant, 77, 86–87
and Lubac, 105, 117
and Plantinga, 150
and Quine, 109, 132, 299
and scripture, 251
and Thales, 22n64, 54
determinism, 94, 149n99, 226–34, 257
divine, 173
factuality, 130–33, 192, 204
holism, 109–11, 214, 299
induction, 25, 152, 225
Newton, 87
noumenal vs phenomenal, 295
of God, 11–12, 188, 231–32, 238
ontology, 120
phenomena, 86–87
philosophy of, 89–90
physis, 55
Puritan view of, 173
regenerate, 300
scripture, 112
supernature, 54, 238
teleology, 94
theory of, 132, 194, 204
Thomism, 103–105, 116
transcendentalism, 201–2, 249, 305
as a synonym for Universe, 69, 122–23
necessity, 1, 59–61, 209–11, 260–63, 320
and Hume, 26
and philosophical method, 111–12
and reason, 60–61
and Scotus, 226
and skepticism, 294
and Strawson, 264
and Wittgenstein, 206
in Christian epistemology, 179
in empiricism, modal logic, 212
in evolutionary theory, 90
grace, 171
in Ockham, 229–30
in Plantinga vs Van Til, 114–15, 163–65
in Van Til, 221
in Van Til vs Warfield, 186

induction, 186
logical, 56, 220–21
naturalism, 89–91
ontological vs conceptual, 249–50, 259, 265, 308, 320
presuppositionalism, 240–42, 252–53
psychological, logical, 23
TAG, 51
theonomy, 170
Trinitarianism, 218
worldview, 260, 266, 306

objective proof, 8, 71
of Christian worldview, 48, 308, 312
objectivity, 71, 92–94, 108–11, 133, 145, 203n27, 204n28, 263, 272, 298

Philosophy, 1, 4, 27, 30–42, 49, 53–57, 60–91, 101–7, 111, 117–18, 119–38, 179–94, 195–96, 223–37, 268–93
Analytic, 64, 64n35
Continental philosophy, 32n94, 41, 320, see also postmodernism
Ordinary Language, 207–8
Oxford School, 246
Pragmatism, 84–86
Romantic, 125, 137, 141
postmodernism, 8, 12, 28n82, 35, 41n122, 44n127, 45, 53–54, 70, 93, 99n168, 100, 112, 113n208, 118, 132n51, 145, 181, 184n229, 195–200, 207, 215n60, 224n27, 262, 274–75, 280, 292, 308, 319
principle of verification, 64–67, 114, 212, 249, 261, 265, 267, 308
psychology, 2n2, 31n91, 34, 44, 49, 62, 76, 84, 86, 125–26, 134, 136, 167, 259n59, 300, 316
behaviorism, 29, 34n98, 76n80, 122n7, 123, 168, 169, 201, 226
evolutionary, 152
transcendental, 86, 134, 247
pura naturalis, 104–5

quantum physics, 92–94, 95–98, 100, 131n45, 298, 311

5

SUBJECT INDEX

rationality, 2, 9, 18, 25–29, 53, 59–61, 69, 75–78, 81, 90, 105–20, 143, 160, 179–213, 234, 294–321
realism, 20, 22, 31n.91, 69, 79, 107, 115, 156, 307
   anti-realism, 57n13, 65n42
   commonsense realism, 80–81, 300, 307
   critical realism, 72, 97n157
reason, 5–22, 35, 39n114, 48–92, 106, 182, 212, 242
   and Ancient Greece, 54–55
   and Aquinas, 102–4, 226
   and Anselm, 95n150
   and Bahnsen, 242
   and Descartes, 209
   and faith, 116, 308
   and Hume, 110–12, 123, 138
   and intuition, 109, 296
   and Kant, 76, 195, 243, 244
   and Kierkegaard, 319
   and psychology, see psychology
   and rationality, see rationality
   and revelation, see natural theology
   and scripture, 301–9
   and Plantinga, 158
   and Strawson, 305
   and Van Til, 305
   and Warfield, 187
   autonomous, 164, 305
   circular, 153, 244, 204–6
   cognitive science, 90
   Enlightenment, 101
   ethical, 167
   evidentialism, 184
   irrationality, see rationality
   mitigated, 243
   models of, 251–52
   naturalism, see naturalism
   practical, 50, 296, see also ethics
   regenerate vs unregenerate, 186–89
   transcendentalism, see transcendentalism
   truth, 144
   universal, 106
reasonable verisimilitude, 97n157; 99–100, 113, see also realism, critical realism

Reformed Epistemology, 61, 61n28, 95n150, 105, 114–15, 161–62
relativism, 56, 62, 74, 128, 132, 195n1, 196–98, 204n28, 206, 209, 214, 271–72, 281, 292

science, 6, 16, 18, 22–63, 76, 84–101, 110–11, 121–28, 130–32, 136, 140, 142, 147, 150–54, 167n174, 182–83, 199–202, 224, 275n.27, 292, 296, 311
   Ancient Greek, 54–55
   and Bertrand Russell, 65
   and Kant, 76, 86
   and Kuhn, 130, 191–94
   and Kuyper, 185, 277–78, 313
   and logical positivism, 63–67, 115, 123
   and metaphysics, 66, 118, 119
   and Neurath, 182
   and philosophy, 120, 123, 297–99
   and Plantinga, 180, 251
   and quantum mysticism, 100
   and Quine, 122, 132
   and the Reformation, 105
   and religion, 106
   and scientism, 68
   and scripture, 251
   and skepticism, see skepticism
   and transcendentals, 240
   and worldview, 214
   Christian view of, 264
   circularity, 200
   common grace, 222
   commonsense realism, 300
   common-sense, reliabilism, 81
   contemporary, 188
   deductive, Popperian, 33n97, 297
   empiricism, 62–67
   ethics as a, 166–69
   evidentialism, 184
   evolutionary, 148, 297
   facts, 129
   fallibilist, 78
   family resemblances, Wittgensteinian, 128
   holism, 200, 299
   hypothetical, 235–36

inductive, 76
Medieval, 101
methodological naturalism, 297
mitigated concerns, 74
modern, 110
natural, 86
naturalism, 56, 57, 190
philosophy of, 7, 18, 23, 120–21, 297
physicalism, 297
positivism, 86
Quinean, 123
regenerate vs unregenerate, 301
secular, 57
speculative, 96
theology as a, 184
totalitarian, 40, 48, 191, 299
tyranny of, 39, 319
use of by Nazis, Communists, 126
Western, 54

sensus divinitatis, 105, 159–63, 205, 223
skepticism, 3, 19n56, 20, 26, 30, 47, 53, 61, 62n31, 68, 72–79, 88–90, 98–101, 108–46, 191, 197, 241–48, 255, 262–65, 294–96, 307, 320
and Bertrand Russell, 73–100
global, 136–37
local, 137–46
subjectivity, 17, 32, 41, 62, 92, 100, 269, 292

theology, 2, 4, 12–14, 20–22, 37, 49, 58, 184, 188, 193, 221–38, 259–83
and apologetic philosophy, 117
and Charles Finney, 174
and Feuerbach, 57
and Heidegger, 127n33
and Plantinga, 159
and worldview, 316
analytic, 107
Christian, 2
liberal, 296
natural, see natural theology
philosophical, 4, 12, 107–8, 160
political, 271–72
Reconstructionism, 176n205
systematic, 184–86
Trinitarian, 14n39, 100–1, 134, 238, 301
transcendentalism, 8, 195–216, 240
Transcendental Argument for God (TAG), 241–67
truth, 2, 9–16, 130, 154, 219. See also belief, Justified True Belief.

"under a description," 35, 132, 204
universe, 2, 18, 26, 37, 47, 67, 83, 92–100 120, 125–26, 132–35 142, 150, 168, 191, 218–22, 253–257, 308, see also nature

Verification Principle. See principle of verification.

worldview, 168, 262. See also beliefs, knowledge.

Index of Names

Anderson, James N., 163, 190, 312
Aquinas, Thomas, 5, 102–5, 114, 160, 226, 234, 239, 257, 310
Aristotle, 19, 57–58, 102, 104, 122, 145, 168, 234, 242, 248, 257, 263, 308
Ayer, Alfred Jules, 26, 33, 64–68, 81–82, 87, 90, 139, 153

Bahnsen, Greg L, 5, 7, 8, 17, 21, 23, 26, 37, 51, 57, 72, 79, 80, 119, 129, 133, 135, 140–41, 147, 160–66, 170, 175–76, 179, 180–84, 190, 196, 205, 212, 219, 231, 234, 235, 242, 245, 251, 253, 257, 279, 312–15
Blackburn, Simon, 45, 70–72, 113, 132, 145–46, 198–99, 203, 209, 250
Butler, Michael, 21, 23, 60–61, 73, 104, 140, 159–66, 180, 192, 213, 218, 224, 243, 246, 255–62, 267, 275, 295, 308

Calvin, Jean, 11, 22, 61, 95, 105, 114, 130, 133, 159–63, 171, 205, 220, 223, 229, 235–38, 269, 275, 280, 285, 291, 302, 311, 315
Carnap, Rudolf, 27, 30–32, 65–66, 72, 78, 86–89, 212, 297
Clark, Gordon, 136, 138–42
Clifford, William Kingdon, 84, 155

Davidson, Donald Herbert, 72, 255, 259, 266

Descartes, René, 19, 45–46, 57, 59, 73–77, 103, 106, 115, 138, 154, 209–11, 215, 226, 253, 266, 295, 302
Dewey, John, 2, 27, 72, 83–88, 108, 278

Feyerabend, Paul, 28–29, 38–41
Finney, Charles Grandison, 174–75, 271, 291
Fraassen, Bas C van, 57–58, 159, 203

Gettier, Edmund, 55, 154–58

Hawking, Stephen, 93–100, 116, 131
Hume, David, 20, 25–27, 48, 63, 66, 75–81, 102, 111–15, 122–24, 137–38, 143, 146, 156, 251, 265, 295
Huxley, Aldous, 124–26, 139–42, 147–48, 152

James, William, 84, 155

Kant, Immanuel, 8, 18–20, 48, 50, 51, 74, 75–78, 86–87, 95, 111–12, 115–17, 134, 171–73, 196–97, 200, 213, 218, 236, 238, 240, 243–49, 253–58, 262–66, 295–96, 302–7
Kuhn, Thomas, 28, 34–35, 39, 110, 122, 130–32, 191–95, 204, 213, 297–99

INDEX OF NAMES

Kuyper, Abraham, 6, 11–12, 23–24, 41, 48–51, 74, 81, 108, 113, 185–88, 193, 222, 225, 277–78, 296, 302, 313–18

Lewis, C.S., 90, 100, 123, 127, 151–54, 249
Lloyd-Jones, Martyn, 16, 269–89
Lubac, Henri de, 19, 103–7, 117, 310
Luther, Martin, 15, 89, 172, 229, 275, 277, 284, 291, 315

Machen, J Gresham, 4, 84, 175, 278–79, 291
McDowell, John, 255, 263, 266–67, 308, 320–21

Newton, Sir Isaac, 25, 63, 76, 87, 131n45, 142n83

Ó Murchadha, Felix, 10n28, 14n39, 54n1, 74n74, 102, 194, 226n30, 230n42, 232–34, 255n46, 260n61
Ockham, William of, 16n46, 105, 227, 229–34, 239
Oliphint, Scott, 19n57, 21n62, 204n28, 312

Penrose, Roger, 93, 97–98, 116, 131n45
Pierce, Charles Sanders, 84
Plantinga, Alvin, 5n8, 6n11, 7, 9, 20–24, 38, 50–51, 58–61, 67, 71, 75, 90–91, 95n150, 102–9, 113–17, 121–23, 127, 129, 134n56, 135n61, 138n67, 143, 149–66, 179–81, 188–97, 204–15, 219–24, 249–51, 257n55, 261–62, 281n48, 294–99, 305–7, 311–14
Plato, 43, 56–58, 102, 129, 139–40, 154, 168
Polkinghorne, John, 92–94, 97n157, 99–100
Popper, Karl, 28, 31n91, 33, 39n114, 110, 297

Quine, Willard Van Ornan, 27–38, 49, 66–67, 76n80, 89–91, 99–100, 109–10, 117, 122–25, 130–32, 135n61, 146, 152–53, 169n179, 191–214, 249, 254n38, 255n46, 261, 297–99

Reid, Thomas, 81, 107, 117, 156–58, 192, 205, 307
Rorty, Richard, 2n2, 4, 28n82, 34–35, 71, 93, 99n168, 112–14, 132, 145nn87, 88, 184n229, 199n10, 204n28, 274n25, 320
Russell, Bertrand, 26, 30–31, 44, 49n139, 55, 59n18, 62–65, 69–70, 73–78, 85–87, 103n177, 104, 112, 124, 126, 135n61, 155n122, 156n125, 179n.212, 258n55

Schlick, Moritz, 27, 31–32, 35–36, 65n42, 78n90, 80–82, 86–87, 138, 169, 200n14, 202n19, 263n71
Scotus, Duns, 16n46, 105, 226–30, 234, 239
Skinner, Burrhus Frederic, 29, 169
Strawson, Peter Frederik, 19n56, 86, 111, 123n12, 138, 160, 197, 243n5, 245, 246–50, 253, 254n41, 255n41, 264–65, 305, 308
Swinburne, Richard, 95n.151, 223n22

Trump, Donald J, 174n195, 271–73, 278n39, 317n13

Van Til, Cornelius, 4–9, 11n34, 13, 19–21, 50–51, 58, 61, 82n106–17, 132–35, 141, n.79, 160–67, 170–221, 222n20, 230–41, 247–57, 261–66, 279, 294, 299–319

Warfield, B.B., 5, 6n11, 21n60, 81, 94n149, 108n195, 183, 184–88, 193, 302, 313–15
Wesley, John, 15, 220n12
Wittgenstein, Ludwig, 30, 38, 39, 45, 64, 79–82, 88n124, 115, 124, 128, 129n40, 143, 145n88, 166n169, 195–97, 206–9, 213–14, 242, 246–55, 264–66, 299, 308, 320

www.ingramcontent.com/pod-product-compliance
Lightning Source LLC
Chambersburg PA
CBHW071149300426
44113CB00009B/1138